LAST NIGHT A DJ SAVED MY LIFE

Also by Bill Brewster and Frank Broughton:

Ministry of Sound: The Manual

LAST NIGHT A DJ SAVED MY LIFE

The History of the Disc Jockey

Bill Brewster and Frank Broughton

Grove Press
New York

Originally published in 1999 by Headline Book Publishing

Published simultaneously in Canada
Printed in the United States of America

Library of Congress Cataloging-in-Publication Data

Brewster, Bill.
Last night a dj saved my life : the history of the disc jockey / Bill Brewster and Frank Broughton. p. cm.
Originally published: London: Headline Book Pub., 1999.
Includes bibliographical references and index.
ISBN-13: 978-0-8021-3688-6
1. Popular—History and criticism. 2. Dance music—History and criticism. 3. Disk jockeys. 4. Discothèques. I. Title: Last night a disk jockey saved my life. II. Broughton, Frank. III. Title.
ML3470 B75 2000
791. 44'028'092273—dc21 00-023968

Design by Laura Hammond Hough

Grove Press
an imprint of Grove/Atlantic, Inc.
841 Broadway
New York, NY 10003

Distributed by Publishers Group West

www.groveatlantic.com

11 12 13 14 15 10 9 8 7 6 5

Whosoever knoweth the power of the dance, dwelleth in God.
—Rumi, Persian dervish poet

Whosoever danceth not, knoweth not the way of life.
—Jesus Christ, in a second-century gnostic hymn

Custom-made double turntable built in 1955 by Edward P. Casey of the Bronx, New York

CONTENTS

PREFACE

"A lot of DJs around now, they need to know about this stuff. Someone should put a book together of all this and then we can give it to people and say, 'Read this before you go DJing.'"
—Ashley Beedle, DJ and producer

"There's not a problem that I can't fix,
'cause I can do it in the mix."
—Indeep, "Last Night a DJ Saved My Life"

The story of dance music resides in the people who made it. Or at least played it. And guess what—most of them are alive and well and full of tall tales. We set out to meet as many as possible and start them talking. Some are extremely famous, some we didn't know were still breathing. Some we found in the phone book. Once we started asking questions, the nuggets came flooding out and we were soon brimming with details no one else knew; finding connections that no one had noticed. We were surprised that this story had never been told in full, and along the way felt a sneaking pride that we would be the ones to do it.

Because, sadly, most writing about dance music just hasn't stuck. We keep on reading the same old repeated mistakes, the same well-worn myths, the same poorly researched articles written completely without context. And we're just too thick to deal with the books that have copied all these together and used them as the basis for a lot of abstract nonsense about postmodern intertextuality and Hegelian Gesundfarbensextenkugelschreiber.

So being simple folk, we wrote a simple book. There are a few sociocultural theories in here somewhere, and we like to think we've done a pretty good job of connecting things together and showing where they fit, but what you're about to read is mostly just great stories from people with big egos, explaining what they did to change music.

We aimed to write a biography of dance music's most important figure—the disc jockey. Our story is of how the DJ's job evolved and how the DJ has been the driving force in popular music. In telling it we've concentrated on his crazier years when he was shaking things up, and given less emphasis to his recent behavior now that he's settled down and become respectable.

Given this emphasis, this is not a history of dance music itself (although it nearly is). We didn't have time or space to explore the evolution of every last subgenre, so as we followed the evolution of dance music we set our limits with the motto, "Remember the DJ" and concentrated on the impact of his DJing role rather than the changes he made purely as a producer. And don't be disappointed if your favorite jock doesn't get a whole chapter to himself. We were looking for whoever got there first, not necessarily the ones who were the best. There are plenty of DJs who, while being amazing, talented artists that we know and love and have danced to on many occasions, are only bit players in the big picture.

We had a lot of fun writing this book. If you've got this far you'll probably enjoy reading it. We'll bet a dollar to a dime you'll find things in it which you didn't know. And some of them might even make you laugh.

Hopefully, it can also go some way to counter the ignorance and snobbery which still prevails in grown-up attitudes to dance music. It really is about time. After all, when it comes to the development of music, the dancefloor has always had more influence than the printed word.

—Bill and Frank, London, 1999

PS. We've called the DJ "he" throughout. One, for grammatical reasons, and two, because 98 percent of DJs have a penis.

PPS. The research for this book continues. For updates and more detailed information, log on to www.djhistory.com. If you particularly enjoy reading this, or if you spot any errors, please e-mail us at billandfrank@djhistory.com

THANKS

And this one's for . . .

Afshin, Vince Aletti, Julian Alexander, Ross Allen, Imogen Aylen, Roy Bainton, Pauline Barlow, Alexia Beard, Rob Bellars, John Bland, Kool Lady Blue, Paul Byrne, Bob Casey, Phil Cheeseman, Matthew Collin, DJ Cosmo, Andy Cowan, Steve D'Acquisto, Jon Da Silva, Fritz and Catherine Delsoin, Ian Dewhirst, Jeff Dexter, Dave Dorrell, Roger Eagle, Mick Eve, Sheryl Garratt, Adam Goldstone, Corey Halaby, Malu Halassa, Gareth Hallberg, Omaid Hiwaizi, Chris Hunt, Danny Krivit, Steve Lau, Sarah Lazin, Dave Lee, John McCready, Jon and Helena Marsh, Mary Maxwell, Sean P, Steve Philips, Rebecca Prochnik, Lucy Ramsey, Richard Reyes, Ranj Sehambi, Nicky Siano, Dan Sicko, Spanky, Lindsay Symons, Tracy Thompson, Emma Warren, Judy Weinstein, Steve and Sylvia Weir, Lesleigh Woodburn, Carl Woodroffe, Doug Young.

And thanks to everyone who helped us set up interviews: Lynn Cosgrave, Jonathan Green, Josie James, Peter Kang, Kay-Gee, Lynn Li, JD Livingstone, Kevin McHugh, Wayne Pollard, CB Shaw, Justin and Katrina @ 40dB, Vez and Wendy @ Ninjatune, Damian Harris @ Skint, Fran @ Strictly Rhythm UK, Aurelie and Jody @ Wave Music.

And thanks to Morgan Entrekin, Amy Hundley, Deb Seager and all at Grove/Atlantic.

Finally, Frank thanks Bill for being anal; Bill thanks Frank for being pretentious.

THE ORIGINS OF THE DJ

ONE
INTRODUCTION

You Should Be Dancing

"You may shake your head, smile, mock, or turn away, but this dance madness proves nonetheless that the man of the machine age with his necessary wristwatch and his brain in a constant ferment of work, worry and calculation has just as much need of the dance as the primitive. For him too the dance is life on another plane."

—Curt Sachs, *World History of the Dance*, 1937, writing about the tango

"Music lives in time, unfolds in time. So does ritual."

—Evan Eisenberg, *The Recording Angel*

Back when man was stumbling around the dusty savannahs figuring out the best way to surprise a woolly mammoth, he found his experience divided sharply between night and day. In the light he was a naked animal, prey to those greater than him; but once darkness fell he joined the gods. Under the star-pierced sky, with flaming torches smearing his vision and armies of drummers hammering out a relentless beat, he ate some sacred roots and berries, abandoned the taboos of waking life, welcomed the spirits to his table, and joined his sisters and brothers in the dance.

More often than not, there was somebody at the center of all this. Somebody who handed out the party plants, somebody who started the action, somebody who controlled the music. This figure—the witchdoctor, the shaman, the priest—was a little bit special, he had a certain power. The next day, as you nursed your hangover, he probably went back to being just your next door neighbor—that guy two huts down who wears a few too many feathers—but when the lights were off and you were heading out into a drum-and-peyote-fuelled trance, he was the don.

Today (no offense to rabbis and priests, who try their best) it is the DJ who fills this role. It is the DJ who presides at our festivals of transcendence. Like the witchdoctor, we know he's just a normal guy really—I mean look at him—but when he wipes away our everyday lives with holy drums and sanctified basslines, we are quite prepared to think of him as a god, or at the very least a sacred intermediary, the man who can get the great one to return our calls.

In a good club, and even in most bad ones, the dancers are celebrating their youth, their energy, their sexuality. They are worshipping life through dance and music. Some worship with the heightened levels of perception that drugs bring; but most are carried away merely by the music and the people around them. The DJ is the key to all this. By playing records in the right way the average DJ has a tremendous power to affect people's states of mind. A truly *great* DJ, just for a moment, can make a whole room fall in love.

Because you see, DJing is not just about choosing a few tunes. It is about generating shared moods; it's about understanding the feelings of a group of people and directing them to a better place. In the hands of a master, records become the tools for rituals of spiritual communion that for many people are the most powerful events in their lives.

This idea of communion is what drives the best musical happenings. It's about breaking the audience/artist boundary, about *being* an event, not just watching one. The hippies in San Francisco knew this when they made the early psychedelic rock shows places to dance. Sid Vicious knew it when he jumped off the stage to pogo in the audience and watch the Sex Pistols. It's the answer to the Happy Mondays question, "What's Bez for?" And it's why the twist caused such a dancing revolution: without the worry of having a partner, you were free to be part of the whole room.

The DJ stands at the apex of this idea. If he does his job right, he's down there jumping around in the middle of the dancefloor, even when he's actually locked away behind a lot of electronics in a gloomy glass box.

The Lord of the Dance

The disc jockey is simply the latest incarnation of an ancient role. As party-starter *par excellence,* he has many illustrious forebears. The shaman were his most resonant ancestors (as no end of misty mystical ravers will tell you); pagan high priests who directed their people by dance to the spirit world and drank drug-filled reindeer piss in order to see God. Since then he has taken many names in many places. He was the music hall's loquacious Master of Ceremonies, he was the Jazz Age's zoot-suited bandleader, the wrinkled Blue

Mountain square dance caller, even perhaps the conductor of symphonies and high opera. He may even have been James Brown and George Clinton. For most of our time on the planet, he has been a religious figure. Most older forms of worship are centered around music and dance, their rituals usually focused on some special person who links heaven and earth.

In fact, only recently was dancing ever separated from religion. The Bible tells us "there is a time to dance." The Jewish Talmud says the angels dance in heaven. It is a commandment by rabbinical law that Jews *must* dance at weddings, and the Orthodox Hasidim are instructed to dance as an important part of their regular worship. The Shakers, a nonconformist sect famous for their furniture, lived as celibates with the sexes completely segregated, but their men and women came together to dance in intricate formations as an act of worship.

Shaken and stirred—Shakers conducting an elaborate circular formation dance as an act of religious worship, 1872.

In calling for a greater sense of festivity in the Christian church, sixties theologian Harvey Cox pointed out very sagely that "some who cannot say a prayer may be able to dance it." Nevertheless, modern religion has often had problems with dancing, usually because of its obvious connection with sex—the perpendicular indication of horizontal desires, as George Bernard Shaw put it. But people will dance regardless. Islam is fairly unhappy about dancing, but Turkey's cult of whirling dervishes do it to praise Allah. Christianity has regularly outlawed it, only to see outbreaks of dance-desperate people sneaking a few steps in when they can. In Germany in 1374, a time and place where hatred of the body and of dancing was arguably at its peak, after eating some ergot-poisoned bread, great crowds of half-naked people thronged in the streets and did exactly what the church had told them not to: they danced like maniacs. As historian of religious dance E.R. Dodds wrote, "The power of the Dance is a dangerous power. Like other forms of self-surrender, it is easier to begin than to stop."

All this is the DJ's heritage. It is the source of his strength. The DJ is today's lord of the dance.

If you think it's a bit rich to put the disc jockey in such exalted company, consider the status our culture awards him. Things have calmed down a little since the crazed idolatry of the mid nineties, but even so, a top spinner can earn four, sometimes even five-figure sums for a few hours' work. He has become a millionaire, he has dated supermodels, he has flown between engagements in helicopters and private jets. All this for doing something which is so much fun, as he'll freely admit, that most DJs would do it for free.

If all that doesn't convince you, you'd better have a word with the hundreds of thousands of people worldwide who are involved in the multi-billion-dollar nightclub economy, and certainly the millions of clubbers who dig into their pockets every week to hear the DJ play. In the words of disco-loving Albert Goldman, one of few writers to understand dance music, "Never, in the long history of public entertainment, have so many paid so much for so little—and enjoyed themselves so immensely!"

So that's why the disc jockey deserves his own history. Even if he's mostly a grumpy, overweight anal retentive who makes a living playing other people's music.

What a DJ Actually Does

"Anyone who can play chopsticks on the piano and knows how to work a Game Boy can be a DJ," wrote Gavin Hills when *The Face* sent him to DJ school for the day. "All you need is some sense of timing and a few basic technical skills and you too could be on a grand a night."

Is it really that easy, or do DJs come anywhere near *earning* a living? Could anyone do it or do you need protective footwear?

What exactly does a DJ do?

At its most basic DJing is the act of presenting a series of records for an audience's enjoyment. So at the simplest level a DJ is a presenter. This is what radio DJs do—they introduce music and intersperse it with chat, comedy or some other kind of performance. However, the club DJ has largely abandoned this role for something more musically creative. Out has gone the idea of *introducing* records and in has come the notion of *performing* them. Today's star DJ uses records as building blocks, stringing them together in an improvised narrative to create a "set"—a performance—of his own. By dramatically emphasizing the connections between songs, by juxtaposing them or by seamlessly overlaying them, the modern club DJ is not so much presenting discrete records as combining them to make something new. And thanks to the power of music, this kind of patchwork performance, when done well, can be very much greater than the sum of its parts. Consequently the DJ, now no longer merely the host for a revue of other people's recordings, is a true performer. Indeed, in his finest incarnations the DJ can be considered nothing less than a talented musician.

Even at the purely technical level a DJ's job is reasonably demanding. Many music colleges now offer DJ courses and they're not just cashing in on a fad: there is a lot about the noble craft that must be learnt and can be taught. In bringing together a series of records to create a single, flowing, meaningful (or at least effective) performance, you do need a certain level of skill. You have to know the structure of each of the songs you're going to play, you must have a vaguely musical ear to hear whether two tunes are in complementary keys, and in order to seamlessly merge two separate tracks, you must have a quite precise sense of rhythm. Other musicians' skills are invaluable: most good DJs will have a highly reliable musical memory and a firm understanding of song construction. And you obviously need to know the equipment involved: your turntables, your mixer, your amplifier and any other sound processing devices you might be using. A quick glance into the DJ booth at any club should convince you that this can be pretty complex. The best DJs can make a dramatic difference to the power and danceability of any song by simply tuning the sound, adjusting the volume and frequency balance (EQing) or playing with the crossovers (which divide up the treble, midrange, bass and sub-bass) to accentuate the dynamics of a record. This is often called "working the system" and is rather like playing the whole speaker system like an instrument. Give a really good DJ just one record to play and he can make it sound vastly better than someone else playing the same record on the same system—literally.

The other basic requirement is music—whatever hardware you're going to use, you'll need plenty of records to play on it. DJs love to discover rare or obscure records, and few are anything less than obsessive about their music collections. To join their ranks you will need a love of records strong enough to make your boyfriend or girlfriend jealous.

In *The Recording Angel*, Evan Eisenberg tells of Clarence, the heir to a Cadillac salesman's fortune who sits in poverty in Bellmore, Long Island with an unimaginably vast collection of records. His toilet has stopped working, he can hardly afford to feed himself, but he still collects music obsessively.

"Clarence opens the door and you enter, but just barely. Every surface—the counters and cabinets, the shelves of the oven and refrigerator, and almost all the linoleum floor—is covered with records. They are heavy shellac discs, jammed in cardboard boxes or just lying in heaps; crowning one pile is a plate of rusty spaghetti... All he had left was the house—unheated, unlit, so crammed with trash that the door wouldn't open—and three quarters of a million records..."

It's not fiction.

To become a good DJ you have to develop the *hunger*. You have to search for new records with the insane zeal of a goldrush prospector digging in a blizzard. You have to develop an excitement for vinyl that verges on a fetish. You shouldn't be able to walk past a thrift store without worrying what classic rarity you might have missed nestling among those Osmonds LPs. Your blood pressure should jump a little at the thought of slitting open a 12-inch square of shrink-wrap. People will find you boring, your skin will start to suffer, but you will find solace in long, impenetrable conversations with fellow junkies about Metroplex catalogue numbers or Prelude white labels. Without wishing to be sexist, we suspect this unhealthy, obsessive, anal retentive behavior fully explains why there have been so few female DJs.

Even after you've mastered your equipment and amassed a fabulous record collection you still might not cut it. Certainly, before you can call yourself a DJ you need to show you can generate a cohesive musical atmosphere. In most cases this means making people dance.

The essence of the DJ's craft is selecting which records to play and in what order. Doing this better or worse than others is the profession's basic yardstick. But while it might sound simple enough, successfully programming an evening of records (or even just an hour) is vastly harder than you might think. Try it. Even with a box full of great tunes, choosing songs to keep people dancing—holding their attention without throwing them off and without making them bored—requires a great deal of skill. For some it comes instinctively, for others it's a matter of experience, an ability gained from years of watching people dance.

To really pull it off you need to understand records in terms of their precise effects on an audience—you need to hear music in terms of its energy. All good DJs can distinguish fine nuances of power and feeling in music; they are sensitive to the complex set of emotions and associations that each song inspires, and they know exactly how each record's style and tempo will impact on the room. This understanding is the foundation of the DJ's improvisation, as they choose which record to play next. This is largely about having an ear for music, about having a critical understanding of what actually makes one song work better than another, and certain songs sound good next to each other. Few DJs are musicians in the sense of playing an instrument, but many display a quite refined musicality.

Most DJs who dare to play outside the security of their bedrooms will have got this far. Where good DJs will start to distinguish themselves is in terms of taste and enthusiasm. Taste of course is as subjective as peach vs. avocado for the new bathroom, and it boils down to whether a dancefloor full of people are at all interested in the same music as you. If they are, great. But if they're not, how far can you win them over? This is where enthusiasm comes in. The best DJs are evangelists about music. They can make their love for their favourite records completely infectious. You could probably play a hit record and get people to dance, but could you then capitalize on that and push things further? Can you find new and amazing songs which your crowd will love even if they've never heard them before. Can you make them appreciate something which is on the edge of their tastes by recontextualizing it and showing them how it fits with an old favorite? The greatest DJs have always been driven by a burning need to share their music. As one DJ puts it, "DJing is two hours of you showing people what's good."

The Art of DJing

So the DJ is part shaman, part technician, part collector, part selector and part musical evangelist. Doubtless he is a craftsman, the expert at making people dance. But is the DJ an artist?

Like the musician, he can be. There are many degrees of technical and emotional artistry which can be added to the basics. Popular understanding of great DJing usually concentrates on the technical aspects: incredibly smooth mixes, fantastically fast changes, mixing with three decks, clever EQing, plugging in some fancy sampling equipment . . . perhaps the busier a DJ is, the easier it is to believe that he's doing something creative. And many DJs gained their fame from doing astonishing things with record decks, just like many musicians, from Mozart to Hendrix, owe their legend to a godlike mastery of their instruments.

However, a great DJ should be able to move a crowd on the most primitive equipment, and several of history's best DJs have been pretty sketchy mixers. Great DJing is not just about flash mixing and clever tricks, it's much more about finding amazing new songs and improvising your performance to exactly suit the moment. More than anything else, it's how sensitively a DJ can interact with a crowd.

The truth about DJing is that it is an emotional, improvisational artform and here the real scope for artistry lies. A good DJ isn't just stringing records together, he's controlling the relationship between some music and hundreds of people. That's why he needs to see them. That's why it couldn't be a tape. That's why it's a live performance. That's why it's a creative act. Music is a really powerful force, a hotline to people's emotions, and what a DJ does is use this force constructively to generate enjoyment. Obviously his medium is music, but that's just a means to an end. In a very real sense his primary medium is emotion—the DJ plays the feelings of a roomful of people.

That's a very egocentric way of putting it. More accurately, perhaps, a DJ is *responding* to the feelings of a roomful of people, and then using music to accentuate or heighten them. "It's communication," says DJ and producer Norman Cook, aka Fatboy Slim, marking the difference between good DJs and bad. "It's whether they're communicating to the crowd and whether they're receiving the communication back from the crowd.

"For me, it's whether they look up or not while they're playing," he adds. "A good DJ is always looking at the crowd, seeing what they like, seeing whether it's working; communicating with them, smiling at them. And a bad DJ is always looking down at the decks and just doing whatever they practiced in their bedroom, regardless of whether the crowd are enjoying it or not."

David Mancuso, disco's founding father, has always believed very strongly that a DJ is never greater than his audience. His ideal is that the DJ is in equal parts performer and listener. In his view the DJ should be "a humble person, who sheds their ego and respects music, and is there to keep the flow going—to participate." On the best nights, he says, he feels like a conduit for the emotions around him, he completes the circuit between the dancers and the music. "It's a unique situation where the dancer becomes part of the whole setting of the music being played." In this, the DJ is as much part of the audience as the dancers. "Basically, you have one foot on the dancefloor and one in the booth."

DJ and producer David Morales agrees, affirming that a DJ can only do his job properly in the presence of an audience.

"I can't turn it on for myself," he insists. "I can't. I got a great sounding studio, but when I make my show tapes for the radio, I can't turn it on. I don't come up with the creative things that come on when I'm playing live to an audience. I can't duplicate it."

However, when the live feedback is there, he knows he is capable of greatness. And when a night is going well, the feeling, he says, is incomparable.

"Ohhh, man, it's like jumping out of my skin," he says, beaming. "I dance in the booth. I jump up and down. I wave my arms in the air, you know. It's that feeling of knowing I'm in full control, I can do anything I want."

When he's on a roll, the feeling is completely sexual.

"Oh, for sure. For me? Absolutely. Pure sex! Absolutely. It's spiritual sex. Classic, spiritual sex. Oh my god, on a great night, man—sometimes I'm on my *knees* in the middle of a mix, just feeling it that way. And then when you play the next record, you can bring it down, you can bring it up, or you can just turn everything off and the people are going *nuts!* And you stand back, you just wipe your forehead and ... *shiit!* Everybody just going nuts and just knowing that you're right there... You could play whatever you want. *Whatever you want.* You got 'em from there."

Sex and DJs are rarely far apart—confirmation, if any is needed, that the act of love and the act of getting people excited through music are close cousins. Francis Grasso, the granddaddy of modern club jocks, was getting blowjobs in the booth back in 1969. "I bet you can't make me miss a beat," he'd tell the girl beneath his decks.

Junior Vasquez remembers some drug-crazed Sound Factory clubber dry-humping the speaker stacks in an attempt to get closer to the music. "He kept yelling, 'I'm fucking the DJ,'" says Junior with a smile.

DJs make love in the same way that they play music," laughs Matt Black of Coldcut. "If you think about it, it's got to be true. And also, great DJs are great cooks, my girlfriend reckons."

The bottom line is that a DJ is an improvisational musician. It just happens that in place of notes he has songs, in place of piano keys or guitar strings he has records. And just like a musician, the DJ's skill lies in how these are chosen and put together. Think of a DJing performance in a compressed timeframe and it might help. Where a guitarist can impress an audience by playing a 30-second improvised sequence of chords and notes, what a DJ does takes a lot longer—a DJ needs to be judged on a two or three-hour narrative of records. And there are now so many records available, and so many mixes of most songs, that a DJ's records are fully analogous to the notes of an instrument.

Back when the main part of DJing was introducing records, a DJ's performance was judged mostly on what he did or said in between them. But now that his job is combining records, we consider a DJ's performance in much the same way as we do a live musician's. Sure, he's playing records made by other people, but he's doing it in a unique and creative way. And because of the complex ways records can be combined (not just played one after the other with a respectful gap in between), and because of the continuous nature of dancing, and because of the relative anonymity of the acts which made the records, and because a nightclub context makes the DJ the most important element, and for a host of other related reasons, we are happy to treat the music in a club as belonging to the DJ rather than the people who originally made it. Dance to a single record and you're appreciating the work of a producer and some musicians; dance to a set of records that have been joined together and you're enjoying the talents of a DJ.

Imagine a grand tapestry made by stitching together pieces of the finest handmade cloth. Seen up close its beauty comes from the skill of the weavers and embroiderers who made the different fabrics, but seen from a distance it has a beauty of a different scale, a more imposing grandeur that comes from the overall pattern or design. Like the maker of such a tapestry, the DJ is an artist of a different order. The DJ is a musical editor, a *meta*musician, he makes music out of other music.

Sure, the DJ gains much of his effect from the musicians and producers who made the records he plays. Few would dispute that. This, however, does not remove him from the center of the picture. Without his artistry in selecting music, in knowing when to play a record, what to precede and follow it with, how to mix it, how to sonically enhance it, and—if he's skilled enough —how to remix it live in various ways, the experience of dancing to records would never reach the transcendent peaks it so often does, and many of today's dance records would seem as dull as dishwater.

The DJ is an improvisational artist who has the world of recorded sound as his palette and the musical pleasure of a bunch of clubbers as his canvas. He is the acknowledged expert at making people dance and so today he also produces and remixes records, and many of the records he plays are made by DJs themselves. The industry of dance music is now a grand conspiracy of enjoyment centered on the disc jockey's expertise.

And if he's doing his job right, the DJ is enjoying himself just as much as the dancers in front of him. "Even if I wasn't working, I'd still keep playing records," says David Morales. "I enjoy doing what I do. I get a lot of passion from it, and to be paid, and to be put on a pedestal for doing something that I love doing naturally, is mindboggling."

The Postmodern Angle

Because his artistry comes from combining other people's art, because his performance is made from other musicians' performances, the DJ is the epitome of a postmodern artist. Quite simply, DJing is all about mixing things together. The DJ uses records to make a musical collage, just like Quentin Tarantino might make a new movie which is just a lot of scenes copied from old movies or an architect might build a skyscraper shaped like a grandfather clock. This is the essence of postmodernism: lifting forms and ideas that are already around and combining them creatively.

Seen on a theoretical level the DJ is fascinating to cultural theorists for a number of other reasons. The DJ's role in our culture illustrates very clearly several key themes of postmodern life. As Dom Phillips, former editor of *Mixmag*, puts it, "The DJ is not an artist, but he is an artist. He's not a promoter, but he is a promoter. He's not a record company man, but he is. And he's also part of the crowd. He's an instigator who brings all these things together."

Basically, the DJ's job is strange in all the right ways. For a start, is it really a job? It's a way to earn a living, but it's also a lot of fun. DJs provide a service that's obviously worth paying for, but most of them go home and do the same thing in their spare time, and many of them will jump at the chance to play at that special party when the crowd is right, for free, just for the thrill of it.

Another postmodern thing about DJing is that it is both consumption *and* production, and this confuses the hell out of sociologists (as if they needed help). A DJ is a consumer of recorded music: he buys a record and listens to it, just like anyone else might. However, because his audience is listening to it too, he is also, *at the exact same time*, making a product—the performance of the music contained in that record. And the choices he makes as a *consumer* (which records he chooses to buy and listen to) are a defining part of his worth as a *producer* (how creative and distinctive he is). Practicing consumption as creativity is a very postmodern thing to do, as we'll demonstrate if you lend us your credit card.

An associated issue is that the DJ is both a performer *and* a promoter. He is entertaining an audience and at the same time he is urging them to go out and buy something—the records that he uses for his performance. Again, people with a PhD find this troubling in the extreme.

Academics are also intrigued by the fact that the DJ makes a living by filtering information; he makes sense of the confusing mass of musical information that bombards us (there are well over 200 dance singles released each week). There's no way that we could find all the great music within our favorite genre, so we rely on DJs to do it for us. They are like personal shoppers who sift through the hundreds of shitty records and find the ones we like. These days, fewer and fewer people buy singles; instead, we decide on our favorite DJs and let them buy them for us. Why spend your life obsessively searching for obscure records (in which case you're probably a DJ anyway) when you can buy a DJ-mixed compilation CD made by someone who does that for a living? You could say that these days we don't buy particular records, we buy particular DJs. Another groovy example of postmodernism at work.

Now these are fascinating angles to think about, but there's not much more to them than that, unless of course you introduce some jargon. If you want to write about DJs without leaving the library, or if you want to pretend you're a DJ even though you can't make people dance, we recommend using "text" or "found object" whenever you'd normally say "song" or "record," and calling the DJ a "*bricoleur*" (French for "handyman") whenever you can. Try slipping the words "signifier" and "discourse" into your sentences (use them however you like, no one will know) and never say "slingin' nuff choons" when you could say "the cutting, sampling and interweaving of discrete media commodities."

A few "avant-garde" DJs have successfully pulled such pretentious wool over the eyes of the more academic music critics. We'd argue that DJ Spooky, the New York-based DJ who coined the genre name "illbient" (among others), owes most of his success to the fact that he can make DJing sound really complicated. It might work on the brains of the chattering classes, but it rarely washes with the bodies on the dancefloor. The DJ should concentrate on "finding good tunes to play" rather than "attracting meaning from the data cloud."

The DJ's Place in History

The DJ has been with us for ninety-four years. In that time he has completely transformed the way music is conceived, created and consumed.

By adapting music to suit his dancers he brought about dramatic stylistic changes and revolutionized the use of recording technology. His power to promote records made him a pivotal force in the formation of the modern music industry. He also greatly advanced the status of recorded music—a record is no longer a representation of some distant "live" event, it is now a thing in itself, the primary incarnation of a song.

And though music historians have largely ignored him, the disc jockey has rarely left the patent office of popular music. Almost every radically new musical form in the last five decades owes its existence to the DJ. He let rhythm and blues and rock'n'roll take their first steps (by popularizing hidden, localized genres and allowing them to combine). Reggae, as you'll see, was totally driven by the needs of the DJ and his sound system. And the DJ was at the very centre of the insurrection which disco wrought on recorded music. Not satisfied with all this, in the last twenty-five years the DJ really set to work: with hip hop, house and their galaxy of satellite genres—musics forged solely by the DJ—he staged nothing less than a complete musical revolution.

The DJ could do all this because he operates with relative freedom. As a gun for hire whose reputation depends on keeping his musical tastes independent of outside control, he works largely free of constraint. Until recently when he was turned into a marketable pop star, the DJ was one of the only people with any power in the music business who was not subservient to the record industry. His freelance status and his promotional strength enabled him to push back musical boundaries, expose the world to new sounds and create entirely new forms of music.

The disc jockey's power has not gone unnoticed by the wider world. His independence and the fact that he can wield considerable influence over a large audience have regularly brought him into conflict with establishment forces, and the DJ's history has a rich subtext of power struggles. Perhaps the most dramatic example is that of rock'n'roll propagator Alan Freed, who was hounded to death (literally) by the FBI, ostensibly for taking illegal "payola" payments—bribes to play certain records. The real reason the U.S. government spent so much energy pursuing him seems to have had more to do with his success in promoting "degenerate" black music to their impressionable white sons and daughters. More recently, DJ-centered structures like pirate radio and the rave movement (especially its "crusty/traveler" new-age offshoot) have all incurred the wrath of government agencies. The stakes are raised when drugs, inseparable from most musical cultures, are brought into the picture.

Frequently, instead of trying to silence the DJ, the establishment has coopted his power, buying the credibility of the underground or adapting its musical innovations for the mass market. Major labels have a long tradition of buying talent from the more forward-looking independents. Similarly, over the years UK establishment radio (especially Radio 1) has drawn much of its DJ roster from pirate stations. Recently, with the rise of club culture as a commercial force, the DJ's image as a maverick artist has been turned into a marketing tool, and he (or she, because here a few female DJs have finally found a toehold) has been squeezed into the tried and trusted "rock star" model in order to sell compilation CDs. The record industry has also found great success in using DJ-led music to inject some much-needed energy into the idea of the live band. Groups like Underworld and The Prodigy are now marketed in exactly the same way as the guitar bands they are supposed to have superceded.

Taking Music Further

Despite his pivotal role, to this day the established forums of music criticism remain almost completely ignorant of who the DJ is, what he does and why he has become so important. If this book aims to do anything, it is to show the rock historians that the DJ is an absolutely integral part of their story. As they find space on their shelves for another ten books about the Beatles, perhaps they can spare the time to read this one.

It is probably the fault of our Eurocentricism that dance music's importance has been downplayed for so long. Just as copyright laws protect the western ideals of melody and lyric but largely ignore the significance of rhythm and bassline, musical histories have avoided taking dance music seriously for fear of its lack of words, its physical rather than cerebral nature (hip hop, with its verbal emphasis, and techno, with its obsessive theorizing, are the rule-proving exceptions). And surprisingly, most writers who *have* explored dance music have written about it as if nobody went to a club to dance before about 1987.

Because of all this, the narrative you are about to read has long existed only as an oral history, passed down among the protagonists, discussed and mythologized by the participants, but rarely set in type, and never before with this kind of scope or rigor.

The desire to dance is innate; it has exerted a constant influence on music. Consequently, the disc jockey has never been far from the very center of modern popular music. From his origins as a fast-operating on-air salesman to his current resting place as king of globalized pop, the DJ has been the person who takes music further.

TWO
BEGINNINGS (RADIO)

Make Believe Ballroom

"The entry of broadcasting into the history of music has changed all forms of musical creation and reception. Radio music is a kind of magic and the radio set becomes a magic box."

—Helmut Reinhold

"I can't live without my radio."

—LL Cool J

Who was the very first DJ?

Forgetting, for now, the witchdoctor, the bandleader and all the disc jockey's other illustrious prototypes, what we're asking is: Who first played recorded music to entertain a group of people?

Thomas Edison, who invented the cylinder phonograph in 1877, hardly conceived of putting music on it, and in any case his equipment could only just be heard by a single person, let alone a group. Emil Berliner, who gave us the flat-disc gramophone in 1887, would still probably fail on the volume test. A decade later the radio waves were tamed, but it would take another full ten years before Marconi's equipment was able to send more than Morse's dots and dashes. However, when the gramophone and radio signal were finally combined, we find our first DJ candidates.

In 1907 an American, Lee DeForest, known as the "father of radio" for his invention of the triode, which made broadcasting possible, played a record of the "William Tell Overture" from his laboratory in the Parker Building in New York City. "Of course, there weren't many receivers in those days, but I was the first disc jockey," he claimed. DeForest was wrong, however—he had been preceded.

At the end of 1906, on Christmas Eve, American engineer Reginald A. Fessenden, who had worked with Edison, and who intended to transmit radio waves between the U.S. and Scotland, had sent uncoded radio signals— music and speech—from Brant Rock near Boston, Massachusetts, and astonished a number of ships' telegraph operators out in the Atlantic. He made a short speech explaining what he was doing, read the Bible text "Glory to God in the highest and on earth peace to men of good will" and played a few solos on his violin, together with some singing, which he admits "was not very good." In between all this, he became the world's first disc jockey, because he also played a record over the airwaves.

What was the very first record played by a DJ? It was a woman (probably Clara Butt) singing Handel's Largo.

The Power of the DJ

Radio is a unique broadcast medium. It has the power to reach millions, and yet it has the intimacy to make them each feel they are the most important person listening. Unlike television, which invades the home with images of the outside world, radio is somehow part of the place in which it is heard, and the voices and music it carries manage to create a strong feeling of community. Sociologist Marshall McLuhan called it the "tribal drum." Arnold Passman, in his 1971 book *The Deejays*, wrote, "The electron tube changed everything, for it returned mankind to spoken communication."

Because of radio's uniquely seductive nature, the disc jockey quickly gained adoration, fortune and notoriety. The power of someone playing records across the airwaves was soon noticed and immediately questioned. It was seen as a great threat to employment by musicians and viewed with suspicion by those responsible for society's cohesion. It was even perceived as an economic threat by the record companies, who thought it would replace rather than promote their products.

And the radio DJ was undoubtedly powerful, almost from his inception. His promotional muscle was the major factor in the creation of the modern music industry (and the broadcast advertising industry, too). He was instrumental in founding new genres of music, by bringing together unconnected stylistic strands and by creating pride and ambition in the local folk musicians who played them. In a similar way, the early disc jockeys were key in fostering understanding between different races and cultures.

The disc jockey's influence was soon so strong that it attracted more than just envy and suspicion. America's musicians went on strike for a full year in protest over the rise of the DJ. And before his profession was very old, a radio DJ would be targeted, investigated and eventually hounded to death by the U.S. government, largely because he was perceived as enjoying too much power.

The Age of Radio

It was in 1922 that radio is said to have begun in earnest. Before that there were just scientists and hobbyists dotted around the world toying with the medium and trying to find uses for the new technology. Radio was broadcast to midwestern farmers with coded weather predictions; it was used to boost the morale of the troops of both sides in the First World War trenches; Thomas E. Clark in Detroit broadcast to ships plying Lake Erie. In San José in 1909, Charles "Doc" Herrold saw himself as the first person to realize the entertainment possibilities of the medium, and gave all his neighbors crystal sets so they could receive the music and interviews he broadcast.

In 1911 in New York City, Dr. Elman B. Meyers started broadcasting a daily 18-hour program which was almost all records. Sybil True, the world's first recorded female DJ, went on air in 1914 with a show she called "The Little Ham Program." She borrowed records from a local music store and concentrated on young people's music in an attempt to encourage youthful interest in the possibilities of radio. Even at this early stage, it was clear that it was a powerful force. Mrs. True noted with satisfaction that her program had a noticeable effect on the store's record sales. "These young operators would run down the next day to be sure to buy the one they heard on the radio the night before."

Radio's advertising potential was soon clear and in late 1920 the first fully-licensed commercial station, KDKA in Pittsburgh, started on air. KDKA—which soon gained fame for its coverage of the 1920 presidential election—had grown out of Dr. Frank Conrad's experimental broadcasts as station 8XK, which, using wartime equipment, transmitted from his garage. WWJ in Detroit also started broadcasts in 1920, as did the Marconi Company's XWA in Canada.

The story of early radio is a very American one because it was only in the U.S. that radio wasn't immediately seized on as an arm of government. The rest of the world saw the medium as a force to inform and educate their populations and the resulting nationalized broadcasting was paternalistic and staid. America, however, after a brief debate, quickly saw radio as a mass advertising medium. Economic function then dictated its form and as it looked for ways to gain a large audience, American radio settled firmly on populist entertainment. After 1922, when the first Radio Conference drew up formal proposals for the use of the U.S. airwaves, radio proliferated wildly. In March of that year there were sixty registered stations; by November there were 564.

This year, 1922, was also when the BBC took to the air in Britain, with a November 15 news broadcast read by Arthur Burrows. Given its founding Director General Lord Reith's lofty public service ideals, it took until July 1927 for the BBC to put the needle to the record and give Britain its first DJ.

His name was Christopher Stone and he had to work hard to convince the BBC to let him construct a program around just playing records. However, once on-air it was a great success and Stone's dry and disarming manner quickly made him one of the first stars of radio. In a distinct contrast to the corporation's rules of decorum, he was allowed to ad lib his introductions and developed a conversational, almost chatty style as he spun American and American-influenced jazz. In 1957 *Melody Maker* declared, as it celebrated Stone's seventy-fifth birthday, "Everyone in Britain who has written, produced or compered a gramophone program on the air should breathe a prayer, or (if it is in more accord with temperament) raise a glass to salute the man who was the founder of his trade."

Despite the early triumphs of such pioneers, radio had a long road to travel before it became anything we would now recognize. In its seventy-

Stone groove—Christopher Stone, Britain's first DJ, at the wheels of steel, or at least Bakelite, in 1931.

fifth anniversary issue in 1969, *Billboard* described the sleepy nature of the medium in the years before 1935. Explaining that the evening was taken up by broadcasts from ballrooms and symphony halls, the magazine described the rest of the day's schedule.

"Daytime programs were dull and repetitious. A solo pianist was heard sporadically around the clock. Stuffy, pompous staff announcers read the news from the daily press. A singer might have his own hour, accompanied by the solo pianist. Weather and livestock reports, farm produce prices, fruit and citrus warnings, poetry readings and interminable lectures on cultural and scientific subjects by boring local academic figures ate up the clock from sign-on to dusk. Records were played too. The same staff spieler who read poetry announced each disc solemnly, impersonally and formally enough to qualify as an adept funeral director."

The DJ vs the Musician

Almost immediately, the presence of records on the radio aroused opposition. In the U.S., the Department of Commerce granted preferential licenses to stations that didn't use recorded music, since there was a feeling that playing records was a rather inferior style of broadcasting—mainly because live music gave far superior sound reproduction. In 1927 the industry's new governing body, the Federal Radio Commission, reemphasized that phonograph performances were "unnecessary."

While the big stations complied, using music from large orchestras and live dancehalls, the smaller broadcaster still relied on the gramophone. During the Depression, as belts were tightened, the use of records increased. Soon only the big new radio networks such as NBC and CBS could afford to broadcast only live music.

Musicians called the broadcast of recorded music "DeForest's prime evil." Stations paid no performance fee to the artists whose records they used, and every time one was played on the radio it was music that would otherwise have been performed by paid musicians. In 1927 their employment prospects worsened further when *The Jazz Singer* ushered in talking pictures. Thousands of musicians who had performed accompaniment for silent movies were now out of a job. In coming years the jukebox would become another rival. Attacked by technology on all sides, it was inevitable that the jobbing musician would fight hard for survival.

The American Federation of Musicians, a tight-knit closed shop union, declared the DJ to be the enemy of the musician and fought long and hard to prevent records being broadcast on radio. The AFM were aided in this by the Federal Radio Commission, who as Arnold Passman wrote, "attempted everything this side of public hangings to curb the practice."

On August 1, 1942, America's musicians actually went on strike over the issue. The AFM ordered a ban on members making records, which would be lifted only when the record labels agreed to pay greater royalties to their artists to compensate for income lost through radio's use of records. They also threw in a few demands aimed at curbing the use of jukeboxes in nightclubs. After more than a year during which virtually no new records were made, the record companies gave in.

In the UK, the Musicians' Union and the record companies fought a similar battle against the disc jockey, but this was more about the public performance of records than their presence on radio.

The DJ vs the Music Publishers

Allied to the musicians were the music publishers, then the most powerful part of the music industry. At the time of radio's birth, sheet music was still the dominant popular musical commodity, and songwriters were the stars of the day. When the world started buying records instead of sheet music, however, power shifted away from the publishers and songwriters and into the hands of the record companies and recording artists. Allowing records on the radio would accelerate this shift, so the publishers fought it every way they could.

As early as 1922, ASCAP, the American Society of Composers, Authors and Publishers, the organization which collected royalties for the music publishing industry (and still does), threatened to prosecute radio stations that played records of ASCAP-licensed songs. Eventually, the radio stations agreed to pay ASCAP an annual fee of between $500 and $5,000 each (depending on the size of the station) to play its music.

To counter ASCAP's power, in 1923 the radio stations bonded together and formed the National Association of Broadcasters. In 1939, with intentions of weakening ASCAP's monopoly on the copyright industry, NAB created its own copyright firm, Broadcast Music Incorporated (BMI). While ASCAP tried to maintain the songwriter's preeminence, BMI worked to encourage an industry centered around records and broadcasting. Most established artists were ASCAP members, so BMI's recruits were almost all younger songwriters and musicians, as well as all the folk and "race" musicians which ASCAP had not allowed to join. This would have serious positive implications for the rise of black music on the radio.

In 1941 ASCAP demanded a royalty increase of nearly seventy percent. Broadcasters resisted the increase and ASCAP called a strike. This lasted from January to October. During this time, no ASCAP songs could be played on the radio.

By the end of the strike, ASCAP had won a significant increase in royalties. However, all the songs played in the meantime had been those licensed by BMI, most of them by upcoming artists signed to independent labels, playing jazz, blues, bluegrass and other less established genres. As a result, strong links had been forged between broadcasters, record retailers and smaller labels, and these ethnic and regional styles of music had gained a lot of exposure.

The DJ vs the Record Labels

For several years record companies remained unconvinced of radio's overall value as a promotional medium for their products, so they too joined the throng in fighting the idea of the disc jockey. They thought people were less likely to buy a record if they could hear it played for free. This fear was borne out by some Depression-era figures which showed that urban areas with popular radio stations were suffering a downturn in record sales (they were actually suffering a downturn in sales of everything). The larger record companies started taking legal steps against selected radio stations and a series of lawsuits ensued. One of these, the infamous Waring case, even reached the U.S. Supreme Court.

"Every label on every record specifically carried the warning that the disk was not to be broadcast," recalled pioneer DJ Al Jarvis in *Billboard*'s seventy-fifth anniversary issue. "And so I had to purchase my own records and gamble that the Supreme Court would throw out the Waring case."

One alternative to records which was successful for a while was the electrical transcription disc, or "ET," which was in use throughout the forties. This was a monster 16-inch disc pressed not on shellac like the usual 78s but on "luxurious lightweight vinylite," i.e. vinyl. It spun at the novel speed of 33 rpm, had a playing time of thirty minutes, and contained a whole program, complete with announcements and a live-sounding orchestra playing the latest hits, all captured using state-of-the-art electronic recording techniques. The transcription disc was aimed at the smaller stations and sold as a monthly subscription service. It lessened the reliance on the announcer/disc jockey and, because it was made specifically for broadcast, it avoided record company litigation.

"Most stations could not afford the orchestras and productions that went into the network radio shows," explained Ben Selvin, who worked for the leading transcription disc company. "And so we supplied nearly 300 stations with transcriptions that frequently—but not always—featured the most popular bands and vocalists."

Selvin recalled that some of the top artists made transcriptions under a phony name. The money was good, but they had to get around their existing record company contracts. Thus Tommy Dorsey became Harvey Tweed, and Ray Noble and Russ Morgan, other big stars of the time, became Reginald Norman and Rex Melbourne respectively.

"A Sure-Fire Audience Builder For Your Station. A Powerful Selling-Vehicle For Your Sponsors" was how the discs, in this case Tiffany Transcriptions, were promoted. And musicians recall the mammoth recording sessions which produced them. In Duncan McLean's book *Lone Star Swing*, Johnny "Drummer Boy" Cuviello, who played with western swing megastars Bob Wills' Texas Playboys, remembers recording nonstop all day long, about a hundred songs in a day.

"We never rehearsed a number. Bob would just recall a tune we knew, next second he'd be up on the bandstand: Ready, set, go! One number after another in the can."

McLean's book also explains how the tiny local stations would use every trick in the book to convince their listeners that the band in question really were broadcasting from nearby. "Radio stations would usually fake up their own programs, making on that all twelve or so of the Texas Playboys were crammed into the tiny studio in Slapout, Oklahoma, or wherever. Announcers would come up with effortfully casual links along the lines of, 'Well, folks, I hear Eldon Shamblin a-banging on the studio door, so let's have Bob and all the boys play "Keep Knockin' But You Can't Come In"—and right after that we'll have a message from our friends down at the Slapout feed store.'"

Despite optimistic predictions, the booming market in transcriptions died off soon after the war, largely because of the rising popularity of the personality disc jockey.

The Professional Announcer

The first recorded use of "disc jockey" was in *Variety* on August 13, 1941, when someone wrote, ". . . Gilbert is a disc jockey, who sings with his records." Jockey has a number of associated meanings. As well as its obvious reference to a horse rider, it can suggest someone capable of skilful maneuvering, a man of the people, or a trickster. In Scotland "Jock" is a nickname for man or fellow; while in America a jock is a sportsman, named after his jockstrap, the article which *protects* his man or fellow. When it was first used it is likely that "disc jockey" was meant to be disparaging. The DJ was jockeying his records —maneuvering them with skill—but he was also seen as jockeying, as in *hustling*, his place in the world.

The DJ's early years were fraught with such mistrust and he met opposition from all sides. The musicians didn't want to see records put them out of a job; the record companies were afraid that hearing records played on the radio would stop people from going out and buying them; and ASCAP, the publishing organization, didn't want its songs broadcast without greater and greater royalties.

Added to this, the DJ was held back for many years by the tendency towards ever more neutral announcing. As radio's audience grew, the style of broadcasting was increasingly dictated by the networks: CBS, NBC and numerous others who, in fine American capitalist tradition, had managed to dominate the market. The networks and their advertisers preferred characterless, functional announcing, which they saw as more professional. They provided their local affiliate stations with transcription discs that included clipped, sterile introductions, further reducing the role of the local announcer. For a while it looked as if the DJ would never be much more than a characterless gramophone technician.

However, the disc jockey's star would soon rise. There was a massive expansion in the market and most of the new stations were independent of the stuffy networks. They were competitive, programming to appeal to regional tastes, and they relied mostly on records for their music. This kind of broadcasting definitely needed disc jockeys. Also, TV had started to take away much of radio's ad revenue, and without the big national sponsors, radio advertising was forced to become much more local. As a result there was a need for snappy talkers to sell up the virtues of chewing tobacco and patent chest tonic. A few talented jocks started to show just how profitable their shows could be.

By the fifties, broadcasters had finally settled most of their disputes with the wider music industry and there were no more legal obstacles to filling airtime with records. In 1948 the transistor was invented, and a radio receiver could now be cheap and portable. And around the same time, society invented the teenager. All these factors combined to encourage the rise of the charismatic, fast-talking disc jockey. The postwar world was going to be a very different place, and records on the radio would play a huge part in making it so.

Martin Block's Make Believe Ballroom

Martin Block was the first real star among disc jockeys, one of a handful of successful characters who paved the way for the rapid postwar rise of the DJ. He started as a salesman, advertising various wares (and playing records in between) from a loudspeaker truck traveling up and down Broadway, until the police and local store owners shut him up.

In 1934 he found work as the staff announcer on WNEW in New York, reading off courtroom bulletins from the "Trial of the Century"—the kidnapping and murder of the Lindbergh Baby. During a long break in proceedings, Block decided to play some records but the station didn't actually own any, so he was forced to buy his own. He rushed out to the Liberty Music shop round the corner, returned with five Clyde McCoy records and played them back to back to make it sound like a live broadcast from a dancehall, complete with introductions that made it seem like he was actually chatting to McCoy, a Louisiana bandleader.

The station's sales department thought it was beneath them to sell ads on a "disc show," so Block had to go out and seek his own sponsor. Unable to find one who would pay, he arranged to promote Retardo slimming pills, and paid for the product's first commercial himself. A day after Block had been on-air imploring overweight women to "Be fair to your husband, take the reducing pill," there were 600 letters, each containing a dollar, requesting a box of Retardo. By the end of the week the ad had drawn 3,750 responses.

Block called his show "Make Believe Ballroom" and concentrated on using records to best effect. In just four months his unscripted, easygoing style, combined with music solely from records, netted him four million listeners, and the show was extended to two and a half hours. Advertisers were now lining up. Over the years, Block's selling prowess grew ever more impressive: one department store reported that his ad-libbed commercials helped them sell 300 refrigerators during a blizzard, and when he made a wartime appeal for pianos to entertain the troops, the USO were offered 1,500. As his influence grew, he held a contest to come up with a new version of his show's theme song. It was won by a band led by a young man named Glenn Miller.

Block had actually stolen the idea for his show—and even the name—from Al Jarvis, a Canadian disc jockey at KFWB in Hollywood (where Block had been a junior assistant). Though just the staff announcer, Jarvis was an eager student of the music business, and by reading *Billboard* and *Variety*—something none of his colleagues did—he was able to tell his audience a little about each record, while his cozy, friendly style won him plenty of listeners. From the early thirties his Make Believe Ballroom was broadcast six hours a day and became very successful.

However, Jarvis enjoyed nowhere near the runaway success of Block, who would become number one in radio for nearly a quarter of a century with the exact same show. Surprisingly, Jarvis didn't hold a grudge against Block for the wholesale theft of his idea. "He was a bright guy who had talent and determination," he told *Billboard* in 1969.

By 1940, Martin Block was the make-all, break-all of records. If he played something, it was a hit. In 1948, while already under a multimillion-dollar contract with ABC, he was able to syndicate his show for nationwide broadcast. This netted him a massive two million dollars. Block had considerable insight into the power of his profession. In 1942 he told *Billboard* that when he played a record, "If the platter is a good one, the most effective type of direct marketing has just taken place. And sales are sure to reflect the airing of the disc."

Block's influence as a disc jockey spawned a new figure in the music industry—the record promoter. In *The Death of Rhythm and Blues*, Nelson George recounts the story of Dave Clark, a young "advance man" charged with the job of warming up a particular city for the arrival of numerous touring bands. In 1938 Clark posed as a chauffeur to gain entrance to WNEW's offices (he was black and would have been denied access otherwise) and delivered a record—Jimmy Lunceford's band playing "St Paul's Walking Through Heaven With You." Clark sneakily told Block that the disc came direct from the station's owner, who was waiting to hear it on the air. He then watched Block put it straight onto the turntable.

Capitol Records formalized this idea of radio promotion in 1942, the first year of the label's existence. With his new company struggling to survive, and unable to press up records because of a wartime shellac shortage (a ship carrying huge amounts of the stuff had just been sunk), Capitol's chairman Glenn E. Wallichs looked to the DJ to keep the company's music in people's minds. A list was drawn up of the country's fifty most influential jocks and they were each personally delivered a special vinyl sampler of Capitol's output. This was the first example of a label servicing DJs en masse.

"It was a service that created a sensation," said Wallichs. "We made the jock a Big Man, an Important Guy, a VIP in the industry. And we published a little newspaper in which we ran their pictures and biographies."

By the end of the war, radio DJs had started to enjoy much greater respect. In the fifties and the sixties, radio DJing would become a fully accepted profession, an integral part of the music industry. The DJ was a powerful hitmaker and his patronage could start an artist's career overnight. In 1949 Cleveland DJ Bill Randle, who went on to discover Johnnie Ray and Tony Bennett, put it in a nutshell: "I don't care what it is. I want to make hits."

Black Radio and Rhythm and Blues

In 1942 *Billboard* introduced a music chart called the "Harlem Hit Parade." Three years later it became "race records." This wasn't meant to refer to any specific musical style, it just meant records made by black people. In 1945, Jerry Wexler, later a partner of Atlantic Records, wrote in the *Saturday Review of Literature* suggesting "a term more appropriate to more enlightened times." Wexler's suggestion, already used in some quarters, would soon be the recognized catch-all term for black pop. *Billboard* adopted it in 1949. It was "rhythm and blues" (R&B).

The biggest impetus in the rise of black music came from the post-war expansion and localization of radio. In the newly competitive market, smaller stations, independent of the national networks, had become the norm. Just as a Texas disc jockey might play The Crystal Spring Ramblers and promote animal feed to ranchers, in New York a DJ would play Red Prysock and rely for his income on advertising hair oil to Harlem. Together with the jukebox, which was serving a similar localized role, DJs and radio gave an incredible boost to the fortunes of less mainstream music and the smaller record labels on which it was released. Black music was the most obvious beneficiary, as the DJ's influence allowed the various splinters of race music to coalesce into rhythm and blues.

In 1947 *Ebony* magazine reported that the "discovery that a voice has no color has opened new vistas to Negroes in radio." Black DJs were hurriedly recruited as radio looked to target the urban black population. In 1947 *Ebony* could only find sixteen blacks employed in the U.S. as DJs, but by 1955 there were 500, and as Nelson George writes, "It was the DJs' roles as trendsetters and salesmen, both of themselves and the music, that made them essential to the growth of rhythm and blues." They talked to their audiences in the slangy "jive" vernacular, they pitched products aimed specifically at the black consumer, and they were playing artists like Louis Jordan, Etta James and Joe Turner.

It wasn't just their music that was important. Their presence was a beacon for the black communities, important examples of black success in what was then a very white world. Al Benson, aka the Midnight Gambler, was a key figure, because he was one of the first black DJs who didn't adopt a white way of speaking. "Benson killed the King's English and I don't know if he did it on purpose or not," recalled another black DJ, Eddie O'Jay. "Everybody had to see Al if they wanted to sell to the black market in Chicago, whether it was beer or rugs or Nu Nile hair cream. He wasn't pretending to be white. He sounded black. They knew he was and most of us were proud of the fact." Eddie O'Jay himself would be massively influential as a DJ (it was after him that the O'Jays were named) both for the quality of his show and the way he integrated his radio persona with his public life.

Although by the fifties there were many influential black DJs, it hadn't been easy for their forebears to gain employment. Hal Jackson, who started broadcasting in 1939 (and who, amazingly, is still on-air weekly on New York's WBLS sixty years later), was told, "No nigger is ever going on the air in Washington," by the management of WINX in the nation's capital. Jackson wasn't going to let plain old racism stop him, however. He bought time on the station through a white advertising agency, hovered outside the studio until just before his allotted slot, and then used his paid-for airtime to interview two prominent black community leaders. The audience reaction was so good he was hired straight away. Within three months he had been employed by two other radio stations as well, working 18-hour days as he drove between D.C., Baltimore and Annapolis and did shows in each. Today he is the chairman of a whole group of U.S. radio stations.

The increased presence of black Americans on radio exposed an entire culture which had previously been closed to whites. There was the music, of course, but the way many of these DJs spoke would also have a huge influence, both on future disc jockeys and on music in general.

"If you want to hip to the tip and bop to the top, you get some threads that just won't stop," rhymed Lavada Durst on Austin's KVET. "Not the flower, not the root, but the seed, sometimes called the herb. Not the imitator but the originator, the true living legend—The Rod," rapped Baltimore's Maurice "Hot Rod" Hulbert.

Biggest of them all, however, was Douglas "Jocko" Henderson, aka The Ace From Outer Space, with his famous 1280 Rocket rhythm review show, live on WOV from Harlem's Palm Café. Using a rocketship blast-off to open proceedings, and introducing records with more rocket engines and "Higher, higher, higher . . ." Jocko conducted his whole show as if he was a good-rocking rhythmonaut. "Great gugga mugga shooga booga," he'd exclaim, along with plenty of "Daddios."

"From way up here in the stratosphere, we gotta holler mighty loud and clear *ee-tiddy-o and a ho,* and I'm back on the scene with the record machine, saying *oo-pap-doo* and how do you do!"

When Yuri Gagarin completed the world's first manned space flight in 1961, Jocko sent him a telegram. This now resides in the Museum of the Soviet Armed Forces in the Kremlin. It reads: "Congratulations. I'm glad you made it. Now it's not so lonely up here."

Jocko, and similar loons, showed that the radio DJ could be a creative artist in his own right, not just a comedian or a companion but a vocalist, a poet. This aspect of the DJ's craft was to have momentous impact. In Jamaica, the sound system DJs emulated this jive rhyming almost immediately and became superstar deejays as "toasters" or "MCs." In New York twenty years later, there emerged the rapper, the descendant of both traditions.

The White Negroes

The other move that the jive-rhyming DJ took was to change color. Rhythm and blues was too good to remain a black secret for long and as the fifties dawned, certain musically adventurous white DJs started to add it to their playlists. By 1956 a quarter of the best-selling U.S. records would be by black singers. This move was accelerated by the dramatic commercial success of some of the new black stations, exemplified by WDAI in Memphis, since 1948 the first black-owned radio station, which, as well as being the home of DJs B.B. King and Rufus Thomas (he of the Funky Chicken), was extremely profitable.

In adopting this subversive music, the white DJs also started adopting black slang. This "broadcast blackface," as Nelson George calls it, let them speak (and advertise) to both the black community and younger whites. Dewey Phillips of Memphis' WHBG was so successful at integrating his audience that the wily Sam Phillips of Sun Records chose him to broadcast Elvis Presley's first single.

The idea of the "white negro" was still born of racism, however. George recounts the amazing tale of Vernon Winslow, a former university design teacher with a deep knowledge of jazz, who was denied a radio announcing job on New Orleans' WJMR simply because he was black. After what seemed like a successful interview, Winslow, who was quite light-skinned, was asked, "By the way, are you a nigger?"

Denied an on-air position merely because of his race, Winslow was hired for a most extraordinary job. He was to train a white DJ to sound black. Winslow had to feed a white colleague—now christened Poppa Stoppa—with the latest local slang, teaching him to say things like "Look at the gold tooth, Ruth" and "Wham bam, thank you ma'am." The show became a smash. One night, frustrated by his behind-the-scenes existence, Winslow snuck a turn at the mic. He was fired immediately, but WJMR kept the Poppa Stoppa name and continued using a white man, Clarence Hamman, to provide Poppa's voice.

The white negro disc jockey was an extremely successful invention, eventually leading to the zaniness of such star DJs as Murray the K and hundreds of other wacky talkers. Perhaps the most famous white negro was Bob "Wolfman Jack" Smith, but the Wolfman was a relatively late incarnation. Before him had been Zenas "Daddy" Sears in Atlanta, George "Hound Dog" Lorenz in Buffalo, Hunter Hancock in Los Angeles, Ken "Jack the Cat" Elliott in New Orleans, Gene Nobles, John Richbourg and Hoss Allen in Nashville, and, in Cleveland, Alan "Moondog" Freed.

Alan Freed and Rock'n'Roll

Rock'n'roll was created by the DJ. The very name comes straight from the title of a radio show, and the music itself was nothing more than what was previously called rhythm and blues, which in any case, as we have seen, owed its emergence largely to the rise of localized radio and the black disc jockey. In a country dramatically divided by race, the term "rock'n'roll" was simply a subtle way of making black music accessible to white kids. The man who changed the name, and who did more than anyone to popularize the music, aroused such controversy in doing so, that he would be investigated by the U.S. government for much of his professional life, an investigation which eventually drove him to his grave.

Rock'n'roll is said to have been born on the night of March 21, 1952, when Alan Freed, a DJ on Cleveland's WJW, hosted his Moondog Coronation Ball, a huge concert of rhythm and blues. Such was Freed's power as a DJ that, with little advertising except for his on-air announcements, the event drew a phenomenal crowd, almost wholly black.

The Cleveland Arena held 10,000 people and Freed had initially worried that he might not recoup his money. However, by 11:30 P.M., as the *Cleveland Press* reported, there was a "crushing mob of 25,000 hepcats, jamming every inch of the floor." Thousands of angry zoot-suited ticket-holders were still outside, and as doors were broken down and fighting broke out, the fire de-

Zooted and suited—on March 21, 1952, Alan Freed's Moondog Coronation Ball drew a crowd of up to 25,000 people, testimony to his great influence as a DJ.

partment and police put the house lights up and stopped the show. As a college student of the time commented later, "It worried the authorities. They'd never seen that many black people in the street." Following the event, the local press campaigned insistently for Freed to leave town.

On September 7, 1954 Freed broadcast his first show on WINS in New York. Within weeks he was the dominant force on radio there, attracting a huge, racially mixed audience for his uncompromising black music (in Cleveland, his constituency had been overwhelmingly black). Ray Reneri, who worked for Freed, claimed that if he played a record it "sold ten thousand copies the next day."

"Rock" and "roll" were euphemisms for sex, both much used in black music since the twenties, and first used together in 1945. When another "Moondog" forced him to change the name of his show, Alan Freed's Moondog Party became The Rock'n'Roll Party, a term coined by his manager Morris Levy. Ever alert to a business opportunity, Levy even trademarked the term "rock'n'roll," thinking he'd make money whenever it was used.

Initially at least, rock'n'roll was merely the name of the show and didn't particularly refer to a style of music. Freed used "rock'n'roll" and "rhythm and blues" interchangeably, and both *Billboard* and *Variety* continued to refer to the music he played as "rhythm and blues." It was only when Elvis Presley's career was launched nationally that the two terms ceased to be synonymous and the music known as rock'n'roll took on a whiter complexion. However, Freed continued to fill his shows with the raw black records he had always done—songs like Hank Ballard's "Work With Me Annie," The Silhouettes' "Get A Job" and Buster Brown's "Fanny Mae."

The reaction to rhythm and blues/rock'n'roll was damning. Some cities banned it from their concert halls, others insisted that under-18s going to a rock'n'roll dance took their parents. The black middle classes thought it would simply reinforce negative stereotypes, with its low-brow, even obscene lyrics promoting an image of black people as gamblers and drinkers keen on promiscuity. White bigots saw it as an attempt at miscegenation, with the Alabama White Citizens Council declaring that rock'n'roll "appeals to the base in man, brings out animalism and vulgarity . . . It's a plot to mongrelize America." Most music critics hated it, too. The esteemed jazz writer Leonard Feather wrote that "rock'n'roll appeals to morons of all ages, but particularly young morons."

Oblivious to such criticisms, Freed ploughed on, using the advantages of his color to promote this nascent black form in a way in which most blacks had been prevented from doing. By 1957 his show was syndicated across the entire U.S. and could even be heard in Britain on Radio Luxembourg. Alan Freed was not the first person, black or white, to play rhythm and blues on the radio, but he was certainly the most prominent.

Payola

Unfortunately, as well as being known for inventing rock'n'roll, Freed was also famous as the first victim of an intensive government investigation into "payola," the practice of record labels bribing DJs to play their records. In an era of Cold War paranoia, and following the shattering revelations about the fixing of popular TV quiz shows, the government decided to turn its attention to radio.

The investigations into payola came as a direct result of the rivalry between the two music publishing organizations, ASCAP and BMI. With the rise of broadcasting and the growing profitability of the black and ethnic music which BMI had championed, ASCAP saw its position dramatically eroded.

Out of spite, it spurred the government to sniff around the financial workings of radio. At the end of 1959 a Congressional hearing into payola was inaugurated. Naturally, there was plenty to investigate: DJs often accepted money and gifts from record labels. Some even had interests in publishing companies and labels themselves.

Despite the moralistic outrage, payola was nothing new. It had existed even before records. In Victorian England, songwriter Arthur Sullivan (of Gilbert & Sullivan) succeeded in having a song, "Thou Art Passing Hence," performed by baritone Sir Charles Santley by giving him a share of the sheet music royalties. This was euphemistically known as "song plugging," and by 1905, Tin Pan Alley (the New York songwriting establishment) was paying out an estimated half a million dollars a year for stage stars to perform certain songs, although the word "payola" did not appear in print until 1916 when *Variety* described it as "direct-payment evil."

The payola investigations coincided neatly with the authorities' increasing concern about rock'n'roll's social effects. FBI Director J. Edgar Hoover declared it a "corrupting influence on America's youth" and the hearings themselves drifted frequently into questions of aesthetics rather than law. The broadcast of forbidden black sounds to excitable white teenagers was seen as revolutionary and profoundly dangerous. In retrospect, the investigation was less an enquiry into financial misdeeds, more a crusade against the unrestricted influence of the disc jockey, here personified by Freed.

Having already been sacked from WINS after a riot during a rock'n'roll concert in Boston, Freed was fired by his next employers, WABC, once the hearings began and he refused to deny that he'd accepted payola. A girl interviewed outside one of his shows was in no doubt as to why he had been removed. It was "the station's way of getting rid of rock'n'roll," she said.

The hearings rumbled on for years, until Freed was eventually convicted on December 10, 1962, fined $500 and given a six-month suspended jail sentence. The *New York Herald Tribune* summed up conservative America's view when it opined that rock'n'roll was "so bad that it's almost a relief to learn they had to be paid to play it."

Freed, arrogant and complacent to the last, admitted accepting payments from United Artists, Roulette and Atlantic Records and distributors Cosnat and Superior. Between 1957 and 1959 he made about $50,000 from payola. Intriguingly, some companies had even given him bogus writing credits (and the royalties they generated) for certain records he promoted—to this day, you'll find "A. Freed" on the credits for Chuck Berry's "Maybellene"; until

Stacks records—in 1959, as the U.S. raged indignant over payola, New York radio DJ William B. Williams illustrated the record companies' "generosity" by posing among the 8,000 free records he received that year.

Berry saw a royalty statement, he had no idea Freed "had written the song with me." Importantly, though, Freed never compromised the quality of his shows, and he was certainly not alone in accepting payola.

"It was nothing for the promotion men to keep the disc jockeys in cars and deep freezes and televisions, and fur coats for the little lady," recalled singer Lou Rawls. "That was the way business was done, and all of them did it until the Man stepped in and busted Alan Freed."

It is interesting to compare Freed's treatment with that of an equally powerful DJ. Dick Clark, as host of ABC's syndicated TV dance show *American Bandstand*, was for decades the most powerful figure in American pop. Clark had a financial interest in many of the songs he played on *Bandstand.* He owned a bewildering array of intertwined music companies, and admitted to owning the copyrights to at least 160 songs. However, in comparison to Freed, Clark's obvious conflicts of interest escaped scrutiny. He was hardly pursued, was never charged, and even had his sworn statement reworded so that he could sign it without perjuring himself. Many have suggested that Clark's much whiter taste in music was what saved him from criticism. Because of his love of black music, Freed was a far more appealing target. Congress wanted a scapegoat and if they could discredit rock'n'roll at the same time, so much the better.

Although Freed had brief stints at other radio stations, his career went into steep decline after the hearings. Not satisfied with his payola conviction, the authorities went after him for tax evasion. In response to a constant barrage of investigation and character assassination, his drink problem quickly escalated and he died on January 20, 1965 from complications brought about by alcoholism. The obituaries largely concentrated on his ignominious departure from the public eye rather than his considerable influence on popular music.

In 1973 his archrival Dick Clark finally admitted that Freed "was the man who made rock'n'roll happen" and that "we owe a great deal to him." Before Alan Freed, rhythm and blues was unknown to the vast majority of white people. Rock'n'roll not only affected music—in that black artists no longer had to water down their style to achieve widespread success—it also had a profound social impact, bringing many their first experience of black culture.

For having such influence, Freed paid dearly. He was a clear example of how much power a DJ can wield, and an even clearer example of the lengths to which the establishment will sometimes go to curb that power.

Top 40 and Freeform Radio

In the long term the payola scandals did little to erode the radio DJ's strength. They did, however, raise the profile of a format known as Top 40. In the wake of payola, the idea of selecting records scientifically and not according to the whims of some corrupt disc jockey had great appeal for station proprietors and their advertisers. In 1961 Murray Kaufman, aka Murray the K, boasted that a Univac computer would select all the music for his show.

The "invention" of Top 40 is much disputed (sales charts had existed since the days of sheet music's supremacy). The most popular account relates that in 1950 Todd Storz, station owner of Omaha's KOWH, was one day watching customers choose records from a diner jukebox. He noted that people wanted to hear just a few very popular songs over and over again. With the capacity of the jukebox in mind, Storz named the concept "Top 40" and applied it to radio programming with great success. WABC in New York adopted it in late 1960 and by 1962 was the city's number one station.

American radio has always put advertising before entertainment (with the exception of the noncommercial public radio and college stations). Ratings are all, and anything that ups listening figures is welcomed eagerly. As a result, since the sixties such "scientific" notions as Top 40 have been taken to extremes. Playlists were trimmed to just twenty-five hit tunes, the most popular of which were "rapidly rotated" and played as often as hourly. Radio stations were "formatted," limiting themselves to a very closely defined genre (e.g. Album Oriented Rock, Top 40, Adult Contemporary, Urban), and only after painstaking market research were new records added to playlists. The DJ's role of selecting records was usurped by a new functionary: the Program Director, who was often little more than a market researcher in the service of the ad sales department.

There was a brief backlash against rigid formatting, in the shape of the hippie-driven dream of freeform radio. In the U.S., FM technology, which allowed hi-fi stereo broadcasts, was first licensed for use in 1961. It was the preserve of "serious" radio, often broadcast from universities, with academic programs, jazz and classical music to the fore. But given the rise of sophisticated (or pretentious) rock music, this too found its way onto the FM band, complete with a new intimate style of presentation, and disc jockeys who chose all their own music and who ignored time restrictions and rotation schedules.

The pioneer in this was station KMPX in San Francisco, one of the many music interests of local label owner and concert promoter Tom Donahue. From 1967 Donahue began playing album tracks, avoiding chart hits and promoting the underground bands of the emerging hippie movement, including then unsigned acts Jefferson Airplane and the Grateful Dead.

As a postscript, British DJ John Peel had been sneaking album tracks onto the air in a UK chart he fabricated on a station in San Bernadino. And in fact, Peel had proposed a format very similar to Donahue's at least six months before freeform was born in San Francisco, though this had been rejected by the station management. In spring 1967, Peel returned to England and introduced the same ideas on his Perfumed Garden show for pirate station Radio London.

Czar of the World's Entertainment

As Marshall McLuhan declared, "The radio injected a full electric charge into the world of the phonograph." And it was in the context of radio that the DJ gained his first victories. From humble beginnings as an experimental hobbyist, via his incarnations as quick-witted pitchman, jive-talking hipster and white negro, the radio DJ showed how much power resides in music and a voice. To this day some of the most influential figures have been found on the dial rather than on the screen, from Murray the K, Gary Byrd, Jimmy Savile, Pete Murray and Alan Freeman, to John Peel, Annie Nightingale, Zoë Ball, Chris Evans and Howard Stern.

"The jock rules the roost," proclaimed *Billboard*. "He is unbeatable. He is, in short, the Czar of the World's Entertainment. Live with him or join the Merchant Marine. That's the way it is and will be until smarter men devise something better."

But smart folk had already invented something better—the club DJ.

THREE
BEGINNINGS (CLUBS)

Night Train

"We ran our own club in a rehearsal room in a Gerrard Street basement and, on the rare occasions we were in town on a Saturday night, organized all-night raves. Mick Mulligan and I were the first people to organize all-night raves. Although today the idea of spending a whole night in a crowded airless basement appears extraordinary, it was very exciting then."

—George Melly, from "King Of The Ravers" in *Owning Up*

"Opium? No! Cocaine? No! The Great American Brain Killer Is Dance Music!"

—*The Oregonian*, 1932

The revolutionary concept of dancing to records played by a disc jockey was born not in New York, not even in London or Paris, but in the town of Otley, West Yorkshire. Here, in a room above a working men's club, we find the very first example of the club DJ.

It was in Otley that an eccentric young entrepreneur with a deep love of American swing decided he would like to play his collection of records publicly. In the U.S. the disc jockey didn't come out from behind the radio until the fifties, and while some of Europe's prewar clubs moved to records, these were played by the patrons, not a DJ. All this lends further credence to the surprising claims of a man who is probably the great-grandfather of today's DJ—Jimmy Savile.

Savile is nowadays seen as an odd fellow who occasionally appears on TV with a cigar the size of Cuba and a mop of platinum blond hair that hasn't been fashionable since the Crusades. He is a classic British eccentric. He's also a revolutionary DJ.

He grew up in the tough working-class districts of Depression-era Leeds. After the war broke out, the teenage Savile was conscripted into the coalmines to assist the Allied effort, though it's hard to imagine him doing anything but hampering it. He was quickly pensioned out of the mines after injuring his back in an underground explosion. It was then, in 1943, that he hit upon the bright idea of playing records live, armed only with brittle piles of 78s and a makeshift disco unit.

The amplification system was gingerly constructed by a friend from salvaged parts of Marconi radios, a gramophone, a wing and a prayer. "It was to present hi-fi sets what the Wright Brothers' first efforts were to Concorde," wrote Savile in his autobiography, *As It Happens*. "I hurried to inspect this important discovery. A short demonstration was all I needed to realize its potential. I mean, music by Glenn Miller and Harry James in larger than life quality: it had to be worth something."

Savile hired an upstairs function room as his venue, and entry was set at one shilling. The evening itself was not without technical difficulties. "Installing the equipment was fraught with great dangers," he wrote. "It was in several pieces connected by wires. These covered the top of a grand piano, glowed red hot when switched on for longer than five minutes, and charred the top of that noble instrument for the rest of its days. By 9 P.M. we had taken eleven shillings, the machine had melted at several soldered points and died quietly, but not before giving a final electric shock to its inventor, causing him to weep openly."

The evening was salvaged by Savile's mother, who performed songs on what was left of the grand piano. He was nevertheless convinced he had created an important new form of entertainment. "Disaster or not, there can be no doubt that the world's first disco, as they have come to be called, took place in the top room of the Belle Vue Road branch of the Loyal Order of Ancient Shepherds."

The night's final takings were £2.10s, and Savile was sure this was just the beginning. "That was the point I knew I was a millionaire. There. Was. No. Question. At all. All I needed, then, was £999,997 and ten bob. And I knew I'd get it. I had the Rollers lined up in my mind."

The technical problems did nothing to deter him and for his next appearance Savile enlisted the help of another pal, Dave Dalmour, who constructed a sturdier mobile system using an electric player, 2½-inch speakers and just one turntable.

So successful was his new live DJ entertainment format that Mecca Ballrooms—who then controlled many of the UK's dance halls—hired him to initiate it throughout the country, first in Ilford, then subsequently in Manchester and Leeds. For his first gig in Ilford, Savile commissioned a proper disco system—albeit rudimentary—built by Westrex. To cut down on the gaps between records, he had the idea of using two turntables. This, the fundamental technical advance on which modern club DJing is based, Savile did in 1946.

His other innovation—not so enduring—was to talk between records. Back then, as he said recently, "It was the latest gimmick."

Savile had to overcome resistance in several quarters, not least from the Musicians Union, who saw the idea of the disc jockey as an incursion onto their members' turf. In 1934 a group of record labels had successfully sued Cawardine's Tea Rooms in Bristol for playing their records. This led to the creation of PPL (Phonographic Performance Limited), which collects a license fee from all British venues using recorded music. In 1946 there was a ruling that such a license would only be granted on condition that "records not be used in substitution of a band or orchestra." The Musicians Union continued fighting against the incursions of records into live venues, hence those rather twee "Keep Music Live" stickers on guitar cases up and down the land. Savile neatly circumvented MU rules of the day, by the simple expedient of paying some musicians *not* to play. As he says, "I gave the band full money, but gave them five nights off a week."

Savile continued to pursue his career as a disc jockey. He was also a professional wrestler for eight years but by the sixties he was a household name in the UK as a DJ on Radio Luxembourg and then as host of the TV institution *Top of the Pops,* the very first edition of which he presented in 1964. Writer Nik Cohn called him "our best disc jockey. Come to that, to me, he was our only disc jockey." Jimmy Savile was Britain's first superstar DJ.

So, as unlikely as it seems, for the idea of playing records in a club, and for the idea of joining together two turntables, we owe a huge debt of gratitude to Sir James Savile OBE. Disc jockeys had long existed on radio, but transposing the idea to a live format required a quantum leap of imagination.

As Savile wrote himself, "Ideas which are considered wild and foolish when one is penniless suddenly become genius and brilliant in the eyes of the world as soon as one starts to make money. Therefore, an idea which would surely have got me the sack before was hailed now as a masterstroke."

To borrow Savile's most famous catchphrase, How's about that then?

The Jukebox

Savile might have been the world's first club DJ, but his experimental evenings were far from the first time people had danced to records. Ironically, the DJ's profession was automated even before it came into existence. His clearest predecessor had existed since 1889 and was a machine—the jukebox.

"Juking" is derived from the Gullah dialect of the sea-island slaves of South Carolina and Georgia. It originally meant "disorderly" or "wicked" but became a common word in black vernacular for having sex. Like "rock'n'roll," which also started life as a euphemism for fucking, the verb "juke" eventually came to mean "dance."

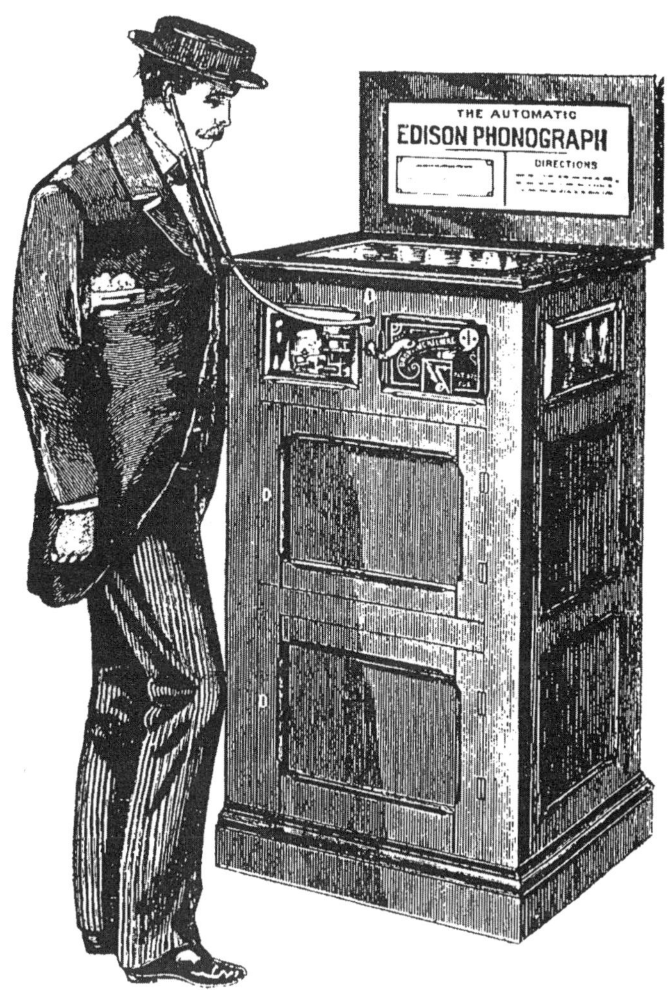

Victorian Walkman—1891 engraving advertising the Edison Automatic Phonograph, the world's first jukebox.

So even their name suggests just how important dancing was for these big chrome monsters. The manufacturers, however, were less than keen on the name "jukebox," since it was obviously both black and lewd. Many operators called them phonographs, and in the American South they were often referred to as piccolos or wurtelisers.

The jukebox was patented in 1889 by San Franciscan Louis Glass, only a couple of years after the record had been invented. The first one was installed in the Palais Royal Saloon in Glass's hometown. Coin-operated and with stethoscope-like ear tubes, it was much like the listening posts in record stores today, except it was the size of a small nuclear reactor. Edison made some similar machines and wheeled them out at state fairs, where up to ten curious folk would plug in and grin at each other. However, these primitive contraptions never grew beyond a novelty.

Only with amplification were the jukeboxes much use and in the twenties, as recording technology progressed, they became fairly widespread. By 1927 an estimated 12,000 were in operation in bars, saloons, speakeasies, roadside rest-stops and cafés across America. In the rural south, black folk partied in "juke joints," shacks where booze and music let them escape from their sharecropping drudgery.

Jukeboxes were perfect for Depression-era America. Bar owners found the jukebox far cheaper than a band, and the mood was perfect for the nickel-priced escapism they provided. In fact, as the Depression dramatically eroded record sales, the jukebox did much to prevent the music industry from reaching bankruptcy. In 1939, keeping jukeboxes stocked with tunes accounted for about sixty percent of total record sales.

It was the repeal of Prohibition in 1933 that really caused the jukebox to mushroom. For each illegal speakeasy, five bars, taverns or saloons opened in its place; most had a jukebox. In 1936, Decca alone operated 150,000. By the Second World War, there were nearly 500,000.

The jukebox was a key instrument of marketing, because it was responsive. By tabulating the number of times each record had been played, its popularity could be accurately gauged. This fact was what inspired the idea of charts; the Top 40 was such because forty records was the standard jukebox capacity. One of the earliest chart-based radio shows was called *Jukebox Saturday Night.*

Additionally, the jukebox put musical programming firmly in the hands of the venue's owners. Thus records of strictly local appeal were given a chance to shine—an important factor in the commercial rise of rhythm and blues and hillbilly forms. And the jukebox positively encouraged the rude stuff. Dirty blues records, completely unfit for broadcast, were a common feature of the jukes.

The jukebox's greatest significance came after the war, when its domain extended beyond bars and clubs and into diners and drugstores—places where youngsters hung out. Music to dance to, once inseparable from alcohol, was now something teenagers could share in. Together with the expansion of radio, the jukebox was a crucial force in the musical explosions of rhythm and blues and rock'n'roll. It eroded the reliance on live music and laid the ground for the DJ to take over.

The Sock Hop

In the U.S., the first live DJ events were the fifties dances known as "platter parties" or "sock hops." Here, the personality radio DJ stepped out from the studio and took the role of human jukebox. These were held in high school gymnasiums (where you removed your shoes to protect the floor, hence the "sock hop" name) and were mainly promotional events for the DJ's radio show. Such events were the basis for *American Bandstand*, the TV program that made DJ Dick Clark an American institution. Broadcast nationally between 1957 and 1963, *Bandstand* was unsurpassed as a promotional medium until the rise of MTV in the mid-eighties.

Almost immediately, amateur disc jockeys took up the idea. Bob Casey, later a Forces DJ in Vietnam and sound engineer on the New York disco scene, ran dances from his first year of high school in 1957.

"A guy would show up, sponsored by 7-Up, so you hung up some 7-Up posters and you promised to serve 7-Up at your dances," Casey remembers. "This guy showed up with a little 45-record changer and a little box of fifty records. He'd take the high school gym system, put the microphone in front of his little loudspeaker, he'd have a little microphone. He'd pick it up and say, "Well, that was Brenda Lee and "I'm Sorry" and now we have Elvis Presley." He's talking while the record's dropping on the repeater, saying, "OK, drink up your 7-Up folks."

When Bob played his own dances he added an important innovation, the double turntable, custom-built in 1955 by his sound engineer father. "I had two volume controls and a switch, 'cause I wanted much more music. I wanted to be able to come out of one record and go right into the next record, turn it down and talk over the record and bring it up."

Paris

Like food, the discothèque, as the name would suggest, is a French creation. Taken from *bibliothèque*, it literally means a record library. Initially at least, that is precisely what it was. The origins of the discothèque lie in the Mediterranean port of Marseilles, where sailors would leave their record collections in the stockrooms of cafés while they were away at sea. When shore leave arrived, they would return to their favorite bar and listen to records on the phonogram in the corner.

The first place to employ the word was La Discothèque, a tiny bar in the rue Huchette in occupied Paris. Because it was wartime there were no bands around. So they played jazz records, music with a potent resonance for the French Resistance because it was played by blacks. The Nazis were even less keen on blacks than they were on Jews. Perfect rebel music.

In cellars and subterranean taverns, Parisian patrons would string up rudimentary public address systems and feed their customers the finest resistance music in all its syncopated glory. To run a discothèque in wartime Paris was to participate in an act of civil disobedience. The discothèque's lasting reputation as a place where outlaws gathered was sealed in smoky basements in occupied territory.

We English-speakers like our few French words, and while *discothèque* may well have originally stood for resistance and struggle, its Frenchness grew to suggest sophistication, style, panache and élan. It was the kind of place to throw on your glad rags, smoke a cigar and sip cocktails from a tall, slim glass.

After the war, the first discothèque that could be recognizably described as such was opened in Paris by Paul Pacine in 1947 under the name Whiskey-A-Go-Go. Pacine had a bit of a thing for scotch whisky, then considered an exotic drink in a nation that preferred the grape to the grain. He decorated the walls with tartan, apart from one which was covered in whisky case covers: Ballantines, Johnny Walker, Dewar's, Cutty Sark and Haig & Haig. The musical menu was equally single-minded. Pacine played jazz, exclusively.

This was soon usurped by another Parisian spot. Chez Castel was located on rue Princesse in Saint Germain-des-Prés and was strictly for the invited only. It was the in-crowd's secret hangout, and with only a small address plaque on the door, you may not have found it anyway. Chez Castel was a favored haunt of the French existentialists. Jean-Paul Sartre and Simone de Beauvoir could often be found there. A typical evening began with a movie or a show, before people repaired to the discothèque in the basement to dance cheek-to-cheek on the copper and steel checkered dancefloor.

In 1960 Jean Castel discovered he had a rival when a carrot-topped girl about town called Régine Zylberberg opened Chez Régine. Régine came from a family of Polish-Jewish refugees and had worked her way up the bar business, starting out as a hostess in her father's joint, Lumière de Belleville, before working in the ladies' bathroom at Whiskey-A-Go-Go.

When the Whiskey began to slump, Pacine, sensing an opportunity in his bright-eyed employee, offered to bankroll her very own night-spot. Régine knew the value of hype. For the first month of Chez Régine, she would dutifully open the doors at 10:30 P.M. and promptly place the DISCO FULL sign outside. For four whole weeks people were regularly turned away, as the empty cacophony of the club echoed outside. The day she opened her doors proper, the place was mobbed.

She didn't need existentialists in her club. She had Jean-Paul Belmondo, Alain Delon and the *nouvelle vague.* Jean Castel remembered Régine as someone with "an easygoing temperament, warm, funny, the life of the party." If discothèques were not initially regarded as the chi-chi spots in which to be seen, they certainly were now.

London

It might have been impossible to buy two ounces of beef or a bag of oranges in postwar London, but there was no shortage of jazz and swing. Club nights would be improvised in underground cellars, smoky backrooms and illegal speakeasies, and here GIs and hipsters would congregate and dance to music provided by players like Chris Barber, Mick Mulligan and jazz-surrealist George Melly. In fact, the first British all-nighters took place in this period—in Cy Laurie's Jazz Club in Soho.

The scene was wild, even by today's standards. Drugs—principally opium and marijuana—had been smuggled into Britain for many years by African and Chinese sailors, for use within their own communities. However, trade in these substances was moving easily into the clubs. In 1950 it was at one such jazz joint, run by Johnny Dankworth and Ronnie Scott, that the very first British drug bust took place. When the London bobbies raided Club Eleven at 50 Carnaby Street on April 15, 1950 they were suitably appalled. "There were on the premises between 200 and 250 persons," reported Detective Sergeant George Lyle of Scotland Yard, "colored and white, of both sexes, the majority between seventeen and thirty. All these people were searched." Among the goodies recovered were hemp cigarettes, cocaine and morphine ampoules. The drug conviction Ronnie Scott received prevented Britain's greatest tenor saxophonist from pursuing a career in America.

There were also gigantic trad-jazz raves at the Alexandra Palace, with thousands of kids kitted out in what was then regarded as "rave gear." Boys, for example, would wear bowler hats (often with "Acker" painted on them for jazz clarinetist Acker Bilk), jeans and no shoes; while the girls would wear men's shirts hanging outside black woolen tights, again often accompanied by a bowler hat. The tradsters' dancing had to be seen to be believed, too. It was antidancing; a reaction to the liquid moves of the modernists. "The accepted method of dancing to trad music is to jump heavily from foot to foot like a performing bear, preferably *out of time* to the beat," wrote George Melly. These elephantine youths were nicknamed "leapniks" by trad musicians.

The growing immigrant community in London was having an impact, too. West Indians, unaware that one was supposed to be tucked up in bed at 10 with a cup of Horlicks listening to the Light Programme, partied all night at places like the Roaring Twenties. The disc jockey here was a hip Jamaican dude called Count Suckle, who introduced the metropolis to bluebeat (so named because of Ziggy Jackson's ska label Blue Beat). Even before he arrived at the Twenties, Suckle had already built a considerable reputation among the black community with his sound system parties (usually held on bank holidays) at Porchester Hall, Kilburn Gaumont State, and other venues in west and northwest London. He brought over another Jamaican innovation, the cover-up, whereby the label would be scraped off in order to disguise the identity of the record. Mick Eve, a musician active on the London all-nighter scene, recalls Suckle steaming the label from a pristine copy of Nina Simone's "My Baby Just Cares For Me."

New York

Jazz clubs were pretty popular in New York, too. In fact, the city was dubbed "The Big Apple" by touring jazz musicians, who considered it the most lucrative place to play. The swing of the big bands filled huge ballrooms, but as bebop started to crystallize, the smaller club came into its own. The city's first bebop club, the Royal Roost, grew out of Topsy's Chicken Roost on Broadway. At the start of 1948, a jazz concert was staged by radio DJ Symphony Sid and entrepreneur Monte Kay. Its success spurred the owners on and soon Miles Davis, Charlie Parker and Dexter Gordon were performing there.

The nights were promoted by a savvy Jewish hustler called Morris Levy. Levy's shadow looms large over the history of dance music in the city. At times, it has loomed large *and dark*, since Levy was eventually convicted of extortion conspiracy (he died before he could serve his sentence).

At the behest of Monte Kay, Levy started a new club on 52nd Street and Broadway, its name a homage to the godfather of bebop, Charlie Parker. Birdland opened its doors for business on December 15, 1949. Such was its success that by the fifties Levy was opening clubs on an almost weekly basis. He had the Embers, the Round Table (a favorite haunt of his buddies in the mob), the Down Beat and the Blue Note.

When Alan Freed arrived in the city to take up a radio show at WINS, Levy began to manage the mercurial DJ and promoted Freed's record parties at the Brooklyn Paramount and Fabian-Fox. On April 12, 1955, Freed staged a weeklong event under the name Rock'n'Roll Easter Jubilee. By the week's end it had attracted 97,000 kids and broken the twenty-five-year-old box office record at the Paramount with receipts of $107,000.

But Freed's events were more like radio roadshows than nightclubs, and the bebop venues were centered around live music. The first New York spot where all the discernible elements of a modern nightclub were assembled was Le Club. Predictably, considering the discothèque's Parisian origins, it was opened by a Frenchman.

Oliver Coquelin's family owned several grand hotels, including the Meurice and George V in Paris. He had been awarded a Purple Heart during the Korean War and became an American citizen. After dabbling in ski resorts, he hightailed it to New York, where, it seems, he arrived at the perfect time. The high society of old money and the social register was on its way out, made obsolete by the dawn of the egalitarian sixties and a new group of the great and good. The jet set had been born and it was landing in New York.

Coquelin knew the right people and found the perfect location: a garage used by a lingerie photographer underneath his apartment in Sutton Place at 416 East 55th Street. He raised the necessary capital from partners Igor Cassini, Michael Butler, the Duke of Bedford and a motor car manufacturer called Henry Ford. He fashioned the club along the lines of a hunting lodge, with Belgian tapestries along the wall, wood-paneling all around the bar, ornate floral arrangements, glass-shaded candles and crisp linen. To one side, an open marble fireplace blazed. The two loudspeakers were so discreet they were barely noticeable. The $150 initiation fee and $35 annual dues ensured the club retained its exclusivity.

Coquelin asked society bandleader Slim Hyatt to find him a DJ, which he duly did. Thus New York's first discothèque DJ was Hyatt's butler, a long-faced, handsome black fellow called Peter Duchin. Coquelin schooled him in the arts of French spinning. Le Club opened on New Year's Eve 1960. The sixties had begun.

The Twist

In the first years of the sixties a revolution took place in the way people danced. The result was to have an enormous impact on youth culture. Reviled by critics and commentators as lewd, lascivious and unseemly, it nevertheless captured young imaginations and went some way to crashing the barriers of racial and sexual prejudice. Dancehalls would never be the same again, as it destroyed everything that came before. It was the twist.

The Russian poet Yevgeny Yevtushenko described a visit to a London nightclub: "Couples were dancing in a stuffy, packed hall, filled with cigarette smoke. Bearded youths and girls in tight black trousers wriggled and twisted. It was not an especially aesthetic sight. However, among the twisters was a young Negro couple dancing with remarkable lightness and grace, white teeth sparkling in the semidarkness. They danced full of joy, as if they had been used to the dance since childhood. I suddenly realized why they danced the twist the way they did.

"The twist is advertised as the miracle of the atomic era. But I remembered Ghana jungles two years ago where I watched African tribal dances. Those dances have existed thousands of years. They were ritual dances that had not yet been called the twist. This miracle of the atomic era is merely a modernized version of what was invented thousands of years ago."

The twist caused a revolution because of its simplicity. It required no partner, no routine, no ritual, no training. All it needed was the right record and a loose set of limbs. It was an invocation to get on the floor and do your own thing. Because it wasn't a couples' dance, it struck a small blow for sexual equality—destroying the concept of the "wallflower," a girl awaiting an invitation to dance (coincidentally, the Pill and the twist were launched within months of each other). Most importantly, perhaps, it unified a group of dancers. Dancing the twist you were no longer just focused on your partner, you were partying with a whole roomful of people.

It wasn't particularly new. Ancient variations of it abound. Part of the nineteenth-century French musichall dance, the can-can, had within its high-kicking sequences a part known as the French twist. There's a routine in a 1933 British musichall comedy film, *Cavalcade*, which bears a remarkable resemblance to the twist. In America, slaves from the Congo imported a similar dance oriented around loose pelvic maneuvers (Groucho Marx even aped these actions in a few movies). And in the early part of this century, there were many other black dance crazes such as the mess around and the black bottom that prefigured the twist. One 1920s song, "Fat Fanny Stomp," even implored girls to "twist it a little bit." Like all good dances, the twist was yet another dancefloor approximation of sex.

The modern twist probably began in Baltimore in 1960 when Hank Ballard recorded the first, and best, version of "The Twist" after spotting black kids doing it on the Buddy Dean Show on local television. When Ballard's record spread the craze to Philadelphia it began to break nationally, thanks to Dick Clark's *American Bandstand*, the most important TV pop show in America.

Clark divested the twist of all of its sexual connotations, its essential *blackness*, and made it safe for white suburban teenagers. A new version was recorded by a pale-skinned black man called Chubby Checker (whose name was a jokey dig at Fats Domino) for a label, Cameo-Parkway, in which Dick Clark happened to have a financial interest. Clark promoted this new version of "The Twist" on *Bandstand*, where Checker explained to the audience exactly how it was done: "Just imagine you're wiping your bottom with a towel as you get out of the shower and putting out a cigarette with both feet." White dancers, claiming they'd originated it, demonstrated how the dance was done. Checker was soon #1 in the Hot 100.

Despite the success of Checker's record, the twist had largely died out by the end of 1960. Then, in a curious anomaly, a small wreck of a bar in midtown Manhattan with an occupancy limit of 178 achieved what Clark's nationwide TV show had failed to do: make the dance into a worldwide fad.

The Peppermint Lounge at 128 West 45th Street was hardly the place on which one would expect New York's high society to descend. Adjoined to the Knickerbocker Hotel just off Times Square, the Lounge was essentially a gay hustler joint, frequented by sailors, lowlifes and street toughs in leather jackets. It had a lengthy mahogany bar running along one side, lots of mirrors and a tiny dancefloor at the back.

Music was provided by a New Jersey outfit called Joey Dee & the Starliters (who at one stage included actor Joe Pesci on guitar), and here the whole of Manhattan's thrill-seeking in-crowd were to be found twisting. It was especially popular with the acting profession: Marilyn Monroe, Tallulah Bankhead, Shelley Winters, Judy Garland and Noel Coward were all spotted. "They started twisting in there, so celebrities started mobbing the place," recalls Terry Noel, a professional dancer at the club. "Then it got very chic."

The reaction from most commentators was not favorable, often using thinly veiled racism to damn the dance fad. *Journal-America*'s John McClain described the Peppermint Lounge as having "the charm, noise, odor, and disorder of an overcrowded zoo," while Arthur Gelb, writing in the *New York Times*, was yet more dismissive. "The Peppermint Lounge and its surroundings are the scene of a grotesque display every night from 10:30 to 3 o'clock. Café society has not gone slumming with such energy since its forays into Harlem in the twenties. The lure is a tiny dancefloor undulating with the twist where couples gyrate in a joyless frenzy."

The twist made its transatlantic leap via a couple of routes. One evening in the autumn of 1961, the touring cast of *West Side Story* made an unscheduled stop at Chez Régine in Paris. They brought a stack of new American records with them. In the pile was Chubby Checker's "The Twist." At the time, the dance craze in Paris was a rockabilly hybrid called "yogurt." One of the yogurt acts, Dick Rivers et Ses Chats Sauvages, swiftly recorded a twist record: "Twist à Saint Tropez." The twist became hugely popular in France. Even exiled former king and Nazi sympathizer Edward VIII had a go. "It was amusing, but a bit strenuous," he reported.

On its arrival in London, the twist caused an outrage. At the Lyceum dance hall a young snake-hipped mod called Jeff Dexter, who'd seen how to do the dance on the cover of the record, was expelled and barred for twisting with a couple of girls. Within a couple of weeks, however, reports had appeared in the press about this dance craze from America and Dexter was a star. "I got captured on film and it got shown around the cinemas on Pathé newsreels," he laughs. "This thing, this *obscenity* that I'd been ejected for, became popular and I got offered a job at the Lyceum. As a dancer!"

Even the BBC had a twist or two. On *Television Dancing Club*, Victor Sylvester's Ballroom Orchestra presented the twist in suitably anodyne form by recasting the Gershwin classic "Fascinating Rhythm," as "Fascinating Rhythm Twist." This sanitized version still drew the ire of appalled suburbanites everywhere. A distressed dance instructor called Mr. Stetson told BBC reporters that "the knees and pelvis are used in such a way that the dancer is making very suggestive movements. I have an extreme objection to the fact that this is not what is called a couple dance. It is a solo dance. A girl can just as easily go out on to the dancefloor without having a partner and exhibit herself in what I consider to be a rather unseemly way for British ballrooms."

Until the twist took off, Europe had remained impervious to the various fad dances that had swept America over the previous decades such as the

Madison, the bop and the stroll. In Britain, the jive—a dance imported by American GIs during the Second World War—had been the one routine that all self-respecting dancers knew (with the jitterbug, also known as the Lindy-hop, as its less popular and more controversial brother).

Now, released from the constraints of formal steps and partners, the dancer was free to build something completely new. Dancing had returned to the original black dances on which most European formal dances were originally based. You could dance however your imagination suggested.

The popularity of the twist set in train a raft of similarly freeform dances —the frug, the mashed potato, the pony, the hully gully, the monkey. Within a few years, dancefloors had thrown up the freakouts of the flower power era and the acrobatic flips and spins of northern soul. The twist had dropped an H-bomb on dance conservatism and stripped away the dancefloor's tightly policed rituals. In doing this, it paved the way for a new kind of dance club. It was time for the discothèque to come of age.

Ian Samwell at the Lyceum

Once the jet set got a taste for the low-rent fun of the twist, they poured into the newfangled discothèques springing up in New York, London and Paris. The tradition of having dance bands as the primary focus of entertainment was being quietly eroded by the ascendancy of vinyl. Up until this point, the DJ had been no more than a minor functionary in the evening's proceedings. He was someone proprietors would rely on to keep the club busy while the next band readied their equipment. But rapidly he would become the focus for the whole night.

It was in Britain that this happened first. Club culture in the UK has almost always been far ahead of its American counterpart, even when musically it may have occasionally lagged behind. The reason for this is largely to do with the way that music is heard. Music in America lives much more on radio than in clubs. The relative freedom of U.S. airwaves has always meant that anyone with a transmitter and a fat wallet could transmit music. You only had to twiddle the knob to the right frequency to get a dose of your favorite records. In the UK, where radio was still seen largely as an arm of government social policy, the only way to hear the exciting tunes emanating from America was to go out.

At the Lyceum in London the resident DJ was Ian "Sammy" Samwell, a handsome, bequiffed smoothie with a long history in rock'n'roll. Samwell's entry into the music business had been as guitarist and songwriter with Cliff

Richard & the Drifters, before he was sacked in preference to Jet Harris. It was Samwell who had penned the first credible British rock'n'roll record, Cliff's "Move It," as well as committing Georgie Fame and John Mayall to wax for the first time. (Samwell later wrote and produced the Small Faces' "Watcha Gonna Do About It.")

As a songwriter signed to a subsidiary of an American publisher, Samwell made regular trips to New York. He brought back coveted rhythm and blues 45s on Atlantic, Chess and Berry Gordy's pre-Motown label Anna, such as Barratt Strong's "Money."

In 1961 he was invited to spin records for Tuesday lunchtime dance sessions at the Lyceum, a baroque Edwardian music hall. Up until then, such was the disc jockey's status, the records had been played by the electrician. Soon Samwell was asked to fill a Sunday slot. "The Lyceum's record collection was pretty pathetic," he recalls. "So I started to bring my own records. I played a lot of stuff you couldn't hear on the BBC, mostly rhythm and blues because it was hip and great to dance to." He would spin records for the first three hours and then play in the intervals between the Mick Mortimer Quartet and Cyril Stapleton's Orchestra, who appeared on the Lyceum's giant revolving stage.

Though he never really realized the importance of what he was doing, his connoisseur-quality music was the last piece in a jigsaw. The Lyceum was the first place in which all the recognizable elements of a modern club—lights, upfront dance records, disc jockey and dancefloor—came together. Dave Godin, later the man to coin the term "northern soul," believes it deserves a place in history: "The Lyceum was very important, I can't stress that enough, because in some ways it was the first place that could merit the name discothèque."

"It changed my life in about three minutes," says Jeff Dexter, the renegade Lyceum twister, recalling his first trip to the club. Walking in through the foyer, past the life-size cutout of Ian Samwell which read "LONDON'S NUMBER ONE DJ," and up to the balcony and the gigantic cloakrooms, the sheer spectacle of it all impressed him: "The sound in such a big place just blew me away. It was great."

The Modernists and Swinging London

The French, yet again, played a key part in bringing the concept of the discothèque to London. Spreading out like a virus from the south of France and Paris, the discothèque arrived in London via French students and the many au pairs working in the capital. Several of the early clubs were opened by the French, such as Madame Cordet at the Saddle Room, and specifically aimed at the patronage of this young constituency. But what helped establish discothèques in England had nothing to do with France and everything to do with one of the many subcultures that postwar Britain had thrown up. They were called the mods.

"Mods go to dance halls, Hammersmith Palais, the Marquee, and various 'discothèques,'" wrote Charles Hamblett and Jane Deverson in 1964's *Generation X*, "clubs where they play gramophone records." Throughout the sixties, British club culture—particularly in London and Manchester—was driven by a uniquely British subculture: the mods. "Mod was the gap between full employment and unfulfilled aspirations, the missing link between bomb sites and Bacardi ads," wrote Julie Burchill in *Damaged Gods.*

The mods had grown out of a split in the late fifties between trad jazz fans (who were mainly middle-class) and the modernists, who favored the modern jazz of Charles Mingus and the existentialist philosophies of Jean-Paul Sartre. Their initial constituency was Jewish, East End and working class. As the cult spread from its arty origins, the mods became noted for an obsessive attention to fashion and a predilection for scarfing amphetamines. They also loved dancing to Jamaican and black American records.

The Lyceum was an important precursor, but if you were a mod and loved black music in 1963 your first port of call would have been the Scene, owned by an irrepressible Irishman called Ronan O'Rahilly. Located in Ham Yard, Soho, it had formerly been Cy Laurie's Jazz Club. As the Piccadilly, it had also been where an unknown group called the Rolling Stones had performed.

As the Scene it was a dank, dingy basement room that was so small there was no option but to dance. A young Jewish boy called Marc Feld was one of the club's "faces." (With the name Marc Bolan, he later became a pop star.) Although it was technically alcohol-free, it wasn't too hard to get a hit of whisky added to your bottle of Coke, and you could certainly get amphetamines, as most of the kids present did.

The main reason most people went to the Scene, however, had nothing to do with hits of whisky or handfuls of pills. It was to hear the DJ. His name was Guy Stevens. If Ian Samwell at the Lyceum was the accidental revolutionary of British club culture, then Guy Stevens was its Lenin, a confirmed believer in the revolutionary power of the disc jockey. He was a frizzy-haired obsessive, permanently bursting with enthusiasm, and his sets of maximum rhythm and blues were as legendary as his drug consumption. Guy Stevens was as keen on purple hearts as his clientele.

"Guy would play all these great rhythm and blues records and we'd groove all night," sixties face Johnny Moke told the *Evening Standard.* "Of course, nearly all of us were doing pills—you had to if you were dancing all night. Same way they take ecstasy now."

"Everybody would come to hear Guy," reflects Ronan O'Rahilly. "The Stones, The Beatles, Eric Clapton—all the major stars. People would come from all over the country on Monday nights, and from France and Holland too; it was that good." Stevens's sets at the Scene were prime source material for both The Who and Small Faces, who reworked many of the records he played.

"Stevens used to carry his records around in a huge trunk," remembers O'Rahilly, "and he was so protective of them that he used to sit on top of it while he DJed. I've seen him sleep on it! It was like religion to him, it really was."

He would often spend days wandering around record stores looking for coveted rarities. Each Friday morning, he would head for the basement of a shop in Lisle Street in Chinatown, where a rhythm and blues enthusiast sold freshly imported 45s from a tiny box on a table. By lunchtime, the records would be sold and the vendor melted into the Soho crowds.

Stevens was part of a growing network of soul fans around the country and corresponded with such people as Roger Eagle, resident DJ at the Twisted Wheel in Manchester. "He was a nice man, Guy. He used to send me up records," recalled Eagle shortly before his death in May 1999.

Stevens also worked for Island Records' sister label Sue, and signed songs by Ike & Tina Turner, Betty Everett and Rufus Thomas. He played a key role in the careers of Free, Traffic, Bad Company, Mott the Hoople and Spooky Tooth, and had a profound influence on the British record business overall. He was also a huge rock'n'roll fan, crazy about Jerry Lee Lewis, and the founder of the UK Chuck Berry Fan Club.

But his full-throttle approach to life had its consequences. He died on August 29, 1981 from an overdose of prescription drugs he was taking to help with his alcohol dependency. Tragically, it came shortly after he had produced perhaps his finest record: *London Calling* by The Clash.

The Scene was not alone. There was the Flamingo, the Purley Orchid, La Discothèque, the Roaring Twenties and the Crazy Elephant (where another black jock, Al Needles, plied his trade), as well as trendy nightspots filled with

London's rapidly growing pop aristocracy—the Ad Lib, Cromwellian and Scotch of St. James. The Sombrero in Kensington was a favored haunt of London's gays.

Jeff Dexter joined Ian Samwell as a disc jockey and the duo spun at many of these places, including playing guest spots at the Scene's hip rival, the Flamingo. This was yet another unlicensed Soho dive, located underneath the (licensed) Whiskey-A-Go-Go on Wardour Street (now the WAG), which featured all-nighters on Fridays and Saturdays.

The Flamingo drew an eclectic mix, including patrons from the American military bases in Hillingdon and Ruislip, as well as newly integrated blacks from west and south London. This cultural mélange gave the music dynamism too. "That was the best gig because the audience were either very hip or West Indian," recalls Ian Samwell. "I played nothing but rhythm and blues or bluebeat."

Another club was Tiles, a Disneyland for pillheads. Once inside it was as if you'd wandered into a covered side street—the club contained a sort of mini-mall of shops including a Ravel shoe store, a soft-drink stand and a beauty parlor called Face Place. Completing the illusion that you were in some unknown London alley was a sign reading "Tiles Street." Each lunchtime, Tiles would fill with office girls in pale lipstick, skiving clerks, young merchant seamen on shore leave and mods who, somehow, never seemed to work—all there to dance in the middle of the day to soul and bluebeat. Tom Wolfe termed this strange mod subculture the Noonday Underground.

One of the backers of Tiles was Jim Marshall, owner of the Marshall PA company. Tiles, therefore, had a decent sound system (something that couldn't be said for any other club in London). By the mid-sixties several DJs had worked there, including a cocky Liverpudlian called Kenny Everett, Mike Quinn, Clem Dalton, Ian Samwell and Jeff Dexter, who hosted his own night, the Record & Light Show.

It became so notorious as a pill palace, the police visited almost as often as the mods. It was finally closed and turned into an aquarium. John Peel, recently returned from a seven-year stint as a radio DJ in America, played the last night there. He was not popular. "There were waves of irate customers coming up over the footlights to try and persuade me to play whatever it was they wanted me to play. Which certainly wasn't the Grateful Dead, Jefferson Airplane and Country Joe and the Fish. They didn't like me at all."

London's culture of all-night dance parties quickly took off elsewhere, proving especially popular in the Midlands and north. While the dance clubs in the south succumbed to the prevailing winds of flower power, the working-class north continued to pursue doggedly its love of black American music. This quirky subculture would, in a few years, transform itself into northern soul.

Terry Noel at Arthur

Now that British club culture was booming, the New Worlders wanted a piece of the action. Energized by the twist, New York's society darlings championed a series of fantastical, theatrical clubs, each more chic than the last. One in particular became the talk of America. It was called, simply, Arthur and was the Studio 54 of the sixties jet set. Its disc jockey was a flamboyant cherub called Terry Noel.

He was the first DJ to mix records.

When actor Richard Burton dumped his first wife Sybil for Elizabeth Taylor, she took the divorce money and ran off to New York for some fun. In May 1965, with a great deal of society support and 80 donations of $1,000 each from her friends, Sybil Burton opened a club, Arthur, named after a line about George Harrison's haircut in the film *A Hard Day's Night.* It was an instant sensation. A photograph of Sybil Burton and Rudolf Nureyev dancing together was splashed across several newspapers the day after it opened and the Arthurian legend was born.

Terry Noel, an art student originally from Syracuse, had danced himself into a job as a professional twister at the Peppermint Lounge. When Sybil Burton came down searching for talent for her new club, she passed Noel over in favor of his flatmate's band, The Wild Ones. Green with envy, Noel gatecrashed Arthur's opening night and informed Sybil in no uncertain terms that the club was great but the music sucked. He must have convinced her because from the next night, Terry Noel was Arthur's resident DJ.

Burton had taken the idea of Soho's Ad Lib club and transplanted it 3,500 miles to 154 East 54th Street. The influence of Swinging London was immediately evident as Burton implored clubbers: "Please dress up daft." They obliged. To an appropriately Mondrianesque pop art backdrop, dancers whirled manically in a gala of man-made finery: plastic jackets, nylon shirts, chain-mail dresses, vinyl suits and fake-fur hot-pants. "WILD NEW FLASHY BEDLAM OF THE DISCOTHÈQUE," trumpeted *Life* magazine. Amid this controlled pandemonium stood Noel, part showman, part shaman.

Sybil Burton's celebrity may have drawn them to Arthur, but it was Noel who kept them on the dancefloor. He took control of everything. Within six months of Arthur's debut he had redesigned the speaker system and taken charge of the lights. The sound engineer, Chip Monk, was asked to create speakers which operated independently of each other, with separate frequency controls. That way, Noel could move the songs around the room like a churning mess of controlled sound. Noel gave them a *show.*

"I wanna thrill," barks Noel, remembering his DJ days. "I want them to feel like they've never felt in their life before. I'd see people's mouths on the dancefloor going "Wow! What was that?" It's like those movie theatres today where you hear the gunshot behind you. It was the same with me. Except I was doing it in the sixties."

Noel mixed records, too. On a primitive setup—he just had a volume dial for each deck—he would take elements from a track and tease and taunt the crowd with them: a Jimi Hendrix guitar lick here or a Chambers Brothers a cappella there—allusive whispers, barely heard fragments. Then he would slam the whole song through the mincer. "People would come up to me and say, 'I was listening to the Mamas and Papas and now I'm listening to the Stones and I didn't even know.' I used to try some of the wildest changes without losing a beat." Noel's reputation had risen to the point where producers would bring test pressings of their latest confections. He still has the metal test disc that Smokey Robinson and Berry Gordy brought down of Smokey's new production, the Marvelettes' "Don't Mess With Bill."

Celebrities assailed the club. Everyone wanted a piece of Arthur, so the new and symbolic velvet rope kept the undesirables at bay, with Mickey Deans as doorpicker (Deans later married Judy Garland, twelve weeks before she died, after meeting her at Arthur). What Burton was looking for was that perfect mix, like a great cocktail, where all the ingredients meshed together perfectly. She singled out what she termed the PYPs (Pretty Young People), the not-yet-rich, "good-looking working girls with lots of dates, models, sub-editors on magazines." Burton even had a phrase for those terminally unhip folk who *still* did the twist: mippys.

Noel didn't suffer fools gladly either. "John Wayne asked me for 'Yellow Rose of Texas,'" he recalls. "I said, 'Gee, I happen to have it.' And I go—snap!—'Oh, it's broken' and I threw it on the dancefloor. He goes, 'You faggot!' His toupée was falling off his head. Sybil was sitting behind where he was; Judy Garland was sitting beside her and Lauren Bacall next to her. They go, 'Teeerrrry!' They loved it, because they hated him."

Soon this new haunt of celebrities was no longer unique. Shepheard's opened in the Drake Hotel with a decor that recalled imperial Egypt; there was L'Ondine where Terry Noel moved after Arthur (and where a young Jimi Hendrix was briefly a busboy); Geoffrey Leeds opened L'Interdit in the

Gotham Hotel; Trude Heller's The Trik made waves downtown. Whiskey Disque in Los Angeles became the first to open up on the west coast, with socialite Mimi London's Le Disque Alexis following swiftly in San Francisco.

As for Terry Noel, he eventually gave his music career for art and today is to be found painting in his downtown studio. However, he had a long run as a DJ, moving from Arthur to L'Ondine and hence to a new Greenwich Village haunt, Salvation, where he continued his experiments, even to the point of mixing with three record decks.

"Salvation was very about the records," he says. "That was when I went into three turntables. I was really into it. Soul. Absolutely. The Chambers Brothers' 'Time' was like the theme song to Salvation. I'd build up to that and everybody would know it was coming. I'd turn off all the lights and you'd hear—thud, thud, thud."

He aimed to control as much as he could. "We had this ball that had a light inside it and it shot out little rays of light and it actually had a string on it and I would pull it to make it rock across the dancefloor. The song's going 'Time has come today,' I'm doing lights, I'm pulling strings. I was like the Wizard of Oz.

"This is a play. You're directing a play. It's very dramatic. It has to be dramatic, and no automatic programming is ever going to be any use, because it's different every night and every time you play the record."

For the DJs who came after him, Terry Noel was the man who wrote the instruction manual. Those in his wake would add considerable layers of artistry and intensity, but Noel was the prototype of the modern DJ. Unlike those later who would dig deep to find the most primal dance tracks, his tastes were resolutely pop; and his love of celebrity and celebrities prevented him from sacrificing everything for the dancefloor, but in technical respects, and in terms of putting on a show, Terry Noel was a founding force.

The DJ owes him a great debt for his obsessive control of the musical experience and for his cunning manipulation of the crowd. And we can never ignore the fact that this was the first DJ to ever mix records. His mixes may have been primitive by today's standards, but it was Terry Noel who first hit on the idea that two records could be sewn together somehow.

Acid

As we know, at some point in history nightclubs became places of grand spectacle—great throbbing systems of sound and light, otherworldly places that can shake reality right out of your bones; and clubbers were transformed from members of an audience into active, reciprocating participants, vital components of the transcendent musical ritual. This change happened gradually for a while, as the club experience trundled on behind technology, musical experiments and social customs. But then, all of a sudden . . . there was acid!

"Who needs jazz, or even beer, when you can sit down on a public curbstone, drop a pill in your mouth, and hear fantastic music for hours at a time in your head?" queried Hunter S. Thompson in the *New York Times.* "A cap of good acid costs $5, and for that you can hear the Universal Symphony, with God singing solo and the Holy Ghost on drums."

LSD arrived on the club scene in the early sixties. Club drugs before had been largely about increasing your energy, but instead of the paranoid frenzy of cocaine or the menacing endurance of amphetamines, LSD went straight to work on your very senses. One acid trip turned most into instant LSD evangelists. Or certifiable basket cases. Or both.

The drug radically changed the complexion of nightclubs. In London, psychedelic vessels UFO and Middle Earth replaced the clenched-jaw dregs of mod's soul dream. In New York, the brain-frying experiences of Electric Circus took the elitism of Arthur and drenched it in blotter. But it was in San Francisco—at least initially—where the effects would be felt first.

Although the scene in San Francisco was by no means DJ-led (in fact, their role was insignificant), much of what happened was about dancing. It was also very much concerned with heightening visual and aural stimulation, and in line with the effects of this amazing new chemical compound, it spurred the creation of incredible light shows and daunting sound equipment.

When acid house and rave culture blossomed in the late eighties, it would find in itself all manner of evocative echoes from the psychedelic sixties—from the feelings of community and the scale of its events to the belief that this combination of drugs and music could really, no honestly . . . if only you'd try it . . . change the world.

San Francisco and the Acid Tests

Novelist Ken Kesey introduced San Francisco to LSD. Kesey had discovered lysergic acid after volunteering for government-sponsored tests at Menlo Park Veterans Hospital in Palo Alto, thirty miles south of San Francisco. In 1965, Kesey and his cabal of Merry Pranksters (a loose aggregation of freaks, drop-outs and former beatniks) began throwing parties under the title "The Acid Test." The acid was supplied by a wild-eyed and very gifted chemist called Augustus Owsley Stanley III, whose product was so coveted that Jimi

Hendrix ordered a run of 100,000 tabs for his own personal use. Owsley was later described by a government official as having done for LSD what Ford did for the motor car. His first batch of acid was available for consumption on March 5, 1965.

The Acid Tests were a series of freeform "events" in which the participants drank Kool-Aid laced with Owsley's finest. Music blared out, lights and slides were projected onto walls and people danced until either their legs or drugs gave out. The first Acid Test took place following a Rolling Stones concert at the San Jose Civic Center on December 4, 1965. Prankster lieutenant Ken Babbs handed concertgoers flyers asking, "Can YOU Pass The Acid Test?" Around three hundred turned up, tuned in and dropped out to a freakshow bombardment of the senses.

The band that day was the Warlocks, playing a wild amalgam of bluegrass, country, and rhythm and blues. They changed their name specially for the event. After considering various options, among them Mythical Ethical Icicle Tricicle and Nonreality Sandwich, they decided to call themselves the Grateful Dead.

The Dead did to rock music what the disco DJs would later do for dance music: they contorted it to within an inch of its life. As Tom Wolfe related in *The Electric Kool-Aid Acid Test*, "They were not to be psychedelic dabblers, painting pretty pictures, but true explorers." Their "songs" became rubberized workouts that were tailored there and then, specifically for the needs of dancers, whose bodies—and, often, clothing—had been loosened from their moorings and set adrift on memory bliss. "At the Avalon or the Fillmore," wrote Joel Selvin in *Summer Of Love*, "the Dead would play songs as long as they felt good, as long as they made people dance, and when most of the audience is high on something, that can be a long time."

There may not have been a disc jockey or a turntable at work, but this was a radical new approach to music, one which today's DJs will recognize immediately.

In the center of the room at one Acid Test, a tangle of scaffolding towered up into the eerie darkness. Kesey, sitting atop it surrounded by projectors, lights and sound equipment, scribbled messages in gels on the projector. He then poured water onto his creation and watched the words dissolve into puddles of nonsense at the bottom. A troupe of conga drummers hammered hypnotic polyrhythms into the heads of the dancers below. Amid this chaotic muddle, there were people with their shoes off counting their toes, or talking to the scaffolding.

Owsley took the Dead under his wing, and began experimenting with electronic equipment for them to incorporate into their shows: tape loops, recording devices, even primitive video equipment. The Acid Tests became increasingly weird. "Allen Ginsberg could be seen wandering around in this white hospital-orderly suit, staring around with a look of amazement," wrote Charles Perry in *Rolling Stone.* "There were *all* these . . . crazy . . . people . . . wearing antique gowns, paisley prints, spacesuits, with paint on their faces and feathers in their hair, dancing, dancing."

The Acid Tests took place all over the Bay Area of San Francisco and, latterly, in Los Angeles. The last one was on October 2, 1966. The San Francisco scene that spawned peace and love slowly began to sink in a pit of heroin. A few days later, on October 6, LSD was finally made illegal in the state of California.

Psychedelic London

The links between London and the growing scene of Pranksters in the U.S. were close, and acid fairly quickly started making inroads into the tight mod scene. (In fact, London's main supplier, Michael Hollingshead, had been the one to turn Timothy Leary on to LSD.) London clubs would soon dissolve in a haze of dope smoke and a rainbow of psychedelics.

A Ladbroke Grove-based group called the London Free School launched a club on December 23, 1966. The LFS was an informal brood of Notting Hill hippies, local working-class people and black activists like Michael X. One of their number was a talented young record producer called Joe Boyd, who went on to work with Pink Floyd, Fairport Convention and Toots & the Maytals. The club was called UFO (pronounced "*Yoofo*").

Housed in a ramshackle Irish ballroom at 31 Tottenham Court Road called the Blarney Club, UFO was not a dance club in any understanding of the word. There was no DJ, only an American electronics wizard called Jack Henry Moore who would play tapes, records by the Grateful Dead or reel-to-reels of electronic music. The Pink Floyd and Soft Machine became the club's twin totems. Other bands would perform there. One was called the Purple Gang, whose Joe Boyd-produced "Granny Takes A Trip" was an underground anthem. After performing there, their leader Peter "Lucifer" Walker disbanded the group to become a witch. It was that kind of a club.

"The Acid Tests were coming over," recalls Jeff Dexter. "All the underground poets were arriving. UFO reflected this. It was totally unstructured. It was a free-for-all. There was no presentation as such, it just happened. For

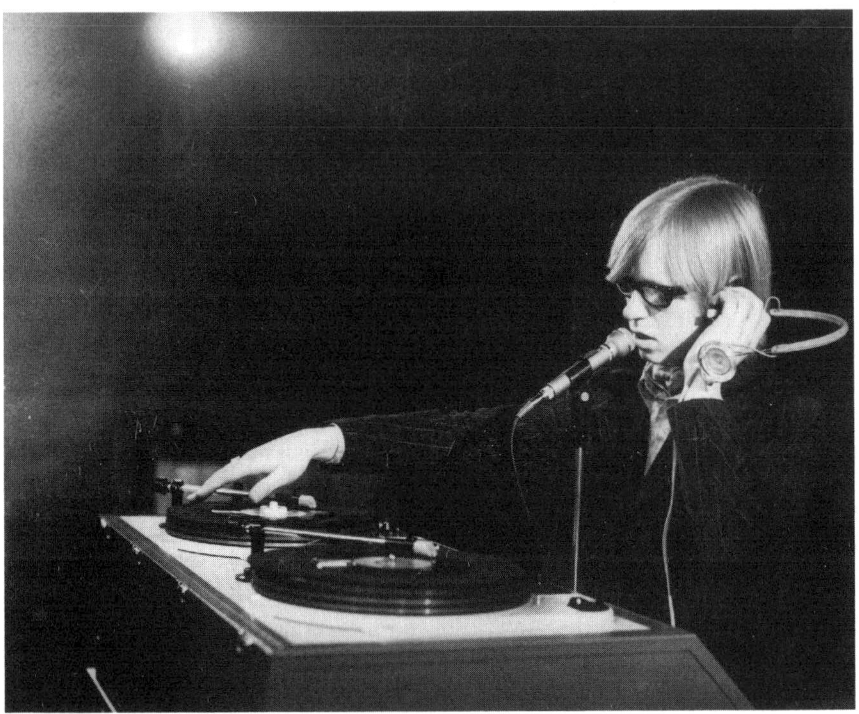

Maximum R&B—mod-about-town Jeff Dexter plays the platters that matter at his Record and Light Show in 1966.

me, coming out of the straight world of ballroom showbiz, this was a brave new world."

Dexter, by now resident at Tiles where his Record & Light Show straddled both worlds, would bring records for Moore to play. Moore reciprocated by introducing Dexter to records that he characterized as "really weird American stuff." Inside this psychedelic cocoon, people would trip out, read books, dance or simply stare at the refracting patterns of lights on the wall. John Peel was a regular visitor. "The only time I took acid deliberately was at UFO because I felt I was kind of safe," he recalls. "It wasn't like clubbing is these days. Rather than dancing around—obviously some people danced about in a fairly idiotic manner—mostly you just lay on the floor and passed out, really." He laughs energetically. "It sounds like fun, doesn't it?"

UFO fell in Tottenham Court Road police station's patch. The cops there would draw straws from broken plastic spoons to decide whose turn it was to visit. "The principal danger was from acid-crazed Hell's Angels," wrote Miles in *NME.* "Anxious to practice love'n'peace in order to pull hippie nookie, they would insist on French-kissing every policeman they saw."

The UFO found an echo in Middle Earth in Covent Garden. Middle Earth took the UFO template and exposed it to a more suburban crowd. Both John Peel and Jeff Dexter DJed there. Dexter may have been entranced by this brave new world, but he was still acutely aware of the purpose of a disc jockey in a nightclub: to make people dance.

"John hated ska and bluebeat and most of those records that I'd lived on," remembers Dexter. "He thought they were awful. I was totally into what he was doing, but he didn't understand what I was doing. The thing is, people still loved to dance and you really couldn't dance to a lot of the new psychedelic records that were around. They were horrible to dance to. So to keep people moving I had to mix it up a bit."

New York

New York's jet set was not immune. It, too, would soon succumb to the pretty category mistakes of LSD.

In 1966 Brooklyn-born Jerry Brandt purchased a beaten-down Polish meeting hall on St. Mark's Place in the East Village. A talent-booker by trade, Brandt was no hippie but he could see an opportunity when it presented itself. He called his new venue the Electric Circus.

Just prior to its sale, another creative opportunist had noticed its potential. Andy Warhol booked it for the whole of April 1966, called it Exploding Plastic Inevitable and installed his latest protégés, the Velvet Underground. He projected lights through gauze and onto a wall. Nico sang "I'll Be Your Mirror," while Warhol showed movies behind her. As she performed, a silver ball sent shards of light scurrying through the room, like glass shattering.

"You trudged upstairs to this place that smelled of urine," wrote John Cale in *What's Welsh For Zen.* "It was filthy and had no lights in it, but Andy took it over and turned it into something totally different. Nobody had seen or heard anything like this before. We transformed this dump into an exciting, jumping place."

Jerry Brandt maintained Warhol's approach when he made it the Electric Circus. After financing the club with an audacious scheme in which the Coffee Growers' Association contributed $250,000, provided coffee was the main drink served in the club, he brought in Ivan Chermayeff who had designed the America Pavilion at the World's Fair. The designer transformed Electric

Circus into a gigantic psychedelic Bedouin tent comprised of white stretch yarn. Projections of home movies, liquid lights and morphing glutinous blobs glowed on the fabric. A gigantic sound system blasted rock freakouts to the St. Vitus dancers.

The Electric Circus trumpeted itself as "the ultimate legal experience" yet it was far from it. Drugs were rife. *The Village Voice* compared it with Rome shortly before the fall. "There was no alcohol served," Brandt told Anthony Haden-Guest. "I was afraid, because everyone was doing LSD." The Electric Circus was immortalized in *Coogan's Bluff* as the Pigeon-Toed Orange Peel Club, where Clint Eastwood chases an errant hippie prisoner into this den of iniquity. He soon collapses in a stoned stupor as the lights pulse and throb around him.

Electric Circus had a rival in the psychedelic stakes called Cheetah. Ironically, this had been opened by Le Club's staid Frenchman, Oliver Coquelin. Situated on the site of the Arcadia Ballroom near Broadway's theatre district, it threw its doors open on May 28, 1966. The cavernous space had a dancefloor with silver circular podiums scattered randomly like outsized polka dots. Each supported a girl frugging. Above, a cavalcade of 3,000 colored lights palpitated gently, while a boutique at the back sold the latest Carnaby Street fashions. And there was smooth and soft black velvet everywhere—except the bar, which was covered in fake fur.

In the basement there was a TV room and on the upper floor a cinema showed the latest, strangest, underground movies. *Variety* got rather excited about this new *boîte*: "GOTHAM'S NEW CHEETAH A KINGSIZED WATUSERY WITH A FORT KNOX POTENTIAL," it declared.

A striking Puerto Rican teenager, Yvon Leybold, clad in hot pants and fishnets, ventured down from Spanish Harlem. "Cheetah was the first real disco club I went to," she recalls. "That was a lot of fun. It was a very mixed atmosphere. It was the first time I went into a place and you see lights and you see atmosphere, instead of the rinky-dink places I was used to."

The End of the Beginning

The psychedelic era, though initially based on dancing, would eventually take the rhythm out of rhythm and blues. Rock, after a trip too many, would soon drift well away from the dancefloor and become *serious* music, sounds for the head rather than the body.

When the hippie dream spluttered to a halt, the same fate seemingly awaited the discothèque. The Electric Circus filed for bankruptcy, and Arthur spun its final disc on June 21, 1969. Under the headline "DISCOTHÈQUES GO-GO INTO OBLIVION AS JUVES TURN TO NEW KICKS AND SOUNDS," *Variety* predicted the end for the nightclub boom. "The closing of Arthur indicates that the day of the discothèque is virtually over," they claimed.

In fact, it was only just beginning.

The whole hippie trip had opened up the doors of perception for club promoters, showing them just how much it was possible to do within the club experience. This brief era also acted as a powerful inspiration in the lives of future visionaries like disco pioneer David Mancuso—indeed disco's early years would be full of the brotherly love which sixties acid seemed to foment. Its styles, its artwork, its decor, and its *psychedelia* would be echoed in the shock waves of acid house twenty years later. And its events added a lot to the DJ's armory, even if he hadn't played much of a part.

Once the disc jockey had come out from the radio and entered the dancing arena, his job had changed radically. He was now no longer a simple record selector and tastemaker, he had the essential fact of audience response to deal with. Now that the relation between music and audience was interactive, the audience had become part of the event—in some sense, the audience *was* the event, and the DJ a responsive controller of their pleasure.

By the end of the sixties, the notion of the discothèque had come a long way. It was now supported by some relatively sophisticated hardware, some very creative disc jockeys and a complex series of interwoven cultures devoted to dance and music. In less than a quarter of a century, the idea of dancing to someone playing records had evolved from a bizarre experiment in a Yorkshire working men's club to an intricate world of nightclubs, DJs, drugs and music.

This world had matured more rapidly in the UK than the U.S.—maybe because Britain seems to invest far more energy in its youth culture, which is somehow more accepting of outside novelties and is usually energetically downmarket in its social makeup. While the café society were twisting in New York's Peppermint Lounge, the kids doing the same dance in the Lyceum were clerks, apprentices and shop girls. Perhaps it's because Britain is a nation based on duty, a country of subjects not citizens, that its young people expend so much effort in trying to escape, but it's here that club culture was built, even if the records which filled it were from across the Atlantic. As the pages turn on the DJ's story, you'll see that Britain made him a home, while America gave him his music.

The connections between the two countries have always been strong, and one theme has a particular resonance—the passionate romance between white working-class kids in the UK and black music made in America. Perhaps the connection is work, perhaps it's the refusal to defer pleasure. If you were black and American you sang about pay day, you waited for the eagle on your dollar to fly. If you were British and working class, you just said Ready Steady Go, the weekend starts here.

2
HOW THE DJ CHANGED MUSIC

FOUR
NORTHERN SOUL

After Tonight Is All Over

"The northern soul scene, to me, was like an eighth wonder of the world. You're looking at the depressed north of England, where there wasn't a great deal there apart from steelworks and coalmines. You had people doing this boring repetitive work during the week; and hard work, too. And when they went out on a weekend, they *really* wanted to go out. Going out until 11 o'clock to the local pub just wasn't going to be good enough.

"When the whole rave thing went ballistic it felt like northern soul twenty years on. Lots of people getting off their heads, dancing to fast music and this *love* attitude. House is this generation's version of northern soul. But what was so revolutionary about northern soul was there was no antecedent for it."

—Ian Dewhirst, aka "Frank," northern soul DJ

"Northern soul exists as a fascinating example of a predominantly working-class, drug-fuelled youth culture which (unlike house) was never controlled by the music industry, because the music industry never understood it. Northern soul was a true and near-perfect underground scene."

—John McCready, *The Face*

You live in a nondescript town somewhere in the north of England. Row upon row of factories fill the horizon with chimneys, scarring the sky with belches of dark gray smoke. During the week, in one of those factories, you work the nine-to-five drudge: manning the production line, sweeping the yard, shoveling shit. The job is unrewarding, but it pays enough for you to live. More importantly, it pays enough for you to go out and dance.

Because though the factory may be your job, it is certainly not your life. Every weekend, you travel to other nondescript northern towns, you dress up, you pop pills and you dance to pacey, obscure soul records, all the time dreaming of singers from impossibly glamorous places like Detroit, Chicago and Philadelphia.

Your uniform is unfashionable but highly practical. From your white Fred Perry polo shirt down to your leather-soled Ravel shoes, everything you wear is built for comfort *and* for speed. The drugs you take are practical too: an array of amphetamines, swallowed with the express purpose of keeping you on the dancefloor till morning.

You dance to records by unknown artists, on labels no one knows about, singing songs that few have ever heard. Yet these records are the ones you treasure; the ones you spend tens of pounds—sometimes even hundreds—from your meager salary to acquire.

Your friends, still stuck on progressive rock or perhaps discovering the glittery pop modes of glam rock and Bowie, laugh at you. They don't understand the secret world you inhabit. They don't understand the clothes, the music, the rituals of your underground existence. For you are a member of a closed order, you belong to one of the most pure and untainted musical movements ever. You are a northern soul boy.

The First Rave Culture

A full fifteen years before rave culture would whistle into existence, northern soul provided it with an almost complete blueprint. Here was a scene where working-class kids came together in large numbers, across great distances, to obscure places, to take drugs and dance to music that no one else cared about. It was a scene in which togetherness and belonging were all important. It was long ignored or treated with contempt by the sophisticates of music journalism and London clubland, allowing it to develop largely undisturbed and unobserved. And, just like the rave movement (in which "hardcore" diverged from the more mainstream side of the scene in an effort to preserve the music's original spirit), northern soul ended with a dramatic split, as the progressive DJs found their more open-minded musical policies fiercely opposed by the traditionalists.

Northern soul has largely been written off as a musical cul-de-sac, but in fact it was a vitally important step in the creation of today's club culture and in the evolution of the DJ. Many of the first records to dent the UK pop charts as a result of club play came from northern soul. It was northern soul DJs who introduced many of the craft's stylistic innovations and it wasn't a coincidence that the first DJs forward-thinking enough to play house music in the UK came from a northern soul background. In fact, until disco emerged in New York, thanks to northern soul and clubs like the Catacombs and the Twisted Wheel, British DJ culture was far more advanced than its American counterpart.

What northern soul brought to the DJ was *obsession*. Because it placed an incredible premium on musical rarity, it made him into an obsessed and compulsive collector of vinyl. It taught him the value of playing records no one else owned, of spending months, years and hundreds of pounds in search of that one unheard song which would bring an audience to its knees. It sent the DJ across the oceans to hunt in dusty warehouses and tiny rural outhouses for unknown classics which his competitors didn't have and couldn't play. Northern soul showed the DJ how to turn vinyl into gold dust.

A Genre Built From Failures

Roughly speaking, northern soul was the music made by the hundreds of singers and bands who were copying the Detroit sound of sixties Motown pop. Most of this was a complete failure in its own time and place—it was the music of unsuccessful artists, tiny labels and small towns, all lost within the vast expanses of the U.S. entertainment machine—but in northern England from the end of the sixties through to its heyday in the middle seventies, it was exhumed and exalted.

And it is named because of where it was enjoyed, not where it was made (though this would make sense, too). The word "northern" in northern soul refers not to Detroit but to Wigan; not to Chicago, but to Manchester, Blackpool and Cleethorpes.

Basing a genre around a love of music that the rest of the world had forgotten was a bit like inviting a bunch of friends around to speak Latin, but in clubs dotted across the British industrial north, this was exactly what happened. It might have been because their drug-taking habits demanded a certain kind of music, or because this fast, escapist style—originating as it did in Detroit, the *motor* city—somehow resonated with their mechanized existence. It might simply have been that they were reluctant to see their favorite music die now that the rest of the world had grown tired of it. Whatever the reason, working-class youngsters (almost all white) in the north of England started to lionize a series of records which had been complete flops in their original context. The worship of such tunes became a thriving underground club scene.

Baggy trousers—northern soul not only pioneered breakdancing but also invented trousers big enough to accommodate a family of four.

For many years, because it was so independent, this scene was also very pure. Northern soul was entirely club-based, so it needed no chart approval, no crossover hits. And because it was a retro movement, it needed no new bands or bright young stars. In fact, since all its records had been made years ago, it needed absolutely nothing from the music industry.

What it did require, however, was an army of dedicated and driven collectors determined to unearth enough good records to keep the scene going. Without "new" records being discovered and played, it would have quickly degenerated into nothing more dynamic than an oldies appreciation society. Luckily, there was plenty of incentive for voyages of discovery.

Northern soul had a particular appeal for collectors since it was built almost entirely from rarities. A record couldn't just be good, it also had to be rare as hell. If a track sounded like it had been recorded in a garden shed in Detroit, then so much the better. (In any case, it probably had been recorded in a garden shed in Detroit.) On top of this, there was the enticing fact that a collection of northern soul was—in theory, at least—*completable*: because only songs made in a certain style during a certain period in a certain place were acceptable, there was a strictly finite number of good records to discover and possess. Work obsessively enough and you could one day own the full set.

Plus, given this vinyl fetishism, the prestige which went with finding new records was enormous. In this closed world, the man who discovered a song like R. Dean Taylor's "There's A Ghost In My House" or "Tainted Love" by Gloria Jones could expect showers of admiration, even public adoration. A DJ with an exclusive tune would watch his crowd swell rapidly and his status increase. The value of records rocketed accordingly.

"When you find an unknown record, it's like seeing a baby suddenly mature," reflects Ian Dewhirst, a key northern DJ. "You listen to it at home and wonder whether it will work. And then you see your vision confirmed. Suddenly it's a hot one. Seeing an unknown record go from zero value to being valuable. It was almost like the stock market."

In the clubs, dancers drove themselves into ecstasies of excitement over the latest treasure from America. Posters for dances advertised not only the DJs who'd be there but also the rare records they would play. Given this unprecedented discophilia, the hunt for the rarest sounds went to comically tortuous lengths. Though the financial rewards were usually scant in comparison, there was no shortage of intrepid explorers scraping together a passage to the new world, confident that they would return not with a box of dusty and forgotten 7-inch singles, but with a casket of priceless pearls.

The Twisted Wheel and Roots of Northern Soul

When Eddie Holland, Lamont Dozier and Brian Holland penned the follow-up to the Four Tops' Motown smash "Ask The Lonely" in 1965, little did they realize that it would be so influential for a strange sect of soul-obsessed

DJs in the north of England. The song was called "I Can't Help Myself (Sugar Pie Honey Bunch)." From its opening salvo of drums, bass and piano to the dizzy whorls of strings, double snare hits and rhythmic vibraphone licks that perch underneath Levi Stubbs's spiraling vocal delivery, it provided a blueprint for northern soul.

"I Can't Help Myself" had *exactly* the kind of sound they liked at the Twisted Wheel. In this spartan basement club near Manchester city center, around 600 kids would squeeze in cheek-by-jowl every Saturday night and dance to some of rarest sounds in the country. And do so until 7:30 every Sunday morning.

The Twisted Wheel began business in November 1963 at 26 Brasenose Street as an all-nighter, playing a mix of blues, early soul, bluebeat and jazz (On 18 September 1965 it moved to a second location at 6 Whitworth Street). The fad for all-night dance parties had been around for some time and it was by no means the first to hold them. But within a couple of years, as the contours of clubland changed significantly around it, the Wheel would become a rare oasis for such music.

In London and the south, the rock underground began to dominate. In northern clubs, this trend caused not a ripple. Perhaps this was because the staunchly working-class north clung onto the escapism of all-night soul sessions. Maybe it was simply that pop culture moved far more slowly than now. Communications between London and the rest of the country were certainly more limited and the only significant music publications specialized in rock and pop. So the Wheelites, blissfully unaware that they were becoming an anachronism, continued to dance to the uptempo soul records that they loved.

There was a good reason for the fast nature of the songs played at the Wheel. Its clientele was wired on speed. They consumed the full range, from black bombers and purple hearts, to prellies and dexys (drinamyl, preludine and dexedrine) either bought from dealers in the club or stolen from pharmacies. It wasn't unusual for dancers traveling to a soul club to stop on the way to break into a drugstore for the evening's sustenance.

"The bad lads must've reconnoitered all the different ways into Wigan," remembers Ian Dewhirst, "and looked at the chemist shops that didn't have the greatest security. And whichever way they came in, you could almost bet your life that a chemist would be broken into."

Fueled by these prescription amphetamines, they danced in a highly gymnastic manner to songs of a very specific type. Tempo was all. To make it at the Wheel, a record had to be energetic enough to keep up with the speed-freak dancers—propelled by an urgent, stomping Motown beat, liberally sprinkled with horns and strings, and finished off with a melodramatic black vocal. This music wasn't funky, but it sure was fast. The lyrics told not of sex, but of love; sentimental tunes that provided a soundtrack of escape from the factory treadmill.

"The Twisted Wheel was an unusual little place with five rooms and stone floors," remembers Dave Evison, who later DJed at Wigan Casino. "Bike wheels everywhere you looked. It took me four weeks to work out where the disc jockey was: he was hiding behind a pile of scrap metal! As part of the dancing, the kids used to run up the walls to see how high they could get. It was young, eager. There was a respect for the disc jockey; there was a respect for what he played. It was a good scene."

What was remarkable was the mobility of the clubbers who started going there. Soul aficionados traveled miles to reach the Twisted Wheel. If you thought no one went further than their home town to dance until the days of raves, think again: these kids were doing this not in 1989 but in *1969.*

"Part of the enjoyment was actually travelling there," remembers Carl Woodroffe, who as Farmer Carl Dene would become one of the scene's pioneer DJs. "And the motorways didn't really exist then as they do now. The M6, for example, didn't start until you went north of Cannock to go to Manchester."

Clad in casual clothes, Wheelites like Dene would journey up to Manchester before changing into their pristine, freshly pressed mohair suits, crisp white shirts and skinny ties. This style, ubiquitous in the Wheel, was handed down to its clubbers from the mods of the early sixties. And, irrespective of the heat in the club, that's the way they would remain until the drive home. "You'd be wringing wet with sweat but still wearing your suit when you came out of the club," laughs Dene. "But a suit was always a good way of endearing yourself to the women. It went down well, that."

The first Wheel on Brazenose Street was where the northern soul sound originated. Its resident DJ Roger Eagle had broad tastes in black music, playing the gritty blues of Little Walter, Art Blakey's rhythm-heavy modern jazz, and mixing in Solomon Burke and early Motown. Although imports were scarce in early sixties Britain, he had been making money importing Chess and Checker records from America, and played such records there right from the Wheel's opening night.

However, Eagle watched as the speeding dancers increasingly dictated the nature of his music. He would eventually leave in frustration at the pill scene at the Wheel, as it forced his quite eclectic playlist towards a single, stomping tempo.

"I started northern soul, but I actually find the music very limiting," he recounted, "because in the early days I'd play a Charlie Mingus record, then I'd play a bluebeat disc followed by a Booker T. tune, then a Muddy Waters or Bo Diddley record. Gradually, there was this blanding out to one sort of sound. When I started DJing, I could play what I wanted. But after three years I had to keep to the same tempo, which is what northern soul is."

Sure enough, by the time the Wheel moved venues to Whitworth Street, its music had narrowed considerably. The club's later residents—Phil Saxe, Les Cokell, Rob Bellars, Brian Phillips and Paul Davies—concentrated on more uptempo sounds. By then, the Wheel was the place to play. "Oh, it was a bit of a cult thing at the Wheel, if you got to DJ there," laughs Bellars. "There were people begging to do it!"

Though there was a considerable variety of styles and tempos, these later DJs played strictly soul. "We were playing more what you'd have called rhythm and blues, but then we were playing new releases like the Incredibles, Sandy Sheldon and all the good Stateside stuff. We were playing imports like 'Agent Double-O Soul' by Edwin Starr. We were playing things on Revilot and Ric-Tic. Everything on OKeh came out of the Wheel. They weren't necessarily frantically fast, but these were the forerunners of what became known as northern soul."

Bellars is keen to dismiss the misinformation that has been spread about the club's music. "People have said that the Wheel only played British releases," he says, "but that's rubbish." In fact, he and his cohorts hunted down records from all manner of places: from London's influential Record Corner, from a raft of sources in the Midlands and from Stateside stores like Randy's Records in Tennessee.

The More Obscure the Better

The reason northern soul jocks were forced to look for rarities was quite simple: by the early seventies, the U.S. had largely stopped producing the right records. Black America had moved on from the snappy pop-soul of Motown, and its producers—alongside the hugely influential James Brown and Sly & the Family Stone—had started experimenting with other rhythms and sounds. Soul begat funk, and the accent transferred to languorous fatback rhythms rather than yearning melody. For Manchester, this wouldn't do at all. Of course, it was still great black music, but it was too funky and slow for a crowd hyped on a head full of pills. They needed something with a bit more urgency than "Say It Loud, I'm Black And I'm Proud." So the DJs started to dig deeper and look for older records that did have the requisite beat and the by-now *de rigueur* helping of strings.

Ian Levine, later to become northern soul's most influential DJ, first visited the Wheel in the final period of its eight-year run. He recalls the change as the search for obscure oldies began.

"People were fed up with the same old songs—like Frankie Valli's 'You're Ready Now' and Earl Van Dyke's 'Six By Six'—that had been played at the Wheel for years. There was a hungry crowd at the all-nighters, pilled out of their heads on amphetamines, who wanted to dance to fast Motown-style records," says Levine. "Rob Bellars discovered that by finding these hard-to-get records, the scene thrived."

It was this hunt that would uncover a vast well of previously unknown black soul records (and, eventually, some pretty execrable white ones, too). Fast enough for jaw-crunching youths to get off on, and sometimes even great enough to cross over and become pop hits.

And just as they went to great lengths to find the right kind of records for their dancefloor, these DJs were also learning how to work a crowd—prefiguring the kind of sophisticated approach which was about to emerge in far-off New York. There was no talking between records, just pure sequenced soul with peaks and troughs to keep the bug-eyed dancers happy. "A lot of the DJs would play records in a certain order, because of the way the people danced," remembers Bellars, describing how he'd play three of Bobby Freeman's discs, "The Duck," "C'mon And Swim" and "The Swim" in that order, because they built up in tempo. "You'd build it up gradually, and then you'd play about five fast records on the run. Then you'd slow it down because it was getting so manic."

Visitors to the Wheel were astonished by what they saw. "The dancing is without doubt the finest I have ever seen outside the USA," wrote Dave Godin, a black music columnist in *Blues & Soul* and the man who started Tamla Motown's UK operation. "Everybody there was an expert in soul clapping. In the right places, and with a clipped, sharp quality that adds an extra something in the appreciation of soul music. There was no undercurrent of tension or aggression that one sometimes finds in London clubs, but rather a benevolent atmosphere of friendship and camaraderie."

Noting the strength of the soul scene in the north, Godin, a Londoner, was the person who gave it its name. Inspired by his first pilgrimage to the Twisted Wheel, he coined the term "northern soul" in a *Blues & Soul* column in 1970.

Godin co-owned a record store in Soho's Monmouth Street called Soul City. He first remarked upon the difference in tastes between the north and south when northerners, down on football trips from the northwest, asked for a specific sound. "What I noticed was that people who came from the north were not buying what was subsequently called funk," says Godin. "So I started using the term northern soul, meaning that when we've got a shop full of people from the north, we should only play northern soul to them. That's how the term took off."

Manchester's Twisted Wheel provided much of the groundwork for what was to follow. As well as helping to inspire the scene's name, it had started the DJ on his obsessive hunt for undiscovered oldies, it had given him a network full of devoted (and musically knowledgeable) clubbers, and it had sparked the start of an intense love affair between white northern working-class youth and soulful black American music.

It had also consolidated the UK's lead in club culture. In the same period, New York had the plushest nightclubs, the most beautiful clientele, and sound systems that put ours to shame. It didn't matter. Culturally and musically, what was going on in the north of England was miles ahead of everywhere else.

Inspired by the Wheel, numerous soul clubs sprang up, serving the growing network of DJs, fans and collectors. Leicester had the Oodly Boodly (later the Night Owl). There was the Mojo in Sheffield (where the DJ was a young Peter Stringfellow), the Dungeon in Nottingham, the Lantern in Market Harborough and the Blue Orchid in Derby. In Birmingham there were all-nighters at the Whiskey-A-Go-Go, a club informally known as the Laura Dixon Dance Studios. However, none of these approached the influence of the Twisted Wheel. It was here, in a dank basement in Manchester, that a generation of collectors, clubbers and DJs fell in love with soul music.

Unfortunately, the Wheel's reputation as a drug haven meant it was finally closed down by Manchester council sometime in early 1971. In its final incarnation, the only way they had been able to open at all was with the co-operation of the local police drugs squad, who insisted on having a presence in the club during the all-nighters.

There were emotional scenes on its final night. "We knew it was going to close," says Rob Bellars, "but people were still crying." Looking back on the

Wheel's legacy in June 1974, one soul-boy told *Black Music*, "Something changed when the Wheel closed. You know, there was never quite the same everything-for-the-good-of-the-music scene."

The Catacombs and Farmer Carl

One club inextricably linked to the Twisted Wheel was the Catacombs in Temple Street, Wolverhampton. Although its early closing (it shut at midnight) restricted its direct influence, it was here that much of northern soul's early musical menu was drafted. Its DJ, Farmer Carl Dene, did more than perhaps any other to build firm foundations for northern soul. He was probably the first DJ on the scene to actually make an effort to unearth rare records, and one of the earliest to realize that having more rarities than your competitors could actually be a creative part of DJing. And by introducing and lending records to the DJs at the new Wheel, he was responsible for breaking many of northern soul's early anthems.

Farmer Carl Dene ("farmer" came from a hat he wore; Dene he felt was a suitably popstarish name) had started life as Carl Woodroffe. He discovered soul as a clubber firstly in his native Birmingham at the Whiskey-A-Go-Go, then at the Mojo in Sheffield and at the Twisted Wheel itself.

"I think it was because you couldn't hear it anywhere else," he says. "It was so unique. You wouldn't hear it on the radio. You wouldn't hear it in a regular nightclub. You'd have to go to a chosen place; and there were only a handful of those." A fervid collector, he started DJing at Le Metro in Birmingham, then at Chateau Impney in Droitwich and then, most famously, at the Catacombs.

Farmer Carl not only had good records, he had *rare* ones, too. Records that no one else seemed to have. Rather than playing the famous version of a song, he would seek out the rawer, more unfamiliar covers and champion those. An example is the wondrously named "I'm Not Going To Work Today" by Boot Hog Pefferley and the Loafers. This had been a minor hit for Clyde McPhatter, but Carl preferred the obscure version. He bought his copy from Roger Eagle. "It really hit me, that one," he remembers. "So I bought it for £1 10s, which was a lot of money then!"

"He was the one that discovered the records that were taken up to the Wheel," says Ian Levine, just one of the DJs who see Farmer Carl as the scene's mentor. "He found this record by Richard Temple called 'That Beating Rhythm' on Mirwood Records. Nobody even believed it existed. You had to go to the Catacombs to hear it." Dene also introduced the Sharpees' "Tired

Of Being Lonely," Gene Chandler and Barbara Acklin's "From The Teacher To The Preacher" and Doris Troy's northern classic "I'll Do Anything" (Troy later provided the background vocals for Pink Floyd's *Dark Side Of The Moon*). "Farmer Carl was the one they all thought of as a god," declares Levine.

There were others influencing the DJs' playlists, including a renowned collector from Gloucester known as Docker. He caused merriment among soul fans at the Wheel by carrying a lockable record box. One of the gems in this high-security safe was the only copy in the country of Leon Haywood's "Baby Reconsider," now regarded as a Wheel classic.

Although the scene was still in its formative years, it was already having an influence on the wider music industry—it was the nascent northern movement which spawned the first chart hits to have broken through the clubs rather than the radio. When a Contours 45, "Just A Little Misunderstanding" (originally recorded in 1965 and cowritten by Stevie Wonder), slithered into the charts in January 1970, it heralded a new era in dance music in the UK. Tami Lynn's "I'm Gonna Run From You" on John Abbey's Polydor-distributed Mojo Records, which reached #4 (UK) in May 1971, soon followed. Abbey, as founder/owner of *Blues & Soul*, was in a privileged position to see the possibilities of this music.

Confirmation of this new phenomenon came when the Tams' "Hey Girl Don't Bother Me," a record Farmer Carl Dene had been instrumental in breaking, peaked at #1 (UK) in July 1971.

"Everybody, particularly the girls, went absolutely wild about it," he says. "The company reissued it and Peter Powell, who was from Stourbridge, near to the Chateau in Droitwich, heard it and brought it on to the radio. He'd heard about the clamor for the record."

The Torch and the Birth of Northern Soul

If the Twisted Wheel was the foundry in which the northern sound was smelted down, and the Catacombs was where it was hammered into shape, then the Torch in sleepy Tunstall, on the outskirts of Stoke-on-Trent, was where it was polished into gleaming stainless steel. The Wheel and Catacombs created a fad; the Torch turned it into a fetish. Although the club only lasted for a year (most of 1972 until its closure in March 1973), it exerts a powerful hold over everyone who remembers it today.

The Torch's precursor, the Golden Torch, had during the sixties been a regular haunt of mods looking for a fix of rhythm and blues (they also had acts including the Graham Bond Organization and Johnny Johnson & The

Bandwagon performing). To get to it required orienteering skills that would have deterred all but the keenest—the nearest branch railway, Longport, was at least a mile away. From the outside it looked like a social club in the middle of a humdrum row of terraced housing (it was actually a converted cinema). Inside it looked like a ranch, and when full of dancers it could get as steamy as a sauna.

"There was an air of expectation going in there," says Ian Dewhirst, recalling his first all-nighter. Dewhirst would later, under the name "Frank" (after Huddersfield footballer Frank Worthington), be a key northern DJ. "It was like a dream. Like suddenly knowing you're home. And this wonderful"—a subtly ironic smile—"feeling of togetherness. All these other enthusiasts, misfits and nutters that had traveled from all over the place. It just felt like a really little, elite, very tight scene."

The Torch's soundtrack was almost entirely American soul imports, many of which were culled from the playlists of the Wheel. Its residents—Alan Day, Colin Curtis, Keith Minshull, Tony Jebb, Martyn Ellis and, latterly, Ian Levine—were all from the northwest.

Kev Roberts, later a resident at Wigan Casino, recalls his first visit there. "I absolutely loved it," he enthuses. "I lived for that particular club. I'd never come across so many unknown records in my life. And every one of them was a stonker. The song element was very important at the Torch, and the record had to have some substance to it. But they were all fast, furious great vocals. Girl groups. Odd labels. Obscurities on the OKeh label. They were great."

One particular night at the Torch will be long remembered by those in attendance, when a packed house gathered to hear a performance by Major Lance, a Chicago vocalist well past his peak. Immortalized on a later recording, Major Lance Live at the Torch was one of the northern scene's most legendary appearances.

With the scene resurrecting forgotten American soul records, it was inevitable that someone would want to dig up the singers themselves. Imagine: you're Major Lance—fallen far from stardom in your own country—and out of the blue you get a phone call from some nutty Englishman with a funny accent, gushing about records that even you have forgotten about. That's pretty much how it went. Singers like Jackie Wilson, Brenda Holloway and Edwin Starr found their careers enjoying a bizarre rebirth as a result.

"It's an opportunity I never got in the States," Brenda Holloway said on Granada TV's *25 Years Of The Wigan Casino.* "It's like a second chance. When I come over here I'm a star."

Major Lance had sung on a series of fantastic tunes on OKeh (mostly written by Curtis Mayfield) that had been resounding flops everywhere in the UK apart from on the floors of clubs like the Wheel (he had enjoyed six Top 40 hits in the U.S.). He had only ever had one minor hit in the UK, "Um Um Um Um Um," and that was back in 1964. The Torch's promoter, Chris Burton, had pulled off the not inconsiderable feat of locating Lance in Chicago and bringing him over for a performance. In spite of his lackluster accompaniment, Lance brought the house down.

"He sang with the worst band you've ever heard! It was some British band who had no concept of what northern soul was," recalls Ian Levine. "But that night was the first night I DJed there and it was the most electrifying night of my whole career." His voice audibly rising, he adds, "You could not have squeezed one more person in that club. They were hanging off the rafters. It must've been 120 degrees. It was so hot and packed, the sweat was rising off people's bodies as condensation and dripping back onto them from the ceiling."

Soul Wars: Wigan Casino vs Blackpool Mecca

Northern soul was too esoteric to ever become a mainstream movement. Its defining feature was rarity: you couldn't walk into Woolworth's and buy any of its records, you had to prove your love for them, either by paying a week's wages for a single dusty disc or by somehow visiting the States and scouring junk shops and cutout warehouses. Even before you could do this, there would be an extended apprenticeship as you studied the names of the most prized tunes, and learned each record's evocative history: who made it, why it was passed over, how it was discovered, who played it first...

The scene did cross over to some extent. There were chart hits when certain records were reissued by major labels; there were new bands attempting to recreate that northern soul sound. On the whole, though, as a retro movement, it had an inbuilt protection against commercialization, since it revolved around collectors not consumers. The converse of this was that it contained the seeds of its own destruction. By definition, a scene based on discovering "new" oldies would eventually run out of fresh music.

The soul scene's golden era was centered around two clubs. In Wigan, a Lancashire cotton town, there was the Casino; an hour's drive away in Blackpool, at the mercy of the Irish Sea, there was the Mecca (more exactly, the Mecca's Highland Rooms). These two cathedrals of soul vied with each other to play the rarest, hottest records. Thousands of kids crisscrossed the country to hear their resident DJs throw down the latest unbelievable discoveries amid a barrage of scorching favorites. Clubbers to this day have fierce arguments over which was the best of the two places, their memories gloriously misted from the music, the people, the emotions and the drugs.

Eventually, these same two clubs would preside over the death of the scene. After sharing northern soul's glory years, the rivalry between Wigan Casino and Blackpool Mecca would accelerate into warfare as they fought over the soul of soul, enduring the scene's bitter identity crisis, disputing the direction to be taken when the world's supply of great lost tunes was finally exhausted.

However, for many years before that, they were both amazing places. Both the Mecca and the Casino still conjure up memories for a whole generation of northern clubbers—memories of walking in, their hearts in their mouths, ready to dance themselves into pools of sweat; memories of dancehalls steamy with gurning soul boys and girls leaping and spinning to stomping drums and pleading voices.

In 1978 *Billboard* declared the Wigan Casino the world's best discothèque, only a year before it awarded New York's Paradise Garage the same accolade. For many, Wigan Casino is synonymous with northern soul. Open between 1973 and 1981, in its heyday it was the biggest, most successful nationally known expression of a solidly regional scene. Many also remember it as the best.

This status is based largely on its huge membership (100,000 at its peak) and the fact that it pulled in the largest number of clubbers week in, week out. It was undoubtedly popular. However, claims that it was actually the *best* of the northern soul clubs need to be taken with a pinch of salt. It wasn't the most influential club, it certainly wasn't the most adventurous and, towards its final years, as it purveyed a procession of sometimes laughable records whose only merit was a snappy northern beat, it somewhat undermined its claims to the northern crown. Writer John McCready has compared it to today's Ministry of Sound, urging that historians shouldn't overemphasize its importance simply because it crammed the most people in. Nevertheless, the name Wigan Casino holds a special place in the memories of thousands and even today, for many it represents the true northern soul club: the Heart of Soul.

If the Casino was the choice of the masses, then the Blackpool Mecca was the connoisseurs' pick. It was here the most devoted dancers, collectors and disc jockeys gathered on a weekly basis to check out the latest unearthed tunes.

Mecca's resident DJ, Ian Levine, had a big advantage over other soul collectors and disc jockeys of the time. He had wealthy parents (they owned the Lemon Tree entertainment complex on the town's Golden Mile, which included a casino, disco and nightclub), and from 1970 onwards he had been making trips over to the U.S. (his parents also owned an apartment in Miami) and unearthing rare records. Levine's first major discoveries were J.J. Barnes's "Our Love Is In The Pocket" and a bunch of other Ric-Tic rarities. "I found them in a joke shop in 110-degree heat in New Orleans," he laughs. Levine is a large, loud, forceful character who now writes for and produces pop acts like boy bands Take That and Bad Boys Inc.

Levine had started DJing at the Mecca in 1971, then played at the Torch towards the end of its tenure in 1973, before returning to his residency at Blackpool. Here he and Colin Curtis reigned for the rest of the decade. Blackpool had other notable DJs including Tony Jebb and Keith Minshull, and another soul club, Blackpool Casino (no relation), but it was Levine and Curtis who wowed the crowds with the most soul discoveries, courtesy of Levine's bottomless pockets and erudite taste.

The Mecca became a weekly must. "If you were a serious collector, the only place you could conceive of going was Blackpool Mecca," says Ian Dewhirst. "Levine was there, and Levine was the arbiter of taste. He always had the most breathtaking array of records. You might not know them all, but you'd know they'd all be good. And he would take *chances*. You'd never have heard 'Seven Day Lover' by James Fountain at Wigan. I have to give him respect, even though he's pretty irritating to be around a lot of the time."

Construction had begun on the Wigan Casino in 1912. It was then known as the Empress Ballroom. As a result of the war effort, it wasn't completed until November 1, 1916, when local mayor J.T. Anson officially opened the vast arena. The Emp, as it was known locally, served various functions over the years, including a period as a billiard hall, but when Russ Winstanley placed the Sherrys' "Put Your Lovin' Arms Around Me" on the platter on September 22, 1973, at the first Wigan Casino all-nighter, the building took on a new life. This was the first chapter in a club story that has become less history than mythology.

In truth, few connoisseurs were impressed with what they found on that first evening. Russ Winstanley had some decent records, but few of them were particularly rare, while his cohort, Ian Fishwick, was nothing more than a local pop DJ struck lucky. Kev Roberts stopped off on the way back from the Mecca that first night. "I distinctly remember it," he says. "The first thing: there weren't many DJs on, and the music wasn't crap exactly, but the records were easily available. There wasn't much I didn't know." After the Mecca, where he could be sure of hearing rare records he didn't yet own, it was an anticlimax to hear such familiar music.

Roberts's friends were so incensed that they harangued Winstanley to give their friend a DJing spot, arguing that his collection was far superior. He got his chance that same night.

"I played an hour's worth of my top tunes and they went down a storm," chuckles Roberts. "They loved them. I was up there absolutely petrified. It was a massive room. And Russ came up to me and said, 'Great. Do you wanna work here every week? Ten pounds.' "

The recruitment of another DJ, Richard Searling from Va Va's in Bolton, helped seal Wigan's place as the spot of the moment, its advantage over Blackpool Mecca aided by the fact that while the Mecca was closing at 2 A.M., Wigan was just opening. Many soulies went to both clubs regularly, rarely caring about any distinction between the playlists of the two. When the Mecca closed, they would often head for Wigan to dance out what was left of the night.

"By Christmas of 1973, no disrespect to Blackpool Mecca but they were running second," claims Kev Roberts. "There were two thousand people at the Casino every week. Even though Ian Levine at the Mecca was the most creative, he was the most innovative, he had the best records, it didn't make any difference. With Russ, myself and, by January 1974, Richard Searling, whatever we played, we had an even bigger dancefloor." Even Levine himself is reflective about their rivalry, freely conceding that "it was Kev, Russ and Richard who took Wigan to great heights."

There's no questioning the atmosphere at the (alcohol-free) Casino. It was electric. The huge maplewood dancefloor would bounce as though it had independent life, while a monochrome blur of dervishes performed ever more complex rituals of drops, backflips, handclaps and spins. The dancers were dressed from head to foot in soul garb: high-waisted pleated trousers with wide flapping legs known as "Brummie Bags," bowling shirts, singlets or Ben Shermans, white socks, flat leather-soled shoes and an Adidas or Gola sports bag stuffed full of the night's essentials. These would include talcum powder to dust the dancefloor, a change of clothes, a few 45s to sell or trade and, of course, gear.

The room took on an opaque sheen from the condensation steaming off the dancers. It was like looking through net curtain. And while the grandeur might have long since deserted the Emp (it didn't bear to inspect the carpets, fittings or toilets for too long), there was no doubt about the ambience. They might not have had the best music. But they had the most fun.

And there is no doubting the influence of both clubs. "You can say what you like," says Jonathan Woodliffe, a respected soul collector and now a DJ on the house scene, "but both places had wicked atmospheres and they were both major players on the scene at that time."

Reissues and Commercialization

A few sharp movers were soon realizing that while the DJs and collectors were only interested in records if they were rare and unobtainable, there was money to be made from reissuing some of the biggest songs.

On visiting the Casino, an old soul DJ called Dave McAleer, who was also an A&R ("Artiste & Repertoire") man for the British label Pye, realized northern soul's sales potential was growing. The success of the Tams and Tami Lynn had hinted as much, and by this stage the Mecca and Torch had broken two other records, Archie Bell & The Drells' "Here I Go Again" and the stone-cold northern monster, "Love On A Mountain Top" by Robert Knight. McAleer set up the Disco Demand label to specifically deal with northern soul. Others followed his lead.

By the mid seventies, commercial successes would happen almost weekly: Betty Wright's "Where Is The Love?," Esther Phillips's "What A Difference A Day Makes," George Benson's "Supership" and Al Wilson's "The Snake" all crashed the charts.

But it was pastiches rather than reissues which crossed over with more force. Despite Pye having the UK licensing rights to some sought-after labels like Scepter and Roulette, the first pop hit was "Footsee" by Wigan's Chosen Few, a faintly risible concoction that had originally begun life as the B-side to a surf record. (The "Wigan" was added to avoid court action from Island Records, who had a Chosen Few on their roster.)

"Footsee," although mitigated by having the credible "Seven Days Is Too Long" by soul-howler Chuck Wood on the flip side, was miles away from true northern soul. However, for the *Top of the Pops* TV appearance in February 1975, they recruited some of the best young dancers from the floor of the Casino. Kids around the country must have wondered what this bizarre quasi-balletic dancing was all about: part jazz dance, part freestyle, with even a foretaste of breakdancing in there, too. As Russ Winstanley said they made Pan's People look like clog dancers.

Then there was Wigan's Ovation. If anything, even worse than "Footsee," the Ovation were a white pop act previously called Sparkle whose cover version of the Invitations' "Skiing In The Snow" (the original record is as rare as hen's teeth), made the Top 20 two months later.

The connoisseurs and true soul fans were disgusted. "They had these horrible pop novelty hits that were masquerading as northern soul," fumes Levine. "Thousands of new people would see these dancers on *Top of the Pops* and a new crowd descended on Wigan, who were really like sightseers and tourists who'd got into northern soul through the TV exposure it got."

To be fair to the Casino, it was breaking other records, too: Frankie Valli & The Four Seasons' "The Night" and Rodger Collins's "Sexy Sugar Plum" were two of the more credible additions to the canon which came from Wigan. And what was undeniable was that it captured the imagination of many thousands of clubbers. In that sense Wigan Casino was probably the first truly national club, drawing dancers from all corners of the British Isles.

Fighting for the Soul of Soul

"There was only one golden era of northern soul," says Kev Roberts. "There was only one definitive playlist. Now, you can argue about how many records were on that playlist—the absolutely stonking mega dancefloor fillers, I'm talking 'Landslide,' 'There's A Ghost In My House,' 'Tainted Love'—but really it's no more than about 200."

Dave Godin agrees. "When the northern soul scene was its most vigorous," he says, "there was this tremendous search for obscurities, and a lot of great records surfaced as a result. But after a while, the chances of discovering some old masterpiece diminish. All the masterpieces have surfaced."

This was the issue that started to face northern soul around the mid seventies. Where could it go when there were no more old records to discover?

At Wigan, the DJs stuck doggedly to what they knew, maintaining the traditional sound by championing oldies of rapidly decreasing quality. Preserving the styles their dancers loved so much led to an unrelenting diet of stompers (the term for the frenetic Detroit-style soul oldies), songs which fitted the northern soul blueprint however crass they were.

Levine's answer, far more controversial, was to look to the present for fresh sounds, adding modern soul tunes, disco 12-inches and jazz-funk to the menu. In the eyes of many, this was a travesty. This was a scene that fetishized the old, the dusty and the anonymous. A northern soul DJ was breaking the rules of his trade if he dared to tamper with its stomping sound and play genuinely new (and easily available) records. As Levine exercised his broad tastes, he found himself carving a deep split into the established scene.

Though Levine was determined to break with the constraints of the music, he had not entirely forsaken the northern sound that had made his reputation. On one of his Stateside forays—Levine claims it was as early as 1971—he returned with yet another rarity. Incredibly, it was on Motown, a label so successful—and available—that its records normally had little cachet on the northern circuit.

"Levine comes back from the States and, of course, I'm on the phone on the Saturday afternoon," recalls Ian Dewhirst. "And he says, 'I've got the greatest northern soul record ever'—but he used to say this all the time—'It's 'There's A Ghost In My House' by R. Dean Taylor.' That night he played it about six times and by the third play everybody realized that, yes, it is the greatest record ever."

Overnight this became the most wanted record in the country. The buzz spread. Levine had done it again. When Tamla Motown reissued it, it shot to #3. Nowadays, because Taylor was white, Levine has less affinity for the record.

"R. Dean Taylor, really, is a nasty white pop record on Motown," he says, surprisingly. "I suppose I should be ashamed of it."

Despite extracting such gems, Levine continued to innovate. He and Curtis brought in records that, although still relatively rare, were new releases. Over the years, certain new releases had been accepted, but only when their sound fitted the soul mold (jazz drummer Paul Humphrey's fluke northern hit "Cochise," being one example). However, at the Mecca, the mold was being defiantly broken.

The division got deeper and more unpleasant as time went on. The die-hards saw their traditions being shattered; the modernizers felt Levine was breathing new life into the scene. Like the 1965 furor over Bob Dylan going electric, it showed just how important this music was to people.

Ian Levine remembers a time when the Blackpool and Wigan crowds were brought together in Manchester's Ritz for an all-dayer put on by Midlands promoter Neil Rushton. The Mecca clubbers were there to hear Levine and Curtis, the Casino dancers to hear Richard Searling. The Wiganites made it clear what they thought of Levine.

"It was like two football crowds: Manchester City and Manchester United. It didn't work," he recalls. "At that time we were playing all this modern disco stuff: Doctor Buzzard's Original Savannah Band, Tavares, *Car Wash*, *Jaws* by Lalo Schifrin. And they were playing anything with a stomping beat. All of these Wiganites with their singlets and baggy pants were shouting, 'Fuck off! Get off! Play some stompers!'"

A campaign was started to get rid of Levine. Casino fans sported buttons with the bald legend "LEVINE MUST GO." One Saturday, two fans even walked through the Mecca with a huge banner bearing the same slogan.

Today, even Levine has his regrets. "I'll go on record here and say: We went too far," he states firmly. "The northern soul scene was very special. We started with the Carstairs and Marvin Holmes, which were equally rare but more modern. Then we're playing Tavares and Crown Heights Affair, Kool & the Gang even. And suddenly, you weren't hearing anything that you couldn't hear anywhere else. It had no uniqueness about it. We should've stopped it before it went too far. Because what we did was split that scene into two with an axe."

Levine was gaining much of his inspiration from his frequent trips to the clubs of New York's underground gay scene. Visiting places like Infinity and 12 West, he saw how the early disco records could generate as much energy on the dancefloor as any northern stomper.

As well as Levine's distinct sensibilities (he would later enjoy a second career as the pioneer of hi-NRG, a fast disco variant with obvious northern soul features), there were other factors encouraging a split. Since the Casino was an all-nighter, it's safe to assume that its dancers were more intoxicated than the Mecca's. There was also the fact that the Wigan dancefloor was much bigger. As Kev Roberts remarks, the size of the venue made a big difference. "On that massive dancefloor, unless the tempo was really kicking immediately the record was a no-no," he explains. As has often happened in dance music, at Wigan the needs of the dancers and their drugs were in the driving seat.

As the music changed, the Mecca's clubbers became noticeably more urban in appearance, wearing more current styles than their Wigan comrades. As clubber and DJ Norman Jay noted on a late-seventies visit there, the fashions wouldn't have looked out of place in London.

Incidentally, the Casino/Mecca split conjures interesting parallels with the evolution of jungle/drum'n'bass many years later. In the early nineties, as the masses moved into the clubs and adjusted their tastes to a less frenetic music, the diehards of the rave scene partied on in their own, largely ignored world and in an echo of the Wigan love for stompers, rave music became a faster, rougher, ever more absurd parody of itself (undeniably an acceleration driven by changing drug habits). The irony is that out of this fierce preservationist attitude and its much-reviled music came jungle and hence drum'n'bass.

In northern soul's case, it was the progressives rather than the traditionalists who came up with the goods. It's hard to imagine such deeply held opinions now, but many considered Curtis and Levine heretics and pariahs for what they were doing. However, they took northern soul out of its fossilized past and into the future.

The new sound emerging at Blackpool Mecca was led initially by records like the Carstairs' "It Really Hurts Me Girl" which, as Levine says, still had "a northern soul feel but with a slightly shuffly beat." But the changes were really crystallized when another record made it to the turntables.

"The O'Jays' 'I Love Music' really opened the doors, I think, to new singles," says Kev Roberts. "It paved the way for things like 'Heaven Must Be Missing An Angel,' which was a northern soul monster, and 'Young Hearts Run Free,' another one perfect for a northern crowd."

Levine was given the O'Jays' record to play by Roberts, who had by now quit Wigan in a dispute with Russ Winstanley and was making judicious use of Freddie Laker's £59 each way flights to New York for record-hunting trips. Somehow he managed to prize a test-pressing out of the hands of New York jock Tony Gioe, who had got it straight from Kenny Gamble, its producer.

The success of this Philly disco stormer on the Mecca's dancefloor encouraged Levine to break completely with any lingering traditions.

"From the moment 'I Love Music' had been accepted, Ian made a pact with himself to say northern is unofficially dead," affirms Roberts. "He went completely into the disco thing. In some quarters it worked a treat, and he captured a different audience. But some of the hustle type records he was playing were not well received in northern soul terms."

As Mecca moved determinedly on, throwing anything from Philly International to Funkadelic into the melting pot, Wigan reacted violently with an increasing horrorshow of pop stompers. Ron Grainer Orchestra's "Theme From Joe 90" got played. As did "Hawaii 5-0" by the Ventures. One DJ, Richard Searling, did his best to preserve some dignity in the music selections, his thumb stuck in the dam, but it wasn't enough. It looked like northern soul was parodying itself. It wasn't a pretty sight.

Cleethorpes

In 1976 a third player entered the fray as the Lincolnshire seaside town of Cleethorpes hosted some golden-era soul. A husband and wife team, Colin and Mary Chapman from Scunthorpe, found a venue on the faded east coast resort, which had staged everything from Leo Sayer concerts to Nolan Sisters summer shows. When the wind blew, the Pier audibly creaked. Stuffed full of several hundred northern soul dancers, it creaked some more. They recruited the roster of disc jockeys mainly from local unknowns like Poke and Chris Scott, and after adding veteran residents like Ian Dewhirst, forged a sound that was essentially an amalgam of the Casino and Mecca.

"That has to be one of the greatest venues ever, as far as mystique goes," claims Dewhirst. "I used to get to the Pier about four in the morning and by that point all you'd hear was this stomp, stomp, stomp from about a mile and a half away. It would be the dancing. It was surreal. There's this place jutting out into the sea. It's four in the morning. And all you can hear is STOMP! Multiplied times a thousand."

Dave Godin championed Cleethorpes. Ian Levine got mad. "Cleethorpes's success grew out of Dave Godin's attention to them," he asserts. "But it was better music than Wigan."

Jonathan Woodliffe recalls a trip there back in its soul days. It was a freezing winter's night. The snow was being blown almost horizontally in from the North Sea. "All I can remember is this door opening in the distance," he says, "a mountain of steam coming out and the smell of Brut talcum powder, and entering the room and hearing World Column's 'So Is The Sun.' Whenever I hear that record, it always takes me back to that smell and that time." Perhaps tellingly, these days the Pier plays host to occasional wild hardcore raves.

The Birth of the Trainspotter

Northern soul's most significant contribution to the DJ's trade was to introduce the idea of connoisseurship. Previously, this had been the exclusive province of the collector of classical music, with a few jazz and blues addicts following behind. But until soul, dance music had been largely about playing the hits of the day. Since the northern scene thrived on rarities, it made the DJ's profession as much archaeology as record playing. The DJ had a new avenue of creativity to explore: he was a musical researcher, an evangelist of obscurities—a "trainspotter"!

Back in the Catacombs and Twisted Wheel, the DJ started to realize that the rarity of his records was another tool with which to build a distinctive performance.

Today's notion of rarity is less about old gems and more about anoraked techno nerds championing unheard-of test-pressings by twelve-year-old geniuses on tiny labels based in garages in Canada, but the prestige of rarity introduced by northern soul has never left dance music.

Clubbers would journey hundreds of miles at the thought of hearing that one elusive disc. Posters included lists of the rare records you would hear at a particular event, and a DJ's standing on the circuit could rocket overnight by the simple expedient of acquiring one desirable 45.

"The more the DJs had got a record that was on a tiny little Los Angeles or Detroit or Chicago label," says Levine, "the more people would travel from Gloucester, Scotland and Yorkshire to hear them, because they couldn't hear them anywhere else."

Ian Dewhirst's big break came when he chanced upon a copy of the Carstairs' "It Really Hurts Me Girl" lying ignored at the back of a London soul dealer's box at the Heavy Steam Machine in Hanley. Although it was a new record, it was incredibly rare since its label, Red Coach, had lost their distribution deal with Chess in Chicago and it had never been released; the only copies being ultrarare radio promos.

"I'm flicking all the way through and the last two records are the Carstairs' 'It Really Hurts Me Girl' and Dena Barnes's 'If You Ever Walk Out Of My Life,'" recalls Dewhirst. "The two biggest records in the country and he's got them at the back of his box in paper sleeves." Dewhirst handed over the £15 for the Carstairs (he didn't have enough for the pair).

"Jesus Christ, man, if you want everything on one record, then this record's got it," he gushes. "The most passionate vocal on it, scintillating beat, brilliant strings, and produced by Gene Redd, the fucking archdeacon of northern soul! Everything compressed into this one record. I spent almost a week looking at the label." He also found his gig rate rocketed overnight.

Kev Roberts tells a similar excited tale. On trading some British releases for a grab bag of U.S. records, he found to his astonishment two incredible and super-rare records: Patti Austin's "Pain Stain" and Sandra Phillips's "World Without Sunshine." "I was the first person ever," he beams. "I mean, Ian Levine didn't even have them. So I started to play them and my reputation went like *WOW*! Suddenly I was getting gigs from all over the place. Really, my reputation grew over the course of four weeks."

The northern grapevine was such that if a hot record was played at the Mecca or Casino one evening, by lunchtime the next day everyone would know about it. The legend of Levine discovering "There's A Ghost In My House" is a case in point. As soon as the record was heard, dealers were sent scurrying to the U.S. Calls were made. Shops were scoured. Nothing. "Then the weirdest thing happened," says Ian Dewhirst. "Someone was coming back from Wigan Casino and went into a motorway service station. They bent down to get a Sunday paper and there was a rack of those old Music For Pleasure budget LPs, and in amongst them was an R. Dean Taylor compilation called *Indiana Wants Me*. Track three, side two, there it was: 'There's A Ghost In My House.' So it's in every record shop in the country and we all fucking missed it!"

The World's Rarest Record

The undisputed champion of champions in the northern soul premier league of rare records is Frank Wilson's "Do I Love You?" For a long time there was only one known copy in existence in the whole world. Wilson worked for Motown, and had already had some success as producer of Checkerboard Squares' "Double Cookin," already a big hit on the soul scene.

"Do I Love You?" had all the ingredients for a dancefloor smash, including soaring production, a zippy vocal delivery and an instantly familiar hook. However, after Wilson had recorded it (and even after the records had been pressed up ready for distribution), Motown boss Berry Gordy somehow convinced him not to put it out. "You don't want all the pressures of being an artist, stick with production," Gordy is said to have told him. Consequently, all but one or two copies of the record were destroyed.

The record came to light courtesy of Simon Soussan, a Burton's tailor who had fallen for soul at the Twisted Wheel in 1969, and who had been the first person to trek to America and sell commercially, via collectors' lists, the rare records he found there. (Some of the great records he introduced were Connie Clark's "My Sugar Baby," Louise Lewis's "With You I'll Let It Be You Babe" and "Dirty Hearts" by Benny Curtis.)

On a trip to L.A., Soussan got his hands on "Do I Love You?" Stories vary as to how. Some say he acquired it from the Motown vaults in Los Angeles. Others claim he was loaned it by Tom dePierro, a Motown employee and former DJ.

Soussan knew immediately the record was a monster and had an acetate copy made and sent to Russ Winstanley at Wigan Casino, who protected its identity by telling people it was by someone called Eddie Foster (Winstanley's claims to ownership of the actual record, as documented in his book, *Soul Survivors*, are entirely false). It was an immediate hit.

The original eventually came to the UK when dance music retailer Les McCutcheon (who later discovered Shakatak) bought Soussan's collection. Jonathan Woodliffe bought it from McCutcheon in a deal worth £500, which was then so much money that he paid in installments. "At that time—I suppose it's like the transfer market with footballers—£500 was the highest anyone had paid for a record," says Woodliffe.

The record became nothing less than legendary. People wanted to see it, touch it, even have their photo taken with it. "I used to go to gigs and people used to ask me to get this record out of my box so they could take a photograph of it," laughs Woodliffe.

Woodliffe sold it to Kev Roberts, who held on to it for the next ten years, until Tim Brown, one of Roberts's partners in the Goldmine reissue label, paid him £5,000 for it in 1991. However, the plot thickened when another collector, Martin Koppel, somehow unearthed another copy in 1993. This one sold to a collector in Scotland in the summer of 1998 for an amazing £15,000. The track was reissued by Tamla Motown UK in 1980, and even copies of the reissue now fetch upwards of £40.

Cover-ups—The First White Labels

Inevitably, competition grew between DJs, and to protect new discoveries they would cover the label and give them false names. "Covering up" can be seen as the forerunner to modern DJs' white label exclusives, or the hip hop DJs' habit of soaking off the labels from their most treasured breaks. The practice actually originated in the early sixties when a West Indian DJ at the Roaring Twenties in London by the name of Count Suckle covered up records like Nina Simone's "My Baby Just Cares For Me," a practice he imported from Jamaica. However, it was soul jocks who popularized it, both to preserve their exclusives and also as a way of throwing bootleggers off the scent.

"It's only really the same as people playing acetates today, but these days instead of covering old records they've gone right to the source," argues Jonathan Woodliffe.

Dave Godin, however, hated the practice. "If I went somewhere and a DJ had some exclusive cover-up I knew, I would immediately blow the whistle and review it. Fuck it. They were putting their own ego above the singer, the composer and everyone else, and I couldn't abide that."

Farmer Carl Dene, the first northern DJ to cover up, would cut out the center of an unused record and place it on top of the record spinning, something he did for Jackie Lee's "Darkest Days," Donald Height's "She Blew A

Good Thing" and others. Rob Bellars at the Wheel was the first person to cover up *and* rename the song. Thus Bobby Paterson's "What A Wonderful Night For Love" became Benny Harper's "What A Wonderful Night." This trend spread like a virus: the Checkerboard Squares' "Double Cookin'" became the faintly ludicrous "Strings-A-Go-Go" by Bob Wilson Sound, while the Coasters' "Crazy Baby" was transformed into Freddie Jones's "My Heart's Wide Open."

Ady Croasdell, a regular at the Casino (and later the man behind both the 100 Club all-nighters and Kent Records), took a Tony Blackburn version of Doris Troy's "I'll Do Anything" and handed it to DJ Keith Minshull, claiming it was Lenny Gamble. Incredibly, Minshull played it. "It was just supposed to be a joke," Croasdell said in *Soul Survivors*. "When he played it and everyone danced to it, I thought that maybe the punters weren't too discerning."

Rip-offs and Bootlegs

The new obsession with rarities provided fertile ground for rip-offs and bootlegs.

Simon Soussan, who had discovered the Frank Wilson record, would bolster his sales lists with fictitious titles, asking customers to always include second choices with their requests. One such imaginary record was "Reaching For The Best" by Bob Relf (Relf was a genuine artist who'd had some success with a song called "Blowing My Mind To Pieces"). With the status of his list enhanced by such a "rare" record, Soussan garnered several offers. None, of course, received the new Bob Relf, though Soussan cleared his stockroom by selling everyone their second choice records.

In a hilarious turnabout to the tale, Ian Levine stole the title from Soussan and wrote a real song for it. It was his first production, "Reaching For The Best" by The Exciters, and it reached #31 in the UK pop charts in October 1975.

It was common practice for DJs to have acetate copies made of their rarest records. Such 7-inch one-off bootlegs were known as Emidiscs and were used by many jocks desperate for the next best thing to the genuine article. However, this was only the tip of the bootleggers' iceberg.

Selectadisc in Nottingham (a crucial store in the development of the northern scene) was supplied with an endless supply of "pressings" by Simon Soussan, based in the U.S. Pressings were, supposedly, legally licensed limited runs of certain sought-after records. Their legality was debated, although in an interview with *Black Music* in February 1976, Soussan denied bootlegging. "You can go to jail for two years and pay a fine of $10,000 for bootlegging. I haven't paid any fine because I haven't bootlegged any records."

There were several other bogus labels, one of which was Out Of The Past. Many original soul records sounded like they'd been recorded in a barn. By the time they emerged on Out Of The Past, they sounded like they'd been recorded in a bucket.

Beach Music

There is a strange echo of northern soul in America called beach music. You won't find any mention of it in guidebooks, but it's a thriving subculture based around a series of resort towns in North and South Carolina, where kids gather to dance the shag to obscure rhythm and blues records. Its initial constituency was mainly working-class whites whose clandestine trips to resorts like Myrtle and Virginia Beaches provided an opportunity in a deeply racist society to dance to forbidden black records. (Beach music was even immortalized in the utterly dreadful 1990 movie *Shag*.)

Although beach music only gained its tag in 1965, it has been around since 1945 thanks to influential radio jocks like John Richbourg, Hoss Allen and Gene Nobles. And because beach music exists apart from the mainstream recording industry, it has retained much of the original integrity of northern soul. Both scenes have several classics in common: Guy Darrell's "I've Been Hurt," The Tams' "Be Young Be Foolish Be Happy" and "What A Difference A Day Makes" by Esther Phillips. Incredibly, there were even a couple of clubs in the Virginia Beach district called the Mecca and the Casino.

Nowadays it's organized around the Association of Beach and Shag Club DJs and thanks to the efforts of DJ John Hook and a specialist record store in Charlotte, North Carolina, called the Wax Museum, the sound of beach music lives on. In a small corner of the American Southeast, the search for rare vinyl and great dance records continues.

From Northern Soul to Nu-NRG

Northern soul was the revenge of the small town. Although it was cradled in metropolitan Manchester, its fabled clubs formed a map of deep geographical unfashionability: Tunstall, Wigan, Blackpool, Cleethorpes. Despite its near-complete isolation from London and from the established music industry, its influence was impressive.

Many DJs schooled in the dancehalls, bingo halls, and discos of the northern circuit ended up playing a role in the early UK development of house:

Mike Pickering, Colin Curtis, Jonathan Woodliffe, Ian Dewhirst, Ian Levine, Pete Waterman.

Musically, its effect has been greater subsequently than it ever was at the time. In tracks like Soft Cell's "Tainted Love" and "What" (originally by Gloria Jones and Judy Street respectively), and M People's "One Night In Heaven" and "How Can I Love You More?" (which owe a debt to Linda Carr's "Highwire" and the Trammps' "Where Do We Go From Here"), the northern songs have lived on. Artists including Paul Weller, Ocean Colour Scene, St. Etienne and Belle & Sebastian openly acknowledge their love for the genre, and Fatboy Slim's huge 1999 #1 (UK) hit "Rockafeller Skank" sampled the northern instrumental "Sliced Tomatoes" by the Just Brothers to great effect.

There is also a direct lineage from northern soul to Ian Levine's hi-NRG and hence to the "nu-NRG" of popular DJs like Blu Peter, Tall Paul and the lamented Tony De Vit.

As a scene built entirely from flops, it has also bequeathed an impressive vault of classic Motown-influenced soul records that would have otherwise remained undiscovered. It also gave careers—albeit brief ones—to singers who'd long since returned to the car plant assembly lines of Detroit. And all thanks to the thousands of dancers from nondescript northern towns who held the torch and kept the faith.

Perhaps the greatest legacy of northern soul was a cultural one. It is impossible to ignore its uncanny resemblance to the house/rave movement of a decade and a half later, and given the number of DJs with a hand in both scenes, it would be hard to claim that this was simply coincidence. Praising its spirit of togetherness, Jonathan Woodliffe compares northern soul to the international network of people who picked up on house and ecstasy on the island of Ibiza. "It's the only scene I've come across in twenty-three years' DJing and clubbing where there was such a close-knit community," he says. "Everybody knew everybody."

Northern soul created a nationwide network connecting clubs, record collectors and DJs. Although it provided the charts with their first club-born records, for every tune that crossed over there were another fifty that never made it beyond the walls of an all-nighter. Northern soul was as pure an underground movement as is ever likely to exist. It encouraged a fierce, tribal loyalty and it provided nights of sweaty drug-ridden escapism for thousands of devoted dancers. For those who think that the rave movement started club culture: Think again.

Nowadays, most northern all-nighters are populated by originals returning after their kids have grown up, looking to rediscover the music of their youth (if not their hair or figure). Even with the rise of the weekender events and their popularity with a younger crowd, the northern scene can never have the same vibrancy it once had. But that shouldn't detract from the great records and special clubs of twenty-five years ago.

"Everybody thought I was crazy," laughs clubber Andy Wynne, when he told friends he intended to buy the sign from the Wigan Casino. "I told the people at work I was taking Thursday and Friday off. They asked if I was going away. I said, 'No, I'm going to Wigan.' You couldn't begin to explain to them. They wouldn't understand. It signified a particularly happy time in my life when I discovered the greatest music, the greatest atmosphere, the greatest scene . . ." Wynne fondles the sign. "It's great. It's a piece of art to me."

And the records speak for themselves: 7-inch slithers of raw emotion. Collectors today are regularly paying four-figure sums for rarities and, while you may question the sanity of someone offering 15 grand for a 7-inch single with a coffee stain on the B-side, ultimately it's the music that compels them to do this. "I'll die of shock if, in twenty years' time, you get out of bed and travel 200 miles to listen to some old Prodigy B-sides," wrote John McCready in *The Face*. "Or pay £5,000 for an Aphex Twin record."

FIVE
REGGAE

Wreck Up a Version

"No matter what the people say . . . These sounds lead the way . . . it's the order of the day from your boss deejay."

—King Stitt, "Fire Corner"

"Dub—verb, to make space."

—Coldcut A-Z

When it was untouched by Europe, the Arawaks called their fertile island Xaymaca, meaning "Land of Springs." When it was the pirate capital of the seven seas, its main city Port Royal was the wickedest in the world. When it was a colonial sugar plantation powered by stolen African muscle, a slave owner could be fined £10 if one of his chattels was caught banging a drum. When it was reborn independent of Britain's imperial rule, in Jamaica the DJ was king.

This tropical volcanic rock only 200 miles long was where many of dance music's most essential concepts were first made flesh. While reggae is often misunderstood and dismissed as a quirky local flavor, the things it inspired—the dub mix, toasting, the version, the sound system and the sound clash—have proved to be momentous.

"Within that small place there is this huge thing," marvels Steve Barrow, a world authority on Jamaican music. "You look at Jamaica, and you think it can't be . . . 'cause the place is too small, it couldn't have that influence. Then you say, what about the remix? What about drum and bass foregrounded in the mix?

What about personality DJs playing exclusive dub-plates? And no one can deny it. The arsenal of techniques at the disposal of someone operating the decks—most of these things were developed in Jamaica."

Unique Jamaica

In Jamaica the DJ stripped the voices off his records and grabbed the microphone. Then he stripped his records apart further, separating out each strand of sound. And from each dissected record he built a hundred more, each made with a different weave of noise. He built a towering skyline of loudspeakers and filled them with quaking bass and piercing treble, and as he used music as a weapon to fight his rivals, he built a whole new culture of dancing; a dancehall with no instruments—just a voice, some dub-plates and a system of sound.

Jamaican music is unique in its nature and crucially important to the craft of playing records. Here on this small island, a completely unprecedented approach to recorded music emerged that was to work its influence throughout the world. This influence has not always been direct, but it has been enduring. It would be extremely important to the birth of hip hop and can be seen in many other musical forms, especially in the production methods that lie behind them.

It was in Jamaica that a record stopped being a finished thing. Instead, in the studio, it became a matrix of sonic possibilities, the raw material for endless "dubs." Thus, the concept of the remix was born (several years before similar ideas would dawn on the disco and hip hop DJs). And when a record was played through a sound system, with a deejay toasting over the top, it was no longer a complete piece of music but had become a tool of composition for a grander performance. This was an important change in the status of recorded music, and again something which wouldn't really occur outside Jamaica until disco and hip hop.

It was in Jamaica, too, that the recording studio was pushed to its limits as an instrument in itself. Here, in the service of the sound system, the producer realized that he could be a creative musician and his work lay as much in modifying sound as in simply recording it.

(*A quick matter of terminology: In Jamaica, the person who plays records is called the "selector," and the "deejay" is now a vocalist, akin to a rapper. Throughout this chapter we will distinguish between the "DJ," who is the subject of this book, and the "deejay" who in Jamaica can be found holding the microphone.*)

The Roots of the Sound System

As the meeting place of African, European, North American and native influences, the Caribbean has an astonishing range of musical cultures. But Jamaica added something more which would make its music radically different—the sound system. Huge mobile sets of amplifiers and loudspeakers designed to play records in the open air with as much impact as possible.

Run by flamboyant neighborhood heroes, a sound system (often just called a "sound") enjoys the same kind of popular support as a local football team. There are regular dances in Kingston itself and, out in the smaller towns, people await each one with real excitement. First the colorfully lettered posters go up, then a few days later the sound arrives, its endless speaker boxes filling the back of a truck. The equipment is set up, usually in a specially built courtyard (a "dancehall" is rarely indoors), tickets are sold and the party begins.

The selector picks out and plays the bass-heavy records, manipulating the volume and the tone controls or adding special sound effects such as echo and reverb to add drama to the music. A selector will also do certain tricks like audibly spinning back a popular tune so it can be played twice in a row

Vantastic!—the rolling thunder of a Jamaican mobile record store. Vehicles like these helped provide the inspiration for the first sound systems.

(the "rewind"). His partner, the deejay, either up on a stage or in the midst of the dancers, will use his amplified voice to further engage the crowd, to add rhymes and singing to records and to generally bring the recorded music to life.

The sound system was a product of a combination of social factors peculiar to Jamaica. In a country with generally low incomes, people were unlikely to spend much money on records to play at home, yet, like everyone, they wanted to get together and dance. On other Caribbean islands, people met this need by partying to music rooted in the nineteenth century—salsa, soca, samba, calypso—but in Jamaica the local folk music, mento, enjoyed nowhere near the same dominance. And when Jamaica began its rapid postwar urbanization, its people looked for a more assertive soundtrack for their new city lives.

They found this largely in American and American-influenced music. There were plenty of emigrants living in the States who would send back records, and Jamaica is close enough to the U.S. mainland to receive radio transmissions from WINZ in Miami, WLAC in Nashville and WNOE in New Orleans, among others.

On clear nights the sound of artists like Fats Domino, Amos Milburn, Roy Brown and Professor Longhair would drift into the AM transistors of thousands of Jamaicans, placing the music of Memphis and New Orleans, with its syncopated shuffle beat, at the heart of the island's musical tastes. (Later favorites who had an important influence were Otis Redding, Sam Cooke, Solomon Burke, Ben E. King, Lee Dorsey and especially Curtis Mayfield.) Much of Jamaica's recent musical history can be seen as a response to such imported American sounds: ska, rocksteady and later reggae grew largely from local interpretations of this music.

The most popular postwar music was big band swing. Although there were "orchestra dances" through the forties, only a few Jamaican bands could recreate this style. And live musicians were an expensive way to fill a dancehall. Since a DJ could play all the best American music—and didn't need umpteen helpings of beer and curry goat—it was hard for live musicians to compete.

The sound system also fitted well into Jamaican political life. With the journey to independence, granted in August 1962, and the tumultuous politics which followed, there was a strong revolutionary spirit on the island. Reggae and its associated forms emerged as rebel music, the sound of opposition. Rastafarianism, with its "Dread inna Babylon" attitude, is the best-known expression of this, but the popularity of local sound systems, independent of government authority and sometimes allied to particular political groupings, owed a lot to it too. The deejays would often satirize current affairs and local events, taking on the old "singing newspaper" role of the mento minstrel. An associated point is that Jamaican radio was extremely conservative, with RJR (a cable radio service) and the BBC-modeled JBC maintaining rather elitist broadcasting policies. The sound systems filled a wide gap left by this establishment radio, which for a long time refused to play reggae, the people's music.

It was the habit of using public music as a method of sales promotion that created the sound system. Liquor stores and shops selling records and electronic equipment would set up loudspeakers on the street and play music to entertain and attract passers-by. Gradually the retailers hit on the idea of enlarging on this and taking the music to the people (and selling them booze at the same time). Sound systems have retained this close connection with the alcohol trade, and the fact that the most popular sound stands to make the heftiest profit from drinks sales has always encouraged fierce competition. It also ensured that it was well worth investing money in having the best records, the loudest speakers and the most entertaining deejays.

The First Sounds

At the beginning of the fifties, in an area of the capital which became known as "Beat Street," on a series of outdoor dance spaces called "lawns," the first sound systems plied their trade, attracting crowds of snappily dressed Kingstonians. The women wore spiraling petticoats and the men put on their best suits and wide-brimmed hats, with a hand towel to wipe their sweat. The dancing itself was lively jitterbugging and there would be several notoriously flashy hoofers on hand showing off their latest steps.

Like the great bandleaders, the sound system pioneers adopted a variety of aristocratic titles, calling themselves "Duke," "Count," "King" and so forth, and like the big bands they had their own theme tunes: exclusive records which were ferociously protected for fear another sound should get hold of a copy. Among the first sounds were Waldron, Goodies, Count Nick the Champ, Count Jones and the most successful of the first generation, Tom the Great Sebastian, named after a famous circus performer.

Tom the Great Sebastian reigned supreme until the rise in the middle fifties of the so-called "Big Three"—Sir Coxsone Dodd's Downbeat, Duke Reid's Trojan, and King Edwards's Giant. As these sound systems injected the island's music scene with the latest American rhythm and blues songs, the modern era of music in Jamaica got its kickstart, and it was these sounds which presided over the rise of such forms as Jamaican rhythm and blues, then ska and rocksteady.

Born in 1932, Clement Seymour Dodd started DJing on a 30-watt Morphy Richards gramophone for the customers of his parents' liquor store, obtaining records from visiting sailors via his father, who was a dock foreman. He went on to build speaker boxes for some of the first sound systems on the island, and by the mid fifties was running his own—Coxsone Downbeat (named after a Yorkshire cricketer)—and had started traveling to New York to buy records. In addition to a wealth of jazz, he would bring back the rocking blues of artists like T-Bone Walker and B.B. King. By 1957 Dodd, now known as Sir Coxsone, had three separate sound systems touring the island.

Sir Coxsone's rivals were Arthur "Duke" Reid and Vincent "King" Edwards. Duke Reid was a bombastic ex-policeman who owned a liquor business. He wore an ermine robe and a gold crown to his dances and had the crowd carry him aloft to the stage when it was time to change a record. He carried a couple of handguns, a rifle and a belt of cartridges at all times, and was said to fire a few shots off over the heads of the dancers if any trouble broke out. His Trojan sound system was named after the Bedford Trojan truck which carried it, a name which would later be used for the famous record label.

King Edwards had started in 1955, bringing records and a sound system back with him when he returned from a brief spell living in the U.S. He was known for having the best records and was the first to really emphasize volume. By 1959 he had the island's most powerful system, known as Giant, and that year he was declared the number one sound in Kingston, overtaking Reid and Coxsone.

At this time, more formalized head-to-head competitions had become popular, with sound systems setting up deliberately within earshot of each other, or even playing in the same dance. These "sound clashes," as they would be known, further dramatized the battle for supremacy. Similar rituals would be adopted by later forms of music, most notably hip hop, but also, as is not widely known, Chicago house.

Competition was fierce and almost any tactic—fair or foul—was used to "flop" the rival sounds and gain the most crowded dancefloor. Building up the power of your system was one approach; having the best tunes was another, and record-buying trips to the States became essential. King Edwards recounts how he "started to ride the plane like a bus" in his search for exclusive tunes. In addition, Coxsone Dodd started scratching off record titles and renaming songs to throw off the competition. Thus "Later For Gator" by Willis Jackson became "Coxsone Hop," the sounds system's theme song. This is the first recorded instance of this time-honored DJ practice and it can be traced, via a series of definite links, from here in Jamaica to the northern soul scene in the UK and to the world of hip hop in New York. (As mentioned above, northern soul took the idea from Count Suckle, who imported the idea from Jamaica; hip hop almost definitely took it from Kool Herc, another Jamaican immigrant.)

Others used simple intimidation to get ahead. Duke Reid's gang were renowned for using strong-arm methods. One tale tells of how they shot to pieces the sound system of a rival—it was actually an extra-amplified jukebox—simply because it had a far superior selection of music. Sabotaging rival dances by starting fights or throwing rocks into the crowd was quite common.

Another gangster was Prince Buster, an ex-boxer originally named Cecil Bustamente Campbell. Buster would later become one of the island's best known vocalists and producers, but he started out by running security for Coxsone's dances. His tough posse and hard-man reputation came in very useful in warding off the destructive efforts of Duke Reid. Buster was instrumental in the rise of ska music and when he set up his own Voice Of The People sound, this quickly rose to be the most powerful of the early sixties. In Stephen Davis's book *Reggae Bloodlines*, Buster recalled the dominance of the sound systems at that time: "There was no radio in those days and sound system was everything. To hear a new record, thousands would go to the dances."

The Deejay Grabs the Mic

As the sound systems put all their creative resources into beating off their rivals, they began to really expand the DJ's range of possibilities. In transforming recorded music into a unique live show, the DJ has always striven to add value and excitement wherever he can. The particular needs of the sound system and its attendant culture would force several crucial innovations. Already the engineers who built the systems had been heavily boosting the bass power of their speakers to increase the physicality of the music. Already the DJs were traveling far and wide to seek out rare and exclusive records. The next steps would have to be big ones.

The first great change was the addition of a live vocal element, in the shape of the rhyming personality deejay. Inspired by the verbal creativity of the U.S.

radio DJs, the DJ divided his role and added a dedicated announcer. Now, instead of a single figure playing and announcing records, there were two: the selector and the deejay, also called a toaster or an MC, for "Master of Ceremonies." Nowadays, these performers are the greatest stars of Jamaican music, with deejays like Yellowman, Shabba Ranks, Buju Banton and Beenie Man enjoying the same worldwide fame and adoration as rock stars or rappers.

The vocalist deejay took his first steps around 1956. Winston "Count" Machuki, who had been playing records since 1950, first for Tom the Great Sebastian and then for Coxsone's Downbeat, decided to do more than just introduce the songs.

"I said to Mr. Dodd, 'Give me the microphone,'" Machuki recalled in Steve Barrow's *The Rough Guide to Reggae.* "And he handed me the mic, I started dropping my wisecracks, and Mr. Dodd was all for it. And I started trying my phrases on Coxsone, and he gave me one or two wisecracks too. I was repeating them all the night through that Saturday at Jubilee Tile Gardens. Everybody fell for it. I got more liquor than I could drink that night."

Machuki was far from satisfied and thought he could add more to his performance. Chancing on an issue of Harlem's *Jive* magazine, he started absorbing the jive slang of black America, the cool rhyming style that the U.S. radio DJs were using to introduce their records. Pretty soon he tried out his own compositions. He remembers the first one: "If you dig my jive/ you're cool and very much alive/ Everybody all round town/ Machuki's the reason why I shake it down/ When it comes to jive/ you can't whip him with no stick."

Machuki also started the practice of adding little vocal clicks and beats—anticipating rap's "human beatboxes" by about twenty years. These became known as "peps" because they pepped up the record. "There would be times when the records playing would, in my estimation, sound weak, so I'd put in some peps: *chicka-a-took, chicka-a-took, chicka-a-took,*" says Machuki. "That created a sensation." He proudly recalls that people often bought particular records they'd heard at a dance, thinking that his live contributions would be included, only to return their purchases once they realized that he wasn't actually on the record. "They didn't realize that was Machuki's injection in the dancehall," he laughs.

The second big deejay was King Stitt, whose energetic dancing led him, in 1957, to become Machuki's stand-in, and whose congenitally twisted features led him to subtitle himself "the ugly one." At this stage the deejay was still selecting the records as well as working the mike, and although Stitt was the first to show that the deejay could transfer his verbal skills to vinyl—he made a few successful records with producer Clancy Eccles in the late sixties, such as "Fire Corner" and "Lee Van Cleef"—it was only as the seventies dawned that the deejay era began in earnest.

As U-Roy, Ewart Beckford took the role of the deejay to the next level. U-Roy was so magnetic a performer that he could hold a crowd's attention even without backing music, a fact proved when a dance he was deejaying was forced by rain to turn off the amplifiers and he kept the dancers enthralled with just his voice. He made a series of records, produced by Duke Reid, that proved how popular the deejay had become. Using the instrumental tracks from existing rocksteady recordings, with his rhymed lyrics recorded over the top, "Wake The Town," "Rule The Nation" and "Wear You To The Ball" were so successful that in one week in 1970 they held the top three places in Jamaica's pop chart.

As Carl Gayle, editor of Kingston's *Jahugliman* magazine, relates, "What separates U-Roy from the rest is the fact that he gave reggae this live jivin' dimension which is so electrifying. With his will-of-the-wisp Kingston jive talkin' he turn the tables on a Jamaican recording scene full of singing talent, paving the way for a dancehall full of imitators." And sure enough, after U-Roy's success came Big Youth, I-Roy, Dillinger, and a hundred more deejays, stealing the limelight from the singers.

Into the Studio

The other great innovation which came from the sound systems' fierce competition was the practice of making exclusive, custom-made records. These were "versions"—new instrumental versions of a song made from a recycled backing track—and later "dubs," where a more radical reconstruction of a song was undertaken. These ideas represent the very first incarnation of the dance remix. They both came about simply because the DJ—in the shape of the sound system operator—wanted a constant flow of exclusive records to play to his dancers.

In fact, all Jamaican music since the fifties owes a considerable debt to the DJ, since almost all of it developed from the DJ's impulse to have better and more exclusive records. Ska, rocksteady, reggae and later ragga all evolved as music intended for use on a sound system, their escalating emphasis on bass making them work increasingly well in the open air where sound carries less. Moreover, the pioneer producers who recorded this music were almost all sound system operators themselves, Coxsone Dodd, Duke Reid and Prince Buster being the most important.

At the end of the fifties, there started to be a noticeable lack of the kind of American records which the dancehalls loved best, as the U.S. began to move to a smoother sound. To fill this gap the sound system men started making their own exclusive tracks. From 1957 onwards Coxsone and Reid, closely followed by Buster, began recording instrumental copies of the southern soul tunes of Memphis and New Orleans. It was here that the distinctly Jamaican sound crept in, as the local musicians who played on these tracks started to overemphasize the slightly crooked shuffle beat of New Orleans rhythm and blues and the producers began to turn up the bass.

"We realized that we were not getting enough stuff from America, so we had to make our local sound," explained Coxsone Dodd in *Reggae International.* "I had a couple of sessions, basically tango and calypso and some rhythm and blues-inclined sounds. After a couple of times in the studio, I found a sound that was popular with the dance crowd in Jamaica, and we worked from there."

These first studio efforts of the DJs-turned-producers were never intended for sale to the public. As Dodd himself confessed, "I didn't realize that this could be a business. I just did it for enjoyment." Indeed, these recordings existed only in the form of one-off soft wax pressings, made at considerable expense, as crowd-pulling exclusives for the producer's own sound system. Such discs can only be played about ten or fifteen times before the grooves wear out. Today's DJs and producers in almost all genres carry out exactly the same process. The soft wax discs are now known as "acetates," "dub-plates" or most recently "slates" and they remain things which DJs get very excited about.

Since these soft wax records were instrumentals, the deejays were able to really come into their own. Previously they could only thread their toasting into the spaces left by the record's singer; now they could cut loose and chat over the whole track.

In 1959 the first 7-inch Jamaican 45s were released commercially, and as they continued their forays into production, the sound system bosses started setting up their own studios and record labels. After several others, Coxsone Dodd started his famous Studio One (on which Bob Marley and the Wailers' first efforts were released); Duke Reid launched Trojan. Soon there was a steady flow of singers and musicians trying their luck as recording stars and Jamaica's indigenous music was gathering a real momentum.

Version

A version is a record with the vocals removed, an alternative cut of a song made to let a deejay toast over the top. By recording such instrumental tunes and pressing them up as soft wax discs, the producers had plenty of hot exclusives with which to wow their crowds. When a sound system played these one-off tracks, with a live deejay "riding the riddim," the audience was hearing something absolutely unique, with much the same immediacy as a traditional live performance. In terms of showmanship, the DJ—represented now by the trinity of producer, selector and deejay—was really delivering the goods.

Version, in a slightly wider sense, is music made from existing backing tracks. These are used as the basis of a new song by rerecording them with new elements, perhaps a deejay's vocals, or an organ melody line instead of a guitar, and so on.

All forms of reggae thrive on the idea of recycling or quoting favorite "riddims" (i.e. rhythms), as these recycled backing tracks with their familiar patterns of bass and drums are known. Such patterns may be copied (or "versioned") on hundreds of different records. Many are so well-known as to have names of their own (usually onomatopoeic). "Death In The Arena," "Waterpumping," "Shank-I-Sheck" are three of the best known. Their thriving, multiplying existence is proof, as Jamaican producer Dermott Hussey pointed out, that "you can copyright a song, but you can't copyright a rhythm."

Many rhythms have their origins, as might be expected, in America. One striking example "Death In The Arena," which can be heard on literally hundreds of records, King Tubby's "The Champion Version" being a good example. This can be traced back to a bassline used by drummer Bernard Purdey on his 1968 track "Funky Donkey."

Although it represents an important concept common to all African-derived musics, version owes its emergence largely to technology. The earliest Jamaican records were captured on simple one-track recorders. This meant that all the instruments and any vocals had to be recorded live, simultaneously. However, when Coxsone Dodd returned from England loaded with new equipment for his studio, he carried with him a *two-track* recorder. With this the instrumental part of a song could be recorded completely separately from the vocal, so any track made in Dodd's Studio One could be recorded free of lyrics.

Once you could isolate the rhythm track, you could use it as many times as you liked and add whatever you wanted to it. Producers eventually realized that they were able to release endless reworkings of the same rhythm, each made fresh by a new melody or new lyrics from that month's hottest deejay. In the seventies, one producer in particular, Bunny Lee, showed how a single rhythm could be creatively recycled into many different forms. For Lee, this was a matter of economic necessity as he didn't own his own studio and wanted to maximize the results he could get from each expensive hour of studio time.

Version fever took hold in 1967 when a sound system operator named Ruddy Redwood got hold of an acetate copy of an established hit tune, "On The Beach" by The Paragons, which was missing the vocals (producer Duke Reid had forgotten to add the vocal track to the final mix). After rocking the crowd with the original vocal pressing of the song, he played them this new voiceless version. The crowd went crazy, singing along, and Redwood played the song so many times that night that by morning the acetate was worn out.

Popular demand soon led the style away from purely sound system use. Joe Gibb's engineer, Errol Thompson, started using rhythm versions as B-sides to commercially released singles in 1971. Eventually there were even whole albums of a single rhythm: ten or more cuts of the same backing track, each with a different vocal.

Dub

Dub is a whole new universe of sound. It is the first instance of the dance remix. It opened up such dramatic possibilities that it is considered a whole new genre. Dub techniques are so powerful that they are now used across the whole spectrum of popular music. And as music made expressly for sound system use, dub owes its existence largely to the DJ.

Dub has been described as "X-ray music." A dub mix is essentially the bare bones of a track with the bass turned up. Dub separates a song into its stark component parts, and adds and subtracts each strand of sound until a new composition is made. By adding space to a track, what is left has far more room to breathe. By boosting a bassline until it's a monstrous shaking presence, dropping out the whole of the song except the drums, sending a snatch of singing into a reverberating echo, stretching out a rhythm with an interminable delay, dub can make a flat piece of music into a mountainous 3-D landscape.

"Dub" comes from "double," as in making a copy. It was essentially just an extension of version—because once the producer had a multitrack recorder he wasn't going to stop at simply removing the vocals (dub styles really came into their own with four-track recording). Dub's most obvious technique involves isolating the rhythm track, the "drum'n'bass," and emphasizing it beyond all nature, adding layers of disorienting echo and a barrage of other sound processing effects.

The story of dub centers on King Tubby. Born Osbourne Ruddock in 1941, Tubby had an almost supernatural understanding of electronics, garnered from years of building sound equipment and fixing radios and TVs. In his later years, it is said that if he was dissatisfied with how something sounded, he would dive into his mixing desk armed with a soldering iron and rebuild a circuit or two on the spot until he had adjusted it exactly as he wanted. Shy and an obsessive perfectionist, Tubby insisted on bizarre levels of neatness in his studio. He even went to the bank to exchange crumpled banknotes for new crisp ones. However, he was very generous, sharing his knowledge with the producers who rose up beneath him. In fact, even when he was considered a superstar producer, it is said he still took in toasters and hairdryers for repair.

Tubby (he was very slim) started operating a sound system, Tubby's Home Town Hi-Fi, in 1964. His was one of a new breed that by virtue of their innovations were starting to overtake the older sounds. He put together a very special system, with a built in echo, the first reverb unit of any sound system on the island, and exceptional power. It didn't hurt, also, that his main deejay was the imminently legendary U-Roy. By 1968 Tubby was crowned as number one sound.

Tubby also worked as an engineer and disc-cutter for Duke Reid and it was here in 1972, inspired by the way the sound systems were using version records, that he discovered ways to bring out the amazing contours hidden in a piece of music.

"I had a little dub machine and I used to borrow tapes from the producers and mix them down in a different fashion," Tubby related. "I used to work on the cutter for Duke Reid and once a tape was running on the machine and I just drop off some of the voice, y'know. It was a test cut."

When this test record was played for an audience, the response was phenomenal. "The Saturday we was playing out and I said alright, I going test them, 'cause it sounds so exciting the way the records start with the voice, the voice drop out and the rhythm still going. We carry them to the dance, man, and I tell you, 'bout four or five of the tune, them keep the dance, 'cause is just over and over we 'ave fe keep playing them."

Tubby's first experiments, as he described, involved dropping out the backing to leave the singers a cappella, and then reversing the process to let the band have center stage. The success of this style encouraged him to delve further and add exaggerated echo and reverb effects. Other producers, notably the musically insane Lee Perry, one of Coxsone Dodd's apprentices, quickly joined the dub express train and a whole barrage of remix techniques was developed and refined. (Perry was the first to use sound effects on records, adding such "sampled" noises as pistol shots and breaking glass.)

Soon, producers were lining up for a dash of the Tubby magic. Augustus Pablo, Lee Perry, Winston Riley and especially Bunny Lee among them. A producer would bring him a tape of their latest track and Tubs would remix it into a staggering number of different takes for different sound systems, each one in a style that best suited that sound or the deejay that would toast over it.

By 1975 King Tubby was given full label credits for the tracks he reconfigured, and not just as an engineer or remixer. Those who really know Jamaican music recognize him as one of its true founding fathers. Tragically, he was shot dead in 1989, only four years after opening his own state-of-the-art studio. And amazingly, despite his huge contributions to his national music, his death didn't even make the papers.

Echoes and Reverberations

Reggae set a great many precedents. It laid down the basic principles of remixing, it made an artist and a star of the producer, it made playing records into live performance, and it showed how music could be propelled into whole new genres by the needs of the dancefloor. Although many of these ideas would emerge independently elsewhere, the fact that it was first means that reggae's influence has been vast.

Hip hop owes it an enormous debt. Kool Herc, its founder, was Jamaican and what he did in the Bronx was based largely on wanting to build a New York version of the Kingston sound systems of his youth, toasting deejays included. And Grandmaster Flash's main influence was the mobile disco DJs from Brooklyn, who almost undoubtedly were following the Jamaican sound system tradition.

The first disco remixers developed their techniques—which were initially more about lengthening and restructuring than about sonic dismemberment—without being aware of what was happening in Jamaica. However, the lessons of dub quickly washed through New York. François Kevorkian admits that it was a major influence on him, and in the weird postdisco styles of producers like Arthur Russell and Larry Levan, a distinct dub sensibility is obvious.

Today's remixers still use principles first developed by Jamaica's visionaries, and almost every dance track has some sort of "dub" mix to fuel the dancefloor. Dub forms are at work in some of today's most popular bands, most notably Massive Attack, Underworld and Leftfield.

Perhaps reggae's biggest impact outside the Caribbean has been in the UK, which has been Jamaican music's second home. The influx of Jamaican immigrants from the late fifties had a dramatic impact on the early London club scene. Sound system parties, or "blues" (named after "bluebeat," the British term for Jamaican rhythm and blues) have been a staple since the sixties and have made major contributions to British music. Soul II Soul, with their massively important "Keep On Movin'" beat, were originally a sound system, and from Bristol's Wild Bunch sound came both Massive Attack and producer Nellee Hooper (Soul II Soul, Björk, Madonna). Finally, without a strong undercurrent of reggae and dub running through the UK's soundtrack, it is inconceivable that such forms as jungle, drum'n'bass and UK garage would have been born.

In return, reggae has kept its keen ears open and absorbed all manner of new possibilities from the wider world of music. In recent years, it has closed the circle with hip hop and taken much from the US. Ragga, the hard electronic style of reggae, is exactly analogous with house or techno: traditional musical forms reconstructed on synthesizers and drum machines. The producers, selectors and deejays are still plundering everything they can use to "nice up the dance," and their dancefloor-driven efforts continue to exert a major influence on the world's music.

"The fact is reggae has nourished dance culture to an extraordinary degree," insists Steve Barrow. "I'm not saying anything so banal as everything sounds like reggae—it's in the conceptualization of what you're supposed to be doing when you make dance music. It's in the practice, it's in techniques, and it's in the forms that have arisen out of Jamaican music. In all of this, this little island has had a profound influence."

SIX
DISCO

Love Is The Message

O body swayed to music, O brightening glance,
How can we know the dancer from the dance?
—W. B. Yeats, "Among School Children"

"Disco was a whole movement—people really felt that. They felt disappointed later on that the idealistic quality of it was being trampled in favor of money and celebrity. As much as disco was glitzy and certainly loved celebrity culture, there was never a sense of it being driven by that. It was much more driven by an underground idea of unity. The manifesto was the music. Love Is The Message."

—Vince Aletti

"We are the Stonewall girls. We wear our hair in curls. We wear no underwear. We show our pubic hair. We wear our dungarees above our nelly knees!"

It's the night of June 21, 1969 and you are out in front of the Stonewall Inn in Manhattan's Greenwich Village. It's a hot New York summer's night and the air is thick with oppressive humidity and the tension of unfolding drama. Around you there are men that look like women, women that dress like men, a few spaced-out hippies, bar staff from the Stonewall and quizzical Villagers coming to find out what the rumpus is here on Christopher Street.

Behind you is the Women's Correction Center, whose inmates have joined the party by dropping lighted tissue papers onto the sidewalk below. In the bar are several police officers, originally there on a routine raid, but now barricaded in, apparently terrified of the sudden and unexpected reaction from the freaks and the queers. A black gay man walks past yelling, "Let my people go!" Pennies and dimes hurtle through the air, along with loaded insults: "Faggot cops!" A rock shatters a window above the bar.

This was the Stonewall rebellion, the night when gay New York took to the streets and threw itself a revolution. But this was a rebellion of a different kind—more vivid street theater than armed revolt. Stonewall was the shrill sound of gays fighting back. It was the culmination of decades of oppression and humiliation. Spurred by black Americans' fight for civil rights, and inspired by the women's liberation movement, Stonewall was the landmark event which initiated the birth of gay pride.

Twelve hours before the disturbance, Judy Garland had been buried, after killing herself with an overdose of barbiturates. Garland was an icon in the tight-knit gay community, and the Stonewall Inn was one of several gay haunts in the Village mourning her passing that night. Being without a liquor license meant that it was run as a private club, a "bottle bar," where you had to be signed in to get a drink and where warning lights were in operation to alert clients of impending raids. The Stonewall's owners could usually ensure it remained relatively free from cop interference. Not tonight.

No one knows exactly why the Stonewall Inn was raided that evening, but there's no doubt that the police would come to regret it. New York cop Seymour Pine later commented: "There was never any time that I felt more scared than then." The *New York Daily News* reported: "HOME NEST RAIDED, QUEEN BEES ARE STINGING MAD." Because this was the night that rocks replaced diamanté; anger replaced camp. A cross-dressing lesbian called Stormé DeLarverie (who many believe kick-started the action) said, "The police got the shock of their lives when those queens came out of that bar and pulled off their wigs and went after them."

This was a revolution in a sequined shift dress.

On that same night, a few yards away from the Stonewall Inn, something else is happening. If you turn and walk down to Sheridan Square, on the site of legendary jazz club Café Society—where Billie Holiday once performed—stands the Haven, a small, illegal after-hours club. You go through the cramped entrance, dip down to the bar and join a phalanx of hucksters and hustlers, drag queens and beauty queens, card sharps and loan sharks. You grab a drink and survey the scene. All human life is congregated in this compact, dimly lit place. Barflys chatter; dancers dance. Ice clatters on glass, as bartenders go about their nightly routine.

All this action is played out to a soundtrack of intense rhythm and blues and funky rock music, powering through the largest speakers you've ever seen. Ensconced at the back, positioned behind a rudimentary set of turntables, is a young Brooklyn-born Italian American. He's wiry, muscular and handsome, and the sweat drips off the end of his nose as he lines up the next record: Chicago Transit Authority's "I'm A Man." Layer after layer of percussion is added to the rocksteady drumbeat, until a steely guitar motif signals the song's start. The dancefloor's tempo is visibly raised. The dancers grind that little bit more, their hips moving in circular motions. While Christopher Street is raging with the fight for gay emancipation, this DJ is busy rewriting the rules on the way we hear records in nightclubs.

Underground Origins

Disco was the revolution. Disco was freedom, togetherness, love. Disco was dirty, spiritual, thrilling, powerful. Disco was secret, underground, dangerous. It was non-blond, queer, hungry. It was emancipation.

Before commercial success twisted the music into a polyester perversion of itself, and wrenched the scene out of New York's gay underground only to drop it into the funkless lap of mainstream America, disco was the hottest, sexiest, most redeeming and most deeply loving dance music there has been. It relied on phenomenal musicianship, it was often poetic and highly lyrical, it could be as experimental and as profound as it wanted, and it was always funky beyond the call of duty.

These days the name "disco" is stuck to *Saturday Night Fever*, to the Bee Gees, Abba and the Village People, to plastic compilation CDs and tacky retro club nights. In its own time, however, for its original family, it was the word of salvation.

In fact, many of the people involved with its early days blanch at using "disco" to describe the music and clubs they knew and loved. They don't really have an alternative name, but they have a strong need to distinguish their music, funky and soulful, and their scene, small, gritty and underground, from what disco eventually became and from how disco is seen by most people today. The last days of disco might have recalled the decadent fall of Rome, but the first days were filled with hope.

Disco presided over an era of dramatic social change. As war raged in Vietnam and an oil crisis and deep economic recession brought further misery, it provided a soundtrack of escapism. Conversely, as restrictions on black and gay people started to dissolve, it was also the music for celebrating new freedoms.

After the Stonewall rebellion, gay Americans felt able to turn up the volume on their existence, and despite the rioting and letdowns of the post–civil rights period, black people were also enjoying the benefits of greater equality. Inspired by these minority freedoms, the majority, too, felt a release. Legal abortion, antibiotics and the Pill meant attitudes to sex had changed: it was for enjoyment, not procreation (this notion definitely helped soften the straight view of gay sex). The "Make Love Not War" ideals of the late sixties were still reverberating; Vietnam and LSD had greatly broadened young people's worldview. It was clear that your experience of life would be very different from that of your parents.

Emerging in New York in the first half of the seventies, disco could still vividly recall the Summer of Love a few years before. Its music grew as much out of the psychedelic experiments of Sly and The Family Stone and Motown producer Norman Whitfield as from Gamble and Huff's Philadelphia orchestrations. Its original spirit—an emphasis on equality, freedom, togetherness and love—was just sixties idealism matured by the experience of Vietnam and refueled by the promise of black/gay liberation. And disco not only reflected these changes, in creating a new and vital subculture—one which was eventually co-opted by the mainstream—disco also, in a very real sense, helped to further them.

Musically, disco was revolutionary to an astonishing degree. It was at the heart of some of the most radical innovations to date in the way music is envisaged, created and consumed. It changed clubs almost beyond recognition, it affected radio dramatically, and it had an important effect on the balance of power in the music industry between the independent labels and the majors. By the end of its reign had been born the 12-inch single, the remix and a host of new studio techniques. And with songs being constructed specially for the dancefloor (longer, more beat-oriented, more *functional*) and records being treated as DJs' tools rather than just representations of a live performance, there arrived a new conception of what popular music could be.

As for the club DJ, the disco era was when he came of age. This was when he became a star, even a god to his dancefloor. This was when he learned his vocabulary of mixing techniques, and this was when the industry recognized him as the person best placed to create dance music rather than just play it.

The Death of Rock

However, before any of this could take place, there had to be a shift. As the sixties ended, club culture was based on the ideals of celebrity, international travel and playboy status, epitomized by places like Arthur in New York and Scotch of St. James in London, or on the inner voyages of psychedelic places like Electric Circus or UFO. While it was thriving, having introduced a new kind of jet-set classlessness, this nightworld of beautiful people was hardly likely to inspire any novel musical movement. Before disco could happen, the night had to fall back into the hands of the energetic underclasses, a prerequisite of almost all clubland innovation.

And with the end of the sixties, this was what happened. In the closing month of the decade, the Rolling Stones' free performance in Altamont was soured by the Hell's Angel murder of a black concertgoer. Four months later, state troopers opened fire on student anti-Vietnam protesters at Ohio's Kent State University, killing four. These two events splashed blood in the flower children's faces and provided chilling symbols for the end of the hippie odyssey. Then The Beatles broke up and Hendrix and Joplin died. Sensing that the party was over, the jet set turned their backs on the psychedelic scene.

Around the same time, organized crime had seen the money-laundering potential of clubs and moved in, further repelling the classier elements and encouraging an atmosphere of violence and seediness. Additionally, the authorities moved against many clubs' blatant disregard for drug and alcohol laws, and a series of busts for liquor license violations took place. This inadvertently encouraged the opening of juice bars, unlicensed all-night hangouts which were subject to far less scrutiny and which could stay open much later. "Juice joint" became a byword for depravity.

As the jet set and their followers moved on and clubs needed to fill the space they left, new faces found their way in. Black, Hispanic and working-class white kids found it far easier to get through the door, and since gay New Yorkers—a sizeable clubland constituency—no longer had to hide in illegal speakeasies, they were a valuable new market. In fact, several clubs "went gay" at this time, largely for financial reasons.

Additionally, the dominant music—rock—was changing. Before the seventies were very old, rock had abandoned its early danceable psychedelic forms for the bloated self-aggrandizement of its "progressive" era. It was the age of the concept album, of the rock opera, the tortuous guitar solo. Set on proving its artistic nature, rock no longer provided much in the way of a dance beat. In its place, clubs reverted to rhythm and blues and more Latin styles, a process encouraged by the greater black and Hispanic presence.

Francis Grasso—The First Modern DJ

If it took many factors to prepare the social fabric of New York for the arrival of disco, to make ready the dancefloor it took but one disc jockey. He is the ancestor of all modern DJs, the godfather of the craft, the first DJ that we would recognize as doing the same thing as DJs do today. On the night that New York's queers decided to fight back, he was playing at the Haven on Christopher Street. The Stonewall Rebellion here started the social revolution that would nurture disco, and he was a stone's throw away, staging the musical revolution that would give it roots. His name was Francis Grasso.

DJ Francis didn't just bend the rules; he changed the game. Before him, the DJ had been a musical waiter, serving the songs required by the crowd and maximizing the profits of the owner by periodically directing them to the bar with a few slowies, much as a good waiter can craftily recommend the most profitable dishes. In the UK, northern soul had initiated a similar change, and some U.S. DJs, like Terry Noel at Arthur, had been more flamboyant and had risen to a status equivalent perhaps to that of a charismatic maitre d'. Noel could trust that most customers would accept his recommendations and had added a few flourishes to the dishes (a little tableside flambé, perhaps), but he had still been part of the serving staff.

Grasso took the profession out of servitude and made the DJ the musical head chef. DJ Francis didn't follow the pop chart menu, and he didn't bring the customer what he'd asked for. Instead, he cooked up a nightly banquet of new and exotic musical dishes which the diners, though they devoured them eagerly and came back for more, might never have known to order.

As a result, he completely changed the relationship between the DJ and his audience. Dance at a club where Francis was playing and though it was a reciprocal thing—with him responding to the enthusiasms of the dancers—you had to submit to his taste, to his choice of music and, most importantly, to the mood journey he took you on.

Francis Grasso was the first DJ to present a true creative performance. He was the first to show that a nightful of records could be a single thing: a voyage, a narrative, a set. Before him the DJ might have known that certain records had the power to affect the mood and energy of the crowd; only after him did the DJ recognize that this power belonged to him, not to the records. It lay in the DJ's skillful manipulation of the dancers, in the way he sequenced or programmed the records, and only to a far lesser degree in the records themselves.

Other DJs still thought of themselves as the stand-in for a band; they still thought of a record as an imitation of a live performance. Francis, on the other hand, saw that records were the vital components of *his* performance.

DJ Francis played music, the disc jockeys before him had just put records on.

You can see that Francis Grasso was a wild one. As he flicks and strokes a long mane of dark gray hair, a sparkle in his eyes, he has stories that only stars can tell. There was a time when strangers would scream out his name as he walked his dogs on the streets of Manhattan. He would take eight or nine of his friends out and they would be whisked into clubs and drink free all night. He dated Liza Minnelli. He was a good friend to Jimi Hendrix (not to mention to Hendrix's "main old lady," who moved into Grasso's bed after the guitarist's death). He used to spend more than his rent on drugs. Though never married, he has been engaged to at least three women—one of them a Playboy Bunny—and during his time as a DJ he screwed hundreds more.

Sitting in a bar in his native Brooklyn, the scars of a life lived to the full are only too apparent. The speed-sped metabolism of his youth has left him skeletally trim, and there are several signs—the gaunt curves of his face, the disarrangement of his nose and teeth which leaves his voice both nasal and slurred—that he has also been visited by violence along the way.

His love for his dogs, he reckons, is the only reason he is still alive: if it wasn't for the duties of caring for them—having to head home each night to walk and feed them—the druggy hedonism of his glory years would have claimed him completely. He has always kept dogs, mostly Great Danes. This week he has a new litter of puppies.

Like Terry Noel before him, Francis entered clubland as a dancer. Injuries from a series of motorcycle accidents had left him with poor coordination in his feet, and his doctor suggested that he take up dancing as therapy. This led to a job at Trude Heller's Trik, a couples-oriented Greenwich Village nightspot owned by socialite Trudy "Trude" Heller, where he performed perched precariously on a ledge at one side of the club.

"Yep, I was one of the original Trudy Heller go-go boys," he grins. "You had twenty minutes on and twenty minutes off, and you could only move your ass side to side because if you went back and forth you'd bang off the wall and fall right onto the table you were dancing over. You'd have a partner, and the band would play 'Cloud Nine' by the Temptations for about thirty-eight minutes. Going home, my muscles were killing me. It was the hardest twenty dollars I ever made in my life."

His debut as a DJ came one Friday in 1968, when he found himself in Salvation Too on the night that (as he recalls) Terry Noel had decided to drop acid before setting off for work. Noel didn't show up until 1:30 A.M. By that time Francis was the new house DJ, having displayed an instinctive command of the equipment—two Rekocut broadcast-quality turntables and a single fader switch—and having watched Noel get fired on arrival.

Francis can't recall the first record he played there, but he knows he had "a hell of a good time." They paid him handsomely and he went home hardly believing what had happened. "I would have paid *them.* I had that much fun."

There couldn't be a clearer example of a DJ snatching the torch from his predecessor. Judging by this first night, DJ Francis must have been immediately and noticeably different. What had distinguished him so clearly from those who came before? Shrugging his shoulders in a cheeky display of false modesty, he says simply, "There *wasn't* really guys before me.

"Nobody had really just kept the beat going," he adds. "They'd get them to dance, then change records, so you had to catch the beat again. It never flowed. And they didn't know how to bring the crowd to a height, and then level them back down, and bring them back up again. It was like an experience, I think that was how someone put it. And the more fun the crowd had, the more fun I had."

In contrast, he remembers that Terry Noel, though he was able to mix records, would often trip up the continuity of the night with an incongruous choice. "He used to do really weird things. Like he'd have the whole dancefloor going and then put on Elvis Presley." Francis would never sacrifice a busy dancefloor. "I kept 'em juiced," he growls.

Before him, people had played records as if they were discrete little performances; Francis treated them like movements in a symphony: continuous elements in a grand whole. By conceiving of his music in this way, he was no longer just providing a soundtrack to sixties social razzmatazz, he was envisaging the far more dance-centered clubs of the future. And with this ideal of an unbroken flow of music, the recent notion of mixing records gained new importance.

Perhaps his effortless success was due to his musicality. Having started with the accordion when he was young, he admits also to playing guitar, drums and saxophone, at least in high school and during college (he studied English Literature at Long Island University). He prefers, however, to attribute the source of his talent elsewhere. "I was a dancer!" he declares, as if it's all the explanation necessary. "I was a dancer, so it was rhythmically . . . not hard."

Ironically, he says he wouldn't have enjoyed being down on the dancefloor —he hates crowds—but, as he puts it, he loved to be in control and to absorb the feeling in the room.

Francis Grasso's choice of music was quite different to his predecessor, too. Seduced by the tastes of the jet set, Noel had played rock and pop with a soul accent: The Beatles, a lot of Motown, The Chambers Bros. . . .

But DJ Francis, though he played a lot of the same music (remember there were far, far fewer releases in those days), accented a harder, funkier sound than Noel's soulful pop, picking up on a lot of British imports and the grittier end of black music.

In his hands the funkier side of rock such as The Rolling Stones or Led Zeppelin met heavy black rhythms like Dyke & The Blazers or Kool & The Gang, and he introduced his audience to the drum-heavy African sound of bands like Osibisa, making a personal signature tune of Michael Olatunji's (much-sampled) "Drums Of Passion" (aka "Jin-Go-La-Bah"). He felt that a Latin beat made most people dance, so Santana was a staple. And Mitch Ryder and the Detroit Wheels, early Earth Wind And Fire, The Staple Singers, Ike and Tina Turner, all found their way into his set.

Soul survivor—outside his local Brooklyn bar, Francis Grasso shows the wear and tear which comes with having invented the modern DJ.

Previously, a DJ's records belonged to the club, but Francis owned the records he played and put considerable effort into buying music, badgering the staff at Colony Records in Times Square to find him exclusives. Like all DJs, he fetishized imports, Brian Auger's English jazz-rock LP *Befour* being one example.

He played James Brown and of course Motown—The Four Tops, The Supremes and especially the longer, weirder tracks being produced for The Temptations by Norman Whitfield, as well as the Stax Memphis sound including Sam and Dave and Booker T. and The MGs. Sly and The Family Stone were a particular favorite, and he unearthed the various records Sly made as a producer. He would close his performance with the sound of The Doors' "The End."

The Sanctuary

When Salvation Too closed, Grasso had a brief spell installing air conditioners, rescuing himself with a successful audition at a club called Tarot. From here he was poached by a spot in the Hell's Kitchen district. This club, the place where Francis would fully hone his pioneering DJing skills, was the Sanctuary.

Sanctuary was splashed in controversy right from its inception. Initially named The Church, since it occupied the shell of an old German Baptist church at 407 West 43rd Street, its decor, chosen by its founder Arnie Lord, stretched the credulity of even the most secular. Across from the altar a vast mural of the devil looked on menacingly; its demon eyes seemingly alive and mobile. Around him were clusters of angels with exposed genitalia, all engaged in some sexual act, each more depraved than the last. "The mural was unbelievably pornographic," recalls Francis. "And no matter where you stood in the club, the devil was looking at you." Drinks were served from chalices, the banquettes were pews and the building's stained glass windows were illuminated from outside. On the altar itself sat the record decks, where the disc jockeys served a new kind of sacrament.

When it first opened, the protests against this blasphemous night spot were so vociferous that it was quickly forced to close (thanks largely to an injunction gained by the Catholic Church). When it reopened, the angels had bunches of plastic grapes gingerly placed over their offending gonads, and the club was renamed the Sanctuary.

Then, after building up a good business as a couply straight club, the day manager ran off with the night manager and $175,000 of the club's money. A rescue plan put it into gay ownership, all the women were fired and, with Stonewall a recent memory, the place proudly became the first public flowering of all the scene's seedy juice bar energy, the aboveground representative of places with names like Thrush, Fabulous, Forbidden Fruit, Together and Superstar. As Albert Goldman described it, Sanctuary was "the first totally uninhibited gay discothèque in America."

DJ Francis found himself the only straight man left. This had its advantages. He'd always had difficulties making toilet runs without letting a record finish (quite a problem since most of the tracks he played were 45s lasting about three minutes). Now this was solved. "I just started going to the ladies' room 'cause there were no ladies," he grins. "One night a reporter came down to do a story on the club. He asked the doorman, 'Do you get any straight people here?' and he just pointed at me and said, 'Yeah, there he goes.'"

As a gay club, Sanctuary grew steadily wilder. Francis developed his skills to the point where he could keep the dancefloor packed far beyond capacity all night, seven nights a week. "It was so crowded, and they were passing poppers around. Even if anybody wanted to pass out, there was no room. They were literally holding each other up, it was so packed." Sanctuary had a legal maximum occupancy of 346 people; Francis remembers nights when the doorman stopped counting at more than a thousand. Eventually it lost its alcohol license and became a juice bar, slashing profitability but allowing it to stay open all night. On Fridays and Saturdays this meant noon the following day.

When a nightclub is poured full of newly liberated gay men, then shaken (and stirred) by a weighty concoction of dance music and a pharmacopia of pills and potions, the result is a festival of carnality. This was the Sanctuary. A 1965 law against "deviant sexual intercourse" ensured gay sex was still illegal in New York State (this law, which applies to all instances of oral and anal sex, is on the statute books to this day), and the American Psychiatric Association still classed homosexuality as an illness (until December 15, 1973). But Stonewall had loosened the lid on an entire oppressed culture, and gay New York ran at life like greyhounds out of the trap.

Tom Burke, writing in *Esquire* magazine, described this new breed of homo: "An unfettered, guiltless male child of the new morality in a Zapata moustache and an outlaw hat, who couldn't care less for Establishment approval, would as soon sleep with boys as girls, and thinks that 'Over The Rainbow' is a place to fly on 200 micrograms of Lysergic Acid Diethylamide."

The Sanctuary was patrolled by Puerto Rican dealers dressed like fifties wiseguys who doled out downers like tuies (Tuinal), reds (Seconal) and

Quaaludes (and their methaqualone mates: Paris 400s and Rorer 714s), as well as amphetamines and a lexicon of psychedelics from LSD to DMT. The downers were so strong they were nicknamed "wall-bangers" (or "gorilla biscuits") because they effected an almost total shutdown of the motor neuron system. Francis bought sealed bottles of 400mg Quaaludes (an aphrodisiac tranquilizer) from a pharmacist friend. Normally $5 each, he'd give them to all his friends for a dollar apiece. *The Daily News* called Sanctuary a "drugs supermarket."

As for sex, though fucking was banned on the dancefloor, the club's dark corners hid many a writhing body and its toilets hosted scenes of all-out orgies. Francis remembers the problems caused in the summer when the club's neighbors would complain about guys using their hallways for sex (this was what would eventually bring the club's closure). On his insistence, women were grudgingly allowed in the club and he began to share in the sexual abandon. "I was caught so many times getting oral sex in the booth it was disgusting," he says. "I would tell the girls, 'Bet you can't make me miss a beat.'"

When Alan J. Pakula wanted to depict a place of sin in his 1971 movie *Klute* (for which Jane Fonda won an Oscar), he chose Sanctuary. Francis is in there for about three seconds, playing a DJ. During filming, the place's genuinely sinful nature invested the proceedings. "To get the feel of real hookers, they had real hookers. Then the cops arrived because there was a lot of drug-dealing going on in between takes. It was a lively crowd!"

Francis started playing at another club, the Haven, in 1969 (he would move between Haven and Sanctuary several times). The Haven is remembered as the last place which the cops smashed up with impunity simply because it was a gay bar.

Here, Francis continued his sonic experiments, redeploying records culled from the freeform rock shows on the burgeoning FM wavelength for his dancefloor. Iron Butterfly's progressive rock epic "In-A-Gadda-Da-Vida" (the album version was seventeen minutes long) and Rare Earth's drum heavy "Get Ready" were, because of their length, accidentally perfect. Using two Thorens turntables, a pair of piggyback Dynaco amps and behemoth speakers "acquired" from the rock band Mountain, DJ Francis grew to the peak of his powers.

Revolutionary Techniques

Francis claims he was able to beat-mix—that is to overlap the ending of one record with the beginning of a second so that their drum-beats are synchronized—almost as soon as he started. Even with today's superior equipment, to beat-mix records containing the tempo fluctuations of a live drummer is an impressive feat indeed.

Whether he really did have this ability straight away, Francis was certainly the DJ who made beat-mixing a required skill. He was not the very first to mix, but he certainly took it to a whole new level, and could hold a blend—two songs playing simultaneously with the beats synchronized—for two minutes or more.

"Nobody mixed like me," he boasts. "Nobody was willing to hang on that long. Because if you hang on that long, the chances of mistakes are that much greater. But to me it was second nature. I did it like I walk my dog."

Beat-mixing gave a DJ unprecedented scope for creativity and would be essential to disco's development. Nowadays, it is fairly easy since most dance songs, thanks to drum machines, have an unwavering tempo, and modern turntables have sophisticated pitch control allowing the DJ to bring one record's speed up or down to match the other. Francis, however, had neither of these advantages.

"Back then, you couldn't adjust the speeds," he remembers. "You had to catch it at the right moment. There was no room for error. And you couldn't play catch up. You couldn't touch the turntables. I had Thorens at the Haven, and you couldn't do that on Thorens. All you had to do was start at the right moment."

He also perfected the slip-cue. This now basic technique requires a felt disc (a "slipmat") between the record and the turntable platter. The record about to be played (the one which is being "cued up") can thus be held stationary while the turntable spins underneath. This allows the DJ to start it instantly, exactly at the point of its first beat. The technique was already used in radio and Francis had been introduced to it by the engineer on his friend Bob Lewis's CBS radio show.

Grasso would use this technique to bring a fresh record in right on the beat of the one that was already playing, as if the musicians had changed tune without stopping. At other times, he says, he trusted his instincts to effect the same move, recognizing the record's desired passage by eye, placing the needle into the correct groove and deftly maneuvering the slide fader to make the switch from one disc to another. "I got so good I would just catch it on the run." Such mixing was essential, considering that the songs of the time were so short, but what he was doing was prefiguring the remixing techniques which would be a vital part of all subsequent dance music.

He would often use two copies of the same record to extend it, a technique he describes with "You're The One" by Little Sister (a Sly Stone side project): "Part one ended musically, part two on the other side would begin with a scream, so you could blend right into the scream side, and then go back to 'You're The One.' Or play the scream side twice, part two, then flip it over and play part one, twice. They didn't know I was playing two 45s."

He would play "Soul Sacrifice" by Santana and put the live Woodstock version of the same song on the other turntable. By moving back and forth, alternating between the two records, he could extend the song and keep the dancers locked in its groove. But then by blending the two songs—overlaying one completely over the other—he could achieve a dramatic echo effect. It sounded, he says proudly, "phenomenal." Skilful DJs today do something very similar called "phasing," where, by playing two copies of the same record very slightly out of synch, they produce a climactic whooshing sensation in the sound.

Another of his signature mixes was a blend of Led Zeppelin's "Whole Lotta Love" with the drum break of Chicago Transit Authority's "I'm A Man." He sent Robert Plant's primal moans surging over the top of a sea of Latin percussion. The dancefloor mirrored the music's ecstatic rite and reciprocated with cacophonous wails. "I just basically tried everything there was to try," he shrugs.

DJ Francis's Disciples

In 1970 Steve D'Acquisto was a recently qualified funeral director, driving cabs on the graveyard shift while his embalming license came through. He dropped a passenger off at 1 Sheridan Square, the Haven.

"I decided I'd try and get into this place. I had long hair right down my back at this point so they let me in, figuring I was some kind of freak."

D'Acquisto was astonished at the music he heard there. It wasn't just the funky and unfamiliar records being danced to; it was the way they were played—they were being mixed. "On radio, basically the fade would arrive and the new one would come in, and here was this guy, playing records, mixing records, doing all these great things that had never happened before."

D'Acquisto, entranced by Francis Grasso's music, would quickly become his partner in crime. He was an immediate regular at Haven, joining the DJ in his drug-fueled nights of wild rhythm and blues. "Francis and I got friendly. By now I'd be going every night and we'd speed together. He was a speed freak as well; loved speed. I always had good drugs; he always had good drugs." Grasso even got his friend hired to work the lights, a job D'Acquisto held for about six months. "Then one night I was at Francis's house and he'd been playing for two weeks straight and his alternate hadn't showed. They called Francis and told him he had to come in; it was a Monday night, one of the off nights." But Grasso was feeling pretty burnt out, and at the Haven there was rarely an early end to the night. "It would depend on how high people were as to how late the club stayed open. So Francis says, 'I can't do this.' And he looked at me and said, 'Do you wanna go play some records? Just make believe you're me.' So I did and I liked it."

Soon afterwards, the Haven added a third disc jockey to its rota, a head-turning Brooklyn Italian called Michael Cappello, another clubber sparked by Francis's DJing. Younger than both D'Acquisto and Grasso, yet extremely streetwise, Cappello completed a troika: three music-crazy youngsters who'd been turned on by flower power and seduced by rhythm and blues. With Grasso as their mentor, the two new apprentices eagerly learned his techniques.

"I had to teach somebody," says Francis. "I was teaching in secret because it was really hard to do what I do. I needed somebody reliable who knew what they were basically doing, at least had an idea. I may teach you the basic moves, but it's your interpretation that makes or breaks you."

The trio became tight friends, often spending day after day together, hunting for records, getting tips from the radio, often not sleeping for days at a time, all fueled by a prodigious intake of amphetamine. "Sometimes Michael, Francis and I wouldn't sleep for three or four days at a time," recalls D'Acquisto. "We'd go on and on, snorting speed and crystal meth. We were very serious about our speed! We had to be, though: we were playing twelve or fifteen hours in a night, every single night."

When reminded of this, Grasso just laughs. "Only *four* days at a time?"

Despite being only sixteen years old when he began DJing, Cappello quickly forged a reputation as a consummate spinner—first at the Haven, then joining D'Acquisto and Grasso when they moved back to the Sanctuary. "As far as I'm concerned, Michael Cappello was the best DJ who ever did his thing," asserts D'Acquisto. "I could listen to Michael hour after hour, night after night, and he never bored me. Always inventive, always genius; extremely clever."

Cappello would later be one of the key spinners of the disco period, playing at the original Limelight, where his smooth, climactic style was much admired. "Michael would peak the crowd," remembers Nicky Siano, another rising DJ star of the time. "He would take it up and it would stay up, and it would go up and up and up and up, beyond where you'd feel you could go. It was great." Siano, like many others, also remembers him for his looks. "Michael was so easy to look at, and he was not a very talkative kind of person. But he was just really good at playing records."

With their revolutionary mixing techniques, not to mention their stalwart drug consumption and adventurous sexual antics, Grasso, Cappello and D'Acquisto were to have a powerful influence on the scene, providing much in the way of inspiration for what would become disco. Their technical skills, their attitude to their performance, and their abilities to manipulate a dancefloor were what gave the nascent club scene much of its momentum. And to hear them play was to realize that DJing would never be the same again. People recall that the impact was as dramatic as first hearing hip hop years later.

Remarkably, the three protagonists survived their adventures to see the present day. Cappello and Grasso are both working in construction, only D'Acquisto is still involved in music, working for an audio manufacturer.

Francis Grasso carried on DJing until 1981, although his career was almost stopped at the height of his fame when he was beaten mercilessly by mafia goons for daring to leave a club residency in order to set up Club Francis, a rather ill-advised project bankrolled on the strength of his name. Ignoring the command to merely scare him, the hoods crushed his face in to the point where he was in hospital for three months undergoing reconstructive surgery. "I was beaten to a bloody pulp," he says. "I was in the emergency room of St. Vincent's hospital in Manhattan, I remember these two doctors, they said, 'Shame, must have been a good-looking guy.'" To add insult to injury, while he was in hospital his neighbor moved away and took all his records.

If this was his worst moment, his best, he says, came after he had just left the Sanctuary for the Haven. Returning to help fix some equipment, he was mobbed by the dancers, who thought he was going to play for them. "I walked in and the customers saw me behind in the booth, they all applauded, there was this big cheer. They loved me. I got immediately humbled. *Immediately.* People didn't want to see me leave."

Ironically, despite laying its groundwork, Francis never much cared for disco, although he carried on playing right through its heyday. He has little time for DJs nowadays, arguing that these days the records do all the work, not like when he was playing for ten hours and changing the record every two minutes.

If you are a club DJ today, Francis Grasso is your forefather; he changed the whole idea of DJing. The disc jockey before him had been a slave to the records. After him the DJ would be, as he was, a slave to the rhythm.

Sound System Evangelists

As well as the existence of pioneering stars like Grasso, crucial to the rapid rise of the club DJ were the innovations in sound processing that were also made at this time. Luckily for Grasso and his colleagues, the sound systems at both the Haven and the Sanctuary had been built by a true loudspeaker evangelist.

Alex Rosner was one of the children spared the horrors of the Holocaust by being included in Oskar Schindler's lifesaving list. By the early sixties, he was in America working as an engineer in the defense industry. As a hobby, he liked to experiment with stereophonic audio systems, indulging his passionate belief in the superiority of reproduced sound.

"To this day, I like the concept of the discothèque," he explains. "I like the concept of reproduced music as opposed to live music. And I thought that the technology was available to make things sound good and sound realistic. I experimented a lot."

Rosner constructed his first sound system for the Canada-A-Go-Go and Carnival-A-Go-Go stands at the 1964–5 World's Fair. This was where he built the world's first stereophonic disco system. "Up until then it had all been mono. There was no equipment available at the time. There were no mixers; no stereo mixers; no cueing devices. Nothing." He swiftly moved into clubs, firstly with a little place called the Ginza and then with the Haven, where he made the first ever stereo mixer, used to devastating effect by Francis Grasso. "The cueing system was one of my old-fashioned adventures," Rosner says. "They called it the Rosie because it was painted red. It was really primitive and not very good. But it did the job. And nobody could complain, because there was nothing else around."

Rosner was also instrumental in building the world's first commercially available mixer, the 1971 Bozak, advising its inventor, Louis Bozak, on the more practical side of nightclub requirements. "I had to invent the wheel until the Bozak mixer came along," he remembers. "But I helped Bozak design his mixer; I gave him suggestions so he could make it better. He already had a 10–channel input mixer. I suggested to him that he only needed to make minor modifications to this unit to make it into a stereophonic disco mixer. And right off the bat, he did it the right way." Bozak's prototype mixer became industry standard for the next fifteen years and is now a collector's item.

David Mancuso and the Loft

If disco—and the music which came after—has an angel, it is the raggedy figure of David Mancuso; if it has a birthplace, it is his club, the Loft. More influential than any nightclub before or since, it was the place where the music you dance to today, and the places you go to do it, were first envisaged.

Mancuso discovered and championed more classic dance records than anyone can remember, he inspired a whole generation of DJs, record collectors, club founders and label owners, he set the standards for club sound reproduction and, in the Loft, he created a place where the equality and love of a thousand corny dance lyrics was a tangible reality. Fortified by the cosmic perspectives of the hippie generation, turned on by a profound love of

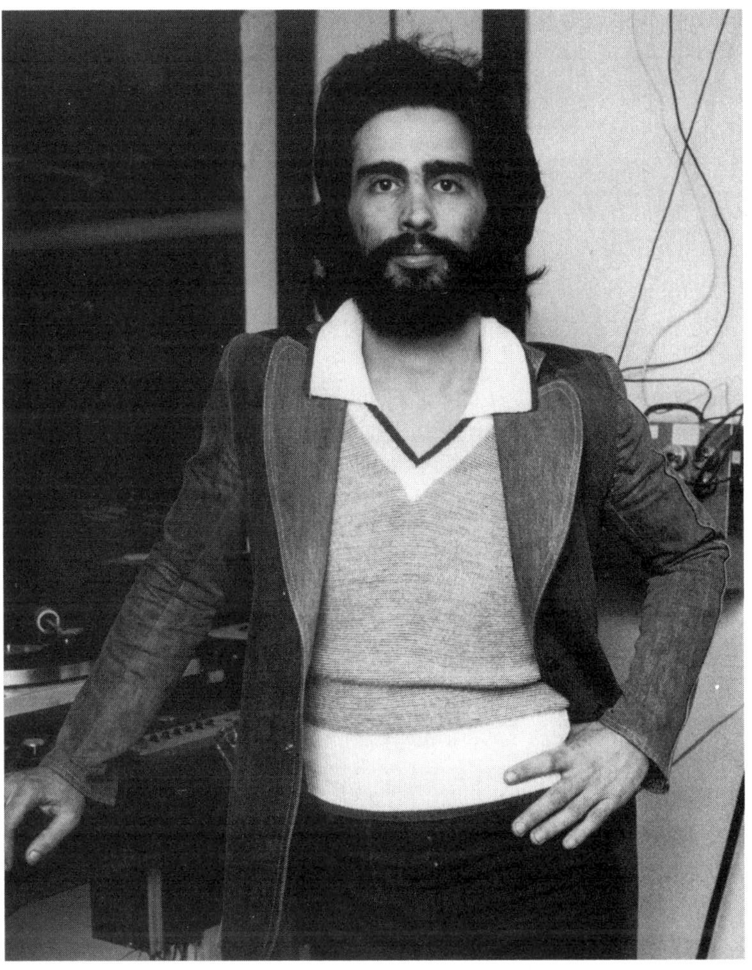

Disco daddio—David Mancuso provided the blueprint for nightclubbing and inspired a generation of DJs.

music and finding himself alive in a time of exciting possibilities, David Mancuso laid the cornerstone of modern clubbing.

While Grasso and his compadres had started to release the creative potential of a DJ and a pile of records, Mancuso would draw up the blueprints for the transcendent dancefloor experience, ideas which have been copied consciously and unconsciously by clubs and clubbers ever since. And though at the time of writing the reality of its next incarnation seems rather precarious, the possibility of the Loft lives on. Up until its most recent closure, Mancuso's club had enjoyed a more or less unbroken quarter-century existence.

Mancuso himself, a shy man who speaks in mumbles from behind wild eyes and a bushy beard, is viewed by many as a crazy musical mystic. He demands perfect sound reproduction, he refuses to mix records, insisting that they be heard entire and unchanged, and when he talks about music his words are usually a universe away from how your average DJ would put things. However, most people who have ever felt the emotional charge of a dancefloor instinctively understand the elusive feelings that he's trying to express.

Mancuso has lived with a lifelong obsession about the relationship between recorded music, the person who plays that music and the bodies and souls of the people listening and dancing. As a DJ he would never lay claim to anything so egotistical as "playing a great set"; for him, a wonderful night is made as much by the dancers as the music, guided as much by the spirit of joy in the room as by the hand which chooses the next record.

David Mancuso, born in Utica, New York, on October 20, 1944, tells of being raised by a kindly nun in an orphanage of twenty kids. To this day, he can recall how she would treat the children with juice to drink and put a stack of records on a big boxy radiogram for them to sing and dance to. He is convinced she had a profound impact on how he conceived the parties he would later create. "I have a feeling part of my influence—why it's communal, why I do it the way I wanna do it—it has to be to do with back then. Sister Alicia would find any excuse to have a party."

By the age of fifteen, Mancuso was working as a shoeshine boy. After moving to New York during the Cuban missile crisis in 1962, he worked at various jobs—including designing towels and as a personnel manager—before he got bored, as he says, "of the nine to five thing." He drifted through life in the city, making friends, struggling to make money, struggling harder to have a good time, until in 1970 he started throwing after-hours parties starting around midnight in the loft where he lived—at 647 Broadway, just north of

Houston Street. Though it was never formally titled, this balloon-filled party space soon became known by all who attended simply as the Loft.

The Loft wasn't much to look at and it wasn't very big. But it was homely, it had a great domestic hi-fi system, and in Mancuso it had a musical director with an acute ear for the dramatic, the atmospheric and the heavily rhythmic. Mancuso, as much a product of the psychedelic era as he was a black music aficionado, conceived the Loft as a series of rent parties, with invites bestowed only on close friends. (In New York it was legal then to hold rent parties, providing the money was used specifically to pay for the rental on the building.)

"I was in a commercial loft," he remembers. "There were sprinklers and everything. I sent out thirty-six invitations; but it took a while to get going. After six months, it opened up every week." He was very strict about the status of his guests, guided by clear aims and well thought-out principles. "When you came in, everything was included in the contribution. You were not a member. It was not a club. I didn't want to be in that category. It meant different things to me. I wanted to keep it as close to a party as possible. It was $2.50 and for that you'd get your coat checked, food, and the music. In those days the bars were only open till 3 A.M. and if anything was open after three, you could be pretty sure it was gambling or liquor and I wasn't into any of that. I didn't want to be into any of that. I wanted it to be private. And you have to remember that the Loft was also where I slept; where I dreamt. Everything."

As well as carefully controlling who came to the parties, Mancuso paid exquisite attention to the music. He understood that the dynamics of sound he projected were as important as the records he was playing. "I wanna hear the music. Once you hear the sound system, that means you're getting ear damage; ear fatigue. So you wanna hear the music, not the system."

Sometime during 1971, he was introduced to Alex Rosner. "A mutual friend said I should stop by and look at David's club, because I could be of some service to him. Which I was. I rebuilt his club for him and made his sound much better. He had what was basically a home system. When I got through with it, it was a disco system."

The precision of the sound system which Rosner and Mancuso created between them has subsequently become the accepted standard for every nightclub in the world. "It's just a matter of quality," says Rosner. "See, I was an audiophile. I applied audiophile techniques—hi-fidelity—to commercial sound, which until then had never been done. Most commercial sound systems sounded lousy. I made it sound good by putting in good components. There were no secrets; it was just a matter of persuading the owner that he had to spend the money to up the ante and put in the proper components. I knew where to put the loudspeakers. I knew how many to use and how to make it sound good."

The two made a formidable alliance, with Mancuso supplying the visionary ideas for Rosner's practical expertise. One day he asked Rosner to create two tweeter-array clusters (tweeters are the speakers which deliver the high-end, or treble, of a recording). "He told me to build them and I said I didn't think it was a good idea," recalls Rosner. "He said, 'I don't care what you think, just make it anyway.' I didn't think it was a *bad* idea, I just thought it was too much. Normally in a sound system, there's one tweeter per channel. He wanted eight. I thought it would be too much high frequency."

But on this occasion, the visionary was right and the expert was wrong, as Rosner admits. "It was so high up, that's not where the pain level is. That's not where the hardness is. The more you have up there the better. So it was actually a terrific idea."

Once completed, the resulting system was peerless. As Mancuso says, "The one thing the Loft did do was set a standard: getting your money's worth, providing a decent sound system." Klippschorn speakers (developed by Paul Klippsch in the 1920s and renowned for their simplicity and purity), JBL bullet tweeter arrays and, later, Koetsu handcrafted cartridges and Mitchell Cotter turntable bases. "He put the Klippschorns in such a way," recalls Nicky Siano, "that they put out the sound and they reflected it too, so they covered the whole area and exaggerated the sound." And the Loft was a great place for sonic experiments. "His room was perfect to do this with. He used to be on the dancefloor, the lights would go out and there would be these little table lamps in the corner and the tweeters would come on and the lamps would go out. It was freaky deaky."

A clientele selected by genuine friendship, music and sound that was out of this world, and a uniquely welcoming environment: no one had ever been anywhere quite like this before. The Loft was a revelation. Only a couple of miles separated it from glamorous clubs like Arthur, Le Club and Cheetah, but it was worlds apart in concept and execution. Since his many friends were drawn from the full spectrum of the counterculture, Mancuso's club became a refuge from the outside world; a secret cabal of the disaffected and disenfranchised. "We used to squeeze fresh orange juice and organic nuts and raisins," he remembers. "We did the place up. Everything was quality. Everyone used to come there: Patti Labelle, Divine, all of them. As people, too, because everybody that came there was able to relax. And, of course, you would not get into this space unless you had an invitation."

Inevitably, Mancuso encountered the West Village triumvirate of Grasso, Cappello and D'Acquisto. "I went to see Steve D'Acquisto at his club," he recalls, "and I liked the way he was doing things. So I walked over to him and said, 'You know, I really like the music. Look, I have this place; it's downtown. It's my place, it's a private party. Do you wanna bring a friend?' And he did. That's how I met Michael Cappello and Francis."

When Steve D'Acquisto discovered the Loft, he felt he was finally home. "I went there on my own one night and I walked into a world of unbelievable sound and tremendous beauty. Just special as can be. There was nothing like the Loft. The Loft was a small little place. But it was just unbelievable."

In return for his hospitality, Grasso and his pals introduced Mancuso to their new mixing techniques: the segue, slip-cueing and beat-mixing, showing him how they created the suites of interlocking sound with which they energized the Haven and Sanctuary. Mancuso had been experimenting with ideas of his own, and already owned an extensive collection of sound effects albums which he would play over the ends and beginnings of songs (an idea he had copied from New York radio station WNAW). Gradually he learned the skills needed to mix records although later, as he formulated his ideas about the purity of the song, Mancuso would refrain from mixing altogether.

"He wasn't mixing when I met him," recalls D'Acquisto. "He had two turntables, but when one was stopping the other was starting. He did mix eventually, for a lot of years. The most popular years of the Loft were when he mixed. I said to him, 'You should never let the music stop.'"

The late Larry Levan, Mancuso's most revered protegé, paid tribute to him in 1983, speaking to journalist Steven Harvey. "David Mancuso was always very influential with his music and the mixes. He didn't play records unless they were serious. When I listen to DJs today, they don't mean anything to me. Technically, some of them are excellent—emotionally, they can't do anything for me. I used to watch people cry in the Loft for a slow song, because it was so pretty."

The Message Is Love

Hear Mancuso spin today and you will probably find it unusual to hear a DJ play records with so much reverence. He leaves space between each track, plays them complete from beginning to end and with no change in pitch or adjustment in EQ. However strange this seems, it will gradually start to make sense as you realize that his skill lies not in tricks and mixes but in using records to tell a story, to generate and reflect a changing mood. Each song follows the last in a profound musical narrative.

"I spent a lot of time in the country, listening to birds, lying next to a spring and listening to water go across the rocks," Mancuso told *The Village Voice*'s Vince Aletti in 1975. "And suddenly one day I realized, what perfect music. Like with sunrise and sunset, how things would build up into midday. There were times when it would be intense and times it would be very soft, and at sunset it would get quiet and then the crickets would come in. I took this sense of rhythm, this sense of feeling . . . "

Aletti, a young journalist who had immediately recognized the Loft's cultural importance, was himself a true devotee of the club.

"Dancing at the Loft was like riding waves of music, being carried along as one song after another built relentlessly to a brilliant crest and broke, bringing almost involuntary shouts of approval from the crowd, then smoothed out, softened, and slowly began welling up to another peak," he wrote in 1975.

Indeed, he was so struck by the magically evolving atmosphere of Mancuso's musical wonderland that he would purposely arrive before anyone else.

"I would go early and hang out with David in the booth, because I loved hearing the music that started out the night," he remembers. "Some of my favorite music was David's early records. He would make this whole atmosphere when people were coming in. Before people started dancing. Oddball things that he would discover, mostly jazz-fusion records or world music. Things that didn't have any lyrics for the most part, but were just cool-out or warm-up records. And I loved that kind of stuff. It was great to see the mood getting set. Little by little, they would get more rhythmic and more and more danceable and people would start dancing. I loved seeing the whole theatre get underway. It was like being at a play before the actors had started."

Aletti had been one of the very first journalists to take dance music seriously. Born in Philadelphia in 1945, he had caught the Motown bug while studying literature at college in Ohio. He got his writing break with one of the many counterculture rags that sprang up in late sixties New York, *Rat.* He was soon writing for *Fusion*, *Rolling Stone*, *Creem* and *Crawdaddy*, usually as a black music specialist. He figured himself an expert in his field; and when a magazine needed a review of the Jackson 5 or Mary Wells, it was to Aletti they increasingly turned. As disco began to surface from its underground

Loft babies—a precious invite to the Loft in New York.

beginnings, he was quickly its most vocal cheerleader, championing the scene and its music whenever he could.

"I heard about the Loft through this group of friends, some of whom were would-be disc jockeys. But I wasn't used to staying up until 12 A.M. in order to go out to some place, so they had to really get me into it. But once they did . . . it was like nothing I'd ever done before. And it was exciting to go to a place where almost every record I heard was completely new and great. So all I wanted to do was write down all the titles. What is this?"

He was struck not only by the music but also by the mix of people. Even today, he remembers disco very passionately as a unifying force, a loving rejection of long-accepted social barriers. For him, the Loft epitomized this.

"It was like going to a party, completely mixed, racially and sexually, where there wasn't any sense of someone being more important than anyone else. It really felt like a lot of friends hanging out. David had a lot to do with creating that atmosphere. Everybody who worked there was very friendly. There were people putting up buffets and fruit and juice and popcorn and all kinds of stuff."

Alex Rosner, too, was struck by the Loft's vividly unifying atmosphere (it was probably about sixty percent black and seventy percent gay). "When I first went to his club and saw the excitement and energy there, it was very inspirational to me. At that point I thought discos were a wonderful idea. There was a mix of sexual orientation, there was a mix of races, mix of economic groups. A real mix, where the common denominator was music. I remember ripping off my shirt and dancing. I loved the music. It was the real stuff. It was terrific."

The club's pansexual attitude was revolutionary in a country where up until recently it had been illegal for two men to dance together unless there was a woman present; where women were legally obliged to wear at least one recognizable item of female clothing in public; and where men visiting gay bars usually carried bail money with them. All were disarmed and united by Mancuso's hypnotic mysticism and quasi-religious karma, all of which permeated his music.

Taking influences from the hippie era, he would play the blue-eyed soul of Rare Earth, white soul singer Bonnie Bramlett (whose "Crazy 'Bout My Baby" was an unlikely Loft anthem), "Glad" by Traffic and the West Coast sound of The Doobie Brothers. Added to the mix would be The Temptations' "Papa Was A Rolling Stone," War's "Country City" or the heavy Afro-funk of Olatunji and Manu Dibango. A panoply of rhythms or an indigo mood. A kind of theme tune was Fred Wesley's "House Party," which summed up the spirit of the place. He would play a lot of instrumentals and lots of more percussive Latinesque tracks. And he would always be drawn to a song whose lyrics carried positive meaning. The rules were simple: it had to be soulful, rhythmic and impart words of hope, redemption or pride. Love was the message.

Because his influence on the nascent disco scene was so great, it's hard to say whether David Mancuso's strong ideals were merely a timely reflection of a common feeling or whether they were actually an important factor in providing dance music with its obsession with freedom and inclusivity. Even if this gentle man is not the definitive source of disco's optimistic faith in equality, his spirit was certainly a catalyst for the powerful feelings which would permeate the music. Certainly, his message of love rarely went unnoticed.

"He's picking a record that's not just a hit record, but he's picking a record that's timely for these particular people; and he's also talking a message," relates Danny Krivit, another Loft regular and a DJ himself since childhood. "There's a story being woven. With, say, Nicky Siano at the Gallery, it would be a vocal story. With David it was a mood story. David in general was always about love, and he'd always try to stay with that."

Krivit had been raised in the nightclub business and was perfectly placed to observe the developing scene. His stepfather Bobby owned the Ninth

Circle, a downtown landmark, and the young Danny had served John Lennon, Janis Joplin and Jimi Hendrix before he was ten, and was making tapes for the place—which, significantly, had "gone gay" in 1971—since the age of fourteen. Krivit was also at that time another aspirant DJ mesmerized by the Loft.

"I just remember it was unique," he recalls. "Before that, my idea of a club was more dressy, the Saturday night out feeling. The Loft was the opposite of that: it was a professional house party. These were eccentric club people who were really into dancing. They knew music, not just the Top 10 hit parade, but they knew music you'd never heard before. That impressed me. The type of music that was being played, it just had a lot more substance to it."

Breaking Records

Mancuso was paving the way for a new kind of club DJ: not necessarily as technically adept as Francis Grasso, but a figure who is librarian, antiquarian, archaeologist, minister. With his zeal as a musical missionary, Mancuso was far from the human jukebox of old. He was driven by a desire to discover great music, to track down records and then share his secrets with other DJs. In truth, he was rarely one to scrabble for them himself: Loft regulars would often bring them to him. But if Mancuso found a record he loved, he wanted everyone to hear it and know its name.

Barrabas' debut LP is a case in point. Barrabas were a Spanish rock-funk outfit signed to RCA in Spain, with members of the band hailing from Cuba, Portugal and the Philippines, a fact reflected in their oddly Afro-Latin sound. "I was in Amsterdam looking for some records," recalls Mancuso. "I'd never heard of them, I just liked the information that was on the sleeve; it looked interesting. I brought it back, checked it out and there were a couple of good things on it." Both "Woman" and "Wild Safari," white-voiced Latino rock workouts, became Loft staples. Mancuso called the record company in Spain and imported several boxes of the album. He would sell them, at cost price, to Loft regulars.

Another record which came to prominence via the Loft was Babe Ruth's "The Mexican," now regarded by hip hop connoisseurs as a defining b-boy hymn. Like Barrabas, Babe Ruth's track record did not suggest they could craft music to make hip hoppers sway or black and Latino gays shimmy. Formed in Hatfield, in suburban England, they had instant success with their first album in, of all places, Canada. This LP, *First Base*, a mainly rock-by-numbers workout, was spared only by the inclusion of "The Mexican." Coincidentally, after some run-ins with club owners in New York, Steve

D'Acquisto was in Montreal when the record broke there. He quickly brought it to Mancuso's attention. "I worked with Rob Ouimet in a place called Love. I was his alternate. And Rob gave 'The Mexican' by Babe Ruth to me; then I brought it back here." Once the record had been popularized in the Loft, DJs across New York started searching it out; news of this obscure gem even reached the closed world of the Bronx, where the DJs who were formulating hip hop would make it an anthem.

"The New York grapevine was so intense," says Aletti. "A record could break in a club one night and next day everybody who cared about it would know about that record and would be running around town trying to find it. At this point, everybody was friendly and it didn't feel like a scene full of rivals. They really wanted to share the music." An infectious camaraderie became the norm, with DJs swapping notes and tipping each other off about records. The loose tangle of jocks would either meet in West Village omelet house David's Pot Belly or, more often, could be found hanging out for hours on end at Downstairs Records in Times Square or Colony on Broadway.

"There was a period, at the beginning, where all the disc jockeys felt like proselytizers. Not just to their audience but to each other," says Aletti. "It was a real community. They were happy to share and make connections with other people. It seemed like a small scene and they were real buddies. They lived and breathed music and didn't talk about anything else. It wasn't like they had a big life outside of the clubs anyway.

"Before clubs became very successful and made a lot of money, a lot of DJs played several nights a week at several different clubs and they lived for nothing else. That was their currency: the newest record. There was a constant trawling of record stores and places where they knew they could find things. It was an active, and great, network, and it was all about sharing."

Another key Loft record was Manu Dibango's "Soul Makossa." The success of this obscure gem showed how powerful the Loft's influence (bolstered by the growing number of underground clubs at that time) had become.

Mancuso had picked up the record, then on a tiny French independent label, Fiesta, from a Jamaican store in Brooklyn sometime late in 1972. With its distinctive Afro-jazz rhythms it was an immediate success with jocks throughout the city, breaking out of the clubs thanks to radio DJ Frankie Crocker at WBLS. Eventually, after Atlantic picked up the rights to the track, it punctured the *Billboard* pop chart. Something was becoming rapidly apparent: that these new clubs not only had power to break songs to the clubbers on their dancefloors, they also were capable of making hit records.

"The best discothèque DJs are underground stars, discovering previously ignored albums, foreign imports, album cuts and obscure singles with the power to make the crowd scream and playing them overlapped, nonstop, so you dance until you drop," wrote Vince Aletti. "Because these DJs are much closer to the minute-to-minute changes in people's listening taste, they are the first to reflect these changes in the music they play, months ahead of trade magazine charts and all but a few radio stations." This piece, from *Rolling Stone*, September 13, 1973, was the first ever story about what would become known as disco.

And so disco was born. Grasso's mixing and mood manipulation, Alex Rosner's sound systems and Mancuso's musical investigations and ideals of togetherness all came together against the background of New York clubland's new black/gay democracy and the wider liberating forces of social change.

Music was changing, too. Funk's "on the one" danceability was meeting crossover soul's prettiness, and a new sound had emerged. Sly and The Family Stone and The Temptations' more psychedelic moments were key points in this, but the thrust of the new music came from songwriter/producers Kenny Gamble and Leon Huff and their Sigma Sound studios in Philadelphia. In the first half of the seventies, with groups like The O'Jays, Harold Melvin and The Bluenotes, MFSB and many more, they produced songs which retained the driving funk beat but which ameliorated its harshness with more complex melodies and rhythm patterns, by adding the soaring sounds of a whole orchestra. As JBs trombonist Fred Wesley put it, "They put a bowtie on the funk." This lush music was both commercially successful and also exactly what the new clubs wanted to hear. All the elements were now in place.

Nicky Siano at the Gallery

Arguably, the first commercial club to bring everything together was the Gallery. Nicky Siano, an energetic, bisexual Brooklyn tearaway, had moved into Manhattan at the tender age of sixteen with his girlfriend Robin. It was 1971 and he had already been exploring the post-Stonewall New York nightworld for nearly a year. By the time he was seventeen, he owned his own club.

He had begun DJing at a club called Round Table after Robin charmed the owner into letting Nicky play records there. Then, with help from his older brother, $10,000 from a friend who had received an insurance payout, and another borrowed $5,000, the Gallery was opened in a loft on 22nd Street (it would be later forced to move, for a lack of fire exits, to 172 Mercer Street, after a Fire Department swoop which closed seven similar nightspots). Siano had been transfixed on his visits to the Loft and aimed to create a place as close as possible to David Mancuso's famous house parties.

"I always feel like I took what David did onto a more commercial level," he says. "Ours was like a club version of David's. That feeling, that atmosphere, was there. The caring about people and stuff like that. The only thing was, we didn't live there. So it was a little different." At 3,600 square feet it was bigger, too. With an Alex Rosner sound system (including copies of Mancuso's tweeter arrays) and with Siano's canny move of opening while Mancuso was on vacation and the Loft was on temporary hiatus, it was an immediate success.

"The wildness is exquisitely wholesome," wrote Sheila Weller about a trip to the Gallery in the *New York Sunday News*. "Furious dancing. Gentle laughter. Crêpe paper and tinsel. Body energy shakes the room, yet sex is the last thing it calls to mind—except, perhaps, hostility. In darkness pierced by perfectly timed bursts of light, Labelle's rousing 'What Can I Do For You?' takes on a frenetic holiness. The floor is a drum to the dancers—many of them gay, most of them black—whose extended fists and tambourines lob the balloons and streamers above at what seem to be collectively chosen intervals."

Weller's guide for the night is another DJ, Richie Kaczor. Noting the direction of the music, he whispers to her, "Get ready for a rush."

"And the song smoothly melts into 'Love Is The Message' over which DJ Nicky Siano—one of the city's best—blares jet-plane sound effects. On every other bar, the lights vanish and the dancers send up a jubilant uniform chant. 'Nicky knows these people like the back of his hand,' Richie says, admiring the rite."

Bob Casey, founder in the mid seventies of the National Association of Discothèque Disc Jockeys, remembers the Gallery fondly. He recalls watching as Siano did his little "Nicky twist" behind the decks while his friend Robert DaSilva, another "young white chicken cherub," as Casey describes him, worked the lights.

"And these two little guys are doing the hottest black club in the world. To me, little conservative me, it was the hottest disco I was ever at *in my life.*"

Larry Levan called the Gallery his "Saturday Mass." Casey has similar enthusiasm.

"Why? Because they began with the basic color BLACK! and they worked it up from there. There was no neon. There was no automated anything, there was a few light switches, a couple of light pedals, that's all it was. They'd grab the mirror ball and give it a spin. And you see the reflections—*sshwwwoo*—

all over the place. That's where the whistles began. That's where everything like that began. But the thing is, they began with black."

Casey, who was a nightclub sound engineer throughout the period, explains that by "black" he's referring as much to the nature of the sound as anything else, detailing how Siano's love for sub-bass drove the atmosphere (and the construction of the system)—another early example of a DJ pushing technology forward for his own ends. (Siano also claims to have been the first DJ to use three turntables, inspired by a dream in which he was mixing two records together and wanted to bring in a third.)

"Nicky Siano took his sub-bass . . . *beyond*," says Casey. "Because of this black . . . He wanted this heavy sound." Siano had the crossover points (the circuits which divide the sound's treble, midrange, bass and sub-bass) engineered so he could wow the audience with just the sizzling highs of a record, then just the earthquaking lows. Casey remembers how the young DJ would use this and have his dancers in the palm of his hand.

"Every once in a while, everybody would be so *together* with it, *so* together—and they'd be singing along—and Nicky would bring it up and then all of a sudden BOOM!, out would drop the center and everybody would be stunned—'Awwwww!'—and then BLAMM!!, in would come this incredible bass. And by that time—and there's essence of amyl nitrate all over the place—it was flawless.

"And the lighting was with it perfectly. When the music went to black, the room would be black. And you couldn't see your hand in front of your face. And yet there'd be a couple of hundred people in there dancing. It'd be so intense. It would be *so* intense."

While Mancuso's influence had worked by way of an underground grapevine, Nicky Siano's was more direct. "When I played a record it was played everywhere," he boasts. DJ Kenny Carpenter, a regular at the Gallery, agrees.

"Nicky was the one everybody would go study at the Gallery," he affirms. "Nicky knew how to talk with music. He used lyrics to send a message to you. I love you, I hate, I miss you. You remember Freddie Prinze, he was an actor in a famous sitcom here. He died and that night Nicky played 'Freddie's Dead' from the *Superfly* soundtrack. Those kind of things." And while Mancuso had used music as a mask for his shyness, Siano was a shameless exhibitionist.

"Everyone basically played the same records back then," Siano recalls. "It was just how people put them together. My style was to link the fillers and let them build and then go into the good ones and just go off, on an hour of good ones, until people were screaming so loud they couldn't stand it any more."

With songs like Diana Ross's "Love Hangover," Harold Melvin's "The Love I Lost," the Trammps' "Love Epidemic," "Where Is The Love?" by Betty Wright, and of course his theme tune, MFSB's "Love Is The Message" (many DJs claimed this as their own; Siano and Mancuso probably have the most rights to it), all mixed through Thorens TD125 turntables and a Bozak mixer, Siano would encourage his dancefloor to completely lose it, creating more abandon than any DJ before.

"People got really out of control," he says. "I remember someone having an epileptic fit one night because they were just driving themself so hard. There were points when the music was taking people so far out and getting so peaked out that people would be chanting, 'TURN THIS MOTHERFUCKER OUT.' That started at the Gallery—they're blowing whistles, and screaming, 'Yeah! Yeah! Yeah! Yeah!' And then I'd turn up the bass horns and the lights would flash and go out, and everyone would *screeeam* so loud you couldn't hear the music for a second."

"He would be like: I'm in the DJ booth. This couldn't be a tape. This couldn't be just a record you like. *I'm* playing this record. He had a presence," remembers Danny Krivit. "He was also very much about drugs, especially towards the end of the Gallery; high, but not too high to play the music. There'd always be a point where it seemed like he'd collapse in a very dramatic manner: fall on the turntables and stop the music. Everyone knew what was going on, and they'd be patient and know that somehow, somebody would help him get it together and an even better record would come on. And usually it did."

"The first year that the new Gallery was open," Siano told writer Tim Lawrence, "we had this huge party on the Fourth of July. We rewrote the Declaration of Independence. Wherever it said, 'We the people of the United States' it was 'We the people of the Gallery' and 'We want to dance all night.' I came out as the Statue of Liberty. I had these draping robes and this big crown, and when they turned out the lights to sing the national anthem, my crown lit up. People went bananas. And my friend Monica, she was so stoned on acid, she starts screaming, 'They're electrocuting him! They're electrocuting him!' We had to drag her off the dancefloor because she was ruining my act—and my hat."

The Gallery messed with people's heads until 1978. On its closure, Siano left for a club called Buttermilk Bottom (he also spun for three months at

Studio 54), playing there until a serious drug problem got the better of him. He has recently returned to New York, having beaten his demons, has published a successful book, *No Time To Wait*, about alternative HIV treatments, and has just opened his own club, Inspira.

To this day he maintains a belief in the vast power of music to unite and heal.

"There is a force that connects us," he insists. "And if I connect with that force, which I think is love, if I connect with that force and I'm playing from that center, we're all gonna get it, we're all gonna get off on it."

A Boom in Discothèques

By the mid seventies, there were an estimated 150–200 clubs in New York. Several were inspired by the Loft (which had by now moved to a larger space at 99 Prince Street): the Gallery, the Soho Place, Reade Street, Tenth Floor and the Flamingo. Many others were updates on the chic niteries that had formed the backbone of midtown nightlife since Le Directoire and Arthur in the sixties. Others still, opening in the city's outer boroughs, were clones of the hottest Manhattan hangouts.

The growth in nightlife was so explosive it was hard to quantify accurately. As Bob Casey told *New York Sunday News*: "It's hard to give a firm number on how many discothèques there are in New York because every Joe's Pizzeria in town is now hooking up a couple of turntables and calling itself a 'discothèque.' I've heard reports that there are as many as 175 in the five boroughs now, but I'd say there are only twenty good, genuine ones."

Like the twist craze before it, disco was forged amid a terrible recession and the deep scars of war, this time in Vietnam. "People have always lost themselves in dancing when the economy's been bad," Casey told the same paper. "The discos now are doing exactly the same thing that the big dance halls with the crystal chandeliers did during the Depression. Everyone's out to spend their unemployment check, their welfare: to lose themselves." This was the "Bad Luck" that Harold Melvin and The Bluenotes had so potently sung about.

Recession or no, David Mancuso and Francis Grasso between them had created a blossoming DJ culture. "The typical New York discothèque DJ is young, Italian and gay," wrote Vince Aletti, referring to the scores of pretty boys with names ending in "O" who were taking over the city's nightlife.

While some resented the newer clubs and upstart spinners, Mancuso welcomed them. "I wasn't really bothered that those places opened. I was glad they were doing it." Ever the evangelist, he was happy to see more people enjoying this music. "There are eight million people in New York. A lot of people want to party. And the more people partying, the better it is. Why not? It was like the civil rights movement: the more people you had marching the better it was."

The Loft had unleashed the greatest period of creativity in the history of nightlife. Early disco inspired great leaps in club sound reproduction, in the equipment available to the DJ, and, of course, in the music and the styles which he played. The waves even rippled out as far as Brooklyn, the Bronx and Harlem, where mobile disco DJs like Ron Plumber, Grandmaster Flowers, Maboya and Pete DJ Jones would put their own spin on the music and help give birth to hip hop.

As disco spread throughout New York and beyond, the DJ's art was gradually and constantly refined. Several key disc jockeys in particular contributed to the refinement of the art; each one adding to the growing accumulation of wisdom.

Larry Levan and Frankie Knuckles at the Continental Baths

Though they are remembered more for their postdisco experiments, both Larry Levan and Frankie Knuckles began their trade during the underground days of disco. The two had been best friends since their teenage years—so inseparable that people confused their names—and as they danced across the city together, they were soon known in Manhattan's clubs as energetic party catalysts. Their adventures started in a tiny gay bar called the Planetarium, but soon they were regulars at the Loft, where Levan was mesmerized by David Mancuso's musical mastery. When Nicky Siano opened the Gallery, he recruited the two club bunnies to put up the decorations, set out the buffet and pop acid blotters into the mouths of arriving guests.

"Part of our job description was spiking the punch," explained Knuckles in an interview in *Muzik*. "We'd be given tabs of acid and we'd spike the punch with them. We'd always have lots of people coming up to us and saying, 'When's the punch going to be ready, when are you going to bring out the punch?'"

By 1971 they were DJs, Knuckles having landed a six-month job at Better Days and Levan having talked his way into a job at the Continental Baths, working the lights for DJ Joseph Bonfiglio—a permanent fixture on the early disco scene—and playing the warm-up slot twice a week. At first Knuckles

Christmas baubles—Frankie Knuckles (left) and Larry Levan (right) pose outside the steam room of the Continental Baths to send their 1974 seasonal message to readers of *Melting Pot* magazine.

refused to visit his friend in the Bacchanalian "Tubs," as it was known, even though Levan was now living in an apartment there. When he finally set foot in it, he didn't leave for three weeks.

The Baths was no ordinary club. Situated below the Ansonia Hotel on 73rd and Broadway, it was an opulent gay bathhouse with steam rooms, swimming pool, private apartments, restaurant and disco. Its owner Steve Ostrow was instrumental in helping to liberalize the city's laws on sex clubs. "We kept thrashing it out with the authorities, the police, the Department of Consumer Affairs, and eventually we got action," he told *New York Sunday News*. "We've done such a good job liberating the city, we've almost hurt our own business. We used to be the only ball game in town."

The Tubs had originally gained fame as the place where Bette Midler had cut her formidable teeth in cabaret (with a young Barry Manilow accompanying her on piano). It would later become the swingers' paradise Plato's Retreat, with a DJ called Bacho Mangual and one of the era's few women jocks, Sharon White. For several years in between, it was also a successful disco, capitalizing on its revered homo decadence by allowing straight folk in to dance at the weekends. It was kitted out by Bob Casey, who gave it sixteen Bose speakers and 3,500 watts of power. "A lot for that small space," he recalls.

"It was very upscale," remembers Nicky Siano. "It was like, 'We're so chi-chi in our towels, cruising each other and slapping each other's dicks.' It was like a kind of orgy, kind of Roman. And then people came out in their towels and everyone would dance."

In 1973 Levan became the club's main DJ, with Frankie playing warm-up and on the quieter nights. Levan left in 1974 to start his own club along with his partner, sound engineer Richard Long. This acted as the prototype for the legendary Paradise Garage. Though it was the Garage that made him a star, Levan never forgot that his roots lay in disco's first heady years.

After Levan left, Knuckles became the Baths' resident, playing there until its closure, when he, famously, moved to Chicago and, as we'll see, forged house music. He never forgot the Continental Baths, however, telling Sheryl Garratt, "Playing there every night, listening to music over and over. That's how I got most of my education."

Walter Gibbons at Galaxy 21

Galaxy 21 was a spectacular concern on 23rd Street, near the Chelsea Hotel, open from approximately 1972 to 1976. The dancefloor ran the length of the building—two brownstone town houses knocked together—with the DJ,

Walter Gibbons, in a cramped booth at the back. It was like a glamour tunnel. Upstairs there was a restaurant, a chill-out area, a movie theater showing X-rated flicks, and on the top floor, a cabaret. It was a saturnalian assault of the senses, with Gibbons conducting the ritual at its center.

"Walter played in a black club and he was as white as can be," remembers Tom Moulton, the pioneer of remixing. "But when it came to black music, he'd give you a run for your money. He was Mister Soul when it came to deep, deep black. He knew his stuff." What was remarkable about Gibbons's style was his use of portentous drum patterns: tribal percussive symphonies played out with religious fervor. Prefiguring the amazing cut and paste skills later developed by the hip hop DJs, Gibbons would take two copies of a track, for example "Erucu," a Jermaine Jackson production from the *Mahogany* soundtrack, or "Two Pigs And A Hog" from the *Cooley High* soundtrack, and work the drum breaks so adroitly it was impossible to tell that the music you were hearing hadn't been originally recorded that way. Few were aware that it was actually being made from two records mixed and spliced together on the turntables. DJs of the time described his style as "jungle music."

"I thought I was the best DJ in the world until I heard Walter Gibbons play," Jellybean Benitez, a young Bronx-born DJ destined for stardom, told Steven Harvey. "Everything he was doing back then, people are doing now. He was phasing records—playing two records at the same time to give a flange effect—and doubling up records so that there would be a little repeat. He would do tremendous quick cuts on records, sort of like b-boys do. He would slam it in so quick that you couldn't hear the turntable slowing down or catching up. He would do little edits on tape and people would freak out."

Alongside Gibbons, the club also hired a drummer, François Kevorkian, who would set up his kit on the dancefloor and play along to the heavy-duty black rhythms pulsing through the club. François had only recently arrived in New York from his native France in the hope of receiving tuition from Tony Williams, Miles Davis's drummer, and putting a band together. His gig at Galaxy brought him right into the heart of the early disco scene and would provide the basis for a prodigious career in dance music. "It was very underground at the time," he recalls. "Very downtown, very black, Latino, and quite a bit gay, too. Those worlds weren't ones I was very familiar with. But it was a very friendly and very sweet scene overall."

Quite often, Gibbons—who was initially annoyed at the idea of a drummer playing in the club over his records—would really put François through his paces, the DJ giving the drummer an accelerating bombardment of different rhythms to try and match. But Kevorkian prided himself on knowing all the drum breaks, and Gibbons was rarely able to trip him up. "Walter had an amazing instinct for drum breaks," says François. "Creating drama with little bits of records, just like a hip hop DJ, but he was incredibly fast at cutting up records. So smooth and seamless that you couldn't even tell that he was mixing records. You thought the version he played was actually on the record, but in fact he was taking little ten-second pieces." In common with most who heard him, François had nothing but admiration for Gibbons's skill. "The whole thing: his selection, his mixing technique, his pace, sense of drama, sense of excitement. And he was featuring all these big drum breaks that nobody else was really using. He was really into drums."

Gibbons's following grew so large that he was eventually powerful enough to influence the running of the club, a rarity for a DJ, even today. Alex Rosner recalls what happened when Galaxy's owner, George Freeman, brought him in to install a separate control to limit the sound system's overall volume.

"I tried to talk the owner out of putting this volume control in. I said you should talk to Walter and agree on sound levels. George says, 'No, I'm the boss, I own this club and I pay you to fix this sound system, so you do as I say.' So I put it in. There was a hidden volume control in his office." The repercussions were dramatic. "When Walter found out, he quit." However, laughs Rosner, "all the people went with him. George had no business, so he had to get Walter back and get rid of the volume control."

Gibbons retained this kind of independence until the end, even, eventually, at the expense of his audience. After a period at the end of the seventies living and DJing in Seattle (in another George Freeman-owned club, Sanctuary), he returned to New York a born-again Christian. As his religious beliefs influenced his music, the size of his dancefloor dwindled.

"By the time Walter had turned into that whole religion thing," says François, "he had stopped playing a whole section of music and only concentrated on songs with a message. There's nothing wrong with that, but it really limited the audience that would listen to his music. Unfortunately, it mainly fell on deaf ears. In fact, it didn't fall on very many ears at all, because there weren't many people going to his parties. At the same time, there's nothing you could say about Walter that was bad, because he followed his vision. It's just his vision was more difficult."

Gibbons, who died in September 1994, outlined his feelings in an interview he gave to Steven Harvey. "You really have to think that every time you change the record, the title or something about the record is going into people's heads," said Gibbons. "For me, I have to let God play the records. I'm just an instrument."

Tee Scott at Better Days

Another club with a reputation for playing the most recherché rhythm and blues was Better Days, opened in 1972 at 316 West 49th Street. By day this was just a bar but by night it transformed magically into a darkened nightclub. The first resident, a lesbian DJ named Bert, was fired soon after the club's opening and replaced by Tee Scott.

Danny Tenaglia, fated to become one of the DJ stars of the nineties, was then a young tentative clubgoer. He remembers Better Days as the first place he encountered people vogueing, and recalls being impressed by Scott's advanced mixing techniques, which included long overlays, or "blends": playing two records simultaneously for an extended period. "Tee Scott was obviously different from other DJs," says Tenaglia. "He would try things like these long overlays. Back then it was so much harder—people really don't realize how hard it was to mix those records with live drummers. And he would do them much longer than other DJs. The fact that the next time you went you'd hear the same mix meant it was something he obviously worked at. But also that it was worth repeating."

Better Days was also one of the clubs where François Kevorkian began DJing after he had made the transition from drumming.

"The crowd there was incredibly intense," he says. "It was very black, very gay. Sometimes I think Better Days was almost better than the others because it was closer and small and more intimate, but the energy level when people were dancing was just so amazing.

"Tee was more focused on the real soulful grooves that would work the dancefloor to an absolute frenzy," adds François. "And very beautiful music, too. He was more into squeezing the last drop out of a record and making it into a hit. It might not be a very strong record to begin with but just the way he would work it, cut it, and make his crowd like it, it would become a hit."

Tee Scott (who died in early 1994) confessed that he felt his priorities were centered on his audience.

"If you come to the club on a crowded night, your hair could stand on end from the static electricity," he told *Billboard*'s Brian Chin. "It rises off the bodies and the hum is in the air. People are going through a particular experience, especially if they go on a regular basis. The music, the people and everything fits together."

In later years, Better Days was known as a more intimate rival to the Paradise Garage. Bruce Forest, who replaced Tee Scott, was a crucial figure in the city's transition from disco to house. He had to work hard to gain the respect of his crowd, however.

"These people loved Tee Scott, they idolized him," Forest explained in 1989. "This was a hardcore black gay club, and the last thing they wanted was a white heterosexual replacement. I busted my balls trying to please them. I had three tables working, cutting records to death." But the crowd remained outraged at his presence. "I needed a bodyguard. I had death threats. People would throw bottles at me while I was working. On the big Friday night, I would have 1,500 people standing in a semicircle on the dancefloor with arms folded." Eventually, revered black DJ Timmy Regisford took over most of the nights, but he was ill one evening and Forest vowed to finally win over the crowd. Pulling a tarpaulin over the booth so no one could see who was DJing, he spun for all he was worth. They danced with abandon.

At 4 A.M. the tarpaulin was taken down. "You just saw 1,500 jaws drop and they just started to applaud."

David Rodriguez at the Ginza

Among the period's most expressive disc jockeys was David Rodriguez. "He is the person who influenced me most," says Nicky Siano. "He was just a wonderful friend and he really helped me launch my career."

Siano recalls how Rodriguez would discover so many great new records that he rarely devoted enough time to break any one of them. "Of the five records that he discovered every week, two were really good. Michael Cappello and I would look at each other and we'd both pick the same two that were good, and then we'd play the same two over and over and really get the crowd going. Now David, he would play all five, and so he never really left an impression on you. But really, he took more risks in playing new music than anyone else back then. He was a real innovator."

Having started out DJing at the Ginza, Rodriguez moved on to the Limelight on Sixth Avenue and 10th Street, where he drew a predominantly, though not exclusively, gay Puerto Rican crowd.

He later made appearances at several clubs, where his combative style resulted in a tendency to blow up sound systems. Nicky Siano remembers him blowing up all of Le Jardin's speakers on his first (and last) night there; DJ trade magazine *Melting Pot* reported that he achieved a similar feat at the Continental Baths.

His propensity for drug consumption was as impressive as his DJing. A favorite confection amongst clubgoers was ethyl chloride, an anaesthetic used to numb the flesh before receiving shots. When sprayed on a handkerchief and inhaled through the mouth, it gave an effect not unlike that of poppers. Nicky Siano recalled a night DJing at the Gallery when a narcoticized Rodriguez destroyed his set. "He's standing there with a rag in his mouth and he's got the bottle in front of the rag and he's just spraying and spraying the rag, and inhaling. All of a sudden—BOOM! Fell right on the turntables. I got 600 people all turning around looking at me and I just looked at him: 'You fat fucking bastard!' And I pulled him by the hair, threw him on the floor and started kicking him. I was like, 'You did this on purpose, you fat fuck!' He cut his head on one of the milk crates in the booth and he had to get three stitches."

Tom Moulton remembers Rodriguez as probably the most aggressive DJ he has ever known. "David played what he wanted to play when he wanted to play it.

"At that time there was a song that everybody liked called 'A Date With The Rain' by Eddie Kendricks," recalls Moulton. "Everybody kept saying, 'Play . . . Rain, play . . . Rain.' So he played 'Make Yours A Happy Home' by Gladys Knight & The Pips, which was a kind of uptempo ballad. Nobody would dance. 'You're gonna hear it all night, then.' The owners are banging on the glass. He plays it over and over again. Finally, he takes the microphone. 'I'm serious. Unless you get up here and dance, this is all you're gonna hear, so you better leave.' So they get up and dance. And he says, 'Okay, one more time with a little more enthusiasm.' Then he played fifteen minutes of these crashing sound effects and all of a sudden you could hear 'The rain, the rain' through the noise. It was Eddie Kendricks. They started screaming and yelling. It was unbelievable."

Sadly, David Rodriguez was one of the first people to die of AIDS, a tragic loss which shocked and touched many on the scene. Siano remembers his extreme bravery in the face of this then unknown disease.

"I view the whole scene as a spiritual congregation," Rodriguez declared in an interview in the mid seventies, exploring a theme that has become recurrent for many DJs. "You've got hundreds of people in a room, and their bond is the music. There isn't any tension between gays and straights; the common denominator is the music. I can get high—literally high—just on the music alone. Sometimes I weave the records together to tell a whole love story in one night. Do you know what it's like to hear the whole room sigh when a record starts? It's like applause to me!"

The Birth of Modern DJing

In many ways, the club DJ of a quarter of a century ago was as fully accomplished as he is today. He had become far removed from his original role—a musical waiter serving whatever the diners requested—and was now almost as exalted as some of our current well-marketed DJ stars. Some, at least to their regular crowd, in their own clubs, had godlike powers.

As he explored the creative possibilities of mixing, programming and sound adjustment (and as his audience explored the creative possibilities of all manner of misappropriated chemicals), the DJ was learning more and more about manipulation. Central to his art was an understanding of his audience and the dynamics of a dancefloor, as well as of the records he was playing. Many DJs, of course, were dancers; some, like François Kevorkian and Francis Grasso, were musicians, too. All had a deep understanding, whether learned or instinctive, of what made people want to dance, and what made people want to dance harder, longer, with more abandon. Without a doubt, disco heralded the arrival of a new figure: the DJ as high priest.

There had been hints of this before, in clubs with names like Salvation and in the blasphemous imagery of a place like Sanctuary. Several earlier DJs, such as Grasso, had been able to whip up their crowds into a devotional frenzy and had been compared with witchdoctors, priests or other religious figures. During the rise of disco, the relatively recent line which the western world had drawn between dance and religion was questioned and blurred.

By the mid seventies, clubs, especially the gay ones, had truly become places of worship. For many, this was where you went to receive your weekly sacrament. "There is a lot to it," agrees Alex Rosner (who, after having built many of the disco era's more revered sound systems, now spends his time designing custom amplification for churches and synagogues). "George Freeman at Galaxy 21 often talked about that. He said he was providing a venue for a spiritual experience."

Interviewed for the *New York Post* in 1975, Steve D'Acquisto asserted, "Disco music is a mantra, a prayer—nobody goes to church anymore, and if you listen to those songs, like "Fight The Power," "Ease On Down The Road" and "Bad Luck," you're getting religious and political instruction."

Albert Goldman, in his insightful book *Disco!*, shared the sentiment: "The disco scene is a classic case of spilled religion, of seeking to obtain the spiritual exaltation of the sacred world by intensifying the pleasures of the secular."

SEVEN
DISCO 2

She Works Hard For The Money

"The first of the disco movies, *Saturday Night Fever*, set a new standard for financial success, and its soundtrack album has doubled the sales record of the Beatles' *Sergeant Pepper.* Disco is a four-billion-dollar-a-year industry, with its own franchises, publications, top-forty charts, three-day sales conventions, catalogues of special equipment, and keenly competitive marketing agents—who are aiming to make every finished basement and rumpus room in America into a mini-disco. The new beat for the feet is sending up all the familiar signals that betoken a new wave of mass culture."

—Albert Goldman, *Disco!*

"They narrowed it down to one beat, to try to corner the market on a particular music, and when you do that with rhythm, talk about something that would get on your *nerve!* Try to make love with just one stroke."

—George Clinton

The disco that drives the latest crop of Broadway musicals, the disco that compels drunken students to don afro wigs and platform shoes, the disco that gets everyone on the dancefloor after a million weddings, has very little to do with disco's roots, or indeed with the larger body of work which comprises disco. It is instead the legacy of a short (roughly 1976–79) period when some of the music crossed over into superprofitable commercialism.

After the disco sound proved to be so irresistible, so universal and so *effective,* disco swept through the wider world like a new kind of fast food. It enjoyed a brief but near-total dominance of the global music machine, it made billions and it brought nightclubbing resolutely into the mainstream. In the process, it also changed much about the music business and the profession of the DJ.

Disco Puts on a Suit

The big-budget music industry as we know it came into being with rock. The Beatles, The Stones and their ilk brought the music moguls a new class of wealth, and for the first time their business was compared to Hollywood. However, by the mid seventies, rock seemed to have died and profits were dropping dramatically. Disco seemed to come to the rescue. It was completely alien to the music biz moneymen—who'd only just started feeling comfortable in the company of hairy musicians with guitars, and were unlikely to want to rip off their shirts in a dark loft full of black homos—but they could still see its potential to become a big fat cash cow.

The reason being: it appealed instinctively to nearly everyone. To this day, no music has bettered disco for its ability to entice the broadest cross-section of people—both young and old, whether nimble or uncoordinated—onto a dancefloor. This was a sales opportunity of golden goose proportions. To see disco's mass market possibilities, you didn't need to know about its loving, sharing spirit, or its special social significance. You just had to see how it got everyone's feet tapping.

Watching the independents who had cultivated the music, larger record labels hurriedly created disco departments or sublabels, and found them immediately profitable. Has-been rock artists knocked out a disco tune or two and found fresh success. Radio stations which abandoned rock for disco saw their ratings skyrocket. Clubs, bars and restaurants found that adding a DJ and a dancefloor drove up their takings significantly. Disco was big business, it was everywhere, and it started wearing a suit.

Though few made any effort to understand the origins or culture of this underground music, everyone loved the associations it seemed to have with decadence, cocaine and sex. Plenty of marketing men would figure it out just enough to rip out its heart and suck out every last drop of its blood. By the end of 1977, when Hollywood got in on the act with *Saturday Night Fever*, it seemed as if the whole world had "gone disco."

In these latter days of disco there were an astonishing number of really bad records produced, mostly exploitative cash-ins by artists who knew nothing about the music (other than the restorative power it might exert on their careers). Greed and cynicism were rampant as the major label latecomers hurried to rake in some disco dollars. It was inevitable, from the weight the industry expected it to bear, that disco would crash.

By 1979 there was simply *too much disco* and people started to hate it. Many who had banked on it were left high and dry and the backlash was swift and enduring. Suddenly everyone remembered that it was faggot music, that it "sucked." This is one reason why today's dance-based pop has had so much trouble getting established in America—it is still tarred with the same brush as disco. For the rock-headed straight masses it still has too many gay associations, and for the U.S. music business too many bad memories of extreme overinvestment.

But of course, it was the postdisco backlash which left the DJ alone to develop dance music further. And even while disco was riding its overground peak, it was building structures which would be invaluable to future DJs. Disco's commercial era resulted in the 12-inch single, the remix, club-based record promotion, and a completely new approach to making records. And though there is a clear theme of the music industry acting to limit the disc jockey's growing power, it was also when the DJ was acknowledged as the expert on what makes people dance, and thus when he was handed the keys to the recording studio.

Fire Island

"We would not stop dancing. We moved with the regularity of the Pope from the city to Fire Island in the summer, where we danced till the fall, and then, with the geese flying south, the butterflies dying in the dunes, we found some new place in Manhattan and danced all winter there." So relates the narrator of Andrew Holleran's gay love story, *Dancer From The Dance.*

If you head out on a train from New York's Penn Station to Sayville on Long Island, and catch the passenger ferry across the thin strip of water on its South Shore, you will arrive at Fire Island, a thirty-two-mile-long isthmus of designated National Seashore. Most of it is out of reach of the automobile, mapped with walks rather than streets. Its remote wildness is a stark and welcome contrast to New York's rattle and hum about sixty miles away.

Here, an endearingly ramshackle cluster of clapboard beach houses and hotels and winding boardwalks was the world's first significant gay community. In Ocean Beach during the 1940s (where Sis Norris's was the favored haunt) and then subsequently at Cherry Grove and the Pines, gays were able to forge a secret suburb intimately connected with but quite apart from the shimmering lights of Manhattan. The geographically isolated Fire Island was where affluent homosexual New Yorkers bought or rented summer homes and escaped to a world where the sun shone and everyone was gay. In areas like the Meat Rack (the informal name for an area of land between the Cherry Grove and the Pines), it also represented the far reaches of gay sexuality. Here, queens would parade themselves among the gently undulating dunes—often completely naked—in search of action.

By the mid sixties, Fire Island had a fully fledged community of largely middle-class, mainly white, gays. Each summer weekend they would flock to the Pines and the Grove to wind down from the stresses of a successful city life, pick up beautiful men and fuck them. Since residents here were wealthy enough to afford a summer home, a rather narrow social spectrum evolved. The scene's lack of a significant black presence meant it also served a slightly different sound from the mainland clubs, with smoother, more sophisticated songs. And as the seventies dawned, at private parties and at clubs like the Sandpiper (now the Pavillion) and Ice Palace—and later the Botel and the Monster—the beautiful and the rich would gather and dance the night away, their perfectly toned torsos glistening under the cascades of stars that shivered in the Atlantic air.

For many, disco had its genesis on Fire Island. "I've yet to hear of another spot in the world where disco came to its formality," claims Bob Casey, "where you had two turntables, so the disc jockey could go from one record to the other and make it a perfect mix." Casey, newly returned from a tour of duty in Vietnam, fell in love with Fire Island right away, and later built a sound system for its most famous nightspot, the Ice Palace.

Bobby DJ at the Ice Palace

That club's DJ was Bobby Guttadaro, born in Bay Ridge, Brooklyn, and known, for simplicity's sake, as "Bobby DJ." By 1971, when he began playing at the Ice Palace, the former pharmacy student had amassed an awesome record collection, and here he put it to propitious use. This streetsmart kid had all the savvy that accompanied growing up in Brooklyn. His neighborhood was later the setting for *Saturday Night Fever*, and if John Travolta's Tony Manero had been a disc jockey rather than a dancer, he might well have been modeled on Bobby Guttadaro. Bobby loved the crowds out on the Island: "They were there for one reason: to party," he told Albert Goldman in an interview in *Penthouse*. "They put themselves completely in the hands of the DJ. They said, 'Do it to us!'"

The Ice Palace was a cavernous, tacky confection, with slanted beams and a "blender bar" where many a famous cocktail has been shaken into life. Huge groups of men socialized, danced together and celebrated their good fortune: not only were most of them well-heeled, they also had all the sex they could want, the best drugs, and some of the finest music in the world.

"The Ice Palace in the Grove was the most fabulous disco I'd ever been to in my life," claimed Fire Island habitué Philip Gefter, "because there were two thousand writhing, drugged, beautiful bodies dancing on this dancefloor. By 6 A.M., we were outside around the pool, and we were dancing under the stars as the sun was coming up. And I believed at that moment in time that we were having more fun than anybody in the *history* of civilization had ever had. Because there was the combination of that sexual tension among all of these men, in concert with the drugs they were taking and the electronics of the music—and the sun coming up. It created a kind of *thrill* and excitement and sensation that I believe no culture had ever experienced before."

It was inevitable that what was happening on Fire Island would impact on New York, whence this gilded island drew most of its clientele. When summer ended, the alliances made here were continued in the city and there were certain clubs—Tenth Floor, 12 West, Le Jardin and, latterly, the Saint and a second Ice Palace (on 57th Street)—where you might see much the same faces.

Society Disco at Le Jardin

On June 13, 1973, reflecting much of the Fire Island scene, a club opened in Manhattan which showed the direction in which disco was headed. Much the same music was played here as in the black lofts of the Village, but in style and ambition it was another world entirely, with the ambience not of a dark cave but of an upscale restaurant. Now that the good ship disco had been shown to be a sturdy vessel, it was time to polish the fittings so the society folk felt comfortable jumping aboard.

Le Jardin opened in the basement of a shabby hotel called the Diplomat at 110 West 43rd Street. It was heavily influenced by Tenth Floor, a private gay club with a similarly sleek appearance, and run by an eccentric South African called John Addison. With his deadpan face, affected English accent and lounge lizard demeanor, Addison, an ex-waiter and juice bar proprietor, was hardly the typical club owner of the time. But then Le Jardin was hardly the typical club.

In its look, it was an echo of the Parisian-style nightclubs of the sixties. There were potted palms, it had nice furniture and the staff wore neat uniforms. The resident DJ was Bobby Guttadaro, recruited specially from the Ice Palace (Steve D'Acquisto later held a residency), and the clientele was the flotsam and jet set of gay Manhattan society. Costumed muscle boys in aviator goggles with clothes pegs on their nipples danced next to famous fashion designers and wealthy hairdressers with just one name. There was a smallish quota of beautiful women and fashionable straights. It was a scene right out of Fire Island: the city's gay upper echelons at play.

In an interview with Johnny Carson, renowned club hag Truman Capote described the scene, emphasizing both the club's elegant surroundings and its highly mobile dancefloor: "It has these art deco couches all along the room, these palm fronds dropping down everywhere, and out on the dance floor, this terrible churning, the whole place churning, like a buttermilk machine."

There had been an element of face-spotting and chatty socializing at all but the sweatiest of disco's early clubs—indeed even the dance-till-you-drop Gallery enjoyed its coterie of gay celebrities—but Le Jardin, in its more refined pretensions, made itself a place where "Look who's here!" and "Darling you must meet..." might push "Let's go dance" lower on the agenda.

Bob Casey pinpoints the opening of Le Jardin as the moment that disco left the underground. "Diana Ross was at the premiere. That hit the papers, and all of a sudden 'discothèque' became in and popular at that point, and came above ground."

The DJ's Power to Promote

As well as helping disco to do a little social climbing, Le Jardin also brought the scene's commercial clout to the attention of the record companies. It was here, thanks largely to the clued-up Bobby Guttadaro, that the industry woke up fully to the promotional power of the club DJ.

Gloria Gaynor's 1973 "Never Can Say Goodbye" had been the first disco record to chart as a result of club play, closely followed by "Do It Till You're Satisfied" by B.T. Express. (Both also highlighted the new phenomenon of the remix, on which more later.) Added to the much-noted success of Manu Dibango's "Soul Makossa" the same year, it had become clear that club DJs could exert impressive influence on the record-buying public. The next club crossover hit would be so big it would change forever the way the recording industry promoted its music.

When Twentieth Century Records promotions man Billy Smith handed Bobby DJ a copy of "Love's Theme" by Love Unlimited Orchestra, led by L.A. producer-turned-singer Barry White, he played it till the groove wore smooth. The city's other jocks spun it just as ardently and the song ended up at #1 on the pop charts. Its success was clearly due to club play, since the LP it was on, *Love Unlimited,* sold 50,000 copies before the song was ever heard on the radio. In recognition of his work on the record, Bobby Guttadaro was the first club DJ to be presented with a gold disc—handed over in person at Le Jardin by Barry White.

"Billy Smith broke Love Unlimited Orchestra and Barry White when they were totally dead," says Nicky Siano. "He literally went down to the basement and pulled out an album they considered a dead record. He had given us these albums and they had black people on the cover, so we thought maybe we can do something with this. And we made them huge hits. Billy Smith became the hottest promotion man in the business."

"GOD BLESS BILLY SMITH" read the headline in the first issue of Bob Casey's disco DJ trade magazine *Melting Pot* in August 1974. The article underneath read: "Billy has not only opened the door for the disco deejay to the record companies, he has knocked it off its hinges."

There were still no radio stations emphasizing disco, yet it was selling in its thousands. The primary sales focus of music changed overnight. For rock it had been radio; now, for disco it was clubs.

Barry White was not alone, either (was he ever?). Hues Corporation's "Rock The Boat," Carl Douglas's "Kung Fu Fighting," George McCrae's "Rock Your Baby" and the Average White Band's "Pick Up The Pieces" were all propelled into the *Billboard* chart on the strength of club play. Even obscure cuts like Consumer Rapport's "Ease On Down The Road" on tiny independent Wing And A Prayer were shifting 100,000 copies before ever getting a taste of radio play.

Exciting though this new avenue of marketing records was, it presented something of a dilemma for record companies, since their promotions people were not the kind to frequent discothèques (or, indeed, to even *know* what a discothèque was like). They were largely middle-aged family folk with houses in the suburbs.

"They realized that they had to deal with these clubs, and they had to deal with the disc jockeys," says Vince Aletti. "Little by little, they realized that they would have to bring someone in, and often they would hire somebody who was an ex-disc jockey, or someone who was working in a club. They were almost exclusively gay."

Aletti noted the change which this recruitment brought to many record companies. "It was really interesting to watch this happen, because they were having to deal with some fairly flamboyant characters who they still didn't know how to handle." This new breed of promotions men would form a crucial line of communication between the DJs and the record industry. They called themselves the "Homo Promos."

DJ Mix Tapes

Le Jardin figures in another small chapter of dance music's rise. Noticing the increased interest in the disc jockeys' performances, John Addison began to make nightly recordings of their sets on reel-to-reel. Through a telephone information line, he sold these to anyone interested for $75 per program—one whole night's set.

In its October 12, 1974 issue, *Billboard* alerted the industry to this illegal practice, pointing out that these tapes were bypassing payment to copyright holders, record labels and artists. "Tapes were originally dubbed by jockeys to serve as standbys for times when they were not in personal use of disco turntables," read the article. "They represent each jockey's concept of programming, placing and segueing of record sides. The music is heard without interruption. One to three-hour programs bring anywhere from $30 to $75 per tape, mostly reel-to-reel, but increasingly on cartridge and cassette." These were not confined to home use. Walk into any downtown bar, café or hip clothes store and the sound of syncopated disco music could be heard blasting out of the speakers.

Billboard claimed that some DJs were making more than $1,000 per month from these sales. In fact, as in Le Jardin's case, it was often the club proprietors who profited. Steve D'Acquisto, who had replaced Bobby DJ at Le Jardin when he moved to play at Infinity, was aware of what was happening: "John Addison used to *sell* our tapes. He'd tape it every night and sell them. We never got a penny from it."

No doubt some of the DJs did boost their income this way. Certainly few were paid well enough to ignore it, and many were turning to more desperate means. "We used to supplement our income by selling drugs," one DJ says. "You had to. We weren't making enough money."

Bob Casey, who set up the National Association of Discothèque Disc Jockeys (NADD) in 1974, tried early on to legitimize the practice of selling mix tapes, contacting ASCAP to inquire what kind of royalty payments would be required.

"I said, 'OK, I'd like to reproduce disc jockeys playing,' and this guy had no idea what I was talking about. I explained that the disc jockeys in the clubs mix the records together. I said, 'Look, I want to send you money for this . . . how much?' He said, 'You can't send it because we're not gonna allow it.'"

Though the copyright organizations wouldn't allow DJs to sell mixed tapes, they were quite prepared to let record companies use the same idea. In the same month that the *Billboard* piece on DJ tapes appeared, Spring Records released *Disco Par-r-r-ty* as the first nonstop dancing LP record. This featured tracks segued together, including James Brown, Mandrill and Barry White. The label said their main concern was creating a "classic" disco album. There was no DJ credit on the record.

Nowadays, DJ-mix albums represent a sizeable portion of the music market. Although they had little idea of how profitable this format would be, the record industry and its copyright organizations acted (largely unwittingly) early on to make sure that the DJ was shut out. Only in recent years, when they had clearly become marketable stars, were disc jockeys allowed a piece of the action.

The Birth of the Remix

Remixing is a vital part of today's dance industry, both as a marketing tool and as a creative outlet for DJs. Its roots lie firmly in the disco era, when DJs learned to transfer the kind of live mixing they had introduced—the extending of intros and breaks—onto tape and eventually vinyl.

The early club DJs learned their phenomenal mixing skills by necessity. Records were short and if they wanted to make them more effective for the dancefloor, disc jockeys were forced to work quite hard. The three-minute pop tune was designed to be perfect for radio. Here the songwriter has to concentrate his mind and deliver a simple message without repeating himself. However, a dancer's needs aren't the same as those of pop listeners—the body makes different demands from the ears. The dancer "wants to get in a groove and stay there until he has exhausted his invention or his body," wrote Albert Goldman in *Disco!* "The time scale and the momentum of any physical activity is vastly different from the attention span of listening." Increasingly, club DJs were searching for longer tracks, songs that gave them the freedom to work the crowd into the required pitch of excitement.

Coincidentally, inspired by the lengthy improvisations of jazz and the lavish epics of prog rock, pop producers had started experimenting with longer tracks, often seen as the sign of greater musical seriousness. Norman Whitfield at Motown was one such producer: his later work with The Temptations was clearly infused with the trippiness of psychedelic rock. Whitfield's notions were taken a step further by another of Berry Gordy's assembly line, Frank Wilson. Working with former Temptations vocalist Eddie Kendricks, he produced "Girl You Need A Change Of Mind," released in early 1973 and arguably the very first disco record.

In *Rolling Stone*, Vince Aletti had written a prescription for great dance music: "The best disco music is full of changes and breaks, which allow for several shifts of mood or pace and usually open up long instrumental passages. If the break works, it becomes the pivot and anticipated peak of the song." "Girl You Need A Change Of Mind" fitted this perfectly. It was seven minutes thirty seconds of sizzling, understated bliss, with a lengthened rhythm passage, vamping keyboard parts and doubled-up snare hits.

The effect was perfect for a dancefloor, but this was not intentional. Wilson himself says the record's distinct structure came from his gospel roots and from his intentions to make the song sound more "live." In the liner notes to a recent Kendricks compilation, he explained: "People always ask me about the breakdown. Well, my background is the church. It's not unusual in a church song to have a breakdown like that. Here, the idea was spontaneous. I stood in the studio with the musicians, giving instructions as we were cutting for them to break it down to nothing, then gradually come in one by one and rebuild the fervor of the song."

The rhythm was a departure, too: "At the time we did think, instead of four on top—which is what Holland Dozier Holland had been famous for—let's start with four on the floor and build it from there. Still, when I began hearing reports about what was happening with the record in the New York disco clubs, I was shocked. That was not what we were going for. We were after radio."

As well as searching out such serendipitously lengthy tracks—and of course, mixing his records live to produce a similar effect—the DJ would quickly take advantage of the opportunity to reconstruct songs, on tape, ahead of time. Reel-to-reel recording offered him the chance to splice and edit his favorite tracks to make them longer and more danceable.

One of the first people to gain attention from this practice was, surprisingly, not a disc jockey but a model by the name of Tom Moulton. The craggy Moulton, who wouldn't have looked out of place in an ad for macho shaving products, had previously worked in record retail and promotion (he worked at Syd Nathan's label King in the fifties, where James Brown cut his most urgent material). Though never a disc jockey, he developed a strong DJ-like affinity with the dancefloor.

His introduction to clubs had been on Fire Island. As a black music freak, he had been impressed by the fact that the largely white crowd were dancing to rhythm and blues, yet appalled at the standard of the disc jockey. It had given him the idea of producing a tape specifically made for dancing. "The reason I wanted to make this tape was that I was watching people dance and, at that time, it was mostly 45s that were three minutes long. They'd really start to get off on it and all of a sudden another song would come in on top of it. I just thought it was a shame that the records weren't longer, so people could really start getting off." Moulton watched what parts of songs made people leave a dancefloor and—just like a good DJ—constructed his music to minimize the dancers' opportunities of escape. "So that way, if they go to leave, they're already dancing to the next record. That was the hardest. I made one side of forty-five minutes. It took me eighty hours."

Strictly speaking, these tapes were re-edits and not remixes. A re-edit is a new version made by cutting up and splicing together chunks of the original song in a different order, usually using a tape recorder, a razor blade and some sticky tape. A remix is a more involved process where the original multitrack recording of the song is used to build a new version from its component parts. If you think of re-editing as making a patchwork version, then remixing is where you actually separate the individual sonic fibers of a song—i.e. separate the bass track from the drum track from the vocal track—and weave them back into a new piece of musical fabric.

Moulton's forays into editing soon led him to studio-based remixing. The first of his studio projects was B.T. Express (the BT stands for Brooklyn Trucking) with "Do It Till You're Satisfied" in mid 1974. His remix doubled the track in length from 3:09 to 5:52, but even so, many radio stations programmed the long version, and it provided the band with their first *Billboard* crossover hit. Despite their success, the group gave Moulton little or no credit. "The band absolutely hated it," he says. "But it reached #1 and they were on *Soul Train.* Don Cornelius interviewed the band and asked them about the length: 'Oh yeah, that's the way we recorded it,' they said. I was so fucking mad!" The record eventually went from #1 on the R&B chart to #2 on the Hot 100.

Such successes further encouraged the labels in their efforts to promote their records through the clubs, and with this in mind they started commissioning more and more remixes with which to entice DJs. And thanks to his growing track record, Moulton quickly cornered the market. When he remixed a previously released song called "Dream World" by Don Downing, his version sold some 10,000 copies without airplay.

By the end of 1974, *Billboard* could report that several labels had started releasing DJ-only vinyl pressings of such remixes as part of their new emphasis on club promotion. A piece in their November 2 issue read: "Specially mixed versions of commercial singles are being offered to discothèques here by a number of labels looking to capitalize on the clubs' growing reputation as record 'breakout' points. At such labels as Scepter, Chess/Janus and Roulette, executives say that the clubs are a definite influence in breaking records and that they consider it well worth the time and effort to reach the disco audience. When airplay on radio stations is missing, the clubs themselves have the power to move sales."

Moulton's reputation grew. His work for Don Downing and B.T. Express led to an encounter with producers Meco Menardo and Tony Bongiovi, who were working on a Gloria Gaynor project.

"I had this idea to make a medley, and the disc jockeys would play it because then they could go to the bathroom," says Moulton. "It would be eighteen minutes long; one song straight into another. It would be perfect." When the *Never Can Say Goodbye* album came out, a whole side of it was a single suite made from three two-and-a-half-minute songs—"Never Can Say Goodbye," "Honey Bee" and "Reach Out"—extended and segued together.

When released as a single, one of them, "Never Can Say Goodbye," became the first *identifiably* disco record to chart. Like B.T. Express, at first Gaynor didn't appreciate Tom's version too much. "I remember sitting in the office and Gloria hearing it," recalls Moulton. "The first thing out of her mouth—I'll never forget it: 'I don't sing much.' I felt so hurt over that."

The evolution of the remix quickly opened up a whole new career path for the DJ. Since disc jockeys had an unparalleled expertise in what makes people dance, it was only logical for more of them to make the leap from booth to studio. DJs like Walter Gibbons, Richie Rivera, Larry Levan, Shep Pettibone, Tee Scott and Jim Burgess would soon join Tom Moulton in refashioning dance music to their own end.

Another jock to move quickly into the studio was François Kevorkian, destined to become one of the world's most respected (and prodigious) remixers. Kevorkian, a talented drummer, started by creating re-edits like "Erucu," an instrumental from the *Mahogany* soundtrack, and "Happy Song" by Rare Earth, which he admits were based largely on Walter Gibbons's own live mixes. In June 1978 he was offered an A&R gig at Prelude. His first job was to remix a record that had been doing good business for the label, Musique's "In The Bush." Despite his inexperience, his deep understanding of the dancefloor made this a huge hit.

"It was really my first experience in a studio," remembers François. "And the record just blew out. I mean, it exploded. Anywhere you would go in the summer, they were playing that fucking record. So my first record becomes a huge hit." As a result, his golden touch was in constant demand. "They put me in the studio night and day. It would not end. I got to pick whatever I wanted. I ended up doing a lot of records for Prelude. Two or three records a week on average. It became like an assembly line."

Though many musicians felt it was sacrilegious for remixers to tamper with their work—a denial of their artistic integrity—the commercial success of many remixes convinced most people that the practice had a place in music. Norman Harris, who produced Loleatta Holloway's "Hit And Run," was one. Although he felt strongly that the album version he produced was "artistically correct," when Walter Gibbons's remixed version was released it sold more than 100,000 copies. Harris was forced to agree that "those figures were an indication that Gibbons's mix had a better feel for what's needed at today's marketplace."

The Birth of the 12-inch Single

Tom Moulton's mixes became famous throughout New York clubland and beyond. However, as they became longer and more complex—more modulating suites than mere songs—it was clear that 7-inch vinyl was not of a sufficiently high quality to do justice to them. The closer a record's grooves are packed together, the lower their volume and sound quality become. When you're talking grooves, bigger is better. A larger record has the added advantage of being easier for a DJ to manipulate.

But the 12-inch single happened quite by accident. Moulton went to have a mix pressed onto vinyl but his mastering engineer, José Rodriguez, had run out of the usual 7-inch metal blanks needed to cut the master disc. "José told me he was out of 7-inch blanks and would have to give me a 12-inch. I said, '*Eeugh*, that's ridiculous.' So he said, 'I know what we'll do: we'll spread the grooves and make it louder.' And of course, when I heard it I almost died." This record, the very first 12-inch single, was "So Much For Love" by Moment of Truth. It was something which Moulton made for a very select group of his DJ friends and although Roulette later released it on 7-inch, the larger format was never commercially available.

For a while, the only 12-inch singles were these handfuls of test pressings which Moulton made of his mixes (the songs were still only actually released in the 7-inch format, usually with the song split into two parts, one each side). Eventually, though, the record companies got wise to the benefits of the 12-inch and started using the format for DJ-only promotion. No one is exactly sure when these label-sanctioned promotional 12-inches arrived on the streets, though the general view is that the first was "Dance Dance Dance" by Calhoun, in spring 1975.

Surprisingly, despite its advantages, the 12-inch was initially greeted with much skepticism; it was seen as little more than a marketing gimmick. "People weren't impressed to start with, because they really weren't putting the best stuff on them," says Danny Krivit. "Everyone was saying, well, there are a lot of hits out there, why are they putting *these* songs on them? It was almost like 12-inches were going to be laughed at."

This derision ended when Salsoul, a small independent label, released a 12-inch that was far too good to ever be a gimmick, "Ten Percent" by Double Exposure, in June 1976. The mix on this was done by Walter Gibbons, who deconstructed the three-minute original and built it back up into a 10-minute epic of sparse conga-led rhythm patterns and strident orchestral sweeps.

Producer Arthur Baker recalls hearing Gibbons play "Ten Percent" at Galaxy 21: "He had this record which just seemed endless, with all of these cuts in it. I was like, 'How is he doing this, he must be so quick.' It was amazing. I went up to the booth and it was one record. It was called 'Ten Percent.'"

Where Tom Moulton had pioneered the remix, it was Gibbons, a DJ, who really showed its full potential. Moulton's early mixes didn't radically change the sonic nature of the songs, they were mostly about extending the better parts and eliminating the weaker ones. Gibbons was much more radical in his approach, stripping songs right down to their most primal elements and reconstructing them into complex interlocking layers of sound. Like his wild, tribalistic DJing, his remixes emphasized the rhythmic essence of a track. Walter Gibbons loved his drums.

With his masterful mix of "Ten Percent," the new 12-inch format finally took off. DJs quickly appreciated its advantages and their enthusiasm drove record companies into adopting it for all their promotional dance releases. And when this single was released to the public, it wasn't split in two and squeezed onto a 7-inch. Instead, it was the very first commercially available 12-inch single.

However, the prognosis of the 12-inch was by no means certain. Two years after its initial introduction, *Billboard* was still questioning whether the infant format had a future at all. In a 1978 piece by Radcliffe Joe announcing that Salsoul, TK, and Vanguard had ceased commercially releasing 12-inches, he wrote: "Several key labels specializing in disco product have begun cutting back on commercial 12-inch disco discs on the ground that they are slicing into album and 7-inch sales, cost too much to manufacture, and exact a high royalty price by music publishers." Record stores like Downstairs and Record Haven saw it somewhat differently. As Scott Dockswell of Record Haven told *Billboard*, "People who want the 12-inches buy them regardless of price, and we have found that many, especially disco DJs, buy both the 12-inch single and the album by the same artist." Only through the sales demand of DJs was the health of the 12-inch single ensured, a fact still true today.

In fact, to date the 12-inch is the only format of recorded music introduced as a result of consumer demand rather than record company marketing guile (although Internet buffs will note that the popularity of downloadable MP3 files are exerting a similar consumer-led pressure).

The Philly Sound

To most music historians, disco begins in Philadelphia. And if one song sums up classic disco it is, with little doubt, "Love Is The Message" by MFSB on the Philadelphia International label. Originally a B-side to the hit "TSOP" (which also became the theme for TV's *Soul Train*), "Love Is The Message" became the era's keynote record, the one which all disc jockeys claimed as their own.

Vince Aletti, in common with many, regards it as a Paradise Garage track; others cite the Loft as its true home. Nicky Siano claims it as his own, too, maintaining he was championing it at the Gallery while others were only playing the A-side.

"I had been the first one to really work that record," he says. "David [*Mancuso*] and Michael [*Cappello*] had been the first ones with 'TSOP' and then I turned the record over and fell in love with 'Love Is The Message.' I had heard it some place else before—Le Jardin, I think. But then I ran with it."

MFSB was an acronym for Mother Father Sister Brother (though some claimed it actually stood for Mother Fuckin' SonovaBitch). They became the Philadelphia house band and, although Gamble and Huff usually take the credit for the Philly sound, this aggregation of musicians, as their track record shows, were clearly a vital force behind it. Bassist Ronnie Baker, guitarist

Norman Harris and drummer Earl Young had already been playing together from the mid-sixties in a group called the Volcanoes. As MFSB (or parts thereof) they played for artists on several labels, going on to provide musical backing for everyone from The Trammps to First Choice, Double Exposure, Salsoul Orchestra, The Three Degrees, Jean Carn, The O'Jays, Harold Melvin and The Bluenotes, and Teddy Pendergrass.

Tom Moulton recalls watching MFSB working in the studio. "When you watched them record a track, they'd be like running it down, and all of a sudden this movement would just *click*. It would lock. 'All right. Let's take it. One, two, one, two, you know what to do!' It was like watching magic; it was scary. You had no idea what the song was or what the melody or the words were going to be, but you knew that that track was *there*." He thinks their influence was profound. "If you took all this stuff, by the same musicians, and put it all under one label, you'd have said Motown who? I'm serious."

The Philadelphia International sound was a complex epiphany of R&B rhythms, classily charted guitar and horn parts and deftly arranged strings. Its home, Sigma Studios in Philadelphia (and later also New York), with its sound honed by owner/engineer Joe Tarsia, became the Mecca for dance producers and singers alike—The Village People, Ritchie Family and David Bowie all used Sigma.

In 1976 Tom Moulton got the chance to remix "Love Is The Message." Moulton's mix—one of several he did for the *Philadelphia Classics* album—took the song to another level, recasting it as eleven minutes twenty-seven seconds of constantly shifting soul-fugue. Progressing from its dramatic minute-long opening, Moulton extended the main part of the song to over five minutes, before gliding the dancer back to the floor with fading strings and then off into the stratosphere for the final saxophone and keyboard vamps. It was and still is a masterpiece of penthouse soul. "That was probably the greatest thing I ever did," he says. "I would have done anything to mix 'Love Is The Message.' They couldn't understand that. And it's still one of my favorite songs. When I got to certain parts of it, it was like being pushed off a cliff and not falling. *Suspended.* Because that's what that song does to you. It's one of the most brilliant songs I've ever heard, for beauty."

Since Moulton recast it so brilliantly, there have been numerous other remixes of the song. Danny Krivit reworked it by taking parts of Salsoul Orchestra's "Love Break," a Gil Scott Heron sample and the second half of "Love Is The Message." This appeared as a bootleg on TD Records and for many is now the definitive version of the song.

The *Philadelphia Classics* remix album confirmed the City of Brotherly Love's place at the heart of disco. Kenny Gamble's socially conscious lyrics resonated with many of the DJs, his meditations on slavery (The O'Jays' "Ship A'Hoy"), corruption (Harold Melvin's "Bad Luck") and spiritual awareness (Melvin's "Wake Up Everybody") summing up the democratic aspirations and upwardly mobile ambitions of the gays, blacks and Latinos who danced to their records.

The Rise of the Independent Labels

Like many successful businesses, the disco empire started with a handful of grass roots entrepreneurs whose profitability was then noted by larger corporations. Double Exposure's "Ten Percent" record had been released by a Hispanic mom and pop concern called Salsoul Records, which had formerly been a ladies' lingerie manufacturer. They went from the bustle to the hustle and, in the process, sealed the incipient 12-inch market for the independents.

As with subsequent new dance genres, at first disco was something which only the indies could really profit from. Many of their employees, like Carol Chapman at Salsoul, were regulars at places like the Loft in any case, and understood both what was happening and how best to capitalize on it. Right under the majors' noses, a locomotive force was gathering speed. As John Brody, Casablanca Records' promotion man, commented at the time: "Before disco there was one pie. Warners, Columbia and RCA had it, and no other record company could get a piece of it."

The smaller labels were quickly carving themselves a slice. Along with Salsoul, there were companies like TK in Miami, helmed by industry veteran Henry Stone, Neil Bogart's Casablanca in Los Angeles and, on the east coast, Roulette, owned by the well-connected Morris Levy, Spring, Wand and Scepter, whose boss, Marv Schlachter, went on to start another important label, Prelude. Philadelphia International was only nominally an independent—it was actually bankrolled by Clive Davis's CBS.

While these indies started enjoying some disco cash flow, the majors were looking the other way completely. Having attempted to push reggae and, later, punk rock as the Next Big Thing, they settled for Peter Frampton. The press were fairly slow as well. As music critic Andrew Kopkind pointed out in *The Village Voice*, "John Rockwell was still writing Hegelian analyses of the Sex Pistols in the *Sunday Times* when two-thirds of the city was listening to Donna Summer."

He always got in—Larry Levan's membership card for Studio 54.

The Record Pools

One of the biggest barriers preventing the majors from cashing in was the DJ. It wasn't that they were against disc jockeys, it was simply that they didn't know what to do with them. Although the new breed of club promotions men and women were making inroads, the current system of distributing promotional records to DJs was not working. It was haphazard, the labels often had ludicrous regulations for collecting records, and there was little prioritization of exactly who should get them.

Vince Aletti sums up the problems many DJs experienced. Aletti, by this time, was working at trade weekly *Record World* and was friendly with many of the DJs; "A lot of what I heard was how difficult it was to get records," he remembers. "And at this point, it was clear that disc jockeys were really breaking records; they were really selling records. Especially selling records that the companies thought they would never sell. Here were all these people coming knocking on their door, saying we want a record, and the labels didn't know how to verify where they were working; didn't know who they were. So it was obvious that there had to be some kind of organization to give the disc jockeys credibility and power in the business. And also to verify who they were."

It all came to a head in 1975 over a record by Esther Phillips called "What A Difference A Day Makes" (as one of the first "modern" records on the northern soul scene, this also had an impact in the UK for entirely different reasons). Kudu Records, Phillips' label, had refused a copy of the disc to Steve D'Acquisto, then playing at Le Jardin. His friends were outraged and a gathering was convened in the club Hollywood.

"The record companies and disc jockeys got together for the first time. It was a total disaster," remembers David Mancuso. Steve D'Acquisto was also at the meeting. "It degenerated into this big screaming match. In the middle of it, David turned round and said: 'Why don't we start a record pool?' We chatted amongst ourselves and I stood up and invited all the DJs down to the Loft. I said it was pointless arguing here. We needed to get our act together. Suddenly we were standing up for ourselves. So we had this DJ meeting and we wrote this declaration of intent."

The idea behind the pool was simple. It would be an organization that provided legitimacy for the disc jockey as well as providing easy access for corporate labels (many of the indies were instrumental in helping to set it up). The disc jockey would enroll into the pool, pay a subscription fee, and in exchange for free promotional records, offer written feedback on the discs supplied by the labels. The DJ got his records; the labels got a line of communication to the clubs.

Mancuso, D'Acquisto and another DJ, Eddie Rivera, set up the first pool, known simply as The Record Pool, in the summer of 1975. It worked well and Mancuso believes it's no coincidence that many great records rose to prominence in this period. "The music that came out when we had the record pool in existence was the best. Most of the classics are right there."

Vince Aletti introduced Mancuso to his friend Judy Weinstein, and she ran the pool from Mancuso's loft. (Weinstein's present pool, For The Record, grew from the ashes of this admirable bout of idealism; she now also heads Def Mix, Frankie Knuckles's and David Morales's production company.) The Record Pool worked well for a while but, eventually, began to fall apart amid recriminations, confusion and arguments among its members. Soon it splintered, firstly with Eddie Rivera leaving and forming his own boroughs pool. "What was sad about that, sad about Eddie Rivera, sad about Judy having to pull away," says Aletti, "was that it had started out as a very idealistic thing pulling everybody together. And, more and more, it became a big business and became more ego-driven and complicated. The more money was involved, the less people got along."

One person vehemently opposed to the pools was Bob Casey. He felt that while the record companies acknowledged the importance of the pool, nothing had been gained for the actual DJs.

"It wasn't the way that disc jockeys were gonna be recognized by the record companies. Your pool is recognized, period. So there was somebody else playing lord and master."

Casey proposed what he saw as a radically different solution: setting up a clearinghouse which would distribute the labels' product to any DJ accredited by his National Association of Discothèque Disc Jockeys. He had formed this in July 1974 and for the next two years published a highly regarded DJ magazine, *Melting Pot*, named after David's Pot Belly, the Village café where the scene's first DJs would meet and swap tips. *Melting Pot*, with its extensive club charts, industry news and a sprinkling of camp scene gossip, illustrated Casey's ambitions of gaining proper respect for the DJ.

"I was trying to formalize the disc jockeys," he says. "I had put together an entire situation; a way a disc jockey is verified, legitimized. To a record company, it would have been the same as being a legitimate radio station. To help them get the product to the right people." Casey insists that under his plan (never put into operation), the balance of power would have been weighted more in the DJs' favor.

It is hard to see what real difference there was between his proposal and the notion of a pool, except that the DJs would have been mailed their records and they would have paid less for the privilege. However, Casey's idea was only a small part of a noble plan to elevate the overall status of the disc jockey profession, rather than just a way of providing record distribution. For example, he labored hard to win pension plans and group medical insurance rates for his members. It seems most likely that his vehement dislike of the Record Pool stemmed largely from friction with the prickly Steve D'Acquisto.

In Chicago in 1979, Rocky Jones (who would later run DJ International, one of the first house music labels) attempted to set up a disc jockeys' trade association. Jones never got this off the ground, claiming the pools sabotaged his plans by preventing their members from joining.

In the end, probably because it was the easiest structure for the record companies to deal with, the pool won out. Despite all the disagreements, The Record Pool was a success and within a few years of its inception, the concept had been copied in every major city in America. By 1978, a National Association of Record Pools was founded, with approximately 150 member pools. Such organizations still thrive throughout the U.S., although the concept never caught on elsewhere (British DJ Paul Oakenfold attempted unsuccessfully to introduce the idea to the UK in the early eighties).

Celebrity Disco at Studio 54

A ruthless scene of life and death at the door, where the ignominy of not getting in is worse than being knifed, and where on his wedding night a man will leave his new wife outside if it means he can gain entrance; Grace Jones arriving completely naked so many times it became tiresome; Margaret Trudeau, wife of the Canadian Prime Minister, caught on camera with her muff getting some air; a famous fashion designer buying sex from a busboy; Bianca Jagger riding in on a white stallion led by a man wearing nothing more than a coat of paint; Liz Taylor photographed having something placed on her tongue; Liza Minnelli chewing the fat (and her inner cheeks) on a banquette. Someone dying in an air vent trying to get inside; Sly Stallone ordering drinks at the bar next to John Travolta while a childlike Michael Jackson sits on a sofa in between Woody Allen and Truman Capote, with Andy Warhol over to the side, Jerry Hall next to him deep-throating a bottle of Moet & Chandon . . .

And all the time the man in the moon watches over, a coke spoon scooping up to fill his nose and a spray of shooting stars erupting as it does. The most expensive light show, the best sound system money could buy. Half a million tax-evading dollars stuffed into trash bags in the ceiling. Cocaine, sex, money, sex and cocaine. Ladies and gentlemen . . . Studio 54.

On April 26, 1977, this is where disco had arrived. Le Jardin had pointed the way and now, upon Studio's opening, disco's social ambitions had brought it right to the top. By cultivating the highest level of glamour, mystique and expectancy of any club before or since, Studio 54 made the most famous people in the world feel completely comfortable about getting fucked up in public. It might not have been the birth of the velvet rope and the elitism it represented (that honor goes to Arthur), but it was certainly the legitimization of it. Those inside felt they had passed some kind of entrance exam, so some bizarre sense of equality and safety was generated. All the club's inhabitants, however recognizable, felt they were part of a great conspiracy of decadence. But the debauched democracy inside depended on fascism at the door. In this, Studio 54 was consciously the antithesis of the original disco clubs. It was not about the mass dancing *en masse.* It was about money, celebrity and *individual* fabulousness.

"The way it was put together was a total atmosphere, like the Loft," says Nicky Siano. "But the thing is, they added this other dimension. It was about

At her infamous 1977 Studio 54 birthday party, Bianca Jagger (left) took some doves with Liza Minnelli (right).

the body; it was about the look; it was about the drugs; it was about sex. That hadn't been the *raison d'être* of clubs before that. And it fucked the whole thing up. It was so self-centered."

Control of the door was not only tight, it was whimsical. Nile Rogers and Bernard Edwards of Chic were turned back, even as their records were riding high on the club's playlist. In protest they went home and wrote a song called "Fuck Off." Later, when they substituted the words "Freak Out," "Le Freak" was born, one of the biggest selling dance records ever.

The sexual antics were legion, for this was the last throw of the seventies dice. Blowjobs in the balcony; adultery in the anterooms below; buggery in the bathroom. Movie star Alec Baldwin was a waiter then. He compares himself to the Humphrey Bogart character in the movie *Casablanca*: "I was the Rick Blaine of well-heeled homosexual balcony dwellers at Studio 54."

The club was opened by Steve Rubell and Ian Schrager—one gay, the other straight, both relative newcomers to the world of clubs. Most of its story has been told far too often to require further detailing here: *Amazing theatrically opulent nightclub full of celebrities misbehaving gets its owners slammed up for tax eva-*

sion. However, in amongst all the spangles, the photo books and the bad movies, little has ever been told of its music.

The principal DJ there was Richie Kaczor, who had made his name at Hollywood, a gay haunt on West 45th Street (it stood on the site of the old Peppermint Lounge, where Terry Noel had danced to the twist fifteen years earlier).

"All these things on Studio 54 recently, and not one of them has talked about the DJs," fumes Nicky Siano. "Never mentioned Richie Kaczor. Richie was a fabulous DJ. 'I Will Survive'? He *discovered* that record. He made a hit out of it. He was incredible. One of the reasons Studio happened was because he was so incredible, and they never even mention him."

"When I heard about the Studio 54 movie I said, 'Oh well, at least they'll have "I Will Survive" on there,'" says Tom Moulton. "When I was told they weren't going to put it on the soundtrack, I thought, 'Well, it can't be about Studio 54 then.' I remember when Richie first played that record. It's the B-side of 'Substitute.' Everyone walked off the floor. He kept right on playing and finally turned it around. Became his biggest record."

Kaczor, who died in the eighties, was remembered as a rare glint of down-to-earth humanity amid the supercharged glitz of Studio.

"Richie was a sweetheart and we all knew him from Hollywood, which was a little more edgy and more underground," remembers Danny Krivit. "So he had a lot of respect from all the underground DJs. When he did Studio 54, instead of thinking, 'Oh, you're just playing that commercial stuff,' we thought of him as someone who does this, but is playing the commercial stuff *there.*"

Nicky Siano also enjoyed a brief residency, playing from the club's second night (and presiding over Bianca Jagger's infamous birthday party). However, he only lasted a mere three months, his drug consumption, by his own admission, out of control. Nicky Siano managed the impossible: to be sacked from a club where drug-taking was almost compulsory. "I was so strung out on heroin," he recalls.

Siano had DJed at Schrager and Rubell's earlier club, a place called Enchanted Garden in Queens, just at the distance from Manhattan where a yellow cab could legally charge you double the fare. Siano laughs as he tells the story of his recruitment.

"Steve Rubell comes to the table and introduces himself and says, 'And this is my fiancée, Heather.' And I'm like, *fiancée*! *You have a fiancée?* I was very confused at that point." When they asked him if he would DJ there, because he didn't want to stop playing at his own club, Gallery, Siano only agreed to play for twice the going rate—$150 a night, when everyone else was getting

$75. "Anyway, after the evening was over, Steve gave me a lift back home; I invited him in and fucked the shit out of him. After that he was at the Gallery every Saturday night."

Siano played at Enchanted Garden for a year but eventually gave it up on account of the trek out to Queens every week. "They were offering me coke and stuff, but by that stage I wanted heroin. I tell you though, honey, Steve Rubell was no longer straight when I got done with him. That fiancée? Fell to the curb shortly after."

Kenny Carpenter, who had started in clubland doing the lights at Galaxy 21, was another DJ who played at Studio 54, spinning there from 1979–81 when Rubell was in jail. He says that under Rubell's stand-in, Mike Stone, he was able to move towards a slightly more underground sound. When Rubell was released and returned, he showed Carpenter just how little he cared about the DJ.

"Steve Rubell comes down with Calvin Klein, Bianca Jagger and Andy Warhol to the booth. And he says, 'Can you play "Your Love" by Lime?'" Carpenter didn't have this, a proto-hi-NRG record. I said, 'It's not my kind of record.' I hated it. He says, 'Well, listen, I own this club and I've got Bianca and Calvin and Andy and they wanna hear that record.' I said, 'Listen, Steve. Sorry I don't have that record, but even if I did have it, I wouldn't play that record because it's not my style.' He got mad. Stormed out of the booth. The following weekend, he hired Lime to perform live. And through the whole show he stood there looking up at the booth."

Danny Tenaglia concurs. "Studio 54 was like going to see a movie, you know? It wasn't about the music. When you went there, it was gimmicky. It was the first club where you had people painting their whole body silver. '*Oh, there was somebody in there on a horse!*' People would talk about that instead of the music. So it was all about *who* was there: Liza Minnelli, Diana Ross."

Le Jardin's John Addison set up a rival at 33 West 52nd Street—New York New York—where François Kevorkian was resident. Another nearby competitor was Xenon off Times Square at 124 West 43rd Street, where Jellybean was resident along with Barefoot Boy's Tony Smith. These two midtown spots attempted to share in the excitement, not to mention the steady stream of customers who had been turned away from Studio itself. Although its success was largely the result of outrageous self-fulfilling hype, François admits that, as a club, Studio 54 provided the goods.

"You cannot say anything other than that Studio had the biggest venue, the best lights, the best sound," he says. "It was quite superior in some respects to New York New York, just because it was so vast, and so spectacular and theatrical. Studio 54 was *nice*, but it was really for the uptown, glitzy crowd."

To the preachers of the downtown underground, for whom music was far more important, there was no doubt Studio 54 was a BAD THING. Many viewed it as the anti-Christ. "I certainly did," says Vince Aletti. "It was not what we thought this was all about. David Mancuso's idealism was very widespread in terms of the way people felt. I think disco was, to some extent, a movement, and a lot of people felt that very strongly. Studio totally got rid of the democracy of the party. It was the beginning of disco becoming a business of a whole other sort. And, I thought, really unattractive."

Like many from the earlier scene, Aletti felt the emphasis on appearance and social standing was simply wrong. "I would never go to a place where I had to worry about whether they would let me in or not. A lot of other clubs aspired to this and were jealous when it happened for Studio. But I think it *was* destructive to have a velvet rope. It was completely against the idealism of disco and the community of disco."

Saturday Night Fever

With Studio 54 generating headlines, it took but one further event to complete disco's coming out. When *Saturday Night Fever* premiered on December 16, 1977, its success took everyone by surprise. It was based on a short story by a Dublin-born writer called Nik Cohn and published in *New York* magazine under the title "Tribal Rites Of The New Saturday Night." It told the story of an aspirant, working-class Italian American from Brooklyn with his sights set on Manhattan and his dancing shoes set on stun. With its partnered dancing rituals, the movie was essentially a clever update of the fifties musical and owed little to the scene which spawned it. Especially since the sexual ambivalence of Cohn's original antihero had changed: John Travolta's Tony Manero was definitely heterosexual.

The success of the movie, its soundtrack and the singles culled from it were the spark that finally ignited major label interest in disco. Much of its triumph can be attributed to three brothers from Australia, via Manchester. The Bee Gees had been one of the better vocal groups of the late sixties, but their transformation to great white hopes in the mid-seventies was nothing short of remarkable.

When they moved labels to RSO from Atco, impresario Robert Stigwood suggested a more American and rhythm and blues-oriented direction. The

Marketing jeanius—in recent years, the superclubs have all launched branded clothing collections, but Studio 54 had its own line of designer jeans way back in 1980.

ensuing pair of albums, *Main Course* and *Children Of The World*, generated three hits: "Jive Talkin'," "Nights On Broadway" and "You Should Be Dancing." Stigwood had discovered the white Temptations.

The *Saturday Night Fever* soundtrack dislodged Fleetwood Mac's *Rumours* from its eight-month residency at #1 in the Billboard Hot 100. The week it reached #1, five other tracks from the soundtrack were dotted about the singles chart: "How Deep Is Your Love," "Night Fever," the Tavares' "More Than A Woman" and KC & The Sunshine Band's "Boogie Shoes." "Stayin' Alive" was #1. To keep it company, Andy Gibb and Samantha Sang also had Bee Gees productions on rotating airplay. *Saturday Night Fever* went on to sell over thirty million copies, the world record for an album until Michael Jackson's *Thriller.*

The Bee Gees did for disco what Elvis Presley did for rhythm and blues, what Diana Ross did for soul, what Dave Brubeck did for jazz; they made it safe for white, straight, middle-class people, hauling it out of its subcultural ghetto and into the headlight glare of the mainstream. Here was something middle America could move its uptight ass to.

This is not to say that the *Saturday Night Fever* soundtrack was an implacable enemy of the underground, since the Trammps' "Disco Inferno" was already regarded as a club classic and the Bee Gees, too, enjoyed downtown club play. Hardly surprising, either, since their taut, muscular productions—aided by some of the best sessioneers in Miami—captured the disco moment far better than the film ever did.

"I remember hearing the Bee Gees' 'More Than A Woman' at the Loft where, I think, it had a special meaning," says François. "You played 'More Than A Woman,' but it was being played alongside things like Barrabas' 'Woman.' It was not the same record that was being played on dancefloors uptown."

Overloading the Disco Bandwagon

Pretty soon the world and his wife (and, on a few alarming occasions, their grandmother) had gone disco. It was a musical panacea and the instant revivifier of any ham entertainer's career: Andy Williams, Dolly Parton, Frank Sinatra, Frankie Valli, The Rolling Stones, Rod Stewart and, bizarrely, Ethel Merman all recorded disco tracks. Percy Faith even recorded a disco version of the Jewish folksong "Hava Nagilah." Anything that could be conceivably recast as disco was, with TV and film themes providing particularly fertile

Disco desperate—this *Billboard* cartoon shows how the industry tripped over itself to promote disco.

grounds. Even James Brown was guilty of cashing in—far from "inventing" disco, as he's often claimed, he made some of his worst records during this period. Ironically, it took a disco producer, Dan Hartman, to relaunch Brown's career with "Living In America" in 1984.

Disco saturation began in earnest when radio realized its potential. In July 1978, a largely unlistened-to mellow rock radio station, WKTU, "went disco." Within two weeks, Disco 92, as it was informally known, had increased its listenership fivefold. By the end of November, WKTU had overtaken the behemoth of New York broadcasting (and the home of Rick Sklar's Top 40 format), WABC. WKTU's Arbitron book rating—the measure of U.S. radio listenership—had gone from 0.9 to 7.8, whilst WABC's had dropped from 8.7 to 7.5. Record stations all over the country would adopt a disco format in their attempts to emulate this success.

It was the broadcasting story of the decade, and WKTU's methods were, initially at least, rooted in the discothèques. Staff would trawl record stores like Downstairs, Disco Disc, Record Shack and Disc-O-Mat looking for hot 12-inches. Program director Matthew Clenott told *Billboard*: "We use our ears and judgment. We let the music happen from the bottom up. It's street-level research. We've got to get on the records when they are happening at the clubs." By the end of the year, its 6–10 P.M. weeknight disc jockey, Paco Navarro, had achieved a personal rating of 15.8, the highest ever recorded. Alan Freed, at the height of his popularity, never exceeded 15.

Disco was now impossible to avoid, and it spread as a "craze" or a "fad" worldwide. By the late seventies there were over 20,000 nightclubs in the USA alone. Some 200,000 people frequented New York clubs every weekend. At the end of the decade, disco accounted for anywhere up to 40 percent of the singles chart. The disco industry's worth was estimated at $4 billion, greater than movies, television or professional sport.

Eurodisco

As disco became a financial force, the music changed considerably. It had begun not as a genre, but as an amalgam of whatever danceable records the DJs could lay their hands on. Rock, soul, funk, Latin: there was no single style or tempo which characterized the music played in disco's underground years. In its commercial period, the opposite became true. Few major label A&R executives had any great understanding of the club scene from which this music had emerged, so they could only see it in terms of its most basic generalities. They looked at the records which had crossed over, noted a few common denominators, and concluded that there was a simple formula for making disco. There soon was. And much of this formula came from Europe. If the Philly Sound became a blueprint for disco's initial propulsion into the mainstream, then Eurodisco heralded a second wave which signaled a departure from the genre's original black idioms.

Giorgio Moroder and Pete Bellotte were two transplanted foreigners set down in Munich; one Italian, the other English. Their first hit together was the faintly ridiculous "Son Of My Father" by synth-pop act Chicory Tip. They then produced Donna Summer's "Love To Love You Baby," a breathy Philly pastiche. Moroder—inspired by, of all things, Iron Butterfly's prog-rock epic "In-A-Gadda-Da-Vida"—lengthened what had originally started out as a four-minute song to fill one whole side of an album, nearly seventeen minutes in all. It became one of disco's first worldwide hits.

The follow-up, "I Feel Love," with its electronic pulse-beat, sequenced throb and thrum and Summer's autoerotic delivery, was a deliberately futuristic record, a Fritz Lang vision for the dancefloor. Black music purists accused Moroder of chlorinating the black sound. American writer Nelson George said it was "perfect for folks with no sense of rhythm." Yet somehow, submerged underneath its nervous electronic sequences, like Kraftwerk, it was still funky. Moroder and Bellotte became Europe's most sought-after producers. They sparked an avalanche of records, many of which really *were* perfect for folks with no sense of rhythm. If this was disco's commercial apogee, it was also its musical nadir. The musical experimentalism that had characterized the indie releases of the early seventies was jettisoned in favor of tried and tested formulas as the major labels sought to suck disco dry. Within a few years, it had crashed and burned.

Disco Crashes

That disco started to suck can be blamed squarely on the majors. They were slow to follow the success of the smaller independents, but once they had developed an efficient line of communication with the DJs (through the pools and the new idea of club promotion), they were soon able to join the party.

However, to make disco work for them, they squeezed it into the star-based marketing structures which had worked so well with rock. They hated the fact that disco was made by anonymous producers bossing a bunch of session musicians around, and that the real star of the show, as everyone kept telling them, was the DJ. (Ritchie Family was named after its *engineer*, ferchrissakes!) Most major labels, used to marketing famous people whose poster you could buy and whose career you could follow, only felt comfortable with this club music if they could dress it up with all sorts of artists and group-based fronts. Naturally, when the wider public saw so much fakery and lip-synching, it reinforced the idea that the music was artificial and inhuman.

There were no bands in disco. No tours. No souvenir T-shirts. Its champions were no more than a bunch of feckless disc jockeys. Critically, outside of the likes of Vince Aletti and Tom Moulton at *Billboard*, disco had little press, and most of what it did have was negative. In the UK, the rock inkies, overwhelmingly middle-class and white, were singularly unable to bring their critical faculties to bear on a music that was made for the body not the mind. This was not music that required a degree to understand. As Danny Baker—one of the few rock journalists to have a handle on what disco was—wrote in the *NME* at the time, how can you critique this music *sitting down*?

But perhaps most destructively, the major labels never got over the belief that disco was only a brief fad to be exploited as quickly and thoroughly as possible. This proved to be self-fulfilling, as the disco bandwagon collapsed from all the expectations which had been piled into it.

In 1980 Marvin Schlachter of Prelude told *Billboard*: "The problem started with the companies which were late getting into the disco scene. When they woke up, they cut lots of disco records and flooded the market."

The story of the shortlived Warner Bros.–backed RFC Records illustrates how quickly the majors pulled out. The launch of the label was a lavish affair at Studio 54, but the hangover was not long coming. "It seemed like everything was happening, then suddenly it was all over," recalls Vince Aletti, who in 1979 joined the label which was headed by veteran promotions man Ray Caviano. "Halfway through our tenure there, disco was over and they changed the department's name to 'dance music.'"

Aletti puts the problem down to the industry's love of instant gratification. "When something becomes so big and so successful, the business thinks it's got to move on. It milks it for all its worth. And then it's over." He also blames the lack of real support from radio. "Radio was still very traditional, very straight, very rock'n'roll, and most of the people there were just not interested. They didn't care about the music, they only played it because it was a hit. And they were only too glad to see it go."

Hi-NRG and the Saint

While the more soulful black and Latin facets of disco evolved, as we'll see, into house music, the whiter, Eurodisco sound of Moroder, Bellotte and Jean-Marc Cerrone lived on in a genre that would eventually be known as "hi-NRG" (Eurodisco would also be an important influence for Detroit techno). Hi-NRG valued melodies over basslines and velocity over funkiness, it professed a love of Donna Summer over Chaka Khan, Amii Stewart over D-Train, and was epitomized in the camp histrionics of artists like Sylvester, Divine and Miquel Brown.

And its influence was huge. Hi-NRG became the *lingua franca* of white gay dancefloors worldwide. It is the music which was appropriated by UK producers Stock, Aitken and Waterman, who then sold this unashamedly gay sound as teen-pop with bubblegum acts like Kylie Minogue, Dead Or Alive and Mel & Kim, among many others. Even today, it remains the predominant pop-dance style, the backbone of supercommercial acts from Aqua and Steps to the Pet Shop Boys and Take That. When combined with the force of nineties European techno, in shirts-off homo-hedonistic clubs like London's Trade, it evolved into "nu-NRG." In this form it is the staple of such hugely successful DJs as Blu Peter and the recently departed Tony De Vit.

The roots of hi-NRG lie in the white, gay, affluent culture of Fire Island, and the scene's favored Manhattan haunts: clubs like the Flamingo and 12 West.

On September 20, 1980, a new place opened which was to drive the competition into the Hudson River. The Saint, on Second Avenue and 6th Street, was for many the city's most eloquent symbol of gay emancipation. "It was the headiest experience I've ever had in my life," said one clubber. "And it is unrivaled still. It was liberating, spiritually uplifting. That's where I learned to love my brothers." $4.2 million was spent in transforming what had been the revered rock venue the Fillmore East into a huge club, purpose-built for its newly liberated gay constituency. Within three weeks of its opening, 3,000 men had paid $250 to become members. In a matter of months, both Flamingo and 12 West closed down.

The Saint was quite the most spectacular club anyone in New York had seen. You walked through a pair of gleaming stainless steel doors through to a massive area with bars, banquettes and cushioned chairs. Upstairs was the vast 5,000-square-foot dancefloor, and above this the club's famous dome. Imagine a hemisphere seventy-six feet across made of aluminum and theatrical scrim. Lit from inside it appeared solid, but when illuminated from above it became formless clouds of psychedelic light. In the center of the dancefloor was a planetarium projector, and when the moment was right this would cast the image of the night sky onto the darkened dome.

The Saint's dancefloor would be a mass of bodies, each sculpted to perfection, moving in tribal unison. To the strains of the club's ornate music, these beautiful men would proceed to get utterly trashed—on angel dust, Quaaludes, ecstasy, cocaine, amphetamines. They were Greek gods with drug habits. The lights would go down, the projector would come on, and as New York went about its Sunday morning chores, a few thousand men would take a snort of their poppers and continue dancing near-naked under the electric stars.

"It was the apotheosis of the underground dance experience," said Michael Fierman, one of the Saint's DJs. "The main point of what we did was to create a commonality of experience for everyone there, unifying several thousand people."

With a night at the Paradise Garage, the Saint's mostly black gay contemporary, you could never be sure what you might hear. But at the Saint you could almost bank on the playlist. The roster of DJs there—Roy Thode, Sharon White, Terry Sherman, Shaun Buchanan, Robbie Leslie and Michael Fierman—favored a very particular sound, playing melody-soaked songs with a heavy kick-drum, richly orchestrated strings and sentimental lyrics that told of love lost and spurned. The Weather Girls were favorites, as was the classic diva soul of Thelma Houston, Phyllis Nelson and Linda Clifford, alongside Eurodisco, especially French acts like Voyage and Cerrone, whose "Call Me Tonight" was a particular favorite.

At about 8 A.M. each week the dancefloor would be offered respite from the pounding beat, as the tempo dropped for what the Saint DJs called their "sleaze records": Johnny Bristol's "Take Me Down," Miquel Brown's "Close To Perfection," "American Love" by Rose Lawrence and, somewhat improbably, Bucks Fizz's "I Hear Talk."

"There never was a club like the Saint," gushes Ian Levine, formerly a leading northern soul DJ and then the founding resident at Heaven, Britain's first purpose-made gay discothèque. "The Saint was unique in the history of disco music," he sighs. "The best ever. At Heaven, all we could even vaguely hope to do was aspire to be a tenth of what the Saint achieved. It was the *ultimate.*"

Ian Levine at Heaven

Levine was determined to bring a slice of the Saint's gay paradise to England. In doing so he would distill the club's musical tastes into a lasting genre.

"We created a new scene at Heaven by playing purely American disco music, but it was at about the same time that the disco market slumped," he explains. "Suddenly there was a shortage of new records. I explained to Howard and Geoff from Record Shack that I didn't want all the funk records they were selling to the straight DJs. I wanted much faster music and they would have to get it."

As well as seeking out speedier tunes, Levine made his own. Already an experienced producer, in the mid-eighties he started to make records tailored specifically for the dancefloors of Heaven and the Saint. These were largely extensions of the Eurodisco sound, but Levine codified and exaggerated the style, bringing to it the aesthetic he'd developed in his northern soul career. The result was fast, stompy music filled with swirling melodies and featuring a series of female vocalists—Eartha Kitt, Hazell Dean, Evelyn Thomas—singing lyrics with which every gay man could identify. One song, "High Energy" by Evelyn Thomas, would clarify the style's name (it was also known as "boystown" and "gay disco").

These records formed the core of Levine's DJ sets at Heaven, founding the tastes of a generation of gay British clubbers, and were an important addition to the Saint's musical canon. In fact, such was his impact on the New York scene that Levine would fly over to debut many of his tracks there.

He recalls just such a trip in Easter 1983, for the first airing of "So Many Men, So Little Time" by Miquel Brown. The song had only been finished on the Monday, but Levine rushed it to the factory for pressing and then flew it to New York for DJ Robbie Leslie's Thursday night at the Saint. He remembers the excitement the record caused: "Three o'clock in the morning, at the peak of the night, he stopped the last record dead, plunged the room into blackness, and then there was boo-boo-boo-BOO-BOO-BOOM! By the Monday, it was the talk of New York."

San Francisco, Patrick Cowley and Sylvester

The Saint was the finest expression of a sensibility which was previously best established on the west coast in the famously gay city of San Francisco. Like Fire Island and the Saint, this was a predominantly white culture. The discothèques here had grown out of a thriving bar scene: the Mineshaft and the Shed on Market Street, the Rendezvous on Sutter Street and the Cabaret on Montgomery, which had become City Disco, the city's first major club. City Disco was a huge entertainment complex that included a restaurant, showroom, disco and several stores. Its first DJ star was John Hedges from Ohio, who began spinning at the Mineshaft under the name Johnny Disco. Another key jock was Frank Loverde, *Billboard*'s DJ of the Year 1976. When Hedges moved to Oil Can Harry's, his place at City Disco was taken by Marty Blecman (DJ of the Year 1978).

Because disco had originated in New York, the San Francisco scene was heavily influenced by the east coast, even to the point of recruiting its DJs. New York–based Howard Merritt was hired to play Dreamland, and Florida's Bobby Viteritti was brought over for a residency at Trocadero Transfer. Merritt came from the original wave of New York disco DJs, having learned his craft at the Cock Ring and been resident at the Flamingo for five years (he was also a promotions director at Casablanca Records). The arrival of Merritt and Viteritti sparked a DJ wage war in San Francisco. Things became so competitive that by the late seventies, the leading spinners were earning $1,000 a night.

Great pains were taken to enhance the dance experience. At Trocadero Transfer, Viteritti and his light man Billy Langenheim would carefully plan the scope of each night's set. "Billy and Bobby would get together at the beginning of the night and plan where they would take the crowd and with what songs," explained a clubber in David Diebold's book *Tribal Rites*. "They believed that if they could totally control the audio and visual environments, then they could actually control the group consciousness and influence people's trips, which they unquestionably did. It was like nothing I've ever seen."

"We'd suddenly go into a wild, frenzied set and we'd beat the crowd with strobes and wild music," said Viteritti. "We'd whip them up with one rough song after another then throw them into a whirlpool, smoothing out with 'Touch Me In The Morning' by Marlena Shaw or 'Rise' by Herb Alpert, and bring everybody back together into the same head space." The Trocadero was quickly the city's most popular club.

As disco took hold in San Francisco, local DJs and producers soon began crafting records specifically for the clubs, capturing on vinyl the atmosphere of places like Trocadero Transfer, the I-Beam, Dreamland, the End-Up and Alfie's. The most talented among them was the light man at City Disco. Patrick Cowley was an intractable, fully liberated white man who lived, as his songs suggest, for sex and music. Cowley grew to fame for his alliance with Sylvester, a well-established black jazz singer turned disco-drag-diva with a piercing falsetto, who he met at City Disco. Cowley became the driving force behind Sylvester's sequenced soul, producing such classics as "You Make Me Feel (Mighty Real)" and "Do You Wanna Funk?"

Cowley was not alone in making records for the scene. Linda Imperial was a local star, as was producer Paul Parker. The Boystown Gang were huge (and even scored a hit in the UK with their horrible cover of Andy Williams's "Can't Take My Eyes Off You"), but beyond Sylvester there was little made in San Francisco of enduring importance. Notable exceptions include the Weather Girls (Martha Wash and Izora Armstead), who started as Sylvester's backup singers and had a huge hi-NRG hit with "It's Raining Men."

Tragedy

The stories of disco and gay liberation run in close parallel. For the core of its devotees, the discothèque boom was more than pure hedonism. It was a movement through which gay people made substantial social gains. Not only was it the soundtrack to their emancipation from years of invisibility, a rallying call for togetherness and tolerance, it was also a Trojan horse by which important aspects of gay culture were pushed into mainstream acceptance. Because of this, when disco collapsed, it seemed like an attack on the freedoms that had been won—especially since the disco backlash was usually voiced with unmistakable homophobia. This effrontery was compounded by all-out tragedy as another force emerged that would have an unprecedented impact on the gay community.

If the disco movement was beaten down by rampant commercialism, it was laid to rest by AIDS. A story that began with the liberation symbolized at Stonewall ended with a disease which seemed at first to discriminate along exactly the same bigoted lines as society at large.

As well as the dance clubs, an important part of gay recreation in urban America (especially for the hi-NRG community) was the baths scene with its charged sexual atmosphere. The bathhouses (or just "baths") were essentially gay sex centers. Based around steam baths, swimming pools and saunas, they were places where men would go to fuck and be fucked by as many men as they desired. Some had music and restaurants, all had endless orgies.

The arrival of the HIV virus meant the hedonism of these places would ultimately result in mass tragedy.

In its early years, the as yet undiagnosed "gay cancer" AIDS was first known as GRIDS: Gay Related Immune Deficiency Syndrome. Novelist David Leavitt described this period as "a time when the streets were filled with an almost palpable sense of mourning and panic." By the time AIDS had become a manageable disaster rather than unmitigated catastrophe, it had claimed fifty percent of all gay Manhattanites.

The abandon with which many disc jockeys approached life saw to it that AIDS ravaged the dance community hard. Many DJs—hedonistic pioneers all—succumbed to the disease. Others lost their lives through drug overdoses. As writer Brian Chin commented, "I wasn't constantly hanging around DJs because the drug-taking *scared the fuck* out of me." In New York, AIDS was initially nicknamed "the Saint's Disease," since so many of the club's members were among the first to die. Over in San Francisco, Patrick Cowley was one of the first well-known people to succumb.

"He was very driven by music," recalled his roommate DJ Frank Loverde. "He really didn't have much of a social life. It was just music and the baths, music and the baths. That's probably how he got sick." So little was known about the disease at the time that when Cowley fell ill on a tour of South Africa, everyone thought he had an acute bout of food poisoning. In the final stages of his life, and after what people thought would be a terminal stay in hospital, Cowley dragged himself into the studio to record "Do You Wanna Funk?" with Sylvester. "He'd be in the studio laying on the couch," recalled a friend, "directing the engineer, really out of it, yet determined to finish that record."

Patrick Cowley died on November 12, 1982. Sylvester was performing at Heaven in London. In an emotional scene, he announced the death of his friend and collaborator before performing "Do You Wanna Funk?" Sadly, Sylvester also died from AIDS six years later, on September 18, 1988.

Despite the first wave of AIDS deaths, and long after it was accepted that it was a transmissible disease, the bathhouses refused to close. Only after July 1983, when the Hothouse in San Francisco shut its doors in recognition of the crisis, did the baths accept their role in the disease's transmission. "Before AIDS, going to the baths had an aura almost like smoking," commented one AIDS activist. "People knew it wasn't too good for them, but it was socially acceptable. Now it has the aura of shooting heroin." One by one the San Francisco baths admitted defeat. New York moved to shut down its remaining baths in late 1985. Finally, on May 5, 1987, the last one in San Francisco, 21st Street Baths, locked its doors.

Its clientele decimated, the Saint closed in April 1988 to the music of Jimmy Ruffin's "Hold Onto My Love" and the final movement of Beethoven's Ninth Symphony (the club reopened briefly without its dome at the end of 1989). The Saint lives on today in massive quarterly parties complete with sex shows and a good deal of bad behavior. When the building was sold, gay campaigners felt very strongly that there should be a memorial erected in memory of the club and its clubbers—for here was a place where gay freedom was shouted to the world, and here was a place where that freedom was weakened by terrible tragedy. Rodger McFarlane, executive director of AIDS charity Gay Men's Health Crisis, reflected on the bittersweet memories the Saint conjures. "We didn't know we were dancing on the edge of our graves."

There was no memorial. Today, the building is a bank.

As disco was declared dead the nightlife dialectic revolved a few more notches, mainstream interest faded and there was space for fresh energy to emerge. As had happened before and would happen again, the clubland motor went back underground and another period of intense creativity was set in motion. Despite the tragedy with which it faded from view, disco would live on in numerous other dance forms. As we'll see, house, garage, techno and hip hop are all reconstructions, deconstructions or selective evolutions of disco—the primal parent of the modern dancefloor.

It would take a decade, but disco would have its revenge.

EIGHT
HIP HOP

Adventures on the Wheels of Steel

"Betwixt decks there can hardlie a man catch his breath by reason there ariseth such a funke in the night..."

—W Capps, 1623

"Think rap is a fad, you must be mad."

—Stetsasonic, "Talkin' All That Jazz"

"It was violent, but the whole neighborhood was violent, you know," recalls Sal Abbatiello, the owner of the Bronx club Disco Fever, open between 1977 and 1985. "I mean, I had three murders in the club in ten years, but if you compare that to the neighborhood . . . I had three in ten years, they had one every week! I thought my percentage was better than theirs. I had one of my bouncers die in my arms, over telling a guy don't sniff blow at the bar.

"But we were open seven nights a week. Monday was like a Saturday. We've got Grandmaster Flash on Monday, Lovebug Starski on Tuesday, I go get this other kid for Sundays called Eddie Cheba, and now I give Kool Herc a night, Kool Herc has a night with Clark Kent. And I always wanted to get DJ Hollywood, but Hollywood wouldn't come to the Fever, he just wouldn't come. Finally I convince Hollywood, and he does a Wednesday. And there's Jun-Bug. So now I got everybody. The club is mobbed every night.

"It was two dollars to get in. Never advertised, never went on radio, just word of mouth and the music and the party. Everybody knew all the customers, and it was pretty wild that a white guy owned the club, and the main DJ was Latin, you know, Jun-Bug.

"I'd have a doctor sitting here, I'd have a pimp sitting here, I'd have a hooker here, I'd have a lawyer here, I'd have a frigging correction officer here, a girl worked on Wall Street here, but in there it was just... *[Acts sniffing coke]* 'Throw your hands in the air!!'

"'Somebody got a gun.'

[*Ducks*]

"'He's gone.'

"'OK.'

"'Ho-ooo!!'

"I'd have a shooting and the whole place would leave. They'd stand outside and then 'Can we come back in now?' Like, 'Did you drag out the fucking body?'

"The rappers would come in and have contests. Jun-Bug would DJ in the booth, and Furious Five, Melle Mel would be lined up, and Kool Moe D, Kurtis Blow, and Sugarhill Gang, and Sequence, and all these groups would be lining up, they'd all be waiting their turn to get on the mic. And try to outdo each other.

"If Flash was in London, he would call up and we had a phone in the DJ booth, we'd put the phone near the microphone and he would rap. They would be rapping on the mic to the people from London.

"This music just had you involved with it from beginning to end. Fever was the biggest neighborhood club in the world. Copacabana was in Manhattan, Studio 54 was in Manhattan, they had all the glamour and the press, we just had that music. That sound. And it was ours."

Fever in the Bronx

The Bronx has not been a fashionable address for sixty years. Carved into unliveable shadows by the great highways of city planner Robert Moses, burnt by riots and insurance arson, and finally rinsed in floods of heroin, by the mid-seventies it had been left by all those who could leave. In places it looked blitzed, in statistics it was the third world. But for half a decade, unknown to the fearful outside, it hid some of the planet's most exciting and concept-breaking music.

Hip hop, or (loosely speaking) rap music, is defined in a hundred proudly self-referential songs as music made with just two turntables and a microphone. As such, like dub reggae, hip hop is DJs' music first and foremost. It grew from the innovations in turntable techniques of a few young Bronx disc jockeys, who taught themselves phenomenal record manipulation skills in order to adapt the music available to them—the disco hits of the day and the slightly older funk tracks of a few years before—to better meet the distinct needs of their dancefloors.

These DJs saw that certain dancers exploded with their wildest moves not only to certain records but also to certain *parts* of records. Following DJ rule one—that such energy should be encouraged—they looked for ways to play only these particular sections, and to repeat them over and over. In the process, they were creating a completely new kind of live music, and not a guitar in sight.

Eventually there were hip hop recordings, but these were records made to sound just like a DJ playing other records. Even now, with a twenty-year body of work behind it and an ever more sophisticated approach to production, hip hop is still about re-creating in the studio the kind of music that a DJ could (and would) make in a basketball park in the shadow of a Bronx housing project.

As music made from other music, with chunks snatched and sampled from existing records, hip hop dramatically affected concepts of musicianship and originality as well as radically changing recording techniques and copyright practice. Of course, sampling, copying, making a version or a cover, has always happened in music, and has been especially important in black music. But hip hop's blatant approach—to steal whatever you like from whatever source and throw it all together (with some rapping over the top)—caused plenty of fuss, especially when digital sampling made such theft as easy as pressing a button.

Hip hop is now a whole culture (indeed, "hip hop" is not now strictly synonymous with "rap music"; instead the term refers specifically to the cultural trinity of rap music, graffiti and breakdancing) and seems to have 10 sociologists for each recording artist. Despite this, its history is often submerged by its mythology. In place of facts there are a few endlessly repeated fables, some respectful nods to its legendary creators and a deal of misty-eyed clichés about "back in the day."

The Bronx DJs who released the creative possibilities hidden in a pair of record turntables were real people in a very real world. All they wanted to do was throw a better party than their rival up the block. In fact, they were creating an entirely new and revolutionary genre of music and sowing the seeds for several more.

Take a Break

Face your partner, holding hands. Tap one foot behind the other and bring your feet together again. Repeat with your other foot. (Your partner does the same in mirror image.) Then take two half steps back and one step forward. Smile.

You are now doing a basic version of the hustle, a dance crystallized in the mid to late seventies by millions of disco-dancing partygoers worldwide. The hustle's undemanding nature lay at the heart of disco's democratic aspirations, and the dance's regular, uncomplicated moves perfectly matched the music's constant pulse-rate tempo and 4:4 beat. It's simple to pick up, requires very little in the way of coordination or concentration, and can be safely practiced by even the most noncommittal dancer, without risk of embarrassment or serious injury, while wearing a suit, tie and sensible shoes.

But you're a teenage boy. Everything in your chemistry says you should be burning energy parading your sexual promise. And you sure as hell aren't wearing a suit. The floor is filled with hustle-busy couples, and while you might love some of the music that's being played, you want to look cool and be noticed. When you venture out to dance you feel uncomfortably unpartnered and inconspicuous. In your mind, the only place you want to be is right in the middle of the dancefloor with a circle of astonished onlookers. You want the hustlers to pause their toe-tapping steps and watch you do something incredible.

Before there was anything called hip hop, there was breakdancing. It evolved, as an expression of peacocking male prowess, from the "Good Foot" steps of James Brown, from the robotic "locking" and "popping" moves of West Coast funk dancers, and from the extrovert dancing of the podium stars on TV's *Soul Train.* It took influences from such acrobatic styles as tap dancing and Lindy-hopping, even from kung fu. Part of an unbroken black dance heritage, breakdancing was far from unprecedented (the flying confrontational moves of capoeira, a kind of choreographed martial art with roots in Brazil, are strikingly similar). It is named after the "break," a jazz term for the part of a dance record where the melody takes a rest and the drummer cuts loose, this being the explosive, rhythmic section of a song which most appealed to the teenage show-offs.

Back in the early seventies, breaking consisted mostly of moves which today's dancers would call "up-rocking," the rapid circling steps and floorwork which precedes their more gymnastic exertions. The "power moves"—such as the headspins and backspins which would capture the world's attention and sweep breakdancing into TV commercials and Hollywood movies like *Flashdance*—were yet to develop, but at clubs and parties in the Bronx, a generation of kids, many of whom would become rap's first stars, were starting the custom of dancing with wild abandon to the breaks; their chance to compete for attention.

"I used to love the roar of the crowd when I would do my moves," remembers Kurtis Blow, an early breakdancer and later the first major label rapper.

"And then I used to go downtown to the disco where there was no competition, no b-boy competition, so I used to reign supreme."

Many dancers would completely forgo the rest of the music, standing against the wall until a song's break came in. They were eventually known as b-boys, the "b" almost certainly for "break" (some say it was also for "Bronx"). The stern "b-boy stance," beloved of rappers even today—with shoulders curved inwards and arms folded tightly under the chin—was not so much a signal of aggression as a b-boy's way of looking cool while he waited for a break.

The dancefloor was soon split between the meandering moves of the hustlers and the youthful explosion of the breakers. When a record reached its break, the entire room's energy level shot up. The same thing was happening when certain oldies, notably James Brown tracks, got an airing. It couldn't be long before the DJ would take notice.

The Labors of Hercules

The DJ was a six-and-a-half-foot Jamaican giant, Clive Campbell, known since school as Hercules: DJ Kool Herc. A suitably mythological name.

One west Bronx night in 1974, Herc tried an experiment.

"I would give people what I know they wanted to hear. And I'm watching the crowd and I was seeing everybody on the sidelines waiting for particular breaks in the records," he recalls.

That night he tried playing a series of breaks one straight after the other, missing out the other parts of the songs.

"I said, let me put a couple of these records together, that got breaks in them. I did it. *Boom! bom bom bom.* I try to make it sound like a record. Place went berserk. Loved it."

Herc recalls the records he used that night. There was the "clap your hands, stomp your feet" part of James Brown's "Give It Up Or Turnit A Loose," "Funky Music Is The Thing" by the Dynamic Corvettes, "If You Want To Get Into Something" by The Isley Brothers and "Cymande" by Bra. All this was topped off with the percussion frenzy of The Incredible Bongo Band's "Apache," a record destined to become Herc's signature tune, a Bronx anthem, and one of the most sampled records in hip hop.

"Took off!" he smiles.

Herc's mixing technique was extremely basic. There was no attempt to cut each record into the next or to preserve the beat. Instead he just faded from one record to another, often talking over the transition, saying perhaps, "Right about now, I'm rocking with the rockers, I'm jammin' with the jammers," or "Party with the partyers, boogie with the boogiers." Sometimes it was just a single word, sustained with the echo chamber he liked to use, or "Rock on my mellow" or "This is the joint." Most of the time, he was actually seated, a boom mic in front of him like a radio jock. But it was his choice of tracks that counted, and the response was incredible. Herc played the older, funkier tracks they loved, and he repeated and repeated the parts they loved most. The b-boys had found their DJ.

Right away, Herc began to always include a sequence of breaks in the music he played over the course of a night, and he started to buy two copies of each record so that he could repeat the same break back to back. He would still play records in full: older funk tracks including a lot of James Brown, and the latest disco numbers. But there would always be a set of records he aimed squarely at the ears of the b-boys. He even had a name for this part of the night: "The Merry Go Round. See, once you hear it, you got to hop on. You're not comin' back, you're goin' forward."

DJ Grandmixer D.ST (now known as DXT), best known for his scratching on Herbie Hancock's "Rockit," remembers being taken by a friend to a club called the Executive Playhouse in 1974 and discovering Herc.

"I stood there, and at the time I was a b-boy, so I was ready to breakdance at the drop of a dime. I'm listening, checking out people doing the hustle, and I'm waiting for 'Apache' to come on, so I could b-boy.

"There was a bunch of guys waiting around for Kool Herc to play the beats. And he was playing the disco for the disco crowd. Then all of a sudden he would play the beats and it's b-boy time. And some of the best hustlers were some of the best breakdancers too. And back then it was still into, you know, asking a woman to dance. With some class. But now you could impress her by doing a spin on the floor.

"Herc didn't cut on time or nothing like that, he just... his variety of music, the songs that he had, it was very clever. It was a combination of the old and new. And it moved the crowd."

Like many other b-boys, D.ST had found a DJ who would give him just the kind of music he wanted to hear.

"Now there's a place, there's a guy, I can go to his party and practice my skills. Herc gave me the opportunity to just go there and work on my moves. So that became it. I became a fan, instantly, of Kool Herc."

To the ears that heard it, Herc's style was revolutionary. He was playing music which you couldn't hear on the radio, reviving the hard funk sound that elsewhere was being displaced by soul and disco. And with his new technique he could extend the excitement found in a piece of music, focus attention on a record's most danceable part, and work the b-boys to boiling point.

"I had the attitude of the dancefloor *behind* the turntables," he says. "I'm a dance person. I like to party.

"I'd come home from dancing and my whole clothes was soaking wet. My mother would be, 'Where you going with my towel?' And I be, 'Ma, it gets like that up in there!' A sweat box."

Indeed, Herc says his decision to try DJing came from frustration as a dancer hearing too many DJs cut records in the wrong places.

"I'm dancing with this girl, trying to get my shit off, and the DJ used to fuck up. And the whole party'd be like, 'Yahhh, what the fuck is that...? Why you took it off there? The shit was about to explode. I was about to bust a nut.' You know. And the girl be like, 'Damn, what the fuck is wrong?' And I'm hearing this and I'm griping, too. Cause the DJ's fucking my groove up."

His other great inspiration was Caribbean sound system culture. Herc is a Jamaican, brought to New York as he entered his teens, who even has a wisp of the islands left in his accent. He has clear memories of living near a Trenchtown dancehall and watching the huge speakers of a sound system run by "King George or Big George" being wheeled in.

"We used to be playing at marbles and riding our skateboards, used to see the guys bringing the big boxes inside of the handcarts. They used to make watercolor signs and put them on lightposts, let people know there's going to be a dance coming."

Too young to get inside, Herc and his friends would listen to the music, watch the partygoers enter and discuss in whispers the guests' reputations for violence.

"We on our skateboards, skating round, you know, and you saw the little gangster kids, and they knew who was from the gangs, or the bad boys. [*He whispers*] 'Yeah, that's such and such, man.' 'Awww!' And you see all the big reputation people come through. We're little kids, and we sit on the side and watch."

The parties Herc was around as a child in Jamaica were at the front of his mind when he was building his equipment and his DJing style. Especially important were his memories of the sound systems themselves.

"Little did I know at the time, that would be a big influence on me," he admits.

The two other leading players in hip hop's creation also have Caribbean roots, but both deny that Jamaican dub culture influenced them directly. Only Herc represents a direct link. New York, specifically Brooklyn, enjoyed large Jamaican-style mobile sound systems before Herc started his parties, but he definitely brought several Jamaican elements to bear. For one, the highly influential rhyming style he and his MCs used was clearly based on Jamaican toasting rather than on the elaborate couplets of the rapping disco DJs. He used an echo chamber, another Jamaican staple. Also, he was ready, in a way reminiscent of dub selectors, to treat records not as separate songs but as tools for composition. And of course, he prized bass and volume.

In his early parties Herc even played reggae and dub, although, he says, "I never had the audience for it. People wasn't feelin' reggae at the time. I played a few but it wasn't catching." New York's West Indians have remained surprisingly separate from the city's main currents of black culture (possibly because they can distinguish themselves as voluntary immigrants). Certainly, as hip hop was being formed in the Bronx, reggae there was either disliked or seldom heard. So instead, Herc moved to the funk and Latin music his Bronx audiences were used to: "I'm in Rome, I got to do what the Romans do. I'm here. I got to get with the groove that's here." However, in choosing records and in tailoring the sound, he emphasized the same factors prized in Jamaican music, the "boonce," as he says his musically minded father would pronounce it, and the bass. "A lot of my music is about bass," he says.

Herc organized his first party with his sister Cindy, who wanted to raise some back-to-school clothes money, in the Sedgwick Avenue Community Center, the public hall attached to the housing project where they lived. The date was 1971, a time when gangs were making their presence felt throughout the Bronx. Around this time, as well as dancing regularly at local clubs the Puzzle and the Tunnel, Herc was building a name for himself as an early graffiti writer, running with Phase II, one of the more famous names of that scene. The party was a success, his sister bought a nice dress and in his next three or four years as a DJ, Herc progressed from 25-cent recreation room jams to block parties to playing in a series of Bronx clubs now considered the sacred sites of hip hop: Twilight Zone, the Executive Playhouse, the Hevalo and Disco Fever.

It is 1998, and Herc stands on Jerome Avenue, where these clubs were all within a few blocks of each other. They are now parking lots and shoe stores;

Twilight Zone is a mattress factory. "This is Herc Avenue, really," he says wistfully, as a subway train rumbles overhead. Then a pronouncement:

"After I who have entered through this door and certain places such as the Executive Playhouse should be known as a parking lot... So it is, baby! After I who have entered through this door. DJ Kool Herc, no one else shall enter, certain places like the Hevalo, should remain a car lot... So it is, baby!"

Herc became a legend. His parties were soon famous throughout "Uptown"—the Bronx and Harlem—and here he enjoyed superstar status. Because he played a radically different kind of music, tailor-made for the teenage b-boying masses, his local crowd-pulling power was nothing short of heroic.

On seeing him play, D.ST realized that Herc had the same kind of marquee value as the local bands. "People go see him just to see *him.* I just stood there and watched him DJ and I was amazed."

As well as trusting his dancer's instincts, Herc added MCs (Masters of Ceremony) to the mix to whoop up the crowd even more and to allow him to concentrate on the turntables. Many people credit Herc and his main MCs Coke La Rock and Clark Kent as being the first hip hop rappers, because they didn't emulate the style of jive-rhyming practiced by mobile disco DJs like Hollywood or Eddie Cheba—a style in turn copied from the personality radio DJs. Theirs was far more like the toasting of Jamaican reggae deejays—hyping up the crowd with short phrases like "To the beat, y'all" or "Ya rock and ya *don't* stop," all with the added drama of Herc's echo chamber.

Herc's other secret weapon was his system. In a time and place when the DJ provided his own sound equipment—just like the club bands he was steadily replacing—Herc had the biggest and the best. Even though the DJs he inspired would eclipse him on technique, no one ever beat Herc on volume. At the heart of his Herculords system (which many mistook for the name of his crew), amassed piece by piece from a lesser DJ who played at the Twilight Zone, were two Macintosh 2300 amps—"The big Macs, top of the line"—and some huge Shure column speakers.

Grand Wizard Theodore, one of the many DJs inspired by Herc, remembers the first time he heard the Herculords' power.

"It made you listen to a record and made you appreciate the record even more. He would play a record that you listened to every day and you would be like, 'Wow, that record has *bells* in it?' It's like you heard instruments in the record that you never thought the record even had. And the bass was like WHUMM!, incredible!"

Herc's later system was so powerful he named it "Not Responsible."

"Every time you play that set somewhere, some shit always jump off, some dispute, some shit, so I call it Not Responsible."

Herc would be a massive, looming influence. Though his style was very different from today's hip hop DJs, in that he mostly played the full thirty seconds or so of a break rather than chopping it up any smaller, he had invented what we now know as the "breakbeat": the use of a record's percussive break in place of playing the whole song.

Suddenly every b-boy dreamt of enjoying the same kind of local adoration; everyone wanted to get their hands on some turntables and throw parties as wild as Herc's. And now that he had shown the way, it all seemed so possible. After all, he was just digging out old records and playing their best bits. As Jazzy Jay, another DJ inspired by Herc's legend, would put it: "All of them was sitting in your house—they were all your mom's old and pop's old records. Soon as Kool Herc started playing, every motherfucker started robbing his mother and father for records."

"I went to the Hevalo when I was thirteen," recalled the Cisco Kid, an early hip hop MC, in Bill Adler's book *Rap*. "It was very dark inside, but there was an excitement in the air, like anything could jump off. Then Herc came on the mic and he was so tough. You'd get transfixed by this shit. You thought, 'This is cool, I want to be like this.'"

Today, though he still has all his records, Herc gets by mostly through manual work. Like so many originators, he has reaped much respect and little remuneration. By the time those he had inspired were signing record contracts and touring Europe, he had retreated from the game and turned to drugs, demoralized by the tragic drowning of his father and discouraged completely in 1977 after being stabbed through the hand at one of his own parties, when he "walked into a discrepancy." Twenty years later, the Chemical Brothers invited him to London to open one of their shows, paying homage to the man who created the breakbeat, the core of their music.

However, most of today's hip hop stars, while knowing his name, would be hard pressed to say whether Herc is even still alive, his absence from what is now a billion-dollar industry only serving to heighten the mythic status of this classically named giant.

Scientist of the Mix

Flash is fast, Flash is cool. If Herc was the DJ who discovered the electricity of the breakbeat, it was Grandmaster Flash who wired it up and put a plug on it.

As Kid Creole of the Furious Five put it, "It's a known fact—the Herculords might cause a disaster, but there only could be *one* Grandmaster."

Flash, aka Joseph Saddler, born in Barbados, was an intense, scientifically minded kid majoring in electronics at Samuel Gompers vocational high school. He would take Herc's raw ideas and subject them to laboratory-style development, emerging with a style of playing that had all of Herc's frenzied b-boy appeal, but that was also polished and continuous. In the process, Flash transformed hip hop from a particularly dramatic quirk of Bronx partying to a genuinely new form of music.

While Herc had given the world the breakbeat, his technique, by all accounts, was pretty slapdash. The excitement of his "Merry Go Round" came from the records he chose and the parts of those records he played—he had no concern for making clean mixes or keeping a steady beat.

But Flash, methodical and obsessed, set himself the goal of playing breakbeats *with precision.* He wanted to take the phenomenal power of Herc's style and deliver it to the dancefloor with a constant, unbroken beat. He had heard disco DJs mix records seamlessly and he wanted to do the same with chunks of the funk tracks beloved of the b-boys. At first, he had no idea whether it was possible, just that it would be amazing—and that if he could get it right, he would make history.

Flash's inspiration came in equal parts from DJ Kool Herc and a disco DJ by the name of Pete DJ Jones. Jones was one of several mobile party jocks who enjoyed a strong black and Latin following throughout New York. Alongside similar figures Maboya, Ron Plumber and Grandmaster Flowers, he was introducing the innovations of disco DJing—seamless beat-mixing and non-stop music—to crowds from the boroughs outside Manhattan. Having seen Jones play at local block parties, Flash had been struck by his continuous dance beat, something that Herc didn't bother with. In his mind he imagined a music which combined the best features of the two DJs' styles.

"Herc was playing the break parts of records, but his timing was not a factor," Flash recalls. "He would play a record that was maybe 90 beats a minute, and then he would play another one that was 110. Timing was not a factor, he would play records and it would never be on time.

"But timing *was* a factor, because a lot of these dancers were really good. They did their moves *on time.* So I said to myself, I got to be able to go to just the particular section of the record, just the break, and extend that, but *on time.*

"I had to figure out how to take these records and take these sections and manually edit them so that the person in front of me wouldn't even know that I had taken a section that was maybe fifteen seconds and made it five minutes. So that these people that really danced, they could just dance as long as they wanted. I got to find a way to do this."

As Flash tells it, this involved a long period of experimentation and research. He became a scientist of the mix (a name he would later take), locking himself away and immersing himself in the technical mysteries of turntable torque, cartridge construction, needle configuration and the like, examining every aspect of the machinery which he aimed to master. For months, during high school and then while a messenger for a fabric company, he spent as much time as possible shut in a room relentlessly pursuing his goal.

"Friends of mine used to come to my house and say, 'C'mon, let's go to the park, let's go hang with girls.' I'm like, 'Naw, man, I can't do that. I'm working on something.'

"I didn't know what I was working on, didn't have a clue. All I know is that with each obstacle there came an excitement on how to figure it out. How to get past it . . . How to get past it, how to get past it."

One particularly thorny problem was cueing—listening to the next record to find the desired passage without the audience hearing it too. At this time, mixers with the necessary extra preamplifiers and headphone sockets were the preserve of custom-built club systems, and Flash was only vaguely aware that such technology even existed. A begged chance to have a go on Pete Jones's system showed him the immense value of cueing and, using his electronics knowledge, he was able to create the device for himself.

"I called it the peek-a-boo system. How do you hear it before the people hear it? The mixer I was using at the time was a Sony MX8. It was a microphone mixer. So I had to go out and buy two external preamps from Radio Shack, and these would take the voltage of the cartridge and boost it to one millivolt, so now it has line output voltage and I could put it inside the mixer and hear it. I had to put two bridges in between the left and right turntable so that I could hear the music before it goes out, so I had a single-pole, double-throw switch, and I had to Krazy Glue it to the top of the mixer." (Soon after this, Flash would note that Herc, though he had an impressive GLI 3800 mixer, didn't use its cueing system until much later.)

His doggedly clinical approach paid off and by the end of 1974 Flash could put into practice a series of "theories" enabling him to cut and mix records exactly as he had envisaged.

"I called my style 'Quick Mix Theory,' which is taking a section of music and cutting it on time, back-to-back, in thirty seconds or less. It was basically to take a particular passage of music and rearrange the arrangement by way of rubbing the record back and forth or cutting the record, or back-spinning the record." He can't now recall the first record he used to practice quick mix theory, but an early favorite in the Flash laboratory was "Lowdown" by Texan blues-rocker Boz Scaggs.

His supporting "Clock Theory" involved marking the record with a line on the label like a hand on a clock face to show where a chosen passage began. This let him speedily rewind the part of the song he wanted to repeat.

"I had to figure out how to recapture the beginning of the break without picking up the needle, because I tried doing it that way and I wasn't very good at it. And that's how I came up with the Clock Theory: you mark a section of the record, and then you gotta just count how many revolutions go by." (To this day, a hip hop DJ's records will be plastered in little stick-on paper lines.)

"I would use what I call the Dog Paddle, which is spinning it back *[fingers on the edge of the disc]*, or what I call the Phone Dial Theory, where you would get it from the inner... *[fingers on the middle of the disc]*."

By teaching himself to flit between his two turntables at breakneck speed, find the first beat of the chosen part of a record in a matter of seconds, and to play, repeat and recombine a few selected bars, Flash became able to completely restructure a song at will. This manual sampling and looping of a record, done without losing the beat, is the fundamental basis of hip hop (as well as all other "breakbeat" musics, i.e. jungle, big beat, trip hop, drum 'n' bass and scores of subgenres). It prefigures the cut and paste techniques of constructing music which would become ubiquitous as soon as digital sampling technology was developed.

To mark his achievements, Flash (a comic book character's name given him by a friend called Gordon) was awarded the martial arts title of Grandmaster.

"That came from a fellow by the name of Joe Kidd. Said to me you need to call yourself a Grandmaster, by the way you do things on the turntables that nobody else could do. It sounded good. It connected with Bruce Lee, which was the leading box office draw for movies at the time, and it connected to this guy that played chess. And these guys were very good at their craft. I felt I was very good at my craft. I found it fitting."

Surprisingly, though, when Flash showcased his new cut-up music, his first audiences were far from thrilled.

"When I first created the style, I played in a few parks in the area but nobody really quite understood what it was that I was doing. A lot of people ridiculed it. They didn't like the idea of it.

"I was so excited, but just nobody would get it. Nobody would get it for quite some time."

Despite his unique skills, Flash found it impossible to make a crowd appreciate the quick mix. While his techniques were revolutionary, he had yet to figure out how they could be best used to drive a dancefloor.

"What I said to myself is if I take the most climactic part of these records and just string 'em together and play 'em on time, back to back to back, I'm going to have them totally excited. But when I went outside, it was totally quiet. Almost like a speaking engagement. I was quite disenchanted. I was quite sad. I cried for a couple of days."

But Flash would soon be vindicated. The initial confused reaction to his music was in fact an indication of its power. Less than two years later, on September 2, 1976, after residencies in two small clubs, the Back Door and the Dixie Room, and innumerable parties in parks, basketball courts and school gyms, Grandmaster Flash was so famous throughout uptown New York that he could fill the massive Audubon Ballroom in Harlem, the theater where Malcolm X had lectured (and been shot). With his MCs the Furious Five to back him, he was introduced by his lead rapper Melle Mel. With screams and cheers, two or three thousand people welcomed "The greatest DJ in the world."

"When we took the crowd to a climax, the floor was shaking," he remembers. "The floor was fucking shaking, it was really something. And next day, man, Grandmaster Flash and the Furious Five was heroes. It was like, after that there was nothing else we couldn't do. After that there was no hurdles we couldn't climb. Anything after that, it was a piece of cake."

Bambaataa, Father Afrika

"Zulu Nation is no gang. It is an organization of individuals in search of success, peace, knowledge, wisdom, understanding and the righteous way of life. Zulu members must search for ways to survive positively in this society. Negative activities are actions belonging to the unrighteous. The animal nature is the negative nature. Zulus must be civilized." So reads the Principles of the Universal Zulu Nation, parts 1 and 2.

In 1975, a high school student from the Bronx River housing project won a trip to Africa in a UNICEF essay competition. He had entered the contest the previous year, for a visit to India, but had missed the judging in favor of giving out invitations to one of the parties he used to throw. After making a special effort the second time around to convince the judges that he needed to visit the land of his ancestors, he found himself spending two weeks in the Ivory Coast, Nigeria and Guinea-Bissau. His reasons for wanting to see Africa were no doubt passionate indeed. As the founder of a quasi-gang breakdancing collective he called the Zulu Nation, and as the proud owner of a colorful self-given African name, Afrika Bambaataa Aasim possessed a powerful identification with the people of the dark continent.

Afrika Bambaataa, "Affectionate Chieftain," was the name of a nineteenth-century Zulu king, and it is on his leadership of Zulu Nation, an organization aimed at giving hip hop culture a unified (and international) foundation, that Bam is most eloquent. He has told the story many times of receiving divine inspiration to form Zulu Nation when he saw Michael Caine and his scarlet-uniformed British soldiers defending themselves against an onslaught of the proud tribesmen in the 1963 movie *Zulu.* Today there are Zulu Nation outposts in such unlikely places as Switzerland and the Canary Islands. It is now the *Universal* Zulu Nation and Bam has said he is ready to offer the hand of hip hop friendship even to extraterrestrial Zulus, should they present themselves.

Alongside his sociological importance—in offering an alternative, post-gang model of comradeship based on music and dance rather than violence, in settling disputes or "beefs" between hip hop crews, in creating a global network of hip hop fans—this courteous, impassive bear of a man is equally important because he is a DJ: Afrika Bambaataa's other self-given name is "Master of Records."

In common with Herc and Flash, Bambaataa can claim Caribbean forebears (his grandparents were from Jamaica and Barbados). However, any link to Jamaica in terms of its DJ culture was not a factor. The sound systems he knew were those of Kool Herc and the mobile disco DJs; he knew nothing of dub, except its records, until much later.

From as young as eleven or twelve, he was throwing parties with his friends in the Bronx River Community Center. Without access to anything more complex than a pair of their home hi-fis, the kids used flashlights to signal across the darkened room to keep the music continuous.

"I would bring my house system down and we would bring out flashlights and we would give parties in the center. You have the lights off and you signal to the other side for them to play the next record. When the flashlight goes on, the guy knows to start his record off. So you put on one record—

Breakers' yard—hip hop's holy trinity, Grandmaster Flash, Kool Herc, and Afrika Bambaataa (left to right) together in 1993. (*Newsday,* Inc. © 1993)

say, 'Dance To The Music' by Sly and the Family Stone—then when you know that it's ending, somebody might put on James Brown's 'It's A New Day' on the other side."

Bambaataa's early years were a whirl of creative mischief. His friends remember him as the catalyst for no end of inspired activities. Whether it was convincing them to buy bows and arrows to hunt rabbits along the banks of the Bronx River, or pouring and lighting gasoline on the sidewalk during a war game siege, Bam could be relied on to fill a day with something memorable. Since his mother, a nurse, regularly worked long and late and owned an expansive record collection, the basis for his own growing music library, Bam's house was often the place for impromptu partying.

In the context of the Bronx at that time, it was almost inevitable that such a charismatic youngster would be swept into a gang. From 1968, tribalistic groupings had emerged to replace the original fifties gangs wiped out by the late sixties floodwave of heroin. The largest was the Black Spades, who dressed in jeans, Levis jackets, military belts and black engineer boots. They existed to fight white north Bronx gangs such as the Ministers, but were also fairly civic-minded in cleansing their neighborhoods of drug dealing. You joined them because you liked their style, because wearing their colors offered you protection, and, simply, because you were a teenager.

During a ninety-two-day confrontation between the Black Spades and the Seven Crowns, another black gang, Bronx River project was filled with enough gunfire to be christened "Little Vietnam." Bambaataa has admitted that he "was into street gang violence," and remains silent on his "negative" past. However, he is remembered by his compadres as mediator rather than warmonger, and as someone who was, in any case, usually off scouring New York for records.

After a peak in 1973, gangs faded fast. The rise of graffiti and breakdancing offered less dangerous ways to express your male competitiveness, and besides, the girls had decided to stand for no more belligerent nonsense from their men. "Get peaceful or get none," seemed to be their message. Bam declared his party-minded friends to be Zulu Kings and Queens, and formed the Zulu Nation, a group of b-boys and b-girls.

"I'd probably be dead if it wasn't for getting straight into hip hop culture, and making a culture out of it, and bringing a lot of my people from that type of way of life," he admits.

He washed his hands of the gangs completely in January 1975 when his best friend Soulski was killed by the police. On his graduation from high school later that same year, his mother bought him a sound system. On November 12, 1976, he played his first official party as a DJ, at the Bronx River Community Center. "I never had a problem in pooling a large army or crowd. So when we shifted right into the DJ thing, I already had a packed house," he grins.

Herc had the head start and the volume, Flash had the techniques, but Afrika Bambaataa had the records. And with no regard for any criteria other than "Will it add to the party?" he was a fearsome hunter of vinyl. While others in the Bronx were wedded to funk, disco and soul, Bam was ready to play anything that would make people dance, ready to buy any record that had just a few seconds of funky rhythm: an intro, a break, a stab of brass.

"His record collection was just *incredible*," recalls Theodore. "He would play the B-52s and everybody in the party would be going crazy. He would play Rolling Stones records, Aerosmith, Dizzy Gillespie. Jazz records, rock records.

"I remember I went to an Afrika Bambaataa party and he played 'Honky Tonk Woman' and I thought, 'Wow, what's that?' And after I went home and thought about it, I was like, 'That's Mick Jagger and them.' It didn't matter if you were listening to a white artist or a black artist, it was any record he could find that had a beat on it."

"We just was comin' out with crazy breaks," enthuses Bam. "Like other DJs would play they great records for fifteen, twenty minutes or more, we was changing ours every few seconds, or every minute or two. I couldn't have no breakbeat go longer than a minute or two. Unless it's real crazy funky that we just want the crowd to get off on—then we would extend it for two minutes, three minutes, four minutes ... I just was finding music from all over the place."

The audiences which gathered around Bambaataa were as open-minded as he, and if anyone dared to get snobbish about music, he delighted in tricking them, whipping in some obscure track and then gleefully informing them they'd just danced to The Beatles or The Monkees. (For the spotters: Bam would play the drum part from "Sergeant Pepper's Lonely Hearts Club Band" and the "Mary, Mary, Where are you going" part from The Monkees' "Mary Mary"). Taped TV themes and commercials, Hare Krishna chants, Siouxsie and the Banshees, The Flying Lizards, even Gary Numan, all made their way onto his system.

Grandmaster Flash remembers Bam's music and shakes his head—he was rarely able to identify the obscure records he heard.

"I couldn't get too much from Bam because Bam's shit was so deep and so powerful I just didn't know where he got it."

"He broke so many records," adds Theodore. "I can't begin to name the records he broke into hip hop." Billy Squire's "Big Beat," Foghat's "Slow Ride" and Grand Funk Railroad's "Inside Looking Out" were just three of the obscure, forgotten or just plain unlikely records which Bambaataa broke to the hip hop consciousness of the Bronx.

Information about records with hot breaks went around like nuclear blueprints and the records themselves were soon plutonium in value. By summer 1978, *Billboard* had noticed this peculiarly localized commerce and ran a story on how Downstairs Records, New York's "leading disco retailer," was doing a roaring trade in "obscure r&b cutouts," mentioning Dennis Coffey's "Son of Scorpio," Jeannie Reynolds's "Fruit Song" and the Incredible Bongo Band's "Bongo Rock." Profiling Kool Herc as the instigator of this phenomenon, the paper noted "...young black disco DJs from the Bronx ... are buying the records just to play the thirty seconds or so of rhythm breaks that each disc contains."

The bigger jocks had learned from the disco DJs to press up one-off acetate discs, putting album tracks (and occasionally even primitive mixes and edits) on more manageable 10-inch dub-plates. It was an obvious commercial move for someone to start printing bootleg copies of the most hard-to-find tunes.

Harlem entrepreneur Paul Winley launched his Super Disco Brakes series of breakbeat compilations (i.e. albums of songs which contained an exciting break). These were notoriously poor quality recordings mastered straight from records in his collection; others, such as ex-chauffeur "Bootleg" Lenny Roberts, offered a better quality product. At the Music Factory record store in Times Square, Stanley Platzer (known as Fat Stanley, King of the Beats) kept a notebook in the store recording for Lenny all the songs that customers requested. On Lenny's Street Beat Records, the *Ultimate Breaks and Beats* series of albums eventually ran over 20 volumes. Many others followed suit, meeting the demand for tracks which by now ranged from expensive to unobtainable.

Each DJ worked to keep their exclusives exclusive, and so took up, probably from Herc, the practice of soaking off or obscuring labels to evade tune detection. Charlie Chase, DJ for the Cold Crush Brothers, perhaps the biggest rap group of hip hop's precommercial days, has many a tale of such happy competition.

"One time I did a party and Flash turned up, and I played this beat that he never heard. So what I did, on one record I wrote, 'For the name of this record, go to turntable two,' and you see this on the label and it's spinning. So Flash went over to the other turntable to look and the other record said, 'Get off my dick!' He was laughing, man. Those were the days."

Charlie also remembers acts of surprising generosity.

"Yeah, we always looked out for each other in the past. Sometimes the DJs wouldn't want to give the names of records up, but at the same time we would always cover them, so it was OK to lend somebody a record because they didn't know what the fuck it was. We just pointed to where the break was, and that was it, that was your cue."

He recalls a time playing on the same bill as Bambaataa. Both had received a promo pressing of Trouble Funk's "Pump Me Up," but each had but one copy.

"So I'm cutting it in with something else because I only had one copy, and all of a sudden Bam says, 'Yo, I got a copy of that. I have one copy of that.' He gave it to me and I went berserk. I had two for the night. I was just cutting it and like, 'Oh god! that was the first.' Then Bam took his copy back, 'cause Bam was the king of records."

Bambaataa's key move, as well as his out-of-state vinyl searches in New Jersey and Connecticut, was to join all the record pools, the disco-born DJ cooperatives through which the labels promoted their dance product. Few in the Bronx knew about these at first, but Bam was in there early. Especially rich pickings came from Rock Pool, where he picked up on such crucial oddities as Kraftwerk and the Yellow Magic Orchestra.

European synth pop, via acid rock, all the way to cartoon theme tunes: even from its very beginnings, hip hop was hungry and eclectic. The DJ had no concern for the genre of the records he played, his only thought was for their effectiveness as sonic components and their effect on a dancefloor.

"This was the only time, this was the only kind of music where you could hear James Brown playing with . . . Aerosmith! You can just fuckin' mix two bands *together*," beams Charlie. "We were there to listen to all eras' music, you could just mix it together. It was really something. It was weird, but it sounded good."

Skills to Pay the Bills

The Bronx is the only part of New York City on the American mainland. Its western half is rippled with steep hills, while the land east of the Bronx River slopes gently down towards the sea. In its forty-two square miles it has a man-made beach, about 1.3 million inhabitants and the busiest highways anywhere in the U.S. In 1976 it was ruled by three people.

"Flash was in the south Bronx, we was the southeast Bronx, and you have Herc in the west Bronx," explains Bambaataa. "Flash was always in the Black Door, or in 23 Park in the summertime. Herc was in the Hevalo, and Sedgwick Avenue Park. I was always in the Bronx River Center, or in high schools or junior high school gyms in the southeast Bronx. But we respect each other."

By this time there were other crews making their way. The mobile disco DJs started adding hip hop spinners to their lineups. DJ Breakout (and The Funky Four) came to hold the north Bronx. Charlie Chase was starting to bring Cold Crush together. And Harlem and Queens were developing their own DJ and MC talent. Crowds at shows were getting bigger as word spread about this new music. Things were quickly more competitive.

"It was basically for who had the most showmanship between Bam, Herc and myself," says Flash. "Bam had the records, Herc had the sound system. My sound system was pretty cheesy, so I knew I had to constantly keep adding things and innovating just to please my audience. Because once they'd go to hear a Herc sound, then heard my sound... eurggh."

Flash tried rapping. He was horrible at it. Then, like any good sideshow circus, he discovered a child star: his DJing partner "Mean" Gene Livingstone had a little thirteen-year-old brother, Theodore. Theodore could do something amazing: he could find the beginning of a break by eye and drop the needle right on it, with no need to spin the record back.

Sure enough, this cute short-stuff standing on a milk crate at a block party in 63 Park quick mixing by needle dropping was a big draw, but he was to develop as a DJ in his own right a whole lot faster than Flash had planned. Calling himself Grand Wizard Theodore, the kid acquired more than just a name. He acquired scratching—twisting the record back and forth while manipulating the mixer's cross-fader to produce a dramatic new percussion noise.

A decade later, as we'll see, this surprising sound would form the basis of an entire style of DJ music, now known as turntablism. Its origins were far less dramatic.

"I used to come home from school and try to practice and try to get new ideas," he recalls. "This particular day I was playing music a little bit too loud. And my moms came and like *[banging on door]* boom, boom, boom, boom, boom. 'If you don't cut that music down...' So she had the door open and she was talking to me and I was still holding the record, and my earphones were still on. And while she was cursing me out in the doorway, I was still holding the record—'Jam On The Groove' by Ralph McDonald—and my hand was still going like this *[back and forth]* with the record. And when she left I was like, 'What is this?' So I studied it and studied it for a couple of months until I actually figured out what I wanted to do with it. Then that's when it became a scratch."

So your mom invented scratching?

"Yeah, God bless my mama."

Scratching is often attributed to Flash, but most people will tell you it was Theodore's invention. The truth, Theodore admits, is that Flash *conceived* of it first but that the Grand Wizard beat the Grandmaster to the decks: "He had a vision of scratching records, but he couldn't really present it to the people."

Scratching, as well as being a huge leap conceptually towards making turntables true instruments, was a massive crowd draw. When people heard familiar songs restructured by the quick mix they might be surprised , but when this was accompanied by a DJ's futuristic *zigga-zigga* scratch percussion, they were really stunned.

"If you knew a record, and you hear that record but you hear a part going *bam, bam, bam,* you walk over to the turntables and go, 'What the hell is that?' So everybody was very astonished about what I was doing.

"People were dancing, and then when I started scratching, everybody would eventually stop dancing and walk up to the front of the stage and try to see what the hell is this guy doing: the arm movement and the cross-fader going back and forth, and everybody was like, 'Wow.'

"They'd be screaming out. Imagine: listening to your favorite record and I'm going *ba-bam, ba-bam, ba-bam, ba-bam, ba-ba bam bam*, and they'd be like... 'WOW!' Our crowd really increased, because everybody was talking about this little short guy Grand Wizard Theodore. Every time we gave a party it was a humungous crowd."

But these crowds were now for himself, not for Flash. Shortly before the scratch emerged, Flash had fallen out with Gene, who formed the L Brothers with Theodore.

The relentlessly innovative Flash was undeterred. He is credited with the important idea of punch phasing, where a stab of horns or a lick of vocals is "punched in" from one record over the top of the other, and he was the first to do "body tricks" like turning his back to the decks or spinning records with his feet. And . . . Flash was on the beatbox—the first to introduce a drum machine to the mix.

"There was this drummer who lived on 149th Street and Jackson, I think his name was Dennis. He had this manually operated drum machine and whenever he didn't feel like hooking up his drums in his room, he would practice on this machine. You couldn't just press a button and it played, you had to know how to play it. It had a bass key, a snare key, a hi-hat key, a castanet key, a timbale key. And I would always ask him if he ever wanted to get rid of it I would buy it off him. A day came that he wanted to sell it and I gave it a title: beatbox. My flyer person at the time put this on the flyer: 'Grandmaster Flash introduces the beatbox. Music with no turntables.'"

He didn't play the machine, a Vox percussion box, over the top of records.

"No, what I would do is play it, play it, play it, *doomm ah da-da uh-hah.* Stop. Zoom. Play in a record. And then, while the MCs was MCing, where you would fade the beat out for a minute, I might switch back to the turntables. It was a real high part of our performance. A real high point.

"I stayed in my room for a month. And once I learned how to play it, myself and my MCs made up routines, 'Flash is on the beatbox.' So the first time we did it, we didn't get screams and yells and whatever. It was, 'Oh shit! Flash got this new toy.' It probably got back to Bam, it probably got back to Herc, Flash is making music—drum beats—with no turntable."

The Reason for Rhyme

Rapping, or MCing as it was then known, was the other great area of competition. As the DJs plundered each other's hot tunes, their playlists (except perhaps Bambaataa's) got ever more similar. Having the most impressive rappers became a new way for a DJ to distinguish himself.

To audiences raised on performers like James Brown, Isaac Hayes, Millie Jackson, Barry White, The Last Poets and Gil Scott Heron, on comedians like Pigmeat Markham, Nipsey Russell and Moms Mabley, on radio DJs like Jocko Henderson and Eddie O'Jay, on local disco DJs like DJ Hollywood and Eddie Cheba, and let's not forget Muhammad Ali, rapping was absolutely nothing new. In 1991, in William Perkins's book *Droppin' Science*, legendary bandleader Cab Calloway reminded us, "I was rapping fifty years ago. My rap lyrics were a lot more dirty than those in my songs." He added, for good measure, "I did the moonwalk fifty years ago, too." The Afrocentrists among us will trace rap from griot poetry, through the dozens and storefront preaching right to the door of the latest gangster group. Black American culture has never been short of oral dexterity.

Hip hop, however, made it def, dope and fresh. When Herc, drawing on memories of dub toasting, used his MCs (who sat with him behind the decks) not strictly as performers but as party energizers, he set off the new era of the

MC. In this way, hip hop took an established form—rapping—and let it evolve from a new year zero. The greatest impetus for this was the fact that the DJ, using the breakbeat, could now provide an MC with an unshakeable beat over which to rhyme. To someone who could rap, the minimal, repetitive, funky-ass drum patterns that emerged from the quick mix were an irresistible invitation. From the initial couplets and "Throw your hands in the air," "Rock it, don't stop it" crowd-raisers and clichés, the form quickly gathered steam.

The rappers drew constant inspiration from rhyming radio DJs like Gary Byrd and Frankie Crocker. Byrd insists that the radio DJ was their main model. "Now I've got a mic, what do I say on it that's gonna make me fly? I'm gonna say what I heard the DJ say. That's my starting point. So the DJ is the seminal influence on the whole piece. You're coming into the seventies, where we've just seen some of the greatest spoken word of the twentieth century: Malcolm X, Martin Luther King, Stokely Carmichael. This is a rhythm that's in the air. So when you get someone who makes a record, Sugarhill Gang or Fatback, what are they doing? They're actually doing what they heard DJs do! Because if an MC is on a mic, what is he going to imitate? He is going to imitate the DJ."

3D b-boys—breakdancers at the Wheels of Steel night at the Roxy, NYC, in 1983.

The Bronx party MCs were soon introducing new elements and styles apace. Cowboy, the late and lamented Keith Wiggins, was Flash's first permanent MC. He is remembered as the first to rhyme about his DJ, and the first to step out in front and act as an actual showmanlike Master of Ceremonies. Flash credits him with adding the human element which finally made his quick mix style palatable to an audience. "If it wasn't for Cowboy, I don't know . . . Cowboy found a way to complement what I was doing." Another of Flash's cohorts, Melle Mel (Melvin Glover), is the MCs' MC: his name comes up more than any other when rappers are discussing their heroes.

Astonishingly, the first person in hip hop to actually sit down and *write* a rhyme was possibly Flash himself. Theodore recalls how, early on, sick of hearing the same old clichés, Flash took it on himself to progress things.

"He said, 'Yo, the only thing you guys say on the mic is "Clap your hands and throw your hands in the air, this person over here, that person over there, this person's in the house, that person's in the house,"' so he wrote a rhyme and tried to get everybody to say the rhyme, but nobody wanted to say it. He actually sat down in a corner, wrote a rhyme and tried to get his MCs to say it. 'Dip dive, socialize, try to make you realize, that we are qualified to rectify and hypnotize that burning desire to boogie, y'all,' that's exactly what he wrote. Couldn't get anybody to say it, so he got on the microphone and he said it himself."

Eventually, as happened in Jamaica, the person playing the records would be eclipsed by the person out front saying the rhymes. But for now, largely because he owned the sound equipment and because rapping was still fairly primitive, the DJ was in control. Herc had Coke La Rock and Clark Kent; Flash collected his Furious Five; Bambaataa garnered several rap crews including the Soulsonic Force, the Jazzy Five and Planet Patrol. DJ Breakout had the Funky Four (Plus One More), Cold Crush came together around Charlie Chase, Theodore would become DJ for the Fantastic Five. But already there were performers for whom the DJ was secondary: Treacherous Three (including Kool Moe Dee), The Nigger Twins from Queens, Kurtis Blow…

From the rappers, this music and these parties—which had previously been referred to as "break" or "wildstyle" music—gained a name: "hip hop."

"The reason that became the name of the culture," explains scenester and impresario Fab 5 Freddy (Freddy Braithwaite), "was because that was the one thing that almost everybody said at a party: 'To the hip, the hop, the hibby-hibby, dibby-dibby, hip-hip-hop, and you don't stop.' And when you would be describing to somebody what kind of party you were at, you would say, 'Yo, it was one of them hibbedy hop . . . you know, that hibbedy hop shit.' So that became the one defining term within the culture that everybody related to."

Although its use was so universal as to defy exact accreditation, popular consensus holds that it was Lovebug Starski, one of the early rhyming DJs, who coined the phrase. Other main contenders include DJ Hollywood, whose regular shows at Harlem's Apollo Theater and Club 371 were the first places many were exposed to hip hop, and Phase II, an early graffiti writer and one of the very first b-boys. Grandmixer D.ST, however, holds that Cowboy was the first to use the term, and that it was a reference to military parade drill.

"The story goes that a friend of his was getting ready to go into the service. And he was saying, 'When you get in there, you're gonna be going, "Hip hop the hip hop, hi hip hi, and you don't stop,"' and that's how the story stuck. Cowboy started it. Lovebug Starski just took it and made it the thing of the day."

Whatever the term's derivation, there was now a name for what was going on in the Bronx and by the last few years of the seventies, hip hop had a well-defined identity. The scene was all about intense partying, and whether this was in the parks, the high schools or in the few clubs like T-Connection, Disco Fever, Club 371 and Harlem World that risked the boisterous crowds it attracted, the driving force was fun. DJs, MCs and the partygoers themselves competed to add as many exciting elements as they could, and hip hop grew to be about improvisation, showmanship, enjoyment and that greatest of party feelings: living for the moment.

Then in the summer of 1979, out of nowhere, riding on the pump of Chic's "Good Times" bassline, came the sinuous rhyme that would change it all.

I said a hip hop
The hippie the hippie
To the hip hip hop and you don't stop the rock it
To the bang bang boogie, say up jumped the boogie
To the rhythm of the boogie, the beat

Sal Abbatiello of Disco Fever remembers the first time he heard "Rappers' Delight."

"I was in my office, I heard the record and I'm like, 'Who's out there rapping?' They said, 'No that's a record.' I said, 'About time somebody was smart enough to put this shit on record. Now they won't be breaking all my microphones.'"

NINE
HIP HOP 2

Planet Rock

"The Bronx is so named because it once belonged to the family of Dutchman Jonas Bronck, who built his farm here in 1636. It is, therefore, The Broncks.'"

—*Time Out Guide to New York*

"A neighborhood is where, when you go out of it, you get beat up."

—Murray Kempton

Hip hop today thrives on a sense of its own past. It is obsessed with "keepin' it real"—grabbing its nuts and proclaiming its thug life, its loyalty to "da ghetto" from whence it came, and to the "old school" pioneers who created it. Ironically, this concern for staying true to its roots (seen by most of today's young guns as a need to appear poorer, blacker and angrier than thou) has obscured a few facts about its history.

In practice, hip hop rarely has any time for its first generation of performers. Its definition of "old school" rarely goes further back than 1982, and while figures like Kool Herc and Grandmaster Flash may be venerated ancestors, they are irrelevant beside next week's young street-corner discovery. As such, the culture prefers to leave them as myths rather than explore their realities.

For similar reasons there have been radical revisions in the story of the genre's musical origins. Hip hop is usually portrayed as some mythical disco-hating force which came out of nowhere; in fact, it was inextricably connected to disco, it has an important debt to Jamaican reggae, and, perhaps most surprisingly, it owes part of its practical success to punk rock.

Most regrettably, perhaps, hip hop has largely forgotten that it was originally all about having *fun.* After years of "ghetto reality" subject matter, with rappers dwelling relentlessly on crime and politics, the culture has lost sight of its original party purpose, its sense of celebration. You might think it's strange when a grumpy, gun-toting gangster asks a concert audience to put their hands in the air ("and wave them like you just don't care"), but all he's doing is displaying a relic from the days when hip hop wore a smile.

Rockin' It in the Park

Born in 1974, it took more than half a decade before hip hop was heard beyond the Bronx. That it remained a secret to white New York for so long was not entirely down to fear and racism; it was also a result of the DJs' narrow horizons. Recording contracts, professionally managed careers, even the simple notion of playing outside your own neighborhood: these things weren't considered. Eventually, the record companies and the cool downtown clubs would catch on and the music would begin its mutation into the worldwide business it is today, but hip hop's first five years were centered on nothing more complicated than throwing the best party.

To poor New Yorkers, block parties were nothing new. Local festivities in closed off streets and in the city's many parks have a long tradition (a New York park can be as small as a single asphalt basketball court, or sometimes even a traffic island). The entertainment might come from a local band playing funk and soul or, in Hispanic areas, salsa and merengue. As well as live music, there were "mobile" DJs who would bring their own sound systems and play a blend of Latin, funk, soul or disco, depending on the crowd.

As hip hop grew in popularity, the new generation of uptown DJs followed these traditions and threw their own events, giving free parties in the parks through the summertime as promotion for paying events in schools, clubs and community centers. In the parks the music would last from the afternoon well into the early hours, with the police usually turning a blind eye, reasoning that it was keeping teenage troublemakers out of harm's way. If they were out of reach of any other power supply, DJs and their crews would break open the base of a street lamp and risk electrocution to hotwire the sound system. "Playing music was more important than our lives," jokes Charlie Chase, confirming that this dangerous practice happened fairly often. "We didn't give a fuck, we wanted to play music."

Basements and abandoned buildings were other favored settings, especially for an older crowd, and here the atmosphere could get much heavier. The scene was far more druggy than today's rap stars prefer to remember, and along with pot—modern hip hop's drug of choice—plenty of less innocent pleasures were enjoyed. In between sixties heroin and eighties crack, the Bronx whizzed along on cocaine, which was then held to be nonaddictive.

Hence names like Kurtis *Blow* and *Coke* La *Rock*, and the fact that Melle Mel's record "White Lines" actually started life as an ironic *celebration* of cocaine, with the "Don't do it" message tacked on for commercial reasons. As well as coke there was angel dust, aka PCP, a manic-making animal tranquilizer which stank like stale sweat when it was smoked.

"It used to be so ill: the energy and the vibe," recalls Fab 5 Freddy, who would travel to Bronx parties from his native Brooklyn. "Back then in the hip hop scene it was very weird. It'd be really dark, the DJ would have a couple of light bulbs rigged up on a board. A lot of DJs had one strobe light and they'd have it on a table, and that was the lighting.

"Motherfuckers used to smoke angel dust on the scene. At least up in the Bronx, that was a popular drug at the time. And it makes a really sickly ill smell, when guys are smoking that in a hot funky room. There used to be a lot of heavy dust-heads. That might have inspired a lot of the sound, I don't know. I'm not saying any DJs were smoking that shit—I never got into it—but the scene was weird.

"That's why you wanted to go. You wanted to be a part of that world, hear that sound, just be in a cloud of angel dust smoke, all that energy, just funky perspiration odor, some stick-up kids that could rob you. I mean, all that shit was a part of the party. It was a whole world. That's what hip hop was at the time."

Battles

In this closed world, competition grew intense and DJs dueled for local glory in what became known as "battles," setting up their sound systems on opposite sides of a basketball court or a school gymnasium, just like their counterparts in Jamaica's dancehalls. They then fought it out with records, technique and volume to see who could win the largest crowd. Their MCs sparred verbally in support, and rapping evolved into complex rhymed boasts about the indefatigable MC and his spellbinding DJ. Likewise, the b-boys who breakdanced to their music fought each other with an escalating vocabulary of impossible moves.

Battles are one of hip hop's great romantic notions. They did happen—frequently—but they had no elaborate tribal customs, just agreements about who played when and for how long. Battles were never for settling disputes more serious than performers' rivalry; on the whole they were just a way of making an event more exciting for all concerned. The loser did not automatically forfeit his equipment (although foolish was the DJ who set up in a Bronx park without a tough crew to protect his system); the winner simply gathered more respect—and more of the audience for his next show.

"It was territorial," urges Charlie Chase. "It was like a cat where it sprays its territory, just to let people know, this area's been taken. Basically, all this shit stems from us wanting to impress the girls."

At first, DJs would simply try to drown each other out. "You play your system, I play my system, a bunch of noise going at the same time," recalls Bambaataa. "You out-louded the next person." But this led to frayed tempers and the possibility of sabotage. "Someone might get mad and go and knock the turntable or something, and it leads into a rumble. So then we started having it where we play an hour, you play an hour, and this way the audience decides, and it got more peaceful."

If the contest was for volume, it was a brave man who battled Herc. As he would rap, "Kool Herc is not a stepping stone. He's a horse that can't be rode, a bull that can't be stopped. Ain't a disco I can't rock."

"Kool Herc used to just destroy people," remembers Jazzy Jay, a key Zulu Nation DJ. "Herc was the ultimate 'cause he had the records, *and* his system was unmatched."

Flash recalled being shamed by Herc's system without even battling. He had popped in to check out the Hevalo one night.

"He'd say, 'Grandmaster Flash in the house,' over the mic, and then he'd cut off the highs and lows on his system and just play the midrange. 'Flash,' he'd say, 'in order to be a qualified disc jockey, there is one thing you must have . . . highs!' Then Herc would crank up his highs and the hi-hat would be sizzling. 'And most of all, Flash,' he'd say, 'you must have . . . bass!' Well, when Herc's bass came in, the whole place would be shaking. I'd get so embarrassed that I'd have to leave. My system couldn't compare."

Many people talk of the time, at the Webster Avenue PAL (Police Athletic League), when Herc's Herculords washed Bambaataa out completely. Herc strolled around casually, taking ages to set things up, so Bam and his DJs carried on playing past their allotted time and were really getting into it. "We was throwing the records on and we was *killing* it," recalls Jazzy Jay. When Herc was finally ready, he warmed up his speakers with a series of polite but booming requests, delivered with the ominous vibration of his echo chamber. With a smile, Jay relates what came next:

"He said, 'Ah, Bambaataa, could you please turn your system down?' So Bam's getting all gassed by the Zulus—'Yo, fuck that nigga, Bam! We got his ass! Throw on them funky beats!' So Bam passed me some shit, I slice that shit up. Herc said *[louder]*, 'Yo, Bambaataa-baataa-baataa, turn your system down-down-down.' 'Fuck you!' Niggas getting on the mic, cursing. Now Kool Herc, he said *[louder still]*, 'BAMBAATAA-Baataa-baataa, TURN YOUR SYSTEM DOWN!' Couldn't even hear our shit. Whoa! We started reaching for knobs, turning shit up, speakers started coughing. And he comes on with 'The Mexican.' You ever hear 'The Mexican' by Babe Ruth? It starts out real low—ba-doom-doom. By about sixteen bars into the song, we just gave up, turned off all the fucking amps. Turned everything off. And the drums didn't even come in yet. When the drums came in, all the walls . . . just like VROOM! That was it."

Bambaataa, however, insists that the Zulus remained unbowed.

"He had a louder system, but when it came to the music they couldn't fuck around. At the battle, we funked them up with our music so much that when we left, the whole crowd left with us too."

Battles weren't always a simple head-to-head. Fab 5 Freddy remembers a battle between seven separate systems in an armory building in Brooklyn. Bambaataa recalls a time at James Monroe High School when a DJ called Disco King Mario put out a call for help in order to battle Flash. Mario ended up fighting the Grandmaster with his own system, plus amps and speakers from Bambaataa's, plus another system belonging to a DJ Tex. "We put our stuff all together. It looked like the wall of Jericho," says Bam biblically.

Charlie Chase, a former musician, had more stage experience than most and with the weighty lyrical skills of Grandmaster Caz, the Cold Crush Brothers used showmanship and theatricality as their trump cards.

"When you saw us perform, it was unforgettable," boasts Charlie. "Nobody else had the stage presence we had. We couldn't just get on the stage and just rap, we've got to give them a show." For the group's entrance, Charlie would use a classical record for a single note: the strike of an entire orchestra.

"When you hear a symphony strike, that shit is intense, so we have to match that visually onstage. So I would take a record and take a strike, and the guys would pose, BAMM! Then you'd see the guys spin round one at a time. I would play 'Catch the Beat' by T-Ski Valley, they would do more dance steps. Once the whole group was on the stage, I would play instrumental breaks that they could do their dance steps to. Then the whole group would do a song together, and then two members of the group would do a chant, and the other three members of the group would do the rap. And then the chant comes in, and then the rap, and the chant . . .

"That shit was not done in hip hop. We dressed the part. We played the part. We had a show called the Gangster Chronicles. We came onstage with pinstripe suits, the hats, and Uzis, plastic toy Uzis."

Cold Crush's mobster outfits made their debut at one of the most famous battles ever: Cold Crush Brothers vs Theodore and the Fantastic Romantic Five, winter 1981 in Harlem World. It was a grudge match, stemming from the fact that two of the Fantastic's MCs had been protegés of Cold Crush MC Grandmaster Caz.

"I remember, we made scenes in the street," laughs Charlie. "We were this close to fighting in the street, fist fights, with them. It was like Muhammad Ali facing Joe Frazier at the time, where he would meet him in public just to humiliate him. Some shit. And the promoters at Harlem World got wind of it and they said, we'll put up a thousand dollar prize if you guys come here and battle. And the buzz was growing in the hip hop community, like, 'Fantastic is better,' 'Hell no, Cold Crush will bust they ass,' 'No, Fantastic is better,' and little tiffs and arguments in clubs and public."

In the end, despite the polished Cold Crush show, the Fantastic Five won the affections of some wild girls at the front of the crowd and were screamed to a dubious victory.

Captured on Vinyl

The idea of capturing these low-rent street thrills on records just seemed contradictory. While the music industry was entranced by disco's glitzy aspirational sound, what would they find of interest in these ghetto parties? The DJs and MCs might be heroes on their block, stars in the neighborhood, but they could hardly conceive of any greater level of fame; none of them thought of making records. The closest these kids—and remember, few were even out of their teens—had come to the music business was a brief negotiation with a local nightclub owner. Partying in the projects was worlds away from the record labels and their midtown mirrorglass.

In late 1978, mere months before the Sugarhill Gang would hit the charts with "Rappers' Delight," Fab 5 Freddy first saw Grandmaster Flash and the Furious Five perform. He remembers, after the show, in the Community Center of the Lower East Side's Smith Projects, talking to Melle Mel.

F5F: "Yo man, wassup. Are you aware of how big this is? You guys should make a record."

MM: "Yo, who would buy it?"

F5F: "Well, at least all the people coming to these parties."

MM *[unconvinced]*: "Yeah?"

Flash himself claims to have turned down some very early offers of record deals, thinking that music made from other people's records was simply not commercial enough. "I was asked before anybody. And I was like, 'Who would want to hear a record which I was spinning rerecorded with MCing over it?'"

In any case, the scene already had an established communication network as DJ-mix tapes were copied and circulated throughout black New York, and played, of course, on "ghetto blasters," the era's suitcase-sized portable radiocassettes (a similar trade had developed downtown in tapes of the disco DJs' performances). The hip hop sound was heard even further away as people sent tapes to relatives outside the city and servicemen took them overseas. In the Bronx, echoing the Pullman railroad conductors who had distributed blues records decades ago, car services helped to market tapes.

"Those were our biggest promotional vehicles," puns Charlie Chase. "You had the OJ cab service and then you had Community Cab service, they were the first cabs that used to drive luxury cars." (The OJ cars were immortalized in several songs, including "Rappers' Delight.") "If they knew you were a DJ, they would come by and buy tapes off you. And then they'd play them in the cars. People would go, 'Yo, whose tape is that?' and the cabdriver would say, 'This is Charlie Chase,' or they'd give them your number." Charlie would sell his tapes from his ground floor apartment. "My window was always being knocked on. They would knock on my window and I would sell 'em tapes. My neighbors thought I was a fuckin' drug dealer for a while."

Cassette technology was also a way for would-be DJs to practice their skills at cutting up songs without the need for expensive equipment. Many of the DJs inspired by Herc, Flash and Bambaataa would begin their careers on a home hi-fi with their fingers hovering over a hot pause button. Grandmixer D.ST was one of them.

"I had pause button tapes all over the place. Everyone had one of my pause button tapes. I was one of the biggest pause button guys." All this despite the fact that his tape recorder didn't actually have a pause button. "I would just cut with the tape on play and the record button halfway down. And then when the part on the tape would get to the cut part, I would just push the record button all the way down." He laughs at the thought of such primitive techniques. "Then when I got a pause button, I was off the hook!"

It would take a handful of independent (and often predatory) entrepreneurs to see the commercial possibilities of committing hip hop to record.

All had experience of bringing money and music together since the fifties; most had a dislike for disco, which kept them away from what was then the most lucrative genre for independent labels; and several saw in the hip hop scene a parallel to earlier forms, especially the street corner harmonizing of doo wop.

1. Vicious Rap

Recalling some of the doo wop groups he had recorded as "real hoodlums," Paul Winley, who was first to put the Bronx sound onto vinyl, saw hip hop as familiar territory. "The doo wop era and the hip hop era, in the beginning it was the same thing. It was kids. Young kids."

The affable Winley, who can greet anyone over forty by name as he ambles down Harlem's 125th Street, had been a Tin Pan Alley songwriter with a number of fifties hits to his credit, had worked for the young Atlantic Records, and had run a successful independent label, Winley Records, since 1956. (He recalls being cursed out by Billie Holiday when he suggested she record for him: "She was a rough woman.")

Winley already knew the hip hop scene from producing compilation albums of breakbeat songs. When his daughter Tanya started coming home from school reciting the raps going through her playground, he decided to put her on record. In 1978 he squeezed her into the studio at the end of one of her mother's vocal sessions. Against a live funk backing and some police sirens, she became Sweet Tee and recorded "Vicious Rap," a great, if rather lo-fidelity record and the first vinyl example of this new music.

Winley didn't necessarily see hip hop as an enduring art form, but he thought it was more than a mere novelty. His view was typical. "It was grass roots people, grass roots kids. Just like the blues, just like gospel. It came from the soul, and it was natural writing, and it wasn't no great productions.

"I saw it as rhyming. Rhyming, with a beat, with music. I just saw it as entertaining. I didn't say that it was music or that it was gonna be a big thing. I saw it as something the kids enjoyed doing, and anything that the masses can participate in could be big."

He would later record Afrika Bambaataa's first records, "Zulu Nation Throwdown" (1980), a rap backed with some minimal guitar and Hammond organ vamps, and "Death Mix" (1981), an exciting but inaudible live show. Bambaataa claims this was mastered from a second or third generation cassette tape—such haphazard quality control meant Winley's early entry into recording hip hop was followed by an equally early exit.

2. Rappers' Delight

Hot on the heels of "Vicious Rap" were records which would have far more impact. An ailing Brooklyn funk band, Fatback, slipped an unknown rapping DJ, King Tim III, onto the B-side of their 1979 single "You're My Candy Sweet," and when New York's powerful disco station WKTU played this track, "King Tim III (Personality Jock)," over the A-side, it became a surprise hit.

Hip hop's breakthrough song, however, was the fatally infectious "Rappers' Delight" on Sugarhill Records, the latest label from experienced soul and funk mini-moguls Sylvia and Joe Robinson (the husband and wife team behind such imprints as All Platinum, Turbo, Stang and Vibration; Sylvia had also enjoyed a long singing career). "Rappers' Delight" stole the bassline of that summer's disco hit "Good Times" to full effect—recreated in the studio by session musicians mimicking the music of a quick-mixing Bronx DJ—and this fourteen-minute groove stormed the clubs and the radio like a police raid.

But the Sugarhill Gang? Who were they? Their record was selling thousands a day, but the Bronx had never seen them pick up a microphone.

"Never heard of them. They didn't pay no dues at all," is how Flash remembers it. "We all thought, 'If they're not from any of the five boroughs, where are they from?'"

Far from veterans of the scene, they were a manufactured group, put together by the wily Sylvia Robinson. She originally claimed she signed them after seeing them perform at her niece's birthday party at Harlem World. Others remember Wonder Mike as a friend of her son, and Big Bank Hank as a bouncer at the Sparkle, one of Kool Herc's clubs. The rest of the time he worked in a pizza shop in Englewood, New Jersey, where Robinson was based.

Although the group was unknown in the Bronx, the rhymes in "Rappers' Delight" were all too familiar—an amalgam lifted, it's said, from the MCs which club doorman Hank had heard onstage. Grandmaster Caz (short for Casanova) of the Cold Crush Brothers has always claimed authorship of most of the lyrics, even to the extent of saying he lent Hank (who had offered to manage him) his rhymes notebook. Since one of the song's lines is, "Check it out, I'm the C-A-S-an-the-O-V-A . . . ," this seems pretty likely.

Whatever its provenance, the record went to #4 on *Billboard*'s R&B charts and #36 in the Hot 100, proving beyond any doubt that this music had a market.

After the Bronx had heard "Rappers' Delight," everyone realized the rules had changed. Bambaataa says he was immediately fearful that hip hop on record would kill the party. "I was one who stood away longer. Flash and all them jumped on the scene. I stood more watching."

Flash, always chasing firsts, was incensed.

"I was like, 'Damn, I could'a been there first.' I didn't know the gun was loaded like that. Blew up. It was a huge record for them." He vowed to turn his anger into action. "It was OK, though. 'Cause we were gonna come later . . . We had the talent, and they didn't."

3. Adventures of Grandmaster Flash on the Wheels of Steel

Soon after "Rappers' Delight," Flash and the Furious Five leapt into the fray with "Superrappin' No. 2" on Enjoy, a Harlem label started by another veteran record retailer and producer, Bobby Robinson. Years ago, Enjoy had been home to saxophone legend King Curtis, just one of the artists Robinson had nurtured for success with larger companies. (Robinson can also claim the discovery of Gladys Knight and the Pips, who he signed to his Fury label.) After "Superrappin'," a funky rip-off of "Seven Minutes Of Funk" by Tyrone Thomas & the Whole Darn Family, Flash would follow this tradition when he moved his deal to Sugarhill, complaining that Robinson had failed to get any radio play for his debut single.

DJ Breakout's group, The Funky Four (Plus One More), had been the first to record hip hop for Enjoy, with 1979's "Rappin' And Rockin' The House," a take on Cheryl Lynn's "Got To Be Real," but they, too, would move their business from Enjoy to Sugarhill, as did Spoonie Gee (even though he was Bobby Robinson's nephew) and the Treacherous Three. Once signed to Sugarhill, Flash and the Furious Five quickly made up for lost time and emerged as recorded rap's first superstars.

Their most famous song is undoubtedly 1982's "The Message," which made #4 in the R&B chart (#8 in the UK) as hip hop's first sociopolitically charged rap. A hugely inspiring record, its conscious lyrics were an innovation of Sylvia Robinson's which the band, armed with a powerful lack of political consciousness, strongly resisted. But Sylvia's uncanny commercial acumen triumphed and rap's enduring sociological agenda was born. With the song's success, a whole series of "message raps" followed.

"'The Message' was the announcement that hip hop was gonna be culturally significant," considers Richard Grabel, one of the first journalists to cover the scene. "White rock fans, and certainly white rock critics, have always been content oriented. Up to that point rap hadn't given them much to write about lyric wise. But now it was doing it. And that's when all the writers started covering it."

From a DJ's perspective, however, 1981's "Adventures Of Grandmaster Flash On The Wheels Of Steel" remains a far more important record. Seven minutes of quick mix excitement starring a host of the period's hit tunes, this was the first track made successfully with records and turntables, not session musicians.

"It took three turntables, two mixers and between ten and fifteen takes to get it right," recalls Flash. "It took me three hours. I had to do it live. And whenever I'd mess up I would just refuse to punch. I would just go back to the beginning."

And how did he react when he heard the playback?

"I was scared. I didn't think anyone was gonna get it. I thought, they *might* understand this. DJs'll probably love it."

"Adventures..." didn't enjoy huge success in America, only managing #55 in the R&B chart, but in clubs, both at home and in Europe, the record was huge.

To those who heard it at that time—a record made from nothing more than other records, a record made by a DJ, a postmodern collage of existing texts, the scratch-filled proof that turntables could be real instruments—it was a revolutionary moment in the history of music. Theoreticians heard the creaking of concepts like authorship, copyright, originality, musicianship—"Adventures Of Grandmaster Flash On The Wheels Of Steel" was the first time hip hop had been captured on record rather than translated; music's possibilities had been expanded dramatically.

4. Planet Rock

Of hip hop's founding trio, only Kool Herc never got the chance to transfer his skills to vinyl. Afrika Bambaataa, after a couple of false starts on Winley Records and a minor club hit with "Jazzy Sensation" (based on Gwen McCrae's "Funky Sensation"), was to emerge with one of history's most influential records. His renowned eclecticism would pay off as 1982's "Planet Rock" lit the fuse on not one but several genres of dance music. It's the source of electro, the root of Miami Bass music, it was an acknowledged inspiration for the genesis of house and was a massive influence on the way future hip hop records would be made.

Arthur Baker, the record's producer, recognized the significance of "Planet Rock" immediately. "Oh, I knew," he insists. "I knew before we even mixed it. I knew before there was even a rap on it. I went home the night we cut the track and brought the tape home, and I said to my wife at the time, 'We've just made musical history.'"

Baker, now one of dance music's most successful producers, had started making records a couple of years earlier, entering production after admitting to himself that he lacked the obsessive nature that makes a good disc jockey. Despite this, he has a DJ's acute instincts for the dancefloor and says he always made records with a particular club in mind, tailoring them to reflect the DJ's style and the feel and energy of the scene.

"Planet Rock," a sci-fi vision of crashing electronic drums and eerie keyboard melodies, was a reflection of Bambaataa's eclectic live performances, the record constructed by recreating elements from a stack of records high on his playlist, notably "Trans Europe Express" and "Numbers" by German synth futurists Kraftwerk. Bambaataa used to overlay Malcolm X speeches over "Trans Europe Express"'s thirteen minutes (Grandmaster Flash put it on when he needed a toilet break). Other elements added included the beat from "Super Sperm" by Captain Sky and a part of "The Mexican" by Babe Ruth.

"I'd been into Kraftwerk and Bam was into Kraftwerk, and we just had the idea of merging the two songs together," says Baker. "I used to hear 'Trans Europe Express' *all over* the place. In playgrounds, clubs, everywhere. At that time, I'd just moved to New York. When I had lunch, I'd sit in the park and there'd be guys with a big beatbox breakdancing to it. I used to hear it all over."

Though Bam had hardly any studio experience, he had very clear intentions for the project.

"I wanted it to be the first black electronic group," he says. "Some funky mechanical crazy shit with no band, just electronic instruments. When I made it, I was trying to grab the black market and the punk rock market. I wanted to grab them two together. I always was into 'Trans Europe Express' and after Kraftwerk put 'Numbers' out, I said I wonder if I can combine them two to make something real funky with a hard bass and beat."

It was probably the first hip hop record to use a drum machine (a Roland TR808), a fact which marks it as the starting point of the spin-off genre known as electro, and makes it a clear inspiration for Run DMC's beatbox workouts, a style which made them the undisputed leaders of hip hop's second wave. Baker, who had no experience with drum machines, recalls hiring a programmer out of the paper. "There was an ad in *The Village Voice*: 'Man with drum machine, $20 a session.' I don't even remember the guy's name or anything. So I got him for $20 and said: 'Program this.'" With its unshakeable beat, making mixing easier, "Planet Rock" couldn't fail to appeal to DJs.

The record's orchestra strikes and explosions were conjured out of a Fairlight synthesizer, "a $100,000 waste of space," as Baker puts it. The Fairlight, an Australian monster machine beloved of prog rockers like Peter Gabriel, was the sampler's hulking prototype, but since its sampling ability was minimal, Kraftwerk's melody lines were masterfully replayed by programmer/keyboardist John Robie.

Though it doesn't use sampling in the digital push-button sense that today's hip hop producers would understand, in conception "Planet Rock," like "Rappers' Delight" and Flash's "Adventures..." is a sampled record. In fact, all three songs show a considerable leap from the kind of organic sampling—the slow transmission of melodies and rhythms—which has always existed in music, to a more unmediated form of musical thievery. Here are songs made from very little more than snippets and snatches of others, not *versions* of other songs, not *improvisations* of other songs, but *copies*, either rerecorded from existing records or replayed note for note as exactly as possible.

And what set "Planet Rock" apart from its hip hop predecessors was that it was more than just a medley of pop hits. Baker and Bambaataa showed that sampled elements didn't necessarily have to be preserved intact: instead they could be collided into each other and woven into an intricate new sound tapestry. Today, this idea is regularly pushed to its limits, as producers make records from a multitude of tiny samples, often distorting and disguising them as much as possible. This process can be seen to have started with "Planet Rock," a record in which the DJ's pioneering ability to create new music from old was on clear display

Another key aspect of sampling was also highlighted: its ability to generate litigation. When "Rappers' Delight" had used "Good Times" so overtly, Chic's Nile Rogers and Bernard Edwards had been able to successfully claim full writing credit. On hearing "Planet Rock," Kraftwerk launched a lawsuit claiming royalties, which continued unresolved for many years. (Baker had in fact anticipated legal problems and had recorded an alternative melody line for the song. When Tommy Boy's Tom Silverman decided to release the record intact, Baker used this as the basis for Bambaataa's next record, "Play At Your Own Risk.")

As for the song itself, Bambaataa recalls the incredible reaction it generated.

"It was faster than any other rap record before, but the crowd was just dancing crazy and couldn't get enough of it, especially when I turned it over to the B-side with the instrumental—it just was a whole different thing to people. They'd heard the techno-pop records, but this was the first thing that had bottom, rhythm, the hard bass and all that." He first played it in the Boys' Club, in the Soundview Section of the Bronx, "a straight-up hardcore party. We had to play it four or five times. Because the crowd just went crazy."

Sampling

There were many other key records, of course. Kurtis Blow's "Christmas Rappin" (late 1979) would become the first major label release (on Mercury); Blondie would show their insight into the scene by releasing "Rapture" (1981), a US #1, important for the fact that it was by an established (and white) group. There was the post-Planet Rock boom of electro records, including the influential sound collages of Mantronix and Double Dee and Steinski, not to mention truckloads of records about breakdancing and Pacman. In the UK charts, the rap phenomenon started as little more than a joke and a series of novelty hits, including Kenny Everett's "Snot Rap" and Roland Rat's "Rat Rapping" (both 1983), were the first rap records to hit the mainstream. Luckily it was a different story in the clubs.

The explosion of recorded hip hop brought the DJ's cut-and-paste aesthetic to bear on studio production and furthered his inexorable move into the producer's chair. As early rap producer Marley Marl said in 1988, "There's not much of a difference between making a record and being a DJ, cutting up beats and stuff." Sampling would become especially important—used these days by everyone from bedroom dance producers to major rock bands—and making records this way is nothing more than using clever studio electronics to exaggerate what a good DJ can do on his turntables.

Indeed, the story of sampling is a tale of technology catching up with the DJ, of equipment being created that could do faster, more accurately and more easily what a DJ had long been able to. After the Fairlight Computer Musical Instrument, which allowed a tiny burst of sampled sound to be played, there was the EMU Emulator, first used in hip hop in 1982 by Marley Marl, who sampled the beat of a snare drum by accident during a remix he was doing. As he told writer Harry Allen, he realized the potential of this immediately: "I could take any drum sound from any old record, put it in here and get that old drummer sound." Old drummer Max Roach realized sampling's promise too, when he declared that, "Hip hop lives in the world of sound, not the world of music, and that's why it's so revolutionary." In contrast, the inventor of the Emulator, Dave Rossum, had little idea how important his machine would be. When asked in the early eighties whether sampling was the "future of the sound industry," he just laughed.

Sampling is now an accepted part of music, and record labels have entire departments selling sampling permissions. For many years, however, it generated considerable confusion, as everyone tried to avoid setting a standard practice. This was partly settled by a landmark decision in 1992 against comedy rapper Biz Markie for sampling part of Gilbert O'Sullivan's "Alone Again, Naturally" on his *I Need A Haircut* album. A federal judge, declaring "Thou shalt not steal," set the precedent by ruling against Biz and instead of having his record label (Cold Chillin', owned by Warner Bros.) pay O'Sullivan a royalty, demanded the offending sample be removed and the records containing it recalled.

The validity of sampling has long been debated, with irate musicians decrying it as noncreative. Hip hop fights back by claiming archivist status, referring to the interest it generates in older and forgotten artists. As Brooklyn rappers Stetsasonic rhymed in "Talking All That Jazz" (1988), "Tell the truth/James Brown was old/'Til Eric and Rak came out with 'I Got Soul'/ Rap brings back old R&B/And if we would not/People could have forgot."

In hip hop, reliance on sampling reached its peak in the late eighties in the wall-of-sound productions of Public Enemy and in the kooky grab-anything styles of De La Soul, before it became too expensive and/or risky to base records on large numbers of lengthy and recognizable samples. Commentator Nelson George makes the interesting point that it was only when hip hop started sampling white music—specifically in the Biz Markie case, and also in lawsuits relating to De La Soul's *Three Feet High And Rising* LP and Public Enemy's *It Take A Nation Of Millions To Hold Us Back*—that the industry perceived a problem.

Uptown Goes Downtown

Obviously, hip hop's graduation to vinyl was what allowed it to develop into an accepted musical genre, but in some people's view, the records were all that saved it from extinction. In the Bronx around 1979, after a peak of interest three years before, there was what Jazzy Jay refers to as "the drought," a time when grass roots interest in the music seemed to be dying. Party attendances were waning so fast that even the DJs themselves were convinced hip hop had already had its day. This before most of the world had even heard of it. "If you wasn't in hip hop, you wouldn't know about the drought," says Jay. "But around 1979 it was dying down. Everybody thought it was a dying art form." With the domination of crossover disco, audiences were turning their backs on hip hop in favor of more glamorous sounds. "Everybody was starting to swing back towards R&B and the club disco type scene. Everybody was getting *sophisticated.* They were through with hip hop: 'Oh, that's childish shit, we don't want to deal with it no more.'"

As well as saving the uptown scene, hip hop's first records had a phenomenal impact around the world; people remember hearing them and feeling they were listening to a completely new musical language. Naturally, there was an intense curiosity about where this music had started. Few were prepared to venture to a derelict Bronx basement to see it in its natural habitat, so hip hop gradually headed downtown. In doing this it became a vibrant part of postdisco clubland, meeting other established scenes and infecting other forms of music with its impressive DJ techniques and its innovative cut-and-paste creativity.

One style of music which is rarely connected with hip hop outside of cultural analysis is punk. And yet punk and hip hop shared a great deal more than a do-it-yourself ethos and a rebellious attitude. In fact, in cahoots with Manhattan's posey art world, punk was what brought hip hop to the world's attention.

Johnny Dynell, then starting his DJ career at the arty punk disco that was Manhattan's Mudd Club, remembers seeing Flash for the first time. It changed his view of DJing completely.

"I was a DJ but I always thought of myself more as a visual artist," he says. "I never saw DJing as artistic or creative. But then in 1979, I went with this friend to this church basement and I saw this battle, with Grandmaster Flash, Hollywood, all those early guys. And Flash was DJing with his toes. He was scratching, which I'd never heard before. He just rocked my world."

With his art school background, Dynell was thrilled by the conceptual implications of what he'd seen. "They were playing the same records I was playing, like James Brown, but what they were doing was taking two copies and going back and forth and making this new thing out of them. To me, coming from the art world, I thought it was brilliant. I thought, I'm going to have to tell Andy [Warhol] about this. This is incredible. It's like Marcel Duchamp."

Dynell was so excited that he tried to bring Flash together with Alan Vega of punk band Suicide, reasoning that Vega's music, like Flash's, was all about repetition. This ambitious attempt at cross-pollination raised little enthusiasm from either side. The collision of punk and hip hop would have to wait a couple of years.

Punks from the Bronx

In 1982 Malcolm McLaren declared, "I think punk rock is more alive in Harlem, in some respects, than it is in Bracknell."

Speaking in *Time Out* to Jon Savage, punk's master hypester spun an unlikely but intriguing yarn: "I was in the Bronx and I saw a boy and a girl, hand in hand, two black kids from the south Bronx, and they were walking down the street and they were both wearing 'Never Mind The Bollocks' T-shirts. Now they may not even have known of the Sex Pistols. They liked the look of it. They homed in on it. They saw something. They liked the words."

In August 1981 McLaren had been introduced to Afrika Bambaataa by Michael Holman, a black video artist who had taken him up to the Bronx to witness this amazing new music scene. The Sex Pistols' ex-manager was then steering the fortunes of pop band Bow Wow Wow, and formulating an ambitious album project based on smelting together the world's folk-dance music (this would become his *Duck Rock* LP). Despite a harrowing night during which he was, by most accounts, completely petrified, McLaren was mesmerized.

"It was like *Heart of Darkness*," laughs Holman. "I go to the hotel and I'm about to take them up to the Bronx on a summer evening—McLaren and Rory Johnston from RCA—and they're dressed like fucking pirates, in all that Vivienne Westwood gear. I thought we were gonna get stuck up or shot at any second. We finally get there and we go from a place that's completely deserted to masses and masses of kids, nothing but teenagers running from one corner to another, watching fights break out in the crowd. It's insane. Bottles flying everywhere. Malcolm's dressed like a pirate—and nobody noticed us. And now he starts to see the special effects DJs and the b-boys throwing down, and he's starting to see it all. So he says, 'Let's get out of here. But I've got an idea.'"

McLaren gave Holman $1,500 to put together a hip hop revue to open for Bow Wow Wow. Holman booked Bam and his cohorts, including the Rocksteady Crew (destined to become the world's most famous breakdancers), to open the band's New York show.

Ruza Blue, an English girl just into her twenties, was fresh off a plane from London for a two-week stay in New York. With her hair dyed in a black and white skunk cut, and with good contacts from her time on the London club scene, she would end up staying stateside. Employed for her fashion sense more than anything, she started working for McLaren and Vivienne Westwood. At the Ritz to see the Bow Wow Wow show, Blue, like most of the audience, found herself transfixed by the support act. A DJ, a stocky black guy with long lashes, was playing some kind of crazy chopped up disco-funk music, and a gaggle of hyperactive Puerto Rican teens were cutting up the dancefloor like demented spinning tops.

"I was like, 'What the fuck is this?' I was completely blown away," says Blue. "I just knew that whatever it was, I wanted to get involved in it."

She introduced herself to the Bronx kids after the show and in the coming weeks this punky British girl started venturing uptown to a club called Disco Fever.

"That was *the* hip hop club. No one downtown knew what the hell was going on up there, and that was wild. Flash was the DJ, Melle Mel was the MC and there were all these other MCs there. All the Sugarhill Gang were hanging out. I'd go up there and I'd be the only white face in the club, and that was wild, and I thought, 'Oh my god, I've got to bring all of this downtown.'"

Zulus take Manhattan—the opening night flyer for the legendary Wheels of Steel at the Roxy, taken from Kool Lady Blue's forthcoming book.

Blue asked Holman to put on a similar night for her at Negril, an East Village reggae joint run by Kosmo Vinyl, manager of the Clash (it had once been Bob Marley's Manhattan hangout). Holman brought down Bambaataa, Jazzy Jay and other Zulu Nation DJs, as well as Theodore and the Rocksteady Crew (who are Zulu-affiliates), and he and Blue began promoting the club to the punky downtowners.

"To get people to come down and check it out, I'd put people like the Clash on DJing," she recalls. "Combining the hip hop scene with the dregs of the punk scene brought the general public down. They were all like, 'The Clash are gonna be there, we'd better be there.' Once they arrived, they'd find what was really going on: the hip hop."

Holman insists that what drew the crowds was in fact the breakdancing. Punk was old news to his trendy Mudd Club friends, but breakdancing had them completely enraptured. "The first gig at Negril was a white guy, Nick Taylor, the High Priest on the turntables, Bambaataa, Fab 5 Freddy. Ramelzee is there putting up giant graf pieces, like armored letters. I had TV monitors showing this breakdancing footage I'd filmed. And Rocksteady Crew came down."

Holman eventually fell out with Blue (now Kool Lady Blue), who then took the concept to the next level. When Negril was closed by the fire department for overcrowding, she moved it to Danceteria, the trendy postdisco new wave club, and then, despite advice that she was mad to book such a huge space, to a 3,000–capacity roller-skating rink: the Roxy.

Everyone remembers the Roxy years as very special.

"The Roxy embodied a certain vision of what New York could be—a multiracial center of world culture, running on a current of flaming, uncompromised youth. The night had a thousand styles, a hundred dialects," recalled club queen Chi Chi Valenti.

Fridays from June 18, 1982 to the end of 1983, Kool Lady Blue's Wheels of Steel nights brought teenage Bronx b-boys together with spiky-haired punks, new wave musicians like Blondie and Talking Heads, and the gentry of the downtown art world, Andy Warhol included. It was one of those rare clubs where a true cross-pollination was happening; the opposite of the selective decadence of Studio 54.

Richard Grabel declared in the *NME*, "The feeling hits you when you walk into the Roxy on a Friday night the way it doesn't hit you in any other New York club. Everywhere else it's hesitation and uncertainty; at the Roxy, you know you're in the right place."

"It was fabulous. It was such a great feeling," says Johnny Dynell, one of the downtown DJs who played there at the time, recalling how the Roxy mixed up cultures and races. "That was the great thing about it. For me it was great; it was like both of my worlds. I would actually see both groups of my friends in the same place. That was really unusual." Dynell is sure that Blue was able to pull this off precisely because she didn't share the usual American assumptions about race. "An American couldn't do that. It took an English person."

Graffiti hung on great canvas sheets. Kurtis Blow, Sequence, Indeep performed. Fab 5 Freddy MCed. Run DMC had their first gig there, as did New Edition. Madonna sang there, starting her climb to stardom. The young Russell Simmons was running around networking. Every week a photographer would take pictures of the partygoers and a huge projector would show the portraits from the week before. With solid residences from the Zulu DJs Bambaataa, Afrika Islam, Jazzy Jay, D.ST and Theodore, and a constant breakdancing presence from the Rocksteady Crew, it drew an astonishing mixture of people, all riding the energy wave of this thrilling new music.

"I didn't have too many MCs. It was very focused on the DJ. I just kept it strictly DJs and dancing," says Blue. "I used to mix it all up. One night I had a whole troupe of American Indians doing sundances on the floor with the breakers. And that was like a really weird thing, but it worked. Or the Double Dutch girls, that was a complete fluke. I just saw them on TV one night in a McDonald's commercial and thought, they'd be good. Double Dutch girls have nothing to do with hip hop whatsoever. But all of a sudden, because it was showcased at the club one night, it was suddenly, "Oh, that's hip hop.'"

Fab 5 Freddy, who was steering Blue around the uptown pantheon of DJs and MCs, remembers the pivotal party as the night they screened *The Great Rock and Roll Swindle*, never released in the U.S., for the downtown glitterati.

"Right after the screening was around the time when the uptown heads from the Bronx, the hip hoppers, would start coming in, and these two scenes had never been mixed on this level. When you went to clubs, the downtown scene was pretty much predominantly white, and the uptown scene was black and Hispanic. And I couldn't imagine it was gonna work. I just anticipated kids from the Bronx beating the shit out of weird-looking punk rockers."

Instead, uptown and downtown were brought wholeheartedly together, a near-impossible achievement, even today. "The fashionable, on-the-edge punk rock people: when the movie ended, they stayed. And sure enough, here come all the little b-boys and b-girls, the fly guys and fly girls coming in. Kids was coming in just dancing, the energy was right. And it seemed to me, from that point on, you had this great mix. You had punk rock kids with mohawks, standing next to b-boys. It was the first time each other was seeing each other."

And the two scenes weren't just cautiously observing each other. A lot of real mixing was taking place. "A lot of fucking going on," laughs Freddy. "In short, a lot of fucking going on, because the hot dance at the time was the Webo, or the Freak. It came out of the Latin scene, where you would dance and you would get all up on a girl and really rub your two pelvic areas together, furiously. Like really wind and grind on each other." Since the white girls didn't know that it wasn't really cool to let just anybody do this, the uptown guys took advantage.

"You would see three or four Puerto Rican dudes all around one chick, and the chick would be like *[dizzy abandon]* 'Aahhh, this is great!' and them guys would be like, 'Yeeeahhhh!' There'd be a lot of energy like that, just people rubbin' on each other and shit. I used to be like, 'Yo! This is kinda hot!'"

Bambaataa has similar recollections.

"At first, people was buggin' when they first seen the punk rockers. Blacks and Latinos looked at them like they crazy. They had the spikes and the hair, and the colors and all the different clothing, but then when that music hit, you just see *everybody* tearing they ass up dancing."

Cold Crush were so taken by punk that they recorded "Punk Rock Rap," one of several records which failed to convert their legendary live shows into a recording career of any note. Cold Crush DJ Charlie Chase remembers the fun of the Roxy, including a night when Bianca Jagger was crowding the DJ booth.

"She was starry eyed, looking at me doing my thing on the turntable. She was fine. She was gorgeous. So I said to Bam, 'Who's that chick down there looking at me?' He says, 'Yo, that's Bianca Jagger.' I says, 'Bianca Jagger, you mean Mick Jagger's wife?' He says, 'Yeah.' I was like, 'Shit, we movin' on up now on the pussy scale! We movin' on up now, kid, this is big time!'"

Fab 5 Freddy was another crucial link between uptown and down. His motivation for bringing the two together was to gain art world respect for graffiti, which had evolved alongside rap music and breakdancing, and thereby further his own career as a graffiti artist. By the early eighties, Bronx spraycan Picassos were painting startling subway-train-sized masterpieces, and with the patronage of Andy Warhol, serious critical respect was being accorded to Jean-Michel Basquiat and Keith Haring, who had both started as graffiti artists. The galleries were jumping on this "street art" fairly quickly, and as he ventured deeper into the art world, meeting people like Glenn O'Brien, editor of Warhol's *Interview*, and Blondie's Chris Stein and Debbie Harry, Freddy soon found himself the Bronx's unofficial cultural ambassador.

This role led him to put together *Wildstyle* with novice director Charlie Ahearn, a film aimed at documenting the nascent world of hip hop. "I was serious about trying to be a painter, and I wanted this graffiti movement to be seen as a serious movement like Futurism or Dada. I didn't want us to be looked on as folk artists.

"I wanted to let people know that this was a complete culture, which I had read somewhere included dance, painting and music. So I wanted this film to be made to demonstrate that this graffiti thing, which was the focus, was a complete culture: that it was related to a form of music and related to a form of dance. Prior to that, nobody had seen these things as being connected."

He also arranged for DJs to spin at gallery events. Thanks to Freddy, Bambaataa had actually been playing for the downtown art trendies since

Boxing match—Tina Weymouth of Talking Heads and Tom Tom Club matches her boombox against Flash's, 1981.

1980, considerably before Holman and Blue's Negril and Roxy nights. Of the Bronx DJs, Bam had the closest connections to the downtown club world (as well as being in many of the record pools, his playlist was published in several dance music newsletters) and Freddy brought him down to play in Club 57 on St. Mark's Place, the Fun Gallery and the Mudd Club, afterdark home of postpunk weirdness. Since he was as flamboyant as anyone on this new wave scene in both his outlandish style (P-Funk goes witchdoctor) and his musical tastes, Bam couldn't wait to play for them. In fact, he soon started dying his hair green and orange and wearing a mohawk (later, he would team up with Sex Pistol John Lydon for a single, "World Destruction"). Make no mistake, Afrika Bambaataa was as punk rock as anyone in New York.

Hip Hop's Debt to Disco

Then there is disco. Musically, hip hop likes to set itself up in opposition to disco. The accepted wisdom is that hip hop was the ghetto's reaction to disco's gayness, its polish and its monotonous beat (all faults which today's hip hop folk are equally happy to ascribe to house). Actually, hip hop's debt to disco as a whole is high (just ask Def Jam mogul Russell Simmons, who was a regular at the Loft and Paradise Garage).

In addition to funk, disco was the music hip hop DJs played in the many years before the scene produced its own tunes. Compare playlists between the Roxy and the Paradise Garage for example and you'd find a huge amount of the same records. You can't get much more disco than Chic's "Good Times," a record deeply embedded in early hip hop, especially in Flash's career.

In fact, even before he knew of Herc, Flash was inspired to DJ by the black mobile DJs who visited Bronx block parties to play disco. Flash's earliest inspiration was Pete DJ Jones, a six-foot-eight stud from Brooklyn who is remembered for his harem of female assistants (including his capable stand-in spinner Ms. Becky Jones) who set up his equipment for him. Bambaataa's first hero was Kool DJ D, who played disco. Another influential mobile disco jock was Grandmaster Flowers, for whom Fab 5 Freddy has a particular affection. Freddy suggests that Flowers, also from Brooklyn, was actually the reason Flash took the name "Grandmaster." And that's not to mention the DJs like DJ Hollywood and Lovebug Starski, who were important to the development of rap but who were playing largely disco.

Flash's revolutionary DJ techniques were as much based on disco's seamlessness as on Herc's sweaty funk breaks. Indeed, the disco scene had actually developed a prototype version of the quick-mixing style even before Flash owned a pair of decks. Walter Gibbons was renowned for using quick cuts and two copies of the same record to extend favorite passages, and for favoring funky percussion-based tracks. Gibbons's style has often been compared to that of a hip hop DJ. He was doing all this around the same time as Flash, and in all likelihood he was even using some of the same records (Flash would have been unaware of these parallels). Before Gibbons, Michael Cappello, too, had a reputation for working fast cuts and extending the lightning short intros of that era's songs. Even Francis Grasso, the granddaddy of them all, can claim that as early as 1969 he was picking out drum breaks to excite his dancefloor.

Finally, without disco it is unlikely that the hip hop scene would have discovered so many of its important vinyl oddities. "The Mexican," a big Loft record long before it was a hip hop anthem, is a case in point, and there are many more. Bambaataa admits that many of his finds (including the all-important Kraftwerk) came about as a result of tips from the disco-based record pools he eagerly joined.

So, far from rejecting disco as some have suggested, the Bronx DJs simply reformulated it. Think of hip hop as an offshoot of early disco which then grew in parallel—a version of disco's dance revolution tailored to the tastes of the Bronx. The formula "hip hop = disco + ghetto" isn't too far from the truth.

The End of the Old School

Hip hop's first commercial flowerings came at the beginning of the eighties; by the middle of that decade, the music—and its culture—was developing into a very different thing. Though its horizon expanded and records streamed out, much of the original party spirit was fading. Blue and Freddy had taken hip hop on tour to Europe in 1982 and the music was beginning to make its presence felt, exerting influence on other genres. Breakdancing and graffiti were (over)exposed to the world in magazines and TV commercials. Around the corner, the next generation of rappers were honing their lyrics, ready to bring in the complexities of social commentary, hard-knocks reportage and character-filled fictions. Rap's first magnate Russell Simmons would soon spring Run DMC, Def Jam and his ruthless commercial instincts on the scene. KRS 1, Eric B. and Rakim, Public Enemy, the Beastie Boys and LL Cool J weren't far behind, not to mention the west coast's gang-obsessed entry into hip hop.

But while the music was establishing itself, its backdrop changed. Many of the new stars had middle-class suburban backgrounds, so the focus moved away from the inner city. Clubs like the Roxy closed or changed promoters and were soon violent ghetto outposts rather than happy melting pots. Reaganomics started biting hard, and crack made Bronx neighborhoods into war zones. Things weren't as much fun as before. It was the end of the old school.

Through these changes, the DJs carried on doing what they knew. And of all the people involved in creating hip hop, it was the DJs who came off worst when the music became commercial. Once there were records to be produced and stars to be created, the spotlight was firmly on the visible and charismatic MC onstage, not on the guy behind the decks. MCs didn't need a DJ to make records, just a studio and a producer. Most of the first wave of rap records were made using session musicians rather than turntables, and fairly soon there was easy-to-use sampling technology which meant anyone could loop up a sample and re-create the effects of a quick-mixing DJ.

After the old school, the DJs who made names for themselves were mostly famous as producers rather than for playing records, even though this was the source of their skill. From Eric B, Marley Marl, through Pete Rock, Large Professor and Premier, to Dr. Dre, The RZA and Prince Paul, to name just a few: these are all artists known for their studio work first and foremost. Hip hop moved decisively into the concert arena and became a performance spectacle more than a dancefloor genre. It maintained a thriving underground club scene, but there are very few hip hop DJs who have risen to fame through playing in clubs (with Funkmaster Flex and perhaps Stretch Armstrong as notable exceptions). Playing in concerts raised the DJ to the status of live musician, but reduced his input to a forty-minute showcase. And eventually there was the dreaded DAT to contend with—mistake-proof digital tapes which all but replaced DJs in live hip hop gigs.

But somehow, the DJ survived.

Turntablism

Hands whipping from one record to the other, stopping lightning fast on the crossfader in between, shoulders dipping slightly in time to the beat, but running no risk of unplanned movement, fingers moving in millimeter-precise formation, each flick or slide or rub controlled to a hair's breadth, and from the speakers a pounding beat with a barrage of skribbles and skratches running in and out of it, the bare bones of a song repeated and repeated and repeated, then let go, dropping into the climax of another.

The hip hop DJ's skills were showy enough to be pursued as an end in themselves, and as the rapper and the DAT stole the attention from the DJ, this is exactly what happened. The essential elements of hip hop DJing were distilled until it became an art form almost completely detached from its original dancefloor function.

It all starts with the scratch. With this technique, instead of playing records, or even recognizable *parts* of records, the DJ was able to chop previously recorded music up so finely that he was manipulating *sounds*—discrete notes or beats or noises—to make compositions, just like any other musician. In the hands of a skilled "turntablist," as these DJs eventually became known, the record deck became a genuine musical instrument. Indeed, with a recent surge of interest in this form of DJing, there are now several ensembles who play multiple Technics 1200 turntables as bands—each DJ/musician laying down component basslines, rhythms and lines of melody until a whole song is constructed. Some have even created systems of turntablist musical notation.

"Manipulating sound with just your hand is like a miracle," urges DJ Q-Bert of San Francisco's Invisibl Skratch Piklz crew, one of today's best-known scratch DJs. "The basic root of scratching is that the turntable is a musical instrument: you're figuring out all these time signatures and rhythms and patterns and notes."

Rob Swift of the X-Men (now, for superhero legal reasons, the X-ecutioners), another leading turntablist, agrees: "With the turntable you can create your own rhythms and sounds. In other words, the turntable can adapt or mimic the violin, the drum, the guitar, the bass. The turntable can morph into almost any instrument. Out of the turntable you can coax high pitches, you can coax low pitches, there are notes involved. If you move the speed a certain way you can create slow noises and fast noises. There are so many things you can do with the turntable, it's definitely an instrument."

At times, though, these scratch DJs seemed in danger of becoming obsessed hobbyists, competing against each other in increasingly esoteric competitions. What saved them from becoming completely isolated was that they were in a very real sense keeping alive the traditions of the "old school" of hip hop pioneers. While hip hop culture was moving fast into the mainstream, the turntablist DJ was preserving the music's roots.

By showing off his tricks, the hip hop DJ retained his status as a star performer and preserved an important aspect of the old school: the battle. Back in the Bronx, the most skilled DJs had been like feudal champions, and even when hip hop left the park for the concert hall, a rap group would find time in the show for the DJ to flex his muscles. In later years, the competition between DJs was formalized in showcase events. DMC, Disco Mix Club, a British-based DJ organization and the founders of dance magazine *Mixmag*, has been staging global competitions since 1987. NMS, the New Music Seminar, a New York music industry forum, ran a well-respected contest for many years. ITF, the International Turntablist Federation, is a more recent grass-roots collective with aims to gain "industry awareness in the future and development of the turntable as a musical instrument." Its contest has been rapidly gaining ground since starting in 1996. These competitions, filled with fast-scratching demons showing off the latest techniques, have kept much of the music's original DJ-based spirit alive. And following a recent resurgence of instrumental hip hop, interest in scratch DJing is greater and more global than ever.

Turntablism (the name is actually a neologism, coined as late as 1995) had been envisaged many years before hip hop's DJs made it a reality. The idea of playing recorded sound like an instrument has existed almost as long as sound recording itself.

French composer Pierre Schaeffer was the founding member of the avant-garde *musique concrète* school, which aimed to create music from natural sounds rather than with musical instruments. Through the forties and fifties, Schaeffer and his friends searched for new ways to record, play back and combine everyday sounds. Schaeffer experimented mainly with the new technology of magnetic tape, but he also messed around with turntables (he, of course, knew them as "gramophones"). Using a group of record players and a series of specially cut discs containing various captured sounds (some of which had been looped), he would produce a musical performance by changing the discs and adjusting the speed and volume controls.

American avant-garde composer John Cage had envisioned turntablism even before Schaeffer. Cage, who wrote that "Percussion music is revolution," had once performed a piece called "Cartridge Music" that involved rubbing a gramophone cartridge against various unlikely things. And in 1937, in a speech to a Seattle arts society, he praised the wonders of record-playing technology in highly prescient terms,

"With a phonograph, it is now possible to control any one of these sounds and give to it rhythms within or beyond the reach of imagination. Given four phonographs, we can compose and perform a quartet for explosive motor, wind, heartbeat and landslide."

Grand Wizard Theodore

Though they acknowledge these conceptual antecedents, turntablists trace their practical roots to hip hop's pioneer DJs, notably Grand Wizard Theodore, who, as we've seen, discovered the basic scratch noise—or at least figured that it could be used creatively—and Grandmaster Flash, who, as well as exploring the possibilities of scratching, started the craze for doing "body tricks" such as scratching with his elbow or using his belly to move the crossfader. There were in fact other, lesser-known DJs who came upon the idea of scratching, including a young spinner called DJ Tyrone, who played the breaks for a mobile disco setup of Cool DJ D. Tyrone, now all but forgotten, would do the simplest of scratching, just rocking the first beat of "Apache" back and forth before starting the song, or catching a break on the beat and doing a few *zik-zak* scratches before letting it go again.

"That's all he would do," recalls Zulu DJ Grandmixer D.ST. "But it was so dope, because nobody ever did it before. That's all he did, but it was enough to go, 'Ohhh, shit!'"

It is Grand Wizard Theodore, however, who most turntablists regard as their forefather. Theodore, surprisingly modest about his contributions, feels it was his adventurousness which set him apart.

"All the other DJs played music the same old way—'Bongo Rock' or 'Dance To The Drummer's Beat,' they played it the same way. I was like, 'You gotta be different.' That's why I started scratching and trying to do tricks with the records. It was so that people can look and say, 'Wow! This guy's really into it; he's not just putting one record after another—he's actually giving us a show.'"

D.ST is less reserved about Theodore's talents.

"He was phenomenal, and he was a prodigy. He was so skilled so young, it was ridiculous. It was effortless, his cutting ability. And remember he was a student of Flash, and Flash was a definite technician, but there was something about Theodore that made him different."

He puts this down to Theodore's highly expressive style.

"Without opening his mouth, he was articulate. He was physically articulate, in his gestures, and in his ability to be so precise, and synchronize. The way he would physically move—it was an expression. It may be esoteric to most, but I understood what he was saying. I'm a DJ and it was a language that I understood."

D.ST and "Rockit"

D.ST would himself have an important role to play, showing that scratching could have a melodic as well as a purely rhythmic impact. Beginning his musical career as a drummer in local Bronx party bands, Derek Showard (named D.ST, or D.St. for the fact that he hung out on Manhattan's Delancey Street) had been a regular DJ at the Roxy.

"By that time I was off the hook," he recalls. "I was doing all kinds of crazy tricks and stunts. I did everything but blow up the turntable. I was running around the place, coming back and cutting on beat with no headphones on. Breakdancing, kicking the mixer, everything."

Jean Karakos of electro label Celluloid hired him for a series of DJ gigs in Paris, and here D.ST's turntable dexterity brought him to the attention of jazz keyboardist Herbie Hancock and earned him pride of place in the grooves of Hancock's 1983 single, "Rockit."

This, more than any other track, was what propelled scratching into the world's consciousness. Aided by a great Godley and Creme video of sexy, robotic legs, it helped break MTV's de facto "No black music" policy and was a very visible video hit, even if it only reached #71 (it was #8 in the UK).

And D.ST's contribution was central to the song. He was providing more than just a few flourishes: his scratches were proper rhythmic, melodic elements—*notes*. Based on ideas he had recorded previously on his own single "Grand Mixer Cuts It Up," his scratching on "Rockit" was a series of climactic manipulations of part of Fab 5 Freddy's record "Une Sale Histoire (Change The Beat)." As it wove expertly between the bassline and melody, D.ST's urgent, insistent vinyl percussion was the essence of the record. Judged as 1983's Best R&B Instrumental Performance, "Rockit" also gave D.ST the honor of being the first DJ to win a Grammy award.

Following "Rockit," he was given a place in Hancock's band, both on tour and in the studio, but it took a long time for the other musicians to treat him as an equal. The penny didn't drop until during a rehearsal when they were badgering Hancock about a particular passage that actually D.ST had created.

"There was some trouble with the song, and they were asking Herbie—I think Herbie was just a little annoyed that day anyway—but they were saying, 'Hey, Herbie, this part?' And he said, 'Yo, man, don't ask me, ask *him*, he did the damn song.'"

However, D.ST didn't feel fully accepted as an artist until veteran producer Quincy Jones paid him a visit. "He took a chair, spun it around backwards and sat in front of me and said, 'Go ahead, play.' Just like that. And when I finished, he picked me up and gave me a bear hug, then it was official for me. He said, 'That's some dope shit you doin', that shit is so bad, it's incredible.' He said, 'You playin' triplets. You playin' a lot of triplets.' He was talking music. I was like, 'Yeah, I play triplets.'"

"Buffalo Gals"

Though "Rockit," by virtue of its MTV visibility, was most people's introduction to scratching, two important scratch-based records had preceded it. Flash's "Adventures on the Wheels of Steel" was crucial, as we've noted earlier, but another record was more widely heard, at least in Britain, than even the Grandmaster's finest hour. Malcolm McLaren's "Buffalo Gals," produced by Trevor Horn, reached #9 in the UK chart in late 1982.

The infectious single was the first release from McLaren's global folk-dance album, *Duck Rock*. A plundered collage based on a western square-dance song by one Peyote Pete, McLaren's version showcased the hip hop sound he had heard in the Bronx, notably the scratching talents of the World's Famous Supreme Team.

By day the Supreme Team, Just Allah the Superstar and C Divine the Mastermind, were a pair of Times Square rogues; by night they became rapping black nationalist DJs on obscure uptown radio station WHBI. Without really knowing what their contribution would be, McLaren brought the duo over to London where, despite some expensive studio shenanigans, they proved to be the essential cement that brought together his sprawling project. When the album was released, McLaren included on the liner notes some brief instructions on how to breakdance, as well as this helpful introduction to scratching:

"The performance by the Supreme Team may require some explaining but suffice to say, they are DJs from New York City who have developed a technique using record players like instruments, replacing the power chord of the guitar by the needle of a gramophone, moving it manually backwards and forwards across the surface of a record. We call it 'scratching.'"

By the mid eighties, hip hop DJ techniques, and scratching in particular, had had a dramatic effect on record production and there was a rash of scratch-like techniques used, made extremely easy by the emergence of the sampler. In the U.S., Steinski, aka advertising copywriter Steve Stein, used the concept of scratching to produce a series of records built around arresting collages of sound, using the studio to transcend his lack of turntable skills. In the UK the scene was greatly energized by these new ideas and many followed suit. And although the overuse of stuttering cutup vocals served to date many a pop dance remix of the time, important new possibilities were becoming clear.

Scratching as a concept was so influential that its impact spread even beyond music. It is possible to see it in the graphic design of the period, and given the new affordability of video equipment at the time, we were even treated to the new "art form" of video scratching, a precursor to TV's now ubiquitous fast-edits.

Transforming and Beat-juggling

Turntablism's next big step came when a pair of Philadelphia DJs found that by cleverly manipulating the mixers' crossfader switch, a basic scratch could be chopped up in all sorts of new ways. "Transforming," as this was called, made the scratch far more flexible and percussive, and gave the DJ more precise control over the sound. From here a whole vocabulary of techniques evolved.

Said to have been first practiced by DJ Spinbad, also from Philly, transforming was perfected through heated competition between DJs Cash Money and Jazzy Jeff. Cash Money showcased the transform to great effect in 1988, winning the DMC world DJ championships in the process. Jazzy Jeff (DJ for the Fresh Prince, aka Hollywood golden boy Will Smith) was the first to put it on record, in "The Magnificent Jazzy Jeff."

"They brought out all these weird styles and ways of scratching that had never been done before," explains Q-Bert. "When transforming came out it just flipped the whole scratching world around."

Today there is rarely anything like a simple scratch. A dedicated turntablist would be able to tell you the difference between the chirp, the tweak, the scribble, the tear, and the stab (or chop), not to mention the more advanced techniques of the transform, the hydroplane, the flare (a reverse transform), the orbit or the twiddle. The crab, a tricky technique which Q-Bert introduced in 1996, is worth describing to give an idea of the complexity involved in all this. To do a crab, your thumb pushes the crossfader to one side while your four fingers (of the same hand) each push it back momentarily to the other. And this is done in just a fraction of a second, while your other hand is doing something equally difficult with the actual record.

Now, if all this talk of scratching is making you itch, you might want to sit down . . . because in 1990 a whole new—*and even more complicated*—arena was opened up when "beat juggling" was invented.

Beat juggling goes a step further than scratching. Instead of using a relatively long noise (a scratch) for your rhythm and cutting it up with the crossfader to make a percussion sound, you use a record's individual drum beats more or less intact, juggling them, as the name suggests, to construct new and untold percussion patterns.

Roc Raida, another of the X-Men/X-ecutioners, explains with deceptive simplicity: "Beat juggling is taking two records, and just rearranging the beat." He clicks on his gold-plated Technics (his prize as 1995 DMC world champion) and demonstrates. With a flurry of little jet-fast moves, he flicks around with two breakbeat records. The result is an impossibly complex pattern of improvised drumming; he seems to be able to put each beat exactly where he wants it. As if that isn't enough, he then speeds up the pattern in a ballistic sequence of funky syncopation and double beats. It sounds, of course, nothing like the original records. Without a doubt, this is an act of musical creation.

Beat juggling was pioneered by "The Cut Technician" Steve D., who introduced it at the NMS Superman battle for world supremacy in 1990, and his mentor "The Cut Producer" Barry B. from Doug E. Fresh's Get Fresh crew. Roc remembers the astonishment it caused at the NMS competition. "People were just fucked up, like all the judges that were on the panel. Like Ritchie Rich, DJ Scratch, all the popular DJs at that time were just fucked up. 'Oaawww, what the *hell* is he doing?'" Steve D. won a hands-down victory and used his sudden notoriety to found the X-Men, for many years the preeminent scratch crew.

Beat juggling is really no more than a superfast version of the basic spinback techniques developed by Grandmaster Flash. The key move is the loop, in which a short drum pattern is repeated and repeated. The other important moves are the breakdown, a manual slowing down of a drum pattern whereby the DJ halts the record in between each beat; and the fill, where beats from a second record are added to the first to give double or triple beats or an echo effect. It's all reminiscent of the early days when one measure of a DJ's skill was how fast he could cut between two copies of Chic's "Good Times." D.ST remembers one of Herc's DJs, a guy named Imperial JC, who could catch it faster than anyone.

"JC was also the fastest out of everybody. Out of *everybody.* JC was the first person to go 'Good . . . good . . . good . . . good . . .' with 'Good Times.' I got this fast: 'Good times . . . good times . . . good times . . . good times . . .' I remember the first night I seen him do that and I went *[sharp intake of breath]* 'I gotta go home and practice.'"

Today's beat jugglers—who practice and practice and practice—can do even better. D.ST recalls judging a DJing competition alongside Flash, and the two being blown away by the phenomenal skills on show.

"I love to go to these new DJ battles and see these guys, 'cause now it's off the hook!" he enthuses. "To actually know that you have inspired a genre, a whole movement . . . I look at these guys and I think, 'We started that shit.' It's incredible what these guys took from us, and there's no end to it."

Turntablism seems to be finally shedding its image as a cryptic cult. All-turntable crews such as the Invisibl Skratch Piklz, the X-ecutioners and the UK's Scratch Perverts are performing as bands and the emphasis seems finally to be on what the finished product sounds like, rather than how many zillion flicks of the wrist a DJ can manage.

As Q-Bert puts it: "Before, when it was just a baby, it couldn't express itself in too many ways. You couldn't have a whole album of just the same baby talk. But now it's maturing. It's twenty years old, I guess it's becoming of legal age, so there's a lot more intelligence put into it, it's got much more of an intellectual life to it now, it can express itself in many more ways."

25 Years of Hip Hop

When it first came to mainstream attention, most people wrote hip hop off as nothing more than a novelty. Hardly anyone, even those on the scene, thought it would grow into an enduring influence on the world's music. Richard Grabel was one of the few believers. When he started writing about hip hop in 1979, he was confident that it was far more than a throwaway gimmick. He saw in it a formidable depth of commitment and musical understanding.

"Part of it was being able to see the dedication that these kids had," he recalls. "You'd see them coming to the Negril to breakdance and they had really practiced. You'd see Bambaataa or Flash come and do a DJ set and it was obvious that it wasn't something they'd just thrown together. The crates of records that they were lugging down to these clubs spoke of a real collector's and connoisseur's knowledge of music that was deep, and wide. Hearing those DJs made me think, 'Wow, it's not just throw your hands in the air and let's throw a party.' These guys really had a deep knowledge of musical history."

In 2000, hip hop is probably the dominant force in music. Two years ago it overtook America's biggest-selling genre—country—with sales of 81 million CDs, tapes and albums. Its vast cultural influence can be seen worldwide in the fashions it has spawned, the way it has made black American English a global vernacular, and in its pervasive influence on other musics.

In the mid eighties, Cornel West, one of many sociologists intrigued by hip hop's rise, asked himself, "Where will rap end up?" His answer was telling: "Where most postmodern American products end up: highly packaged, regulated, distributed, circulated and consumed."

Such is hip hop's mastery of marketing that its current kingpin, Sean "Puffy" Combs of Bad Boy Records, seems able to have hits in his sleep, most of them cynical karaoke-style remakes of tried and trusted pop hits with the latest ghetto sensation rapping over the top. Amazingly, despite having no studio experience, Puffy became the world's highest paid remixer overnight, simply because of the selling power of his name and his unapologetically commercial ear. He personifies the crass materialism that has infused hip hop (a result, no doubt, of twenty-five years of escalating bragging), but he has an undeniable insight into the business of music.

Giving his impression of hip hop's cultural power, he told *Time* magazine, "In five years, if Master P. and I were to endorse a presidential candidate, we could turn an election. Hip hop is that deep."

All this from just two turntables and a crate of your mom and pop's old records.

TEN
GARAGE

I'll Take You To Paradise

"I'm not a fan of disco. I find it mindbending... It's a contributing factor to epilepsy. It's the biggest destructor in history in education. It's a jungle cult. It's what the Watusis do to whip up a war. What I've seen in the discos with people jogging away is just what I've seen in the bush."

—Harvey Ward, Director General of the Rhodesian Broadcasting Company

"I know that it is not one record that makes a night, it's the combination of all things together that leaves the person satisfied."

—Larry Levan

Homer Simpson once confessed that few songs had moved him as much as Lipps Inc.'s "Funkytown." However, when the eighties dawned, he happily applied a DISCO SUCKS bumper sticker to his car.

Homer sums up the mainstream's engagement with disco. Its brief crossover pop phase gave people songs they would hum forever; but as a style of music, few saw it as more than a glittery craze that outstayed its welcome.

In Chicago, radio DJ Steve Dahl hated disco so much that he raised a "disco destruction army" and mobilized it to attack disco wherever possible. His followers rallied around the overtly homophobic "Disco Sucks" slogan and fought the evil faggot music by haranguing club DJs whenever it was played. "Disco music is a disease. I call it disco dystrophy," Dahl ranted over the airwaves. "The people victimized by this killer disease walk around like zombies. We must do everything possible to stop the spread of this plague."

One stunt saw Dahl—who had quit radio station WDAI in disgust when it switched to an all-disco format—giving away one hundred tickets to a Village People concert provided the recipients took marshmallows bearing the words "Disco Sucks" to throw at the band.

Dahl's greatest moment came on July 12, 1979 when he whipped up thousands of baseball fans into a full-scale antidisco riot resulting in injuries and arrests. A joint promotion between Dahl's all-rock station WLUP and the Chicago White Sox, his "disco demolition" rally at the team's Comiskey Park was centered around giving fans reduced admission to a doubleheader against the Detroit Tigers in exchange for depositing a disco record at the turnstile. More than 10,000 discs were collected and then at halftime blown up inside a container in the center of the field. Middle America's antidisco feeling couldn't have been made clearer as a violent crowd invasion ensued, with chanting protesters fighting, starting fires and digging up turf. Police failed to restore order in time for the second game and the White Sox forfeited it.

Dahl's campaigning was far from unique. Dislike for disco was everywhere. The rock generation saw it as the antithesis of all that was holy: no visible musicians, no "real" stars, no "live" performances. It was music based wholly on consumption, music with no aesthetic purpose, indeed with no purpose at all other than making your body twitch involuntarily. Dehumanizing, expressionless, contentless—the judgements were damning.

"Kill Disco" became a popular piece of graffiti. New York's WXLO held "No Disco Weekend." Pasadena DJ Darryl Wayne made his show's motto "Abolish disco in our lifetime," and took calls from listeners suggesting how this could be done. "Cut off the Bee Gees' estrogen supply," was one idea. All over the world, the disco menace was confronted; right-wing Americans denounced it as morally degraded and probably a form of communist mind control; communist countries banned it as decadent and capitalist. Perhaps the most bizarre expression of antidisco sentiment came from Turkey, where scientists at the University of Ankara "proved" that listening to disco turned pigs deaf and made mice homosexual.

Given the depth of this backlash, it's hardly surprising that the story of popular music has largely been revised to disavow its debt to disco. This often has to do with homophobia, but usually it is because those writing the history, like their readers, equate the genre with the overexposure of a few whitewashed and commercialized acts, and are ignorant of much of the artists and music which either came before or lay beneath. If you wanted to sum up the spiritually powerful (and highly influential) dance music which rocked clubs like the Loft or the Gallery, you might talk about MFSB, Chaka Khan or Eddie Kendricks, or a host of lesser known names who created raw, earthy and uplifting disco; you certainly wouldn't leap to mention Donna Summer, KC and the Sunshine Band, the Village People or (of all people) Abba. The poppy, flat-footed rhythms of disco's most formulaic moments might be what most people remember, but they should hardly be seen as exemplary.

Indeed, reports of disco's death were always greatly exaggerated. Its brief commercial era may have ended in dramatic collapse, but the music that originally drove the scene remained alive and reasonably well and has been with us ever since. Such global forms as house and techno are really nothing more than disco continued by other means. Disco simply underwent some cosmetic enhancements, changed its name a couple of times, and had its mail forwarded to a less glitzy neighborhood.

From Disco's Ashes

In the early eighties, in keeping with the well-worn dialectics of nightlife, as the wealthy and celebrated left the clubs, the young and unsung flooded into their place. In New York, the gay dancefloors which had produced disco began to project a new underground vitality, as did the straight black and "ethnic" (the city's racial code for Italian and Latino) places where the city's Latin music flourished alongside the newer forms of hip hop and electro. The DJs in these clubs were suddenly producers and remixers; they now had the power not just to tailor their music live for their dancefloor, but to record original material and have it released commercially. With the support of a growing network of independent dance labels and with the inevitable attention of key radio DJs, they could even use their clubs to push records (including their own) into the mainstream charts. The DJ had proved he knew more than anyone about making dance music. Now, thanks to the structures set up during disco, he could increasingly put this expertise into practice.

The other crucial developments were technological. As the silicon revolution brought studio equipment crashing down in both size and price, the leap from DJing to producing was narrowed even further. And in the first half of the eighties, eager to nourish their dancefloors with something new, a generation of young jocks jumped this line. Several such DJs proved to be so innovative, both behind the decks and in the studio, that they would later be credited with kickstarting entirely new genres of music. House, techno, garage, hi-NRG and electro were all sired by DJs around this time, and though each took a dramatically different set of chromosomes from its mother, all were born from disco's broad hips.

As the age of the DJ-producer began in earnest, dance music entered one of its most fertile periods. In Chicago, the experiments of Frankie Knuckles and Ron Hardy gave us house, aided by legions of bedroom superstars laden with cheap synthesizers and drum machines.

In nearby Detroit, a similar process brought the world techno as Juan Atkins, Derrick May and Kevin Saunderson programmed their music machines and intellectualized about the bittersweet futurism of the decaying motor city.

In New Jersey, Tony Humphries was championing the more soul and gospel-influenced side of disco's remnants and planting the roots of what would become known as the Jersey sound, or (courtesy of a slight misnomer by British journalists) as garage.

And by focusing on other components of disco—this time its fastest, campest elements—a group of DJs and producers set the stage for hi-NRG, or boystown as it was first called.

After Bambaataa and the Zulus' Roxy years, the raucous sounds of hip hop and electro were incubated, together with the city's Latin dance sounds, in a vast New York club called the Funhouse. Here a cult of personality emerged around a young Hispanic DJ, John "Jellybean" Benitez, who would become a star remixer and the first DJ to sign a major label album deal as an artist in his own right. Meanwhile, over at Danceteria, Mark Kamins, Johnny Dynell and Anita Sarko exerted a considerable influence on the city's music as they exposed it to the freaky sounds of European postpunk funk and American new wave (Kamins also steered the young Madonna into a record contract).

Larry Levan and the Paradise Garage

One club more than any other was to pave the way for disco's many offspring to take their first steps: New York's Paradise Garage. Open from 1977 to 1987, the Garage was the crucial link between disco and the musical forms which evolved from it.

Here a young DJ, Larry Levan, exemplified his profession's new possibilities—consolidating the club DJ's new role as producer, remixer and commercially powerful tastemaker. Levan showed just how much creative control a DJ could exercise, and with one of the most devoted and energetic groups of clubbers ever, used the Garage to preserve and amplify much of disco's original underground spirit. In doing this he carved out an oasis of shared pleasure in a city that was becoming increasingly ruthless, and grew to enjoy such a passionate relationship with the people on his dancefloor that they worshipped him more or less as a god. The Garage sound system is reckoned by many to have been the greatest of them all. Elements of the club have been carefully copied by many which came after it. It even has a genre of music named after it. Today, Larry Levan is regularly hailed as the world's greatest ever DJ, and his club elevated to mythic status whenever it is mentioned.

"This is the Paradise Garage in a nutshell," says New York DJ Johnny Dynell. "One night, Chi Chi, my wife, was bartending at the Garage. And, having worked at Danceteria doing the same, she couldn't believe it when she saw these boys making everything so clean. They would take the garbage out and then wash and scrub the garbage can, then dry it, and put a new garbage bag in. She was in awe at the *love* these kids showed that garbage can. Because to these kids, it's the temple. It's sacred. This isn't just a garbage can, this is a garbage can *at the Garage.* It's very Old Testament. And for everyone there, it really was the temple. It was sacred ground."

The Paradise Garage inspired an unparalleled reverence. It dominated gay New York's dance vista for a full decade, with only the Saint—which catered for a very different crowd—as a serious rival. For its members the Garage was a sanctuary from an increasingly cruel and voracious city, a role made more poignantly necessary as AIDS' viral vapor trail drifted over New York. Dance there and you were treated as an honored guest, with a level of courtesy and respect that is virtually unheard of in clubs today. "You felt special," says Danny Tenaglia, one of many DJs inspired by early visits to the Garage. "You felt like you were an elite group, with people who were on the same level of understanding about music as you." In a drab district in southwest Manhattan, its owners created a private world based on disco's original ethos of loving equality. In stark contrast to the harsh city lights outside, the Garage represented freedom, compassion and brotherhood. It was as much community center as discothèque.

Dave Piccioni, owner of London's Black Market records, then living and DJing in New York, was a regular at the Garage in the late eighties. "It was New York cutthroat money time," he remembers. "Everybody was sticking knives in each other's backs. It was dog eat dog. Aggressive. Dealing, 60,000 people living on the street. It was a dog of a place to live in. And then you'd go to this little oasis, where people were really well mannered and friendly to each other. You just felt completely comfortable. People of a like mind who shared something, and that was an open mind. America is a very narrow-minded place. The thing they had in common wasn't just getting high, like it is here—it was much more than that. That was what was so great about it."

Whether the club's central figure, Larry Levan, was really the greatest DJ ever—as is often stated—is irrelevant. What is more important is that he acted as the central inspiration for almost every DJ above the age of thirty in New York, many of whom are now titans of dance music. David Morales, Danny Tenaglia, Cevin Fisher, Junior Vasquez, Danny Krivit, Kenny Carpenter, François Kevorkian, Joe Clausell—they all owe a debt to Larry Levan. All readily acknowledge it.

Junior Vasquez built his whole career on following the lead he set.

"I idolized Larry," he says. "I still do to this day, he was the greatest. And I do live in the past when it comes to that, and I keep striving, wanting to create that feeling, that lounge, that booth." Junior's Sound Factory was a conscious copy of the Garage and at its best came close to the same level of courtesy and feelings of community. When the Factory first opened, the Garage's illuminated sign was hung over the entrance (a rather presumptuous move which was quickly stamped on by irate Garage-heads). The Shelter, now Vinyl, home of the well-known Body And Soul nights, was another club founded more or less wholly on preserving memories of the Paradise Garage.

Garage lore has been made more enduring by the fact that Levan died at the tragically young age of thirty-eight, after suffering heart failure (Levan had a life-long heart condition, though his legend-affirming drug habit can't have helped). Music mythology loves nothing more than a good-looking corpse, which lends Danny Tenaglia's description of Levan as the Jimi Hendrix of dance music yet more aching resonance.

Reade St.

Larry Levan was born Lawrence Philpot on July 21, 1954 in Brooklyn. By the time he was a young teenager he had started to make the magical trek across the East River to Manhattan with his boyhood friend from the Bronx, Frankie Knuckles. The pair, both black and gay, were inseparable, their personalities a perfect yin and yang—Levan excitable, childlike, eccentric; Knuckles laid-back, personable, just *nice.* After they had worked together at the Gallery and then, as DJs, at the Continental Baths, Knuckles moved on to Chicago, where he catalyzed house music. Levan moved firstly to the Soho Place, then to the Garage prototype Reade Street.

At 143 Reade Street, this two-floor warehouse space was one of many clubs that had sprung from the idealism of David Mancuso's Loft. Levan was invited to spin there by its owner Michael Brody. This is where the seeds of the Paradise Garage were sown. It was also, according to those who went, even better than the Garage.

Like the Garage, Reade Street was a predominantly black club, with a clientele that comprised everyone from telephone operators to dancers from local ballet company Alvin Ailey's, to singers on downtime like Teddy Pendergrass, Rick James and Chaka Khan. It was almost exclusively gay. The top floor was a cavernous loft space, with balloons, gently pulsing lights and a gigantic silk parachute draped above the dancefloor. At the end of each Saturday, balloons would be released from above and cascade on the dancers below. Reade Street was a wild scene.

It was postgay rights but pre-AIDS; it followed the Loft and anticipated the Garage. Everything came together perfectly and for a brief disco moment, Reade Street was the place to be.

"The punch was always spiked," chuckles clubber Yvon Leybold. "Someone was always passing a joint around. Somebody's passing around the opium pipe. Somebody's handing out the blotter. It was very free and open. I remember going there dancing *topless*. It was hot in there, but it was so much fun that *you wanted* to take your clothes off. I even remember having sex there a couple of times!"

Reade Street finally closed in the early summer of 1976, after the fire department had made one too many visits. Michael Brody and Larry Levan's next venture, in tandem with sound man Richard Long and aided by Brody's lover, West End Records' Mel Cheren, would be a much more professional affair.

The Garage

Walking up the darkened ramp, with tiny flickering egg-strobes running down each side, was like heading along a darkened runway—with the lift-off chemically, rather than mechanically, provided. Inside there was an alcohol-free bar decorated with murals of Greek and Trojan warriors locked in battle—from where you could catch a tantalizing glimpse into the huge DJ booth—changing rooms, a cinema—through which you could ascend up to a roof garden—and a giant, relatively spartan dancefloor.

The Paradise Garage was located on 84 King Street in west SoHo in—you guessed it—an old parking garage. It opened in the autumn of 1977 with a series of "construction parties," held when it was nothing more than a raw space and an amazing sound system. Building work continued, and gradually the club began to take shape—and as it grew, so did Levan's reputation.

Larry Levan's greatness is proof that technical prowess is but a tiny part of DJing. Technically speaking, he was no match for the likes of Walter Gibbons or, indeed, most of the early disco-mixers. His mixing was slapdash, and he'd often prefer to slam something in awkwardly rather than seamlessly blend. What made him great was his sense of drama, his obsessive control of all aspects of his clubbers' experience, and his heightened ability to transmit his personality through the very grooves of his records.

Levan was an audacious programmer. His high-octane, seat-of-the-pants DJ style was the aural equivalent of a highwire walk across Niagara Falls. He was a dazzling sound man and the crystalline system, although constructed by Richard Long, was honed, manipulated, tweaked and *loved* by Levan.

He had a fierce controlling instinct, as well as a self-destructive streak that manifested itself in tireless drug abuse. This lent the Paradise Garage an aura of intense drama. And thanks to his different club jobs—from spiking the punch at the Gallery to doing the lights at the Continental Baths—he understood how to make a visit to his nightclub a total experience. Each week was a lesson in improvisation, an unscripted performance on the emotional level of high opera. What would be served up on a particular night depended on any number of variants, with only one thing certain: Levan gave good show. He could shock you. He could thrill you. He could amaze you. He could even appall you. The only certainty was that he would surprise you.

Rarely has a DJ's mood been broadcast quite so powerfully to a dancefloor. By the records he played and the order he played them in, you could tell whether Levan was feeling good or bad, whether he'd just had an argument, whether he was tired or whether he was ready to party.

David Morales, who was lucky enough to play at the Garage as a young DJ, says Levan's mood swings were dramatic. "He could be *shit* for seven hours and he could take fifteen minutes and kick the shit out of you, and that made your night! That's what it was about. There was nobody that was able to do that."

Simply by force of will, Levan could take records that every other DJ in the city was playing and make them recognizably *his*, "Love Is The Message" being the most famous. Levan made this firmly a Garage record, just as David Mancuso had long before made it a Loft record and Nicky Siano had claimed it for the Gallery.

Unquestionably, Siano and Mancuso were his main inspiration (he'd had brief affairs with each) and in the early years it was possible to trace each of Levan's records back to either the Loft or Gallery. But he never hid his obvious debt to his forebears. "Nicky Siano, David Mancuso, Steve D'Acquisto and Michael Cappello, David Rodriguez," Levan told Steven Harvey. "This is the school of DJs I come from."

Levan could drive dancers wild with desire or work them into a fury of frustration, often at the same time. Sometimes he would simply disappear from the booth. Occasionally, he would play an hour of dub reggae, or the same record three times in succession. Once (while sitting on a rocking horse), he had the whole club dancing to nothing more than a few of his live keyboard doodles, unaware that the record he was accompanying had finished minutes ago. Occasionally he would collapse in a stupor; somehow always managing to keep the party—if not himself—going. One time François Kevorkian, a regular guest DJ there, remembers him putting on a movie instead of music. "What are you gonna do? There's two and a half thousand people there and you suddenly play *Altered States*. That's the kind of freedom that I think people need to know exists."

"He had *attitude*," remembers Cevin Fisher, another DJ/producer whose formative years were spent on the floor at King Street. "He would leave the DJ booth and the record would end and just spin around. Who knows what he was off doing . . . Actually, we all know what he was doing! And he would come back into the DJ booth totally trashed, lift the needle off the record and start it again. People got off on that."

Although the Garage had a very talented and experienced light man in Robert DaSilva—who had also worked the lights at the Gallery and Studio 54—Levan had a second set of controls fitted on a rail along the top of the booth. When the mood took him—when he was ready to take people for a *ride*—he would draw the console towards him and decant the booth of its occupants. It was like clearing the flight deck for takeoff.

"They used to do these blackouts and they would switch *all* of the lights out," recalls Johnny Dynell. "Exit lights and everything. Totally illegal, you can't turn exit lights out! You couldn't see a hand in front of your face." He would build the intensity to a peak and then let fly with an a cappella or sound effect—one time Dynell recalls him playing the Wizard of Oz—before the system would crank up and—BAM!—he'd hit the crowd with another favorite. "Oh, man, it was fabulous. He would just take control," sighs Dynell.

"The difference between the Garage and other places, was that he was controlling the entire environment," says Danny Krivit.

This was a club poured full of love and devotion. It was reflected back from its members. "I feel like I'm part of something important, a nightly musical happening, when I come to the Garage," commented Robert, a Garage regular, in the book *Nightlife*. "Something that goes beyond the people and the dancing. For me, it has mostly to do with the music. The songs Larry plays are so new, so different from what's going on in other clubs. I know when I come to dance here that I'm hearing songs that very few people outside the Garage, even in New York City, have heard yet."

Levan's life revolved around the Garage. When it first opened he even lived there, a fact which drove Michael Brody to distraction. During the day, Levan's coterie would assemble at King Street and hang out, do drugs, play on that pristine system and roller-skate around the dancefloor. Johnny Dynell recalls receiving DJing lessons from him during these languid afternoons. Levan, conscious of the lineage from which he'd sprung, was keen to pass on disco's traditions. "You don't realize how much power you've got up there," he would tell Dynell, pointing up at the DJ booth.

On Friday and Saturday evenings, Levan's booth took on the role of private party zone where only the Garage famous were granted access. "The Garage had a very social DJ booth," recalls Krivit. "It was huge; like another club in itself. There was a real scene going on there. You were right above

Happy as Larry—inside the booth at the Paradise Garage with its loving driver Larry Levan, 1986. © Tina Paul.

the dancefloor and you'd get the whole feeling of the crowd. The light show, everything."

Boy George wrote about the scene in his autobiography, *Take It Like a Man.* "We made friends with DJ Larry Levan and hung out with him in the booth overlooking the dancefloor. That's where all the drugs were. I took my first line of coke in that dark disco cocoon."

The Power Behind the Myth

The mythology of Larry Levan increases with each passing year. As critic Vince Aletti says, "The Larry legend is beyond any reason; it feeds on itself to some extent." Sadly, it's doubtful whether he would be held in such high regard if he had remained alive. Dave Piccioni is skeptical about the hype surrounding him. "I hate this shit that just because someone dies, they have this mythology that grows around them. If he was alive now, he'd probably be playing the same stuff that Tony Humphries plays."

Much of his fame came from simply creating the best club in town. In both 1979 and 1980, the *Billboard* Disco Convention voted the Paradise Garage best club and best sound system. "There's nothing else that will remotely compare to what the Garage was," says François Kevorkian, marveling that Levan managed to re-create the generosity and intimacy of David Mancuso's Loft (as well as the precision of its sound system) on such a large scale. "He understood everything about what the Loft did, but very quickly took it beyond all that into his own domain. I think what Larry did was nothing short of absolutely astounding."

But many have criticized his technique—or at least his consistency. "Larry was awful, he was too loud, he'd leave big gaps and let records jump, he'd play ballads in the middle of the night," said DJ Bruce Forest, one of Levan's contemporaries. "But that was only five percent of it. On the other hand, he had an atmosphere nobody will achieve ever again. He made it seem like he was playing records to you in his living room. His rapport with the crowd was immense. If you went to the club one week and a light bulb was red and the next week when you returned it was blue, people would say, 'Larry changed the bulb this week.'"

Nicky Siano, never a DJ to restrain the energy of his dancers, feels that Levan could be a little *too* controlling at times. "If I saw it getting out of hand on the dancefloor, I would think, 'Oh, this is cool, show me how I can go further than this.' That would scare Larry. He would try to bring it back. My thing was [*Siano laughs uproariously*]—*out of control!*"

And clubbers Yvon Leybold and Terry Hayden insist that Levan's previous club was far superior to the Garage. Things were never really the same once AIDS cast its dark shadow. The abandon and freedom they'd experienced at Reade Street would never be recaptured.

"Don't misunderstand me," says Leybold. "The Garage was a nice place—for the lack of having anywhere else to go—but it was certainly no Reade Street."

"The Garage was more focused on making money," adds Hayden.

In truth, Larry Levan's prominence derived from several sources besides his DJing. As well as the majesty of the Garage, his friendship with radio DJ Frankie Crocker gave him influence unprecedented for a club DJ. A record could go from the floor of the Garage one night and find itself on the platter at WBLS the next. After that the rest of America would join the party. It became an informal industry test center.

"Larry had the ear of Frankie Crocker at WBLS," explains Vince Aletti. "At that point it was *the* radio station and he was *the* big disc jockey. So Larry became incredibly important. Beyond the fact that he was a good disc jockey and he had a great club, he had the ear of the most important radio disc jockey in the city."

In stark contrast to much of American radio programming—which moves at a notoriously ponderous pace—Crocker was swift in bringing records to the airwaves. Arthur Baker recalls bringing "Walking On Sunshine" by Rocker's Revenge to the Garage for Levan to play. The following day, Crocker gave it its first airing on WBLS.

The two were both mavericks, kindred spirits. Nicky Siano thinks the fact that they were both black had a lot to do with their closeness. "Larry was the only really successful black DJ, so they became friends, I think, because of the race issue." In any case, Crocker was no ordinary radio hack. Born in Buffalo in upstate New York (a city that produced many great black radio DJs, including Eddie O'Jay and Gary Byrd), he surfed the wave of post–civil rights opportunity, getting his first break on Pittsburgh's WZUM and moving swiftly to WWRL in New York. Here he built up a considerable female following, with his racy patter and throaty velvet delivery. Oozing out of the speakers like maple syrup, he was the airwave equivalent of Barry White, and known variously as "Lover Man," "Fast Frankie," "Chief Rocker" and "Hollywood."

Crocker became one of the first DJs to make the crossover from black radio to white when he joined the all-white "Good Guys" team on WMCA in 1969, but it was at WBLS in the seventies where he had his most successful reign, championing the jazz-fusion of Grover Washington Jr. and Miles Davis, and the socially conscious soul of Donny Hathaway and Marvin Gaye, as well as incorporating white records like those of the Bee Gees and Queen into his playlists. The Garage was the perfect hunting ground for a smooth operator like Crocker, who appreciated the catholic tastes of Levan. "The Garage was the place he knew he could go and be comfortable and hear new things," says Aletti.

Levan naturally shot to the top of the list of DJs when it came to receiving new product. One record promoter pointed out, "He's someone to whom top record industry people hand-deliver new albums. When a record goes here, we know we've got a hit."

The Garage's power was equally apparent in its effect on the local record trade. In late 1978 a husband-and-wife team, Charlie and Debbie Grappone, opened a compact little rock music store called Vinylmania on Carmine Street in Greenwich Village. It happened to be just around the corner from the Paradise Garage and Grappone soon noticed the bedraggled hordes streaming towards the subway each Saturday morning. People started asking for strange records that Grappone—who prided himself on his knowledge of music—had never heard of; the stuff "that Larry played."

As soon as they could, the Grappones opened a dance music shop next door to their rock store. They were the first retailers to capitalize on the desirability of 12-inch singles, especially the new promo-only releases aimed at club DJs. They recruited two Garage devotees, Judy Russell and Manny Lehman, and once the store began to orient its stock towards the Garage, sales went through the roof.

"You should've seen Saturday morning," says Grappone in a thick Brooklyn accent. "Thirty-five, forty, fifty people *waitin'* for me to get there. I'd open up the door and Manny would put somethin' on, because Manny had been *there* the night before. 'Shit! That's what he played last night.' We'd sell sixty copies of a record between ten and eleven in the morning. *Sixty copies!*" The crowds were unbelievable. "You would look in the store and think there was something wrong. There was guys crushed. *Crushed!*" The store would sell hundreds of copies of Garage favorites. "Larry was the king," grins Grappone. "If Larry played the record, it was going to sell at Vinylmania."

One such record was "Heartbeat" by Taana Gardner. Originally produced by Kenton Nix for West End Records, it was remixed by Levan and broken at the Garage. "Heartbeat" was an oddball song, with a slow, capricious tempo, dizzy vocal delivery and off-key accompaniment. The first time Levan played it, the reaction was not favorable. "When 'Heartbeat' came out there wasn't hip hop on the radio like there is today," recalls Danny Krivit. "There wasn't any downtempo music like 'Heartbeat.' And when he put that record on, a full club of people left the room to get food. There was not one person left on the floor." But Levan persisted, often playing it several times in an evening. Soon people would run to the floor when it was aired. "By the end of the month, there was no one left *off* the floor when they played that record," says Krivit. "And now, of course, they had to go to Vinylmania and bug Charlie for it." Vinylmania went on to sell over 5,000 copies of "Heartbeat." It is still their biggest-selling record.

The Music of the Paradise Garage

The Garage presided over the death of disco and its rebirth in a hundred forms. Although it charted a route out of what had become an increasingly commercialized music, its roots were firmly embedded in disco—after all, the club opened in 1977, just before *Saturday Night Fever* brought it tearing into the mainstream. But then disco boomed and busted and DJs had to search that little bit harder and that little bit longer to find the right records to feed their ever hungry dancefloors.

Nowhere did this happen more spectacularly than at the Paradise Garage. Here Levan showed that dance music could be made from a multitude of sources, that in the wake of disco there was a whole world of possibilities.

He married solid gold disco classics, burnished at the Gallery and the Loft, with disparate elements that took in rock, pop and weird electronic oddities, as well as the more obvious soul, rap, funk and postdisco releases. The music we now call "garage" has evolved from only a small part of the club's broad soundtrack. The Garage was Yaz as well as Loleatta Holloway. The Garage was Steve Miller Band. The Garage was Grandmaster Flash. The Garage was MFSB, Gwen Guthrie, Marianne Faithfull, Talking Heads and The Clash. The fact that all of this converged so seamlessly and effectively is testament to Levan's forceful personality. "Garage music was kind of breaking the rules," says DJ Danny Krivit. "It was what he felt like playing. It was really about having no boundaries."

Levan took this to extremes and was a determined manipulator of his clubbers' tastes, forcing unusual, sometimes bizarre records on them and making them work through his immense force of will. One such record was Yoko Ono's sonic sonnet, "Walking On Thin Ice." A rock mantra in which

Yoko's dissonant eastern wail weaves around a wall of heavy percussion, it was the song John Lennon had been working on the night he was murdered. Levan loved it.

When Johnny Dynell DJed at Sean Lennon's tenth birthday party, he told Ono about her new-found popularity among the dancers of downtown Manhattan. He even took her down to the Garage one night. "It was a big thing for Yoko to see all these black kids dancing to her record," he says. "But she loved it. I think she went back a few times, too."

Levan's willingness to go against the grain meant he would just as easily champion a commercial record as the most obscure underground cut. Dave Piccioni remembers him playing "Fascinated" by Company B, a real electro-pop commercial record. "It was tacky in the extreme. But, fuck me, he played that for twenty or twenty-five minutes and you could not help but get into it. He thought, 'I like this record and it's gonna sound great in the club, and I don't really care if you like it or not.' And he got away with it because he had talent and creativity."

Another example was Pat Benatar's "Love Is A Battlefield," one of several extremely unlikely Garage anthems. "Someone said he could never play that there," chuckles Danny Krivit. "*That* was reason enough for him to play it—and make it happen, too."

Tony Humphries and "Garage" Music

"Garage is the main thing in the States, and I'm the granddaddy of it," claimed Levan in 1985. However, if you name a genre of music after a club which was open for ten whole years and which was known not for one style of music but for its wild eclecticism, you're going to run into problems of definition pretty quickly.

What garage meant to Levan was very different from how we understand the word today. What is now called garage—most likely pronounced British-style as "*garridge*"—is music which has evolved from the more soulful, more gospel-inspired parts of disco: soaring vocal tracks with lush, melodic production, or jazzy instrumentals with a good deal of sizzling hi-hat cymbals. This was but a tiny part of the broad range of music which Larry Levan played at the Paradise Garage.

In fact, the meaning of the word has slipped dramatically. Today's garage sound was born twenty-five miles away from the Paradise Garage in the city of Newark, New Jersey. It is more accurately called "the Jersey sound" and owes its emergence to the taste-making of DJ Tony Humphries at his club Zanzibar.

"I would focus on more of the gospel part, or more of the jazzy part or melodic part," says Humphries, describing his very particular style. "The closer it sounds to a real band or something from the past, then the more I'm going to lean towards that."

Though he already had a radio mix show on New York's Kiss FM, Humphries had been unable to break into the competitive Manhattan club arena. In 1981, however, he started spinning at Zanzibar and there, with its loyal, tight-knit crowd, he spent a decade creating a sophisticated outpost of the New York scene. In the process he nurtured a stable of local acts including Adeva and Phase II, and championed local producers such as Paul Simpson, Smack Productions and Blaze. These are the real roots of what we now call garage.

In the UK, amid the 1988 boom of interest in U.S. music sparked by house, garage became a convenient shorthand for "current New York dance music," a way of distinguishing the city's more vocal, more soulful take on things from the more minimal and robotic house tracks flooding out of Chicago and Detroit. Originally, to British ears garage just meant "housey stuff from New York."

To anyone pedantic enough (and to most American DJs), Adeva and her cohorts were actually flowerings of the Jersey sound. However, thanks to their success on British shores, and thanks to a number of compilation LPs with names like *Garage Trax*, on which they were featured, they were firmly garage. The name stuck and a generation of UK music journalists spent a decade being confused about the geography of east coast America. Some even told their readers the Paradise Garage had been in New Jersey. (Just to add even more confusion, Larry Levan actually played at Zanzibar on several occasions).

When, around 1997, some London DJs took the descendant of this music and latched it to some cavernous, half-tempo basslines, "speed garage" or "UK garage" or "the London sound" was born. Just to make things even more complicated, this actually took its first steps thanks to records by New Jersey producer Todd Edwards and adopted New Yorker Armand van Helden. Now you wish you'd never asked.

Freaky Disco

As the eighties dawned and New York left disco to the masses, there were hectic collisions of underground music and energy. Hip hop and electro were blossoming onto record, new wave was rising from punk's corpse, and after Bob Marley's passing in 1981, reggae was about as popular as it would ever get in Gotham City.

When Larry Levan began to incorporate his renowned eclecticism into his remixes and productions, the city's new culture clash sensibility was set in vinyl. As he'd shown at the Garage, dance music need no longer be constrained by rules of tempo or style—anything which worked a dancefloor was ripe for plundering.

"If you could see my collection, you'd know I like all music—you'd think it belonged to four different DJs," he explained. "And because of this, I found myself taking things from here, from there—reggae, pop, disco, jazz, blues—and using lots of things as a base to take things from."

Levan's late seventies remixes—such as Cognac's "How High" and Dee Dee Bridgewater's "Bad For Me"—sound much like the regular disco mixes of his peers. But by the turn of the eighties, he was experimenting with drum machines and synthesizers and, like François Kevorkian around the same time, forging a new electronic, postdisco sound.

This was epitomized by his group Peech Boys—Levan, keyboard player Michael de Benedictus (who had worked on "Heartbeat"), and vocalist Bernard Fowler—and their digital-funk excursion "Don't Make Me Wait."

"'Don't Make Me Wait' is about sex, and *everyone* can relate to that," Levan told *NME* journalist Paolo Hewitt. "It was very, very passionate, very rough, then it was tender, then it was cold and then it was sparse. It touched on all bases."

The song was a significant breakthrough for Levan; one that gave him worldwide acclaim in the dance community (it was even a minor pop hit in the UK).

"*Everyone* was influenced by the Peech Boys record," says veteran producer Arthur Baker. "When those handclaps started whipping around the place... oh, man." Fired by this new sound, Baker produced "Walking On Sunshine" by Rocker's Revenge. "'Walking On Sunshine' was specifically *made* for the Paradise Garage," he says emphatically.

Although Peech Boys' eventual album was a disappointment, they furthered their stripped-bare soul with the much-sampled "(Life Is) Something Special." This record, while not garnering the same plaudits as its predecessor, actually pushed their razored bass-heavy sound deeper still, offering a tantalizing glimpse of the future.

With reggae making its presence felt, New York started to absorb Jamaican dub as an influence. Dub is all about space—what's not on the record is as important as what is. Dub's warping basslines and luxuriant wide-open spaces suggest much by saying little and demand supreme confidence in your

Card sharp—Danny Krivit's treasured membership to the Paradise Garage.

abilities as a producer. It's all nuance, a nudge and a wink. The rest is left to the dancer.

Levan's interest in dub came, no doubt, from the people he encountered at Island Records, a label for which he did many remixes. Jamaican producers Sly Dunbar and Robbie Shakespeare, and in particular the engineer Steven Stanley, were to exercise an important influence on his tastes. He started airing many of the tracks coming out of Nassau's Compass Point studios—records like Will Powers's "Adventures In Success," Ian Dury's "Spasticus Autisticus," and a succession of Grace Jones singles.

Levan would use echo and reverb to dramatize records in much the same way that Jamaican sound system DJs had done. The flitting handclaps on "Don't Make Me Wait" were an approximation of a reverb trick he would often do live. And on the Garage's superb system, certain dub-inflected records sounded simply awesome.

One such was Funk Masters' "Love Money," which François Kevorkian introduced to the Garage. The record's reverb, echo and spatial decay were nothing short of thrilling when played there. Greatly inspired, Kevorkian incorporated these ideas into a series of remixes that sound classic even today: D Train's "You're The One For Me (Reprise)," Sharon Redd's "Can You Handle It?," Yaz's "Situation" and, most spectacularly, on the Arthur Russell-produced "Go Bang" by Dinosaur L.

Russell, an avant-garde cellist with an obsession for echo, is oft-cited as a pioneer of this dub-style disco, yet his music was often undanceable. "I will not deny that Arthur was an absolute visionary," says François, who honed Russell's genius into more palatable form, "but I don't think he really knew how to sort out what he had created. When I remixed 'Go Bang,' I really focused that record. I stripped it down. I spent hours and hours going over it."

Russell was a crazy-eyed mystic who worked with everyone from Allen Ginsberg (who he taught to play guitar), to Laurie Anderson and Philip Glass (and also CBS A&R legend John Hammond). His interviews were as abstract as his music, often filled with comments that made Phil Spector sound normal. "In outer space you can't take your drums—you take your mind," he told David Toop in 1987.

Russell had discovered disco music on a visit to Nicky Siano's Gallery in the early seventies and collaborated with several of the scene's pioneers, firstly with Siano himself on Dinosaur's "Kiss Me Again," then later with Steve D'Acquisto on Loose Joints' "Is It All Over My Face?" "He had this energy and the beauty of his music; such strength and tenderness," raves D'Acquisto. "He was an abstract painter, really." Although his work was largely overlooked at the time, it has been recently exhumed by such fans as DJ Gilles Peterson.

Time Waits for No One

Larry Levan treated the recording studio in much the same way he treated the club and everywhere else. It was another good place to have a party. "He was a record company's nightmare," laughs Danny Krivit. "Basically, he'd show up really late and while he was there it was about socializing and drugs. Eventually he would get to the mix, but he would be distracted very easily. And the mix, instead of taking a day or whatever, it would go on for weeks."

Just such a session was the one which resulted in Gwen Guthrie's "Padlock" EP, a mini-album of six songs which spiraled out of a simple project to remix "It Should Have Been You." As Levan's druggery took hold, this became a sprawling marathon. "Island were so pissed off at the price and how long 'It Should Have Been You' took that they just shelved it," recalls Danny Krivit. "For a year or two he was just playing it at the Garage and kicking it there."

The one constant in the kinetic chaos of Levan's daily life was Judy Weinstein. She acted as manager, A&R source, guide and mother figure. "She was totally enamoured of him," says Nicky Siano. "She really did a lot for him." Weinstein's position in charge of For The Record, the most important record pool in the country, meant she heard about records before anyone else. "She would hear about things before they were even made," claims Vince Aletti. Johnny Dynell recalls the reaction of Levan when Weinstein made her weekly entrance. "When she used to walk into the Garage, all of a sudden Larry would start really playing. She was a goddess."

Towards the end of the Garage's life, Levan had entered into a steep decline in which his DJing was running a distant second to his drug use. In the final year, he was relying increasingly on the club's alternate DJs, David DePino, Joey Llanos and Victor Rosado. The club finally closed when its lease ran out on September 26, 1987, after a momentous two-day party in which an estimated 14,000 passed through the club's doors to tearfully bid it goodbye. Although its closure was long anticipated, it nevertheless had a deadening effect on New York clubland. "It was like somebody had died in my family," says Charlie Grappone.

The Garage, especially towards its final years, had developed a significant inner clique of heroin users, of which Levan was one. "He was definitely into drugs," says Krivit. "But, as opposed to the drugs having a handle on him, it seemed like it wasn't running his life. Toward the end, say the last year or two, it was probably clear to him that the Garage was closing. I think at that point the drugs seemed to be more obvious and he was there less."

"He lost his home when the Garage closed, but he would have gone the way he did anyway," says Dave Piccioni. "You can't say, 'The club went and Larry died inside.' I'm sure it was a big disappointment, but he caned it. He was a very bright bloke and he made a decision to do it like that: get fucked up."

People recall him selling his records—unthinkable for a DJ who loved music so much—in order to finance his escalating habit. After the closure of the Garage, whenever Levan was booked to DJ, his friends had to trawl the rummage sales to buy back his collection, just so he could fulfill the date. Danny Krivit remembers finding Levan's unique acetate remix of Syreeta's "Can't Shake Your Love" on a record stall and realizing that most of the other records there were his also.

Justin Berkman, an English wine dealer and DJ who had lived in New York, opened a club in London that was directly inspired by the Garage and Larry Levan. It was called Ministry of Sound. He booked Levan to come over and play.

"We brought him over for three days," recounts Berkman. "He arrived eight days late with no records and ended up staying for three months. I was like, 'Larry, where are your records?' He said, 'I haven't got any. I've sold them all.'" But records were scraped together and even in the depths of addiction, Levan still pulled off a great set.

His final trip abroad was on a tour of Japan with François Kevorkian in August 1992. They played together at a club called Endmax. "Larry went into a set of Philadelphia classics," recalls Kevorkian, "which was just so poignant, so emotional, because the message of all the songs said he was really hurting. We all felt it at the time—I think he pretty much knew he was dying—and all the songs he played were so deeply related to how fast life goes, how temporary it is. He played a song by Jean Carn called 'Time Waits For No One' and the Trammps' 'Where Do We Go From Here?' and all these other things. I was just standing there in the booth looking at Larry playing these records, and then I realized that this was one of the best moments of greatness that I had ever witnessed in my life. It was so obvious, so grand. There was such drama to it, that you just knew." Three months later, on November 8, 1992, Levan died.

Party starter—an invitation to Larry Levan's birthday bash on July 18–19, 1986, drawn by his good friend Keith Haring.

Each year, on Larry Levan's birthday, a party is held in New York to celebrate his life.

Levan's Legacy

With his epic club and his grandiose personality, Larry Levan made an impact that few DJs have known. His legacy includes an element of being at the right place at the right time, but no one can deny the profound effect he had on the New York dance scene. Musically, he dramatically bridged the uncharted territory between disco and house. He inspired more world-class DJs than anyone before or since, and in terms of club culture, he showed that with the right effort and attention to detail, a club could express the ideals of togetherness and love, no matter how large it was.

"Larry could take 2,000 people and make them feel like they were at a house party," says Mel Cheren, co-owner of the Garage. "That was his magic."

Nicky Siano points to Levan's many classic remixes as proof of his genius. "'Can't Play Around,' 'Ain't Nothin' Going On But The Rent,' 'Is It All Over My Face?' 'Heartbeat'—incredible work," he says. "There are certain things he did that will live forever."

Johnny Dynell believes that Levan showed him what DJing was really all about: "When you're creating that magic on the floor. When they've thrown their hands up in the air, and they're totally lost and abandoned into this other world. And *you've* taken them to that other world. *That's* what DJing is. Before that I was just playing records, which is not DJing at all."

ELEVEN
HOUSE

Can You Feel It?

"It really is much better than it sounds."
—Mark Twain (on the music of Richard Wagner)

"I view house as disco's revenge."
—Frankie Knuckles, 1990

Many DJs speak of their work in religious terms, few with as much clarity as Frankie Knuckles. "For me, it's definitely like church," he explained on Chicago's WMAQ TV. "Because, when you've got three thousand people in front of you, that's three thousand different personalities. And when those three thousand personalities become one personality, it's the most amazing thing. It's like that in church. By the time the preacher gets everything going, or that choir gets everything going, at one particular point, when things start peaking, that whole room becomes one, and that's the most amazing thing about it."

In Chicago, as the seventies became eighties, if you were black and gay your church may well have been Frankie Knuckles's Warehouse, a three-story factory building in the city's desolate west side industrial zone. Offering hope and salvation to those who had few other places to go, here you could forget your earthly troubles and escape to a better place. Like church, it promised freedom, and not even in the next life. In this club Frankie Knuckles took his congregation on journeys of redemption and discovery.

"In the early days between '77 and '81, the parties were very intense," he remembers. "They were always intense—but the feeling that was going on then, I think, was very pure. The energy, the feeling, the feedback that you got from the room, from the people in the room, was very, very spiritual."

One day a week, from Saturday night to Sunday afternoon, a faithful crowd gathered, waiting on the stairway to enter on the top floor of the building and pay the democratically low $4 admission. The club held around 600, but as many as 2,000 people—mostly gay, nearly all black—would pass through its doors during a good night. They dressed with elegance but in clothes that declared a readiness to sweat. Many would sleep beforehand to maximize their energy. Once in the club, some stayed in the seating area upstairs. Others walked down to the basement for the free juice, water and munchies. Most people, however, headed straight to the dark, sweaty dancefloor in between. For them there was no need for distraction: they came here for Frankie Knuckles's music. They came to the Warehouse to dance.

"It was amazing because you had those down-to-earth, corn-fed midwestern folk," recalls Frankie, "and yet the parties were very soulful, very spiritual." He smiles his big-hearted smile as he remembers the feeling of communion, the intense focus his club created.

"For most of the people that went to the Warehouse, it was church."

DJ/producer Chez Damier was one of the people mesmerized by the Warehouse. "It was something you couldn't re-create," he remembers. "It was like no other sensation: being in a club full of kids that you didn't know but you knew. To try and understand it, all I can say is you have to imagine all the fabulous feelings you've had over your own partying years."

To reach the dancefloor at the Warehouse you had to enter through a stairwell from the white, plant-filled lounge above. Heat and steam drifted up to meet you, generated in the murk of the underlit room by the glistening black bodies that were down there "jacking" away. And as you descended into the shadowy cavern, you were hit by the power of the sound system; sparked by the energy of the dancers, many of whom were energized further by acid and MDA powder (a precursor to ecstasy). Frenzied bodies were packed in wall-to-wall throughout the space, their clothes reduced to a minimum of athletic gear, their bare skin dripping with sweat and condensation.

"That room was dark," Frankie told writer Sheryl Garratt. "People would say it was like climbing down into the pit of hell. People would be afraid when they heard the sound thumping through and saw the number of bodies in there, just completely locked into the music."

And Frankie's music was something completely new to most of these people. He would work the crowd into a frenzy by twisting songs into frantic new shapes with mixes and edits: New York DJing skills of which Chicago clubs had little experience. And at a certain stage in the evening he'd black out the room and throw on a sound effect record of a speeding steam locomotive, panning the stereo sound from one set of speakers to another so it felt like a real express train was thundering through the club. Chez recalls the effect of a night at the Warehouse: "Kids would totally lose their minds."

Frankie Knuckles had learned his craft playing alternate for his great friend Larry Levan in New York's Continental Baths, becoming the club's main DJ when Levan left in 1974 and playing there until the Baths closed, bankrupt, in 1976. Around this time, Levan was contacted by the owners of the Warehouse in Chicago, a warehouse party which had built itself a permanent home, and offered a residency. Since he was committed to the idea of the Paradise Garage—and was busy cultivating its forerunner, Reade Street—he declined. In his place he recommended Frankie, and told his friend that it would be a great opportunity.

In March 1977, Knuckles went out to play for the opening night and also the following week. Both nights went well and he decided he liked Chicago. He was offered a permanent job; the terms included a financial interest in the club.

"At that point I realized I had to think about what I wanted to do. If I really wanted to uproot from New York City and move there. Then actually when I looked at it, I didn't have anything holding me here. I figured, what the hell. I gave myself five years and if I couldn't make it in five years, then I could always come back home."

Before those five years had passed, Frankie Knuckles had become famous in Chicago. As well as popularizing the funky, the soulful—the dangerous—side of disco, which the city had rarely heard, he also imported its spirit, fostering among these polite, godfearing midwesterners the communal, emancipating hedonism of disco's gay underground. In doing this he was the catalyst for an unprecedented explosion of musical creativity.

His club would give its name to a new genre of music; he would become known as its godfather. The music was house.

The Meaning of House

"In the beginning there was Jack, and Jack had a groove, and from this groove came the groove of all grooves, and while one day viciously throwing down on his box, Jack boldly declared, Let there be house." So booms "My House" by Rhythm Control.

For a long time the word "house" referred not to a particular style of music so much as to an attitude. If a song was "house" it was music from a cool club, it was underground, it was something you'd never hear on the radio. In Chicago, the right club would be "house," and if you went there, you'd be house and so would your friends. Walking down Michigan Avenue, you would be able to tell who was house and who wasn't by what they were wearing. If their tape player was rocking The Gap Band, they were definitely not house, but if it was playing Loleatta Holloway or (surprisingly enough) the Eurythmics, they were, and you'd probably go over and talk to them.

One day soon, Chicago kids would invent a stark new kind of dance music, and because of where this came from, and because of where it was played, it would steal the name for itself. But for several years, house was a feeling, a rebellious musical taste, a way of declaring yourself in the know. Certainly, the word house was used long before people started making what we would now call house music.

Chip E, an early house producer, claims that the name came about from his methods of labeling records at the Imports Etc record store.

"People would come in and ask for the old sounds, the Salsoul that Frankie used to play at the Warehouse," he explained, "so we'd put up signs that said 'Warehouse Music' to get people's attention to reissues and collectors' items. It worked so well that we started putting it on all sorts of records and shortened the label to 'House.' And 'House' became the name for music that was happening, that was hot, whether it was old or new."

Frankie Knuckles says that the first time he knew of the term was in 1981. Driving south through the outskirts of his adopted city to visit his goddaughter, he noticed a sign in the window of a bar: "WE PLAY HOUSE MUSIC." Bemused, he turned to his friend and asked, "Now what is *that* all about?" She looked at the sign and told him, "It means music like you play at the Warehouse."

The name fit for all sorts of reasons. A "house record" could be one belonging to a particular club, one which was exclusive to that DJ. It could be a song which simply "rocked the house." A "house party" was more intimate and friendly than a club, and of course "house" conjured the idea of family, of belonging to something special. If you were part of it, house was your home. Later, as an army of young kids started producing electronic dance music in their bedrooms, it enjoyed another resonance: it was simply music you made in your house.

These meanings made it appropriate, but they were not where the word originated (some will try and tell you otherwise). The word "house" came from the Warehouse, referring to the music played there, the DJing manipulations which Frankie introduced, and the underground vibe the club engendered.

Frankie Knuckles at the Warehouse

If house music was named at the Warehouse, it started as disco, pure and simple. Frankie Knuckles began spinning in Chicago around the time that disco was reaching its commercial peak, and he would have been playing the same records as his peers in New York: songs from labels like Salsoul, West End and Prelude. His audience took to this music immediately, but he soon faced a drought of good material as the major labels felt disco burning their fingers. In New York, this problem was solved for many DJs by the blossoming of new styles, notably hip hop and electro, but in Chicago Frankie looked for ways to keep his beloved disco alive. This encouraged him to look backwards and emphasize older music in his sets.

"Songs lived in people's consciousness a lot longer than they do now," he says. "So a lot of the stuff that came out in the early seventies on Salsoul and Philly International, I was playing a lot of stuff like that, that was still working pretty strong in '77 when I moved to Chicago. And a lot of the popular disco R&B club stuff and dance stuff that was coming out then."

As the eighties began, he played the weirder dubbed-up postdisco sounds emerging from his hometown, the Peech Boys and D Train, and added obscure imports, especially from Italy, where disco—albeit a more mechanical version of the genre—was refusing to die. He also started working on reedits of songs in an effort to rejuvenate old favorites, experimenting with the remixing ideas he had seen DJs do back home. He started playing these publicly around 1980.

"A lot of the stuff I was doing early on I didn't even bother playing in the club, because I was busy trying to get my feet wet and just learn the craft. But by '81 when they had declared that disco is dead, all the record labels were getting rid of their dance departments, or their disco departments, so there was no more uptempo dance records, everything was downtempo. That's when I realized I had to start changing certain things in order to keep feeding my dancefloor. Or else we would have had to end up closing the club."

Using a reel-to-reel tape recorder, and assisted by his friend Erasmo Riviera, who was studying sound engineering, Frankie would take weird tunes like "Walk The Night" by the Skatt Brothers (which sounds like the Glitter Band on angel dust) or jazzy disco records like "A Little Bit Of Jazz" by Nick Straker, or "Double Journey" by Powerline and reedit them, extending intros and breaks, adding new beats and sounds, to make them work better for his dancers.

"Even stuff like 'I'm Every Woman' and 'Ain't Nobody' by Chaka Khan, just things like that, completely reedit them, to give my dancefloor an extra boost. I'd rearrange them, extend them and rearrange them."

Chez Damier remembers how Frankie would rework the ballsy disco song "Can't Fake The Feeling" by Geraldine Hunt: "Frankie would do something like, 'You can't fake it . . . *voom*, you can't fake it . . . *voom*, you can't fake it . . . *voom*,' and it would go three times, and the stop was really hard, VOM!! And then it would go 'L.O.V.I.N.' and it goes into 'You can't fake it . . .' eight times, and then it would hit, and it would break into something else, 'L.O.V.I.N.' which is Teena Marie."

Another record Chez remembers is "So Fine" by Howard Johnson, an uptempo disco tune. "It goes, 'So fine, blow my mind,' and then, 'Throw your head back, move it to the side,' and Frankie would change it to 'Throw your head backbackbackback . . .' *Dum! Dum! Dum!* move it to the side DUMM!! Little tricks like that were such sensations. We were like followers."

The receptive audience loved all this DJ alchemy and Frankie reveled in the chance to work with such a blank canvas. "Those type of parties we were having at the Warehouse, I know they were something completely new to them, and they didn't know exactly what to expect," he says. "But once they latched onto it, it spread like wildfire through the city."

Eventually, his tape projects would become complex remixes, as he ran completely new rhythms, basslines and drum tracks underneath familiar songs. This kind of DJ creativity was at least half a decade old in New York, and was certainly being done in other American cities, but in Chicago it was very new. "I'm sure there were other people that were doing it, but to my audience it was revolutionary," Frankie recalls.

It is these experiments which constitute the roots of house music. As these ideas and techniques were copied, often in much-simplified ways by far less skilled DJs using far more basic equipment, the house aesthetic was born.

At first, the Warehouse was seen by the wider Chicago club world as marginal—it was a club for black gay people (of both sexes) with a black gay DJ—and Frankie's music was written off as "fag music." The disco backlash was building steam and the straight dancefloors in the city were moving to new wave rock and European synth pop. Eventually, though, by virtue of it being the only after-hours club in the city, some adventurous straight kids started going. Many were swept away by the power of the music they heard.

One such visitor was Wayne Williams, a young DJ from the city's south side, who was so stunned by the energy he saw that he became a regular. "For two years or so I would go and stand by the DJ booth and ask the guy next to Frankie to give me the name of the record he was playing so I could write it down and go back to the record store and get them," he recounted. "Being in a gay club, I was a bit scared to ask Frankie." Williams, shopping at Sounds Good, then the only store in Chicago which sold such records, bought as many of Frankie's tunes as he could find and introduced them to his south side audiences. Used to more current sounds, his crowd at first completely cleared the floor. However, he persevered and, by playing music that none of his peers would touch, quickly became one of the city's most successful DJs. "I was the only one who had balls enough to go there and bring back this music to the south side and play it to the straight kids." His success had a considerable influence and in the early years of the eighties, the older, funkier sound known back then as "house" started to spread far beyond the gay clubs.

Ron Hardy at the Music Box

By late 1982, the Warehouse had become a victim of its own success, its gay clientele increasingly diluted. Frankie remembers "a lot more hard-edged straight kids trying to infiltrate what was going on." The owners got greedy and doubled the entry fee. Knuckles left and opened the Power Plant, a former electrical substation. His crowd followed him loyally, but the owners of the Warehouse had an ace up their sleeve: renaming the club the Music Box, they hired another young DJ, black and gay like Knuckles and with similar tastes, but with an even more orgiastic approach to music.

Because, in fact, the Warehouse wasn't the first place Chicago had heard underground disco. At a gay club called Den One, a crazy young DJ had played nights of hard black disco at least two years before Frankie arrived. Around 1977 he had left town to work in California, leaving the clubland gap which Knuckles would later fill. But at the end of 1982 he returned to play at the Music Box and retake the Windy City by storm. His name was Ron Hardy, and to many in Chicago he was quite simply the world's greatest DJ.

"Ron Hardy? Everybody hated him, he was mean and nasty, a drug addict. He had a huge ego, that's how he was. But, oh man, he was GREAT! He was the greatest DJ that ever lived," remembers veteran house producer Marshall Jefferson.

Sharing a house—Ron Hardy (left) and Frankie Knuckles (right), the two founders of Chicago house music, in 1986.

If Frankie Knuckles is the godfather of house, he shared the raising of his child with Ron Hardy. Knuckles's arrival had started a period of intense experimentation. He had created an excitement and a thirst for underground music, and he had shown that a DJ could be a truly creative force. Returning to Chicago to find this energetic laboratory, Ron Hardy was to become its mad scientist. While Frankie's dancefloor experiments were conducted with characteristic level-headed momentum, Hardy was fueled by a far more demonic appetite—for both music and narcotics. Knuckles was already changing the face of dance music, but Hardy was ready to tamper with nature, eager to release musical forces beyond his control.

Seasoned clubber Cedric Neal recalls the effect Hardy had on an audience. "He was like an idol. The first time I saw him spin, it was his birthday, and just to see people literally crying because this man had them so hyper, seeing people pass out, I was like, 'Hey, this is my type of party!' I'd never been to a place where the DJ had a control over the people where they would dance and scream, and at some points cry. Depending on how high they were, they were passing out from pure excitement. It was the energy that was there."

The two DJs' sharply distinct personalities soon took effect. The older, smartly turned out partygoers followed Frankie to the Power Plant. The younger kids left for the craziness of the Music Box, which Chez Damier describes as "more the ghetto version of the party." For Hardy to change the scene like he did was no mean achievement. Knuckles had enjoyed a five-year supremacy in Chicago's underground.

"Frankie was ruling the roost," recalls Marshall. "They were calling it house music now, and that was because of Frankie. And for Ron Hardy to come in there and steal Frankie's thunder, it was really something." Power Plant gave up Saturdays and only opened on Fridays, and eventually the week was divided between the two clubs, with Wednesdays and Fridays being Power Plant nights, and Tuesdays, Thursdays and Saturdays belonging to the Music Box. "They were competitive," laughs Marshall. "Like two gunslingers."

Both DJs were able to generate incredible energy levels on their dancefloors. They would both extend everything for ages, stretching out their dancers on an endless beat, teasing them in a highly sexual way with a repetitive rhythm until the final release of the actual song. Both used a reel-to-reel to play edits and rhythm tracks, and for many this was the best part of the evening. "I used to love it when they went to the reel," says Earl "Spanky" Smith of acid house group Phuture. "'Cause that's when you knew they were gonna play something exciting."

Frankie's style was more orderly and he kept his tempo much lower. He paid greater attention to the quality of his sound and his sets were more technically precise and structured, with the pace rising and falling in waves throughout the night. Ron Hardy, on the other hand, played with a raw, lo-fi energy that left you in no doubt which moment he was living in. All he cared about was energy, about pushing his dancers to their limits. He had little time to plan anything. As Marshall puts it: "He didn't give a fuck about programming or none of that. Hardy did every single drug known to man. How the fuck you gonna program *that*?"

Their playlists were quite similar—favorite songs like "Let No Man Put Asunder" by First Choice, "I Can't Turn Around" by Isaac Hayes, "There But For The Grace of God" by Machine, "The Love I Lost" and "Bad Luck" by Harold Melvin and the Bluenotes, "I'm Here Again" by Thelma Houston and a good deal of Loleatta Holloway found their way into both clubs, as did dubby mutant disco—ESG's "Moody," Dinosaur L's "Go Bang," Atmosfear's "Dancing In Outer Space"—and European synth tracks like "Frequency 7" by Visage, "Dirty Talk" by Klein and MBO, and "Optimo" and "Cavern," both by Liquid Liquid. However, Hardy played his music much faster, stripped it down more, and would even add overtly commercial tracks like "It's My Life" by Talk Talk, "Sweet Dreams" by the Eurythmics, and songs by new-wave glamsters ABC.

Hardy's music was about bombshells and surprises, an onslaught of sound reaching climax after funky climax. He upped the energy levels using anything at his disposal, playing the EQ avidly, dropping out and slamming up the bass or the treble for extra effect (this would become a Chicago trademark, though Knuckles was far less blatant with his EQing), or speeding everything up as fast as he could, pitching records to plus six or plus seven percent. Detroit techno pioneer Derrick May remembers a visit when he heard Stevie Wonder played at plus eight.

Marshall Jefferson had been led to the Music Box by a wild girl he worked with at the Post Office. She was a stripper as well as a letter carrier and Marshall says he wanted to see her body in action on the dancefloor, so he told her, "I want to see the wild clubs you go to." Previously a die-hard rock fan with Thin Lizzy records in his collection and a tendency to believe that disco sucked, he was converted to dance music immediately, such was Hardy's power. "She took me to this place called the Music Box. I was touched by God! The volume, man, just BOOM!!! It penetrated through my chest and took hold of my heart."

Above all, Hardy loved to crank it up. "The *volume*, man!" Marshall exclaims. "It was really amazing. I have never heard music at that volume since. In fifteen years I have not heard a single club that even came close to that volume, and the reason, I would suspect, is there would be loads of lawsuits from damaging your hearing. The Music Box was so loud that anywhere in the club, the bass would physically move you—not just on the dancefloor, but *anywhere* in the club!"

Cedric Neal and his friends would always arrive early so they could sit outside drinking and getting high before they went in.

"The front opened up at a quarter to one. And Ron would always start with 'Welcome To The Pleasure Dome.' This was '84, it just came out, and he would play that for twenty minutes. And you'd just sit around and wait till the crowd just built. Come five o'clock in the morning you gain the momentum, and come six you'd pick up speed. People would come in there and just dance all night."

After its first incarnation in the old Warehouse space, the club moved into a second venue, in an industrial cave beneath an elevated highway called Lake Shore Drive. With a capacity of around 750, it was at least half gay, and in the years immediately preceding awareness of AIDS, a culture of sexual abandon prevailed for gay and straight clubbers alike. Cedric grins as he describes "the big speaker," ten feet tall, all the way at the back of the club, where couples would get under the stage. "We'd take girls in there: get a blowjob, a quickie. It was still the end of the sexual revolution." He remembers how there were pillows in the girls' bathroom. "There'd be guys in there, getting high, having sex together. Maybe you'd see two lesbians in there."

This sexual openness enabled the club to be unusually free of aggression. There was little or no sense of homophobia. "If you couldn't stand to be around gays, you didn't party in the city of Chicago," Cedric recalls. "They would ask, 'Are you a child or a stepchild?' Meaning, are you gay or not? If you were a stepchild it meant you were straight but we accept you." It became fashionable for a time to act gay even if you weren't. Cedric recalls people who would experiment with bisexuality as an attempt to get closer to the true meaning of house.

Music was undoubtedly the central focus, but club drugs like pot, poppers (known as "rush") and LSD were present (with a smattering of MDA, and the pricier intoxicants like cocaine and ecstasy). Music Box had more of everything in its veins than Power Plant, notably a lot of acid and also PCP. A popular high was "happy sticks," joints with a sprinkling of PCP, or "sherm sticks," joints dipped in formaldehyde. With the resulting manic energy, the Music Box could be an intimidating place indeed. Derrick Carter, DJ and producer, remembers being truly scared after sneaking in aged seventeen.

"It weirded me out. There were speakers hanging from the ceiling, Mars lights spinning. For some reason the place made me think of junkies. I didn't know anything about the drugs, but Ronnie would play something like Eddie Kendrick's 'Going Up In Smoke' and everybody would be . . . going up in smoke! It would just lift everybody off the ground, people would be crying, and just freaking out, they got so charged."

"The way Ron Hardy spinned, you could tell how he was feeling," says Cedric. "The way he played records, the sequence he played them, how long he played them. You could tell if he was depressed, because him and his loverman had had a fight. You could know if he was up and happy or you could know if he was just high, out of his mind because of the drugs."

The emotional intensity of the city's dancefloors, combined with the twin genius of Hardy and Knuckles, gave Chicago a nightlife whose energy and focus was unrivaled. With no Studio 54 celebrity scene to fuck things up, and without New York's overbearing industry presence, music in Chicago stayed dirtier, funkier, more about dancing till you dropped. And without any competing scene, the house underground managed to spread beyond its gay origins without losing direction or momentum.

A recognizable house style soon developed: baggy Girbaud jeans and sports sweatshirts were popular (a look later taken up by the world of hip hop, which

at this stage was dressed in tracksuits and Kangols). And since house kids were outsiders, the punk look was appropriated, so bleach-splashed jeans and spiky hair could also mean you were "house." Punk styles of dancing came in, too: it was quite normal to see the younger kids slamdancing to house. Another crucial look was the "pump": a tall, flat-topped haircut. You'd get extra credibility for the height of your pump, and the sharpness of its corners. DJ Pierre was known for his: "People'd be like, 'Damn! Look how high his pump is,'" he laughs. The most distinctive fashion, however (and this would seem to have parallels with London's New Romantics), was a sort of Ralph Lauren preppie meets English country gentleman style, with cardigans, woolen jodhpurs and riding boots being an indisputable sign of house-ness. Some people even remember carrying a horsewhip.

The Hot Mix 5

Those who were too young to go to the Music Box or Power Plant were switched on by another vital impetus: radio. From 1981–86 on station WBMX (and later on WGCI), a racially diverse quintet of DJs introduced mixing records to Chicago airwaves. Captained by Kenny "Jammin" Jason, the Hot Mix 5, as they were called, included at first Ralphi Rosario, Steve "Silk" Hurley, Mickey "Mixin" Oliver and Farley Keith Williams, aka "Farley Jackmaster Funk." They played mostly new wave European pop, including British groups like Depeche Mode, Human League and Gary Numan, the German technopop of Falco, and even the hi-NRG of Divine.

This musical diet had profound influence on the tastes of the city, forming the backbone of the more commercial clubs' playlists. More sophisticated DJs searched out obscure imports along similar lines like Wire, Yello and D.A.F. DJ Pierre, later to pioneer acid house, recalls Italian tunes like Doctor Scat's "You Must Feel The Drive" and Capricorn's "I Need Love," Trilogy's "Not Love" and "Brainwash" by Telex. Much is made of the importance of European records to the development of house, but it is important to note that this was hardly a Chicago anomaly. In 1983 nearly a third of all U.S. chart positions were taken up by British acts.

Such was the dominance of this European synth-driven sound that there was at first a real prejudice against the blacker songs which Knuckles and Hardy were championing. Pierre remembers his friend Spanky introducing him to Isaac Hayes's *Chocolate Chip* LP, and feeling there was no way he could ever play it. "I was like, 'I ain't playin' this old song. Do people even dance to this?'"

The Hot Mix 5, as well as being important taste-makers, mixed like maniacs—far better, it is said, than either Knuckles or Hardy.

"All of the Hot Mix 5 were amazing, technique-wise," agrees Marshall. "They would have two records of everything, everything was phased, then they'd do backspinning and things on every song. Perfect, no mistakes, slamming shit, man." For many, the Hot Mix shows were the first time they'd ever heard records mixed. DJ Pierre was one of them.

"I used to have a tape player and make edits of stuff by using the pause button, but when I used to listen to the Hot Mix 5 and I heard two songs playing at once, I had no idea how they were doing it." Like many others, hearing these radio jocks show off their skills was what pulled him into DJing. And the power they enjoyed was phenomenal. WBMX claimed audience figures of up to half a million—a sixth of the city's population. Maurice Joshua, then a suburban DJ, remembers the excitement whenever the Hot Mixes were on.

"Everybody used to listen, especially when they brought it to lunchtime. Twelve o'clock you'd be glued to the radio. People would even skip school to tape the mixes." At Imports Etc., then the city's leading specialist dance music store, there was a noticeboard describing the songs that had been played in each mix, to save the staff from a barrage of Hot Mix questions.

The membership of the five was fluid and many of the city's DJs took a turn. Frankie Knuckles was even included for a while, but there was constant infighting and people recall the backbiting politics which surfaced whenever it was time to choose a new Hot Mixer.

As the only long-term black member of the ethnically mixed five, Farley enjoyed the most influence among the house kids of the south side. He also had a residency in a club called the Playground, where he capitalized on his radio success. Here he tried playing an 808 drum machine under old Philly records like "Love Is The Message," something he also did on the radio. The boosted beat was known as "Farley's Foot."

"I brought my drum machine to the club and learned to play records that used the same machine, like 'Dirty Talk' by Klein and MBO," he says. "Frankie Knuckles and I used to play many of the same records, but whereas he would make a reedited version at home, I played my drum machine along with the records, so that the crowd could really feel that heavy, heavy foot. To play a record like Shannon's 'Let The Music Play' that didn't have a really driving foot was to get tomatoes thrown at you. You had to drive them with your beat. Call me the foot doctor."

In fact, though Farley reaped the most acclaim for the idea, Frankie Knuckles was also trying it, using a Roland 909 he bought from Detroit's Derrick May. The 909 drum machine, with its distinctive kick-drum sound, would become a standard component of house records. However, rather than playing an actual drum machine in his club, Knuckles says he preferred to play rhythm tracks *made with* drum machines. These tracks were what became house music.

Jamie Principle, Jesse Saunders and the First House Tracks

House was disco made by amateurs. It was disco's essence—its rhythms, its basslines, its spirit—re-created on machines that were as close to toys as they were to musical instruments, by kids who were more clubbers than they were musicians. The DJ, aiming to preserve a music which had been declared dead, had created another from its ashes. And in Chicago this new music even shared the name of its forebear, because remember, the disco that Ron and Frankie played was called "house" even before house was.

As house culture boomed its arrival in this lakeside city, the DJ's aim was to drive dancers into states of drum-hypnotized fury, using endless thundering rhythm tracks to work the dancefloor towards the orgasm of a great vocal song. This style demanded a steady supply of simple, repetitive drum tracks. People had seen how basic a track could be. Studio equipment had just become small and affordable. Suddenly, everybody in Chicago became a producer, eagerly pushing tapes under DJs' noses.

It was inevitable that these would eventually be committed to vinyl, and in 1984 there were two defining moments:

1. Byron Walton was shy and religious, could play the drums and had a thorough college grounding in sound engineering. His favorite musicians were Prince, Bowie, Depeche Mode and Human League. Calling himself Jamie Principle, he created "Your Love," an achingly beautiful musical poem so good that every DJ in the city wanted a cassette copy of it to play, so good that few people believed it had been made by anyone in Chicago.

2. Jesse Saunders was a chancer, wanted to gain recognition in order to get girls, was a big Chicago DJ, and had a friend, Vince Lawrence, whose father owned a local record label and who egged him into making a record. Under his own name, Jesse created "On And On," a rhythm track so basic that everyone knew it had been made by someone in Chicago; so basic that everyone with a drum machine and a four-track recorder felt sure they could do better.

These were the first significant homegrown Chicago house artists.

Jamie Principle's music was heard first, his songs played from tape for more than a year before being records (produced, on vinyl, by Frankie Knuckles), but his work was too accomplished to spark an avalanche of copyists; most people thought "Your Love" and "Waiting On My Angel" were songs from Europe. It took Jesse Saunders's success with "On And On," a far inferior track, to open the floodgates.

"That's what inspired everybody. It gave us hope, man," says Marshall Jefferson. "When Jamie was doing it, nobody thought of making a record. His shit was too good. It was like seeing John Holmes in a porno movie. You know you can't do better."

Continuing his penile analogy, Marshall compares Jesse's track, on the other hand, to a rather less endowed figure. "But if you saw a guy in a porno movie with a three-inch peter, and all the women are swooning all over him and he's a fucking millionaire, you would seriously consider having a go yourself, wouldn't you!" Marshall booms with laughter at his comparison. "That's what inspired everybody about Jesse. They saw somebody make it big . . . *But not be that great.* When Jesse did his stuff, everybody said, '*Fuck! I could do better than that!*'"

After more howls of laughter, he says, simply, "Jesse changed music, man."

Jesse Saunders was one of the city's most successful DJs, having learned to play in the late seventies alongside his half brother Wayne Williams at the Loft, which he describes as the straight version of the Warehouse. By 1983, as well as guesting in other clubs and doing a radio mix show on WGCI, he was spinning at the 2,000-capacity Playground, favoring a Hot Mix 5-type style heavy on turntable tricks, and playing commercial new-wavey pop like the B-52s alongside a few more underground sounds. A night there could last twelve hours, and to stretch out his material he would use a drum machine (a Roland 808).

"A lot of the time I would take the drum machine to the club and just leave it playing the same beat the whole time and just mix things in and out," he says. There was one track in particular that he liked to use for this, the B-side of a 1980 bootleg (the A-side was a megamix of popular tunes) credited to Mach, called "On And On." This consisted of a funky bassline, the "hey, beep beep" part of Donna Summer's "Bad Girls" (looped), and a horn part from "Funkytown" by Lipps Inc. "Whenever I played, my first record would be this bootleg 'On And On' because that was like my signature tune," he recalls. "So I had a drum machine going, 'On And On' going on one turntable, and I'd be bringing in another record like 'Planet Rock' on the other."

When this was stolen from his DJ box, he vowed to re-create it. As he told Jonathan Fleming, "I was so pissed off 'cause now I didn't have my signature record and I couldn't make the crowd go wild the way I used to when I came on. So I was like, 'Well, I'm gonna make one myself.'"

Despite having had music lessons all his life—his mother was a music teacher and he'd learned piano, trumpet, flute, guitar and drums—he had never before thought he had the skill to create the kind of music he was playing as a DJ. "I hadn't really associated the fact that someone actually writes a song, goes in the studio, records it and then presses it on a record—that never really occurred to me at that time. But by the time I got a drum machine I was thinking, maybe I can do a record."

In 1983, with his 808, a Korg Poly 61 keyboard that his mother bought, a TB 303 bassline machine and a four-track cassette recorder, he started making tracks. "I just kinda used the feel from a lot of the songs and records that I played that were hits, to kinda concoct them and embrace them into this one thing." The first he called "Fantasy" and another he called "On And On," in tribute to his stolen signature tune.

Jesse negotiated the task of releasing records with help from his friend Vince Lawrence. As Vince tells it, the alliance was forged with one thing in mind. "I was just trying to get pussy," he declares. "You know—trying to get laid!" As one of the city's biggest DJs, Jesse had an instant promotions network. As for Vince, he knew about getting a record made since his father Mitch owned Mitchbal, a tiny independent blues label, and a year or so earlier, as Z Factor, he and some friends had recorded a pop-rocky electronic single, "(I Like To Do It In) Fast Cars." Though it enjoyed a few airings on Chicago radio, "Fast Cars"—a distant approximation of the lush style of Vince's idol Trevor Horn—had little to do with what was happening in the clubs. However, some—especially Vince—like to think of it as the first house record.

In January 1984 "On And On" came out on vinyl on Jesse's Jes Say label. A month or so later, "Fantasy" came out on Mitchbal (Fantasy should have been first—it was due for release at the tail end of 1983, but Vince's dad was a great procrastinator). Vince then hooked up with a jazz pianist Duane Buford and both Vince and Jesse watched the cash roll in as they released a stream of local hits.

"Jesse was first," remembers Farley. "He put out records before anyone conceived of doing it, got all the girls, and all the fame. Jesse wanted to be the next Motown."

"What we did was gather all the right ingredients," says Jesse, "and luckily, I was lucky enough to be able to take all of that and make it into the sound we know today as house."

"Jesse got all this shit played on the radio," recalls Marshall. "And next to songs like Prince it would sound like bullshit. It would sound like tin cans, man! *But*... everybody knew Jesse, so it was popular shit. By the time he finally did 'Real Love,' which was *one fifth* the quality normally necessary to make the radio—everything else was about one twentieth!—when that shit came out, it was huge! In Chicago, man, Jesse was bigger than Prince."

The Floodgates Open

Almost overnight there was a frenzy of releases as everyone realized that with a few pieces of home studio equipment they could make a track, and with a few hundred dollars and a bit of legwork they could even have it released on vinyl. Whereas only a few months before, DJs were racking their brains to fill a whole night with the uptempo music their crowds demanded, now they had an army of young clubbers-turned-producers thrusting tapes under their noses, and a growing stream of actual vinyl releases as the more successful of those tracks made it onto record.

"Our sound is so different because we can make just a bassline and a rhythm track and we can sell 10,000 copies of that just in the city," Farley told *The Face*'s Sheryl Garratt in 1986. "All you need is a feel for music. There are people who've been to college to study music and they can't make a simple rhythm track, let alone a hit record. It's weird. And it seems like a waste of time to learn that, because now a little kid can pick up a computer, get lucky with it, and write a hit."

The first wave of house tracks broke in late 1984 and early '85. Farley put out early efforts like "Aw Shucks," which was basically a drum machine and some dogs barking, and his "Funkin' With The Drums" EP—a drum machine and some MFSB basslines. Chip E's "Jack Tracks" EP and "Like This" were similar concoctions put together with the Power Plant's 909. Adonis was one of many who were unimpressed and therefore inspired by Jesse Saunders's "On And On." He jumped into the fray with "No Way Back." Musician Larry Heard brought his more sophisticated jazz influences to bear on the music and began his Fingers Inc project with vocal star Robert Owens. Recorded in 1984 but released in '85, Heard's "Can You Feel It" and "Mystery Of Love" added jazzy, soulful flavorings, while his track

"Washing Machine" was an early Chicago example of the more chilly, angular style of house which would eventually be called techno and for which Detroit would be most renowned. Amazingly, he claims to have recorded all three of these tracks the same day.

With Heard as a rare exception, most of these youngsters had no musical training and until a few months before had never even dreamed of making records. Marshall Jefferson's story is typical. After being "baptized into house" at the Music Box, he maxed out his credit and simply bought everything he would need to make a track. He says he spent about nine grand getting kitted up, leaving the store with: a Roland JX8P keyboard, a Korg EX8000 module, Roland 707, 909 and 808 drum machines . . . a TB 303 and a Tascam 4-track recorder. After unpacking them, he couldn't play a note. His colleagues at the Post Office laughed long and hard.

But in two days, impelled by the ridicule showered on him, he had made a track. He realized quickly that the technology he was using opened up all kinds of possibilities. For example, though he couldn't play keyboards, it was simple to make his efforts sound like a virtuoso: he just recorded the melodies at a third of their final speed.

"'Move Your Body' was 122 beats per minute. I must've recorded those keyboards at 40, 45 beats per minute." He mimes playing the stretched-out keyboard line. "*Dum dum DER DER DUM bombombom.* Then I speeded it up." The effect was impressive. He recalls the reactions: "'Oh Marshall's jamming! Oh man!!!' You know."

Marshall's debut release was the "Virgo Go Wild Rhythm Tracks" EP, made with the help of Vince Lawrence. This was mostly just 808 drum machine lines, but it contained elements that would later become Jefferson's 1986 classic "Move Your Body," the first house record to include a piano melody. One of the first tracks he produced, 1985's "I've Lost Control" by Sleezy D, was huge at the Music Box, becoming an anthem for the wild abandon of the club. Marshall recalls the first night that Ron Hardy played his tracks from tape. "He played seven of my tracks in a row. Seven! And by the time the fifth one got on, it was 'I've Lost Control' and that was the biggest reaction. They *ran* onto the dancefloor. It was like a stampede. Everybody going *aaaarghhh*, and I was thinking, 'Oh, man. Yes!'"

A system of patronage had evolved whereby a producer would construct tracks for a particular DJ, with the big guns, Knuckles and Hardy, getting the cream of the crop. Frankie favored the more polished material and, with his greater emphasis on sound quality, was unlikely to play the really rough cassette mixes which were the most common currency. Ron Hardy, on the other hand, would play anything that he thought would get his crowd moving, regardless of what format it arrived in.

"I used to take my tapes down to Frankie," recalled Steve Hurley. "That's how you got your score, that's how you found out if that song was gonna make it or not; by giving it to Knuckles and if the people screamed, if you got that crowd going, it gave you a feeling like there was no stopping you."

House Hits

House quickly grew from its underground beginnings into a thriving local scene. "Us Chicago kids thought we were listening to a different music from anyone else on the planet," says DJ/producer Derrick Carter. Carter was part of the music's second wave, rising to success as a DJ by playing in the warehouse parties which continued in Chicago into the nineties. He, like many of his peers, was from the city's sprawling suburbs, and joined the party as it got into full swing.

Perhaps the most memorable events of that time were the "marathons," explosive two-day dances populated by as many of the city's DJs as could be squeezed into one bill, the big names included. Also notable were the huge parties which Lil' Louis (later to gain international fame as the producer of seminal house track "French Kiss") organized in the ballroom of the Bismarck Hotel. Louis had in fact been DJing in the city since the late seventies, and drew as many as 8,000 kids here to rock the night away, sweating and slamdancing to this music that few others in the world knew about.

By the time his example had started to bear fruit, Jesse Saunders had signed a major label deal with Geffen and moved to Los Angeles. But the founders of the music, Knuckles and Hardy, sustained the energy which had propelled the scene, and with a whole generation of kids trying their hand at DJing and producing, house looked set to accelerate. New clubs opened to capture the growing house constituency. Record shops like Imports Etc and later Gramophone thrived, and Farley and the Hot Mix 5 drove around in fancy cars as their mix shows drew enormous ratings. House in Chicago would never be truly mainstream, but now it was no longer underground.

In JM Silk (Steve "Silk" Hurley and vocalist Keith Nunally), house found its first hitmakers. Hurley, who had risen to prominence as a DJ at the Playground alongside his erstwhile friend Farley Keith, put out "Music Is The Key" in August 1985. This was pumped so much in the clubs and on Farley's radio mix show that on the day it was released, it reputedly sold 2,000 copies in Chicago alone.

It was another of Hurley's tracks, a reworking of Isaac Hayes's "I Can't Turn Around," which propelled the music even further. Hurley's own version, although he had long played it in the clubs, was pipped onto vinyl by his friend Farley, now calling himself Farley Jackmaster Funk. (Hurley claims the name "Jackmaster" was originally his, too, hence the "JM" in JM Silk.) Farley renamed the song "Love Can't Turn Around," and with a vocal sung in the mountainous Darryl Pandy's six-and-a-half-octave vocal range, it made house international. It was accepted as a pop record in the UK, reaching #10 in September 1986. Hurley had his revenge, however, as in January 1987, "Jack Your Body" became the UK's first house #1.

Chicago's Hip Hop

Intriguingly, house took on exactly the same cultural role as hip hop had done in New York. Its original constituency was poor and black. Its energy came from DJs competing on a local level. Its aesthetic was a result of DJs, dissatisfied with the prevailing sound, rediscovering older music and recasting it in new ways.

Just like hip hop, house stole basslines and drum patterns from old songs (both musics were initially about creating a very minimal and repetitive version of disco). Its creative progression was a result of DJs constantly introducing new elements to their performance to outdo the other guy. And house, like hip hop, depended on a fierce "do-it-yourself" spirit. Even the clothes which characterized house in Chicago—baggy and functional—were what would later be identified as hip hop styles throughout the world. The only fundamental difference was the tempo of the music, and that house accepted rather than rejected disco's gayness and its four-on-the-floor beat.

Some Chicago DJs, like Pierre, can even recall battles, just like those between rival hip hop crews in New York, where a series of house DJs would perform for the honor of having impressed the largest number of dancers—complete with MCs!

"A DJ had to bring his own sound system, his own MC, and bring a big sign with his name on it. And it'd be in a big school gymnasium," he recalls. "Then another DJ, he'd bring his sound system, and a third DJ'd bring his sound system. And you had to do your thing for like thirty minutes or an hour, and whoever's sound system and DJing skills sounded the best won the competition." Pierre even remembers losing a battle because he didn't have a particular record, "Time To Jack" by Chip E.

Given the nature of the house subculture, it's no wonder, then, that for many years hip hop was virtually unheard in Chicago. Only in the middle nineties, after house as a local phenomenon had gone resolutely back underground, could hip hop claim any kind of listenership in the Windy City. Today, the musical spectrum on Chicago radio still has a high ratio of uptempo dance music compared to other American cities, but increasingly it is succumbing to the swingbeat-style R&B and hip hop which now chokes the U.S. music business.

Chicago, City of Gangsters

As Chicago's homemade music started making money, the rip-offs began. In the furious competition of the time, copying and bootlegging was the norm, ownership of tracks was shaky, and few people profited financially from their talents. The music business—dance music especially—is one of the most corrupt there is. In Chicago, things were worse.

Two men came to dominate virtually the whole output of house: Rocky Jones of DJ International and Larry Sherman of Trax. Jones was a veteran DJ who ran the local record pool, Audio Talent. His label's first release was JM Silk's "Music Is The Key." When the first batch sold out, legend has it that he paid for a second pressing of 10,000 records with the keys to his car, a souped-up Corvette.

Larry Sherman was a Vietnam veteran and local businessman with a taste for acid rock. He started his label, Trax, with advice about the local scene from Vince Lawrence, who designed the Trax label. The key to Sherman's success was the fact that he not only owned the city's most profitable house label, he also owned the only record-pressing plant in Chicago. Even if you ran your own label, you still had to pay Larry Sherman to make your records. And as people found out, there was nothing stopping him from making some more copies that you didn't know about and selling them himself.

Marshall Jefferson recalls how his song "Move Your Body" miraculously changed labels at the pressing stage, appearing on Sherman's Trax imprint instead of his own Other Records (he still has the original, unused printed labels). Jesse Saunders recalls that although Sherman was very helpful at times, often financing tracks by pressing records for free in exchange for a cut of the wholesale price, he would forget who had the rights to the masters.

"If he happened to get an order from somebody who asked if he had any 'On And On' records, he'd go, 'Oh, no, but I'll press some up and get them over to you.'"

Chicago pressings were also renowned for their poor quality, a result of Sherman's habit of recycling old vinyl. "They used to put all sorts of things in there. People say you'd even get bits of old sneakers in the record," says one Chicago producer.

In early reports about the developing Chicago house scene, Jones and Sherman come over as enthusiastic supporters of the local music. And certainly, they invested a lot of time and money turning the city's musical hobby into something resembling a business. Hundreds of artists were signed, records flooded out and many of the young producers saw their work translate into success and hard cash. However, when it became clear that this music was capable of global impact, their rather casual business practices started to look less than helpful.

It was common practice to buy tracks outright with a minimal contract and no mention of royalties or publishing. Ask any of the house pioneers whether they ever received a royalty check and they'll probably laugh. The kids were too naive to protest, indeed they were only too happy to take a one-off payment of a few hundred to a couple of thousand dollars for a track, never imagining that in time it might be worth ten times that. To be fair, even after they got wise to the way it was supposed to work, many continued selling music to Trax and DJ International, happy to get some quick cash for a quick track.

Perhaps more damagingly, though, Trax and DJ International seemed to do little to invest for future success, concentrating instead on quick foreign licensing deals, the proceeds of which were kept secret from most of the producers. It's often claimed they frightened away almost all the major label interest in Chicago. "They took the money and ran with it," insists Farley, "instead of developing any artists."

In a city with a long history of organized crime, there are plenty of rumors flying round about mafia connections and hidden agendas, and the house scene is no exception. One conspiracy theorist claims that some figures wanted house to remain merely a local success because they had such murky pasts that they needed to avoid unwanted attention. One is alleged to have operated under a false name for years since he was on parole, something which should have prevented him from leaving Illinois, let alone flying all over the world. Another is whispered to have been under the FBI witness protection scheme after involvement in some dramatic mob saga—a fine reason for not wanting too much publicity. Ask someone in Chicago to tell you about the record business there and you'll hear no end of entertaining tales.

Acid House

No one in Chicago had expected their music to have an impact outside the city, let alone over in London, but it was in the UK that this music would rise to its greatest heights. "Love Can't Turn Around" and "Jack Your Body" led the way, but the export market was secured when Nathaniel Pierre Jones discovered the super-synthetic sci-fi squelch noises hidden deep within an otherwise redundant music machine. Jones is better known as DJ Pierre, his group was Phuture, and the music they pioneered would become known as "acid house."

The invention of acid house is a perfect example of an available technology being creatively perverted in the name of dance music. The Roland TB 303 bassline machine was designed to provide an automatic bass accompaniment for solo guitarists. At this task it was fairly useless. When Pierre and his friends Herb Jackson and Earl "Spanky" Smith started messing with the controls, however, they managed to find some remarkable new noises which were perfect for the druggy dancefloor at Ron Hardy's Music Box.

"I wanted to make something that sounded like things I'd hear in the Music Box, or I heard Farley play on the radio," says Pierre. "But when we made 'Acid Tracks,' that was an accident. It was just ignorance, basically. Not knowing how to work the damn 303."

In late 1985, by turning up all the 303's controls past the point at which any pub guitarist would dare to venture, Herb and Spanky made the 303 produce a sort of tortured alien bleep. Pierre then leapt on the machine and turned things up even more. "I started turning the knobs up and tweaking it, and they were like, 'Yeah, I like it, keep doing what you're doing.' We just did that, made a beat to it, and the rest is history." The resulting record would be called "Acid Tracks." Its name and its sound would be the basis of an entire subgenre of music.

The first thing the young producers did with their revolutionary track was take a tape of it over for Ron Hardy to play, waiting for two freezing hours outside the Music Box for his arrival. "Because he was the man. If he said he loved something, that was it. But if Ron Hardy had said he didn't like it, that would have been the end of acid."

When Hardy played it, the results were astonishing. "The fuckin' floor cleared," recalls Pierre with a laugh. "We just sat there thinking, 'OK, I guess he won't be playin' that ever again.'" But Hardy waited for the dancefloor to fill up and then forced the song on his clubbers again, gaining a slightly better reaction. He waited a while and then played it a third time. By the fourth time he played it, at 4 A.M. when everybody's drugs had kicked in, the crowd went ballistic. "People were dancing upside down. This guy was on his back, kicking his legs in the air. It was like, 'Wow!' People were going crazy, they started slamdancing, knocking people over and just going nuts."

Spanky, Herb and Pierre had originally titled the track "In Your Mind," but the clubbers at the Music Box, tripping on the club's spiked punch, had other ideas. It fitted so well with their LSD-infused frenzy, they called it "Ron Hardy's acid track." It caused a storm.

And it was only a reel-to-reel tape. Pierre and his friends had no idea how to have it released properly. "We was running around trying to ask people, 'How do you make a record? How does a record come out? Who do you go see?'" In the end, he scribbled a note to Marshall Jefferson, by then a recognized force on the scene. It read, "My name is DJ Pierre. I'm in a group called Phuture, and we did a track called Acid Tracks, and Ron Hardy has been playing this track off a reel. Could you help us make a record?" Marshall helped them mix it and told them to slow it down considerably—the original track was pitched at 130 bpm. For New York to get into it, he advised, it should be slowed down to around 120.

With the success of "Acid Tracks," the 303 became a coveted piece of hardware, and its aggressive bubblings quickly drenched the house scene. Part of its attraction was that its circuits will quite literally write the music for you, courtesy of the machine's randomizing function. Turn it on and there are a series of mutant basslines all ready to go. If you want a new pattern, you simply remove and replace the batteries and there'll be a whole new composition ready and waiting. Spookily, Pierre says, the line used in "Acid Tracks" is preserved forever in the bowels of that particular machine.

Moving House

Chicago produces a constant supply of church-trained vocalists. These angelic voices are kept in steady work because the city is also the advertising jingle capital of the world. A similar happy mix of the sacred and profane is exactly what powered house. It was a genre inspired as much by the classic spiritual dance songs of the seventies as by basic consumer computer technology. Thanks to this combination, in a process that owed virtually nothing to the musician and almost everything to the DJ, Chicago was the clearest example of disco being lovingly continued under another name.

But by 1987 the Chicago scene was faltering. Rap's belated arrival in the city caused some tension as the two rival cultures clashed, not least over the presence of gay clubbers. Many blame the rise of hip-house, a hybrid of the two genres popularized by artists like Tyree and Fast Eddie, for a weakening of the club scene (and a drop in the quality of the music). Marshall pins similar blame on the success of acid house, suggesting that because it was so easy to make an acid track, there was a flooding of the market and a massive fall in the number of records you could expect to sell locally. Acid's manic qualities also served to edge out the less frenetic styles of house.

The mafia, too, had a role in house's downfall, exerting their influence on the city's revitalized venues and accelerating clubland's cycle of openings and closures. After Power Plant closed in 1986, Frankie Knuckles went to CODs, a smaller, short-lived club. From there he opened a place called the Power House, but in 1987 the city authorities moved against after-hours clubs and he returned to New York. The Music Box closed in 1988.

Hardy got caught in a downward spiral of drug abuse. He started injecting, and would sell his mix tapes for a fix, his ravenous appetite for excitement degenerating with the years into a sickness that drove him to sell the rarest of records for a few dollars apiece. He died in 1992.

House, driven by its success overseas, became an export business. Because back at the end of the eighties, just as the music seemed to wither in its birthplace, across the ocean it was being championed to unforeseen heights.

TWELVE
TECHNO

The Sound

"The race which first learns to balance equally the intellectual and the emotional—to use the machines and couple them with a life of true intuition and feeling such as the Easterns know—will produce the supermen."

—Paul Robeson, 1935

"There are millions of people in Detroit. I'd say about thirty of them have heard of techno."

—Marc Kinchen, 1990

Detroit is only 300 miles from Chicago. You can drive between the two cities in four or five hours. And during the mid eighties, Juan Atkins, Derrick May and Kevin Saunderson would do just that, making the journey sometimes every week, to sell tunes to the city's hungry record buyers and to visit Ron Hardy's Music Box. Back home in Detroit, these three producers were constructing a new electronic vision of what dance music could be, a pure modernist style of synthesized soul that would take the name techno. However, it was only in Chicago that they could see the full power of their compositions. Their trips to the Music Box were where they garnered much of their inspiration, and it was here that they brought many of their tracks to see them tried out on Ron Hardy's maniac dancefloor.

Detroit techno is an ambitious sonovabitch. It is a music which aims at evolution. It wants to free itself from the baggage of all the world's previous music and take a few brave steps into the future. Where other forms are engaged in the routines of copying, emulating, recycling—returning to favorite themes and trusted basslines—techno hopes for the clarity of pure creation. It has rejected representation in favor of abstraction, thereby trying to achieve something newer and bolder. High ideals indeed. In a city wiped out by the loss of faith in progress, techno tried to construct a new belief in the future. Its basic notion was this: if house is just disco played by microchips, what kind of noise would these machines make on their own?

After the Fact

Techno's ideals can prove misleading, however. Its theories and manifestos were only formalized after its first records had been made. And though many commentators have emphasized its properties as cerebral listening music, it was undoubtedly constructed, at least at first, purely for the dancefloor. It would quickly gain a reputation as an auteur producers' medium, as something detached and experimental, but initially at least it was propelled by the same DJ-led dynamic as house and garage: of bedroom producers creating new music to feed the DJ and his hungry dancefloor.

However, because the Detroit scene had far less velocity than Chicago's or New York's (and because techno's pioneers were fairly peripheral to the Detroit club world in any case), techno's arena was rarely the city of its birth. At the beginning it was more or less a satellite of the Chicago scene. In fact, when techno emerged, it was just seen as house that had been made in Detroit. And later, as it found its biggest market over the Atlantic, Detroit techno was driven, to a considerable extent, by the reactions of DJs and clubbers in Europe.

Nevertheless, the Detroit sensibility was distinct in many ways. The city's posturban landscape—an important inspiration—was dramatically different from Chicago's bustle. Its musical background was surprisingly different, too. It had been washed by a far whiter strand of disco than Chicago, and enjoyed a significant love affair with the many European synth-pop acts of the time. In addition its airwaves carried a heavy dose of Parliament-Funkadelic's sci-fi cartoon funk. And there was much less of the furious backbiting competition which drove many of Chicago's music-makers.

Perhaps the most important difference was that Detroit's producers, were never fully immersed in a forceful club scene, and consequently had more time on their hands to be reflective. So, spurred by the critical interest in their music, they ended up being far more analytical about what they were doing. In Chicago, it was all about being *effective*: see what works, throw it into the pot (stealing anything you don't have), and get it onto the dancefloor before anyone else. The Detroit approach grew to be far more serious and self-aware. As their fame grew, and as they were pressed for the ideas behind their music, these people didn't want to be just kids throwing tracks together, they were thinkers, musicians, artists.

This has meant that the way techno has been written about has been quite atypical. Dance music is usually explored in terms of club cultures and collective styles; techno is more often discussed with reference to the genius of individual producers and with lengthy critiques of individual records. There is also a tendency to extrapolate its construction methods and its supposed subject matter to support some rather overblown critical theorizing. While it's easy to be carried away by its intellectual baggage, bear in mind that techno's poetic search for the soul of the machine is just a brainy way of saying, "We wanted to make funky dance music on cheap synthesizers."

Whether intentionally or not, techno's protagonists did a good job of rewriting the music's history, retrospectively adding layers of intriguing philosophy to their work. And journalists, enamoured by the idea of degree-level dance music, were keen to let them. Admittedly, it was music from a different place, with all that entails, but techno came to light as a colony of the Chicago house empire; it grew because it was another source of tracks for Ron Hardy's ravenous Music Box and for the UK acid house explosion. Only when British journalists came knocking did the Detroit producers formulate the "underlying" aims and ideas that made techno's aesthetic mission so radically different from that of house.

Even the name "techno" was bolted on at a relatively late stage. It might have already been a descriptive term, as in "my tracks are very techno," but it only came to be a fully distinct genre title in 1988 when Virgin wanted to market a compilation LP of Detroit tracks in the UK, and the British style press wanted a name so it could distinguish the music from house and hype it as the next big thing.

"Juan threw the term techno in our face," Derrick May confided to British journalist Kris Needs in 1990. "When I first did 'Nude Photo,' I said, 'I'm not calling my shit techno.' As far as Kevin and I were concerned, techno was considered hip hop. I didn't want to be lumped in with hip hop. Juan did an interview in *The Face* and Stuart Cosgrove said he needed a name for the music and the concept. Juan stood up and said, 'techno!'"

The Mojo and The Wizard

Detroit—the motor city. Here Henry Ford had pioneered mass production, planting the roots for the world's most concentrated center of automobile manufacture. Here many years later Berry Gordy had powered up another conveyor belt, that of the pop factory of Motown, from which came the op-

Mirror man—Derrick May reflects on the true nature of techno.

timistic soul of sixties America. Motown was the music of full employment, the sound of black blue-collar workers enjoying their fat auto company paychecks. The same Detroit affluence was at work a little later, allowing George Clinton to connect raw soul to some Marshall amps, add a heavy dose of acid and create the black funk rock of Parliament-Funkadelic. And here in the eighties, as the factories were downsizing and the city beginning to die, a trio of techno renegades would develop yet another new form of music.

Juan Atkins, Derrick May and Kevin Saunderson lived in Belleville, a leafy community to the west of Detroit, and met at junior high school. They were black living in a white suburb, so this brought them together. Derrick and Kevin both had dreams of playing pro football, another link. What really cemented their friendship, however, was music.

The three teenagers would listen to a nightly show "The Midnight Funk Association" and find themselves transfixed by the hypnotic voice and compelling music of DJ Charles Johnson—"the Electrifyin' Mojo" (over the years, his show has been transmitted from six Detroit-area stations). Mojo dispensed a variety of futuristic sounds, linking the galactic funk of hometown heroes, Parliament-Funkadelic, with a constant stream of soundtracks, classical music, white rock acts like J. Geils Band, along with the latest European synth pop.

Mojo gave Detroit a strong taste for Prince, so much so that in 1985 the Purple Rain tour played seven nights there. The music Mojo showcased would be an important focus for the Belleville Three, a shared reference for their future explorations, and there is no doubting the seductive, spaced-out authority of his shows. At a certain point every night, he would make an appeal, P-Funk-style, for the mothership to land, instructing his listeners to flash their lights on and off to guide the cosmic Afronauts home.

Another great influence on techno's pioneers was The Wizard, another important radio DJ of the time, who was later more commonly known as second generation techno producer Jeff Mills. His mix show on WDRQ threw together a breathtaking array of records, all stitched together with the ultra-fast dexterity of a hip hop veteran, a style he later brought to bear on his incendiary club DJ performances.

Cybotron

Of techno's three founders, Juan Atkins was the first musician. He had made music throughout his suburban childhood, playing bass and drums in garage funk bands. His tastes were wide, but he found himself entranced by the synthesized sounds that Parliament-Funkadelic had introduced to their work (thanks to keyboardist Bernie Worrell's innovations, the band was the first to use synthesized basslines). When one night on Mojo's show he heard this aesthetic taken to its limits in the funky computer music of Kraftwerk, he was stunned. "I just froze in my tracks. Everything was so clean and precise, so robotic," he told Sheryl Garratt in her book *Adventures in Wonderland.*

On graduating from high school in 1980, he bought himself a Korg MS10 keyboard and spent the summer putting rudimentary tracks together. After playing these to his new classmates at his college music course, he hooked up with Rick Davis, a rather shellshocked Vietnam veteran, eleven years older than himself, who went by the name 3070 and had an Aladdin's cave of sound equipment. Davis had already made an avant-garde electronic album *The Methane Sea*, which Mojo used to open his show. He and Atkins immediately formed a band, Cybotron.

Cybotron's first release, "Alleys Of Your Mind," came out in 1981 on their own Deep Space label. It was a sparse, pulsing electro track which convinced everyone who heard it that it was made by someone white someplace in Europe (in fact this was no accident, since it owes a considerable debt to a cut from Ultravox's *Vienna* LP called "Mr. X"). The record also displays parallels with Afrika Bambaataa's "Planet Rock," released in 1982, which pursued an almost identical vision of electronic funk, but was vastly more successful. "Alleys Of Your Mind" was only a local hit, aided by regular airings on the Electrifyin' Mojo's show, but after a couple more singles, "Cosmic Cars" and "Clear," they landed an album deal with Fantasy in California.

As important as the music were the ideas behind it. Davis had a distinct personal philosophy based on elements of Jewish mystic numerology (hence his name "3070"), selected science fiction texts and the futurological theories of Alvin Toffler, whose popular book *The Third Wave* niftily predicted a postindustrial future where information was the main currency. Toffler also claimed that the future would belong to society's techno renegades—rebels able to turn technology to their own ends. Such thoughts resonated powerfully with Atkins's dreams of futuristic music made with mass-produced electronic instruments. He and Davis spent hours discussing all this, applying these ideas to the postindustrial cityscape which was Detroit, and making it the driving force inspiring their music.

Cybotron, with a third member, guitarist John Howesley (christened "John 5" by Davis) made an album, *Enter*, but when the Hendrix-loving Davis made it plain he wanted to pursue a more rock-oriented direction, the band split. Atkins set up another label, Metroplex, and, as Model 500, which he felt was a suitably "nonethnic" name (and which was probably a nod to Davis's numerology), recorded techno's founding record, 1985's "No UFOs," a dark challenge to the dancefloor built from growing layers of robotic bass and percussion, with dissonant melody lines and barks of disembodied voices. It was undeniably the sound of Detroit's future.

The Belleville Three

Initially, Derrick May found Juan Atkins, his friend Aaron's older brother, to be very withdrawn, always playing music and rarely speaking to anyone. Eventually, though, the ice broke and the two teens forged a deep friendship. Juan had recorded some Gary Numan and Kraftwerk onto a tape that Derrick had left at his house. Juan was sure he wouldn't like it and offered him a blank tape as a replacement. Derrick took the cassette anyway, heard the music on it and came back bugging Juan to educate him in the wonders of this eerie European sound. Juan happily obliged, and the two of them would burn long hours listening to songs, discussing their origins and meanings, and the intentions which lay behind their creation.

"We used to sit back and philosophize on what these people thought about when they made music," May told Simon Reynolds in his book *Energy Flash*, "and how they felt the next phase of the music would go. And you know, half the shit we thought about, the artist never even fucking thought about!

"Because Belleville was a rural town, we perceived the music a little bit different than you would if you encountered it in nightclubs or in watching other people dance. We'd sit back with the lights off and listen to records by Kraftwerk and Funkadelic and Parliament and Bootsy and Yellow Magic Orchestra, and try to actually understand what they were thinking about when they made it. We never took it as entertainment, we took it as serious philosophy."

Completing the trio and bringing a broader outlook was Kevin Saunderson. With family in Brooklyn, including a brother, Ronnie, who was a sound engineer on the New York disco scene (he wrote a song for Brass Construction), he was able to spend his high school summers discovering the city's most influential clubs, including the Loft, the Paradise Garage, and in nearby New Jersey, Tony Humphries' Zanzibar. As his friends Juan and Derrick started making music together, Kevin remained an interested observer. Eventually, though, he would join them in setting up a studio and making records, and with his more club-based aesthetic would enjoy the greatest commercial success of the three.

The Prep Parties

The Detroit club scene at the time was small and far from influential in the normal sense. It was, however, highly distinctive, both musically and in terms of the nature of its events. Centered largely on the middle-class quarters of northwest Detroit, promoters (who were often still in high school) threw a succession of affectedly chi-chi parties. These were influenced by a combination of Italian high fashion and the English "new romantic" movement, and adopted names that reflected these rarefied aspirations: Plush, Funtime Society, Universal, GQ Productions and, later, Gables. One of the most successful was Charivari—promoter Kevin Bledsoe had appropriated the name from a chain of clothing stores in New York. This would provide the title of one of Detroit's early forays into electronic music, "Sharevari" by A Number Of Names (the spelling altered to avoid conflict with Bledsoe's organization). The "prep" parties, as they were known, were run like private clubs, pretty exclusive ones at that, and the dress was as important as the music, with the "preppy" look to the fore. By the turn of the eighties, these parties were regularly attracting anywhere up to 1,200 kids.

As disco suffered a meltdown, its sister sound, Eurodisco, had taken a hold on clubs in Detroit, mirroring its popularity in nearby Chicago (although in

Detroit it was more usually known as "progressive"). Producers like Jacques Fred Petrus (Peter Jacques Band/Change), acts like Capricorn, Klein & MBO and Telex, danceable new wave groups such as the B-52s, and British synth groups like Visage, Human League and ABC also enjoyed success on dancefloors. Listen to Visage's "Frequency 7" today, with its pulsing rhythm and harsh analogue sounds, and it could quite comfortably pass for an early Detroit techno record.

Along with "Sharevari" and "Alleys Of Your Mind," other locally made records found their way on to the party circuit's turntables. A pair of producers signed to Michael Zilkha's leftfield Ze Records, Don Was (Donald Fagenson) and David Was (David Weiss), released a series of inventive and playful dancefloor-oriented tracks under the name Was (Not Was), although they would have no significant commercial success until 1988's "Walk the Dinosaur." During studio downtime, Don Was produced a disc under the name Orbit called "The Beat Goes On," a popular local hit. He would also occasionally get together with the city's leading disc jockey, Ken Collier, and remix his own tunes under the name Wasmopolitan Mixing Squad (Collier and Was are credited as remixers on "Tell Me That I'm Dreaming" by Was Not Was).

The party scene was driven mainly by the promoters and their ever-changing fashion notions, but certain DJs were important, too. Of these, Collier was the most influential. Having learned his craft during the disco era, he was a fixture on both the prep party scene and in the city's gay clubs, and was widely seen as a powerful unifying force. He would also be among the first DJs in Detroit to play techno records like "No UFOs" and "Strings Of Life." Prep party promoter Hassan Nurullah recalled Collier in Dan Sicko's excellent book, *Techno Rebels*: "He was awesome. He'd get that big booty going, have a little glass of cognac . . . and he didn't do anything fancy, he just had a sense of what worked. He kept that party booming the whole time." Tragically Collier died in 1996 to a late-diagnosed diabetic ailment.

It was into this scene that Juan and Derrick launched themselves in 1981 when they set themselves up as DJs with a couple of other friends including Eddie "Flashin" Fowlkes (Saunderson would join them in 1984). They called themselves Deep Space Soundworks and played on the competitive party circuit.

By the end of 1983, the fragile peace that existed on Detroit's dancefloors began to evaporate with the intrusion of the "jits" (a local term for the more roughneck elements on the scene, most of whom came from the city's eastside and who favored a more electro-driven soundtrack) on to prep party territory. In an attempt to exclude "jits," prep party flyers would often included coded messages; "no hats and canes" was one popular invocation, a reference to gang members' penchant for carrying walking canes.

As Juan and Derrick's skills grew, the DJing process helped further crystallize many of their ideas. "We built a philosophy behind spinning records," May explained. "We'd sit and think what the guy who made the record was thinking about, and find a record that would fit with it, so that the people on the dancefloor would comprehend the concept. When I think about all the brainpower that went into it! We'd sit up the whole night before the party, think about what we'd play the following night, the people who'd be at the party, the concept of the clientele. It was insane!"

Because of its limited size, the club/party scene played only a peripheral role in Detroit techno's evolution. However, Sicko believes it's uniqueness was key to how the music mutated the way it did. "There *was* a scene in Detroit, albeit a very small one," he asserts. "It just wasn't anywhere near as developed as Chicago was. But it was that much more idiosyncratic. Detroit was very small cliques and very quirky, and that's why Detroit ended up sounding so different."

Techno Recorded

Whatever significance the Detroit club scene had in inspiring techno, it must be added that the Belleville Three were only very minor players on that scene. Their importance as DJs was minimal; only as producers did they start to get noticed.

Throughout the Deep Space period Atkins was making records with Cybotron. Then in 1985 and '86, after the band split, the first flurry of techno records was released. Following Model 500's groundbreaking "No UFOs," Eddie Fowlkes made "Goodbye Kiss," the second Metroplex release, and Derrick May, collaborating with Atkins, put out "Let's Go," a web of computerized Latin percussion and driving bass melodies.

Kevin Saunderson, as Kreem, released "Triangle of Love" and started his own label KMS (Kevin Maurice Saunderson), taking on a perplexing armory of aliases (Reese, Reese and Santonio, E-Dancer and Intercity, to name a few). His work is more obviously dance-driven, shown in such underground classics as "Just Another Chance," "The Sound" and "Rock To The Beat," and he went on to great success as Inner City in 1988.

Derrick May, too, created a label for himself, Transmat. On this, as Rhythim Is Rhythim he released timeless classics like "Nude Photo" and

"Strings Of Life," abstract compositions of bittersweet synthesized sound which evaded most established rules of dance music—"Strings Of Life," built from orchestra samples, had no bassline—but cleverly managed to drive clubbers wild. May furthered his reputation with "The Dance" and "It Is What It Is."

If at first this music was seen as a continuation of what was happening in Chicago, it soon became clear that it was something strikingly different. It was inevitable with all that sci-fi imagery, Alvin Toffler theories and affection for stark European synthesizer music that Detroit's music would end up someplace different to that made by the more obviously dancefloor driven party kids of Chicago. In common with many, Dan Sicko believes that techno as a genre began with "Nude Photo."

"The first x number of records, you can definitely argue that Detroit was an adjunct of Chicago," he says. "Until 'Nude Photo,' where it was like, 'Okay, this isn't house music anymore.'" Sicko argues that it was the radical construction of this record, the attention to detail in its instrumentation and its unwillingness to simply throw preexisting elements together, that made it such a turning point. "All the instrumentation was tweaked and altered purposely. If you want to get technical, I think that's when the first proper techno record was. With 'Nude Photo' Derrick May and Thomas Barnett, his collaborator on that track, changed the course of the Detroit sound."

A Suburb of Chicago

As Detroit's musical output gathered steam, it found its most important market in Chicago. Derrick May's mother had lived there since his last year in high school. He visited her regularly through the first years of the eighties and eventually stayed for almost a full year around 1984, soaking up the underground club energy that was lacking in Detroit: "Some people took me to the Power Plant where I heard Frankie Knuckles play," he remembered. "Frankie was really a turning point in my life . . . When I heard him play, and I saw the way people reacted, danced and sang to the song, I *knew* this was something special. Not just being a DJ and playing music and being on a mission, but playing music with love. This vision of making a moment this euphoric . . . it changed me."

He reported back to his friends at home, telling them of hearing Frankie Knuckles play the first house tracks on reel-to-reel at the Power Plant and witnessing the phenomenal abandon of Ron Hardy at the Music Box, playing his custom remixes and working a live drum machine over his records.

Like many of his Chicago peers, Derrick May considers Ron Hardy to have been the greatest DJ ever.

"The reason I think I progressed in dance music was because I had a chance to see a little bit of the future—gay black kids, straight black kids, everybody just going for it, and that was something you didn't see much in Detroit."

Although Derrick remembers Juan being quite dismissive about the Chicago scene—"At first he was like, 'Oh man, fuck that fag shit'"—eventually all three of the techno pioneers paid regular visits to the house clubs, and as they began producing records, they would drive carloads of them over to Chicago's record stores.

Derrick even played a small part in the avalanche of tracks which had started to flow out of Chicago, since he provided Frankie Knuckles's Power Plant with a 909 drum machine. Initially, Knuckles used this to boost the kick-drum sounds in older records, but the machine found itself in constant use as a series of would-be producers borrowed it to record tracks with, Chip E and Steve Hurley among them.

Juan Atkins has actually claimed a little more in the way of Detroit's influence on Chicago, suggesting that "No UFOs" was what inspired the first wave of house producers to make tracks. Since "No UFOs" came out in 1985 and Jesse Saunders's "On And On" was made as early as 1983, this can't be true, although Atkins's earlier records with Cybotron were certainly played on Chicago radio.

As well as Chicago, the early Detroit records made a dramatic impact on European dancefloors. However, they failed to ignite much interest in their hometown which to this day has an ambivalent attitude towards its latest, greatest export. As the precious cargo of Transmat, Metroplex and KMS records started traversing international borders, the trio found their greatest market overseas.

Techno Defined

For a long time, "techno" was more of an adjective than a noun. The word was first used as the name for a completely separate genre as late as 1988. Before that, its creators were happy to be labeled "house" and thrown in with the Chicago scene. In the *NME* in August 1987, Simon Witter described Derrick May as "one third of a team of Detroit house obsessives." May himself nonchalantly referred to his own music as house and didn't once mention anything about machines, computers or science fiction: "House represents basement music, club music, and if they forget that and go soft, kids will think that's what house is about. We're diehards."

What led to the music of Detroit being considered distinct from that of Chicago was initially largely a marketing ploy. By 1988 Chicago's music was big business in the UK, especially now that its acid house subgenre was causing such excitement. In 1987 Neil Rushton, a Birmingham northern soul DJ (who set up Kool Kat and later Network Records), started licensing tracks from the Detroit producers.

"As the house explosion started to filter through, I was drawn more and more towards it," he recalls. "But people like Damon D'Cruz at Jack Trax and the majors like Pete Tong, they'd already got Steve Hurley and Farley and all those guys. So the Chicago thing was already sewn up." Thanks to his connections to Detroit as a northern soul collector (Kool Kat was named after a big Detroit soul record by Joe Matthews), Rushton was immediately drawn to records appearing in England bearing a 313 area code.

"When the imports started coming in on Transmat, KMS and Metroplex I was probably more interested than the average person. So I rang up the number of one of the Transmat releases—'Nude Photo' I think—just before 'Strings Of Life' came through. I rang up Derrick and asked about releasing records and it all started from there really."

Rushton started licensing tracks for UK release, and quickly realized there was enough material for an album. He convinced Virgin to let him put together a compilation showcasing tracks from the Motor City. Its working title was originally *The House Sound Of Detroit.* However it became apparent, despite obvious similarities to house, that the music was very different from its elder brother in Chicago. Eventually, the title would be changed to reflect this, "We realized that the working title would be inappropriate because the music was so different and 'techno' was the obvious phrase to jump onto. We didn't come up with the phrase; it was the Detroit guys themselves, but they weren't using it as a description for the records they were making. It was just a phrase that they used." The fact that Juan Atkins delivered a last-minute tune to the compilation called "Techno Music" may well have tipped the balance. So the label decided to package it not as house but as a new subgenre. *Techno! The New Dance Sound Of Detroit*, screamed the title.

Rushton took journalists Stuart Cosgrove and John McCready to Detroit to write articles for *The Face* and *NME* around the album. Cosgrove elicited some fine poetry from the Belleville three as he prodded them to explain their music. Derrick May came up with the very elegant and much-repeated phrase,

"The music is just like Detroit, a complete mistake. It's like George Clinton and Kraftwerk stuck in an elevator." Kevin Saunderson explained that he had once been sacked from a local radio station for being "too ahead of his time," and Juan Atkins told him, "Berry Gordy built the Motown sound on the same principles as the conveyor belt system at Ford's. Today their plants don't work that way—they use robots and computers to make the cars. I'm probably more interested in Ford's robots than in Berry Gordy's music."

Voila! Techno was born. With its new name, not only was it now a distinct musical form, but it had an enticing philosophy behind it, neatly connecting the city to its sound. The journalists laid the postindustrial imagery on thick and the producers saw that intellectualizing their music would help them promote it. "Derrick was very articulate," says Rushton. "and was quick to see what people wanted. It did lend itself to these articles about Detroit being the forgotten city; the inner city being completely empty. So it can come across as a bit pretentious." Juan Atkins piled on all the Alvin Toffler sociology and weirdie sci-fi stuff his Cybotron partner Rick Davis had gotten him into (they had recorded a track called "Techno City" in 1984), and armed with this novel view of themselves as futurologist musical explorers, Atkins, May and Saunderson started making sure their work fitted the new game plan.

"We intellectualized it," says John McCready, "with Cosgrove gleaning those fantastic quotes. They weren't ready for us to come over and do that to their music. They were making dance records for themselves, and suddenly they found themselves having their music described as being 'a listening experience.'"

Probably if the Chicago producers had been quizzed at such length, they would have devised equally elaborate theories to explain their music. Journalists visiting Chicago had plenty to write about—its booming club scene and its cut-throat record business, its connections to the disco, soul and gospel traditions. The producers in Chicago didn't need to justify the fact that they used machines to make dance music—the machines were cheap and they couldn't play regular instruments. There was nothing more to it than that.

But in Detroit, thanks to some overefficient UK journalists, techno was set off on its express route to intellectualism. "Derrick, Kevin and Juan were all clever blokes and they switched on like light bulbs when they realized this was the way to play it," says McCready. "They realized, 'Oh, that's what you want then,' and hence all these mixes started appearing with no drums on them, and Derrick was encouraged into ridiculous tuneless noodling over the beginnings of his records."

Actually, despite techno's futuristic aspirations, the British trio were drawn by the music's historical links. "One of the things I always thought was the techno stuff had a jazz feel to it—as Carl Craig proved later," says Rushton. "And when we were over there we kept saying that. We kept making comparisons to the past. They were pressing records at Archer's Pressing Plant—which was a tiny little company, and the guy there was the son of the guy who used to do all the independent northern soul classics, so I was seeing all of those comparisons.

"And the other thing people got completely wrong is this image of techno being a new wave of dance music made in super studios. In fact, it was all made on old equipment. There were a lot of paradoxes going on there."

Kevin Saunderson and "Big Fun"

There was an unlikely hit buried on the *Techno!* album, a track that was to make Kevin Saunderson techno's first pop star. "Big Fun" by Inner City (Saunderson and vocalist Paris Grey, the same lineup as on his first single "Kreem") sold six million copies worldwide and entered the UK Top 10 in September 1988. It was a relatively happy techno track, one that undoubtedly owed a lot to Saunderson's exposure to the dancefloors of New York. A follow up, "Good Life," showed that it had been no fluke.

Rescued from obscurity by their British success (Atkins had moved briefly to L.A., Saunderson had enrolled at college), the Detroit producers renewed their music careers. Atkins was less than prolific, but the other two went on to define a full spectrum of techno: May as the thoughtful favorite of the cognoscenti, Saunderson with Inner City proving that techno was always going to have its feet on the dancefloor.

In the summer of 1988 Alton Miller and George Baker opened a small club called the Music Institute (or more correctly, "The Detroit Musical Institution") where May, Darrell 'D' Wynn and Chez Damier (Anthony Pearson) played. Although only open for just over a year, the Institute served to catalyze a little more of an actual scene in the city. Carl Craig, the leading light of techno's second generation of producers, remembers May's powerful dance sets there.

"He played the craziest edits of the wildest music. When Derrick DJed, you didn't know whether he was playing records or manipulating equipment.

People would go crazy. He would play 'Big Fun' three or four times and every time it blew my mind, as well as everybody else's." The Music Institute closed on November 24, 1989, to the sound of Derrick May mixing recorded clock bells over the top of "Strings Of Life."

European Techno and Trance

Around 1990, techno started to recombine with the German industrial genres which had helped to inspired it, to make a distinctive European style of techno. Belgium's R&S label was a key exponent of this sound, and artists like Jam and Spoon and Joey Beltram laid down a new schematic for the genre with records like Beltram's "Energy Flash." Another important label was Sheffield's Warp which rose from acid house with acts like LFO and Nightmares on Wax, and found direction with its 1992 *Artificial Intelligence* compilation album. On this, tracks by Autechre and Alex Paterson (of the Orb) greatly furthered the idea that techno could work away from the dancefloor as listening music.

Another European techno offshoot is trance, a bombastically uplifting form that fuses hard, fast rhythms to driving melodies, with an emphasis on drug-friendly arrangements such as the climactic snare-drum roll and the floaty, atmospheric breakdown. Trance originally found a home with the more mystical antiestablishment scenes such as the nomadic "travelers" (aka "crusties") and developed a focal point on the Indian Ocean coastline of Goa. At time of writing, trance, favored by DJ stars like Judge Jules and Paul Oakenfold, has a near-complete dominance of the UK commercial club scene and is making serious inroads worldwide.

Techno's most extreme incarnation is gabber (Dutch for "mate"), an impossibly fast style with all the musical charm of a steamhammer. The gabber scene is centered in Rotterdam, where a record of 160 b.p.m. is considered downtempo.

Computers Talking to Each Other

While house was happily based on reheating black disco, techno strove consciously to reject tradition and avoid copying previous forms. To be more accurate, techno copied previous forms—European synth pop and experimental music—which had already rejected tradition. Where house rejoiced in funky, soulful disco, techno was transfixed by Giorgio Moroder's computerized version. Where house stole melodies and basslines wholesale, techno preferred to compose new ones from synthesized notes and layers of tiny sampled sounds, supporting claims that it is a genre with greater musicianship. Techno is about going back to first principles, to notes and composition, to sounds and structure—continuing the synthetic agenda laid down by artists like Depeche Mode, Gary Numan and Kraftwerk.

In *Music Technology*, Derrick May said that he considered his music a direct continuation of the European synthesizer tradition, suggesting that English bands of the early eighties "hardly knew what they were doing. They left us waiting. Somebody like Gary Numan started something he never concluded."

"I want my music to sound like computers talking to each other," declared Juan Atkins. "I don't want it to sound like a 'real' band. I want it to sound as if a technician made it. That's what I am: a technician with human feelings."

Techno's love of the machine brought it an obsession with sounds rather than music, with texture and timbre rather than musical form. "If I can't create a sound that I like, I find it very hard to create a song," said Kevin Saunderson, who named one of his early releases "The Sound." "I get inspired by a good sound. It's like a message to me. It gives me a feeling for a rhythm or a melody. The sound's the most important thing."

Techno's vocabulary is often centered around the emotional content of its sounds.

"For my music, I'm not looking for commercial, warm sounds," explained May. "My string sounds are very cold, very callous. I give them a sort of warmth through the way I overlay them, but it's not really warmth, it's just a dreamy sort of feel."

An associated distinction is that techno often places far more emphasis on its melodies than on its rhythmic motor. Taken to its conclusion, this emphasis results in ambient techno, in music made for listening rather than dancing. In this form, techno became the inheritor of a long tradition of avant-garde music—Satie, Stockhausen and Steve Reich—and connected with such seventies electronic pioneers as Brian Eno and Ryiuchi Sakamoto, not to mention the more sixties tradition of "new age" music, complete with whale songs and cheeping birds.

Certainly techno's makers intend their music to be worthy of proper critical analysis and not just to make people dance. "I make my records in the hope that people will go and buy them to listen to as well as dance to," said Atkins in 1988. "A good dance track is going to grab your attention, but on top of that I want something that's interesting and different enough to make you take notice of it. I want to be as far on the edge as possible without going over. I want to stand out whatever I do, but not be so far ahead that people won't relate to it."

Dance Music with a Degree

Detroit techno's purity is very attractive. After detaching itself from Chicago, the music emerged unencumbered by a club scene, so its records could be critiqued as ends in themselves, rather than as expressions of a particular subculture. And because its declared aims were to cleanse itself of influence, it fooled critics into considering its antecedents largely irrelevant. Add the fact that its creators gave it plenty of intellectual backing—ten manifestos for every record—and here was the perfect form for anyone who wanted to get all literary about dance music.

This explains why techno appeals to the trainspotters so much. It also explains why what little intelligent dance music criticism there is shows a heavy bias toward techno. The more cerebral scribes have concentrated on techno, often to the exclusion of everything else, since it gives them more room to flex their academic skills. They love its postindustrial background and all its "soul in a microchip" ideologies. Finally, here's something worthy of all the critical theory they learned at college.

"It's been hijacked," maintains journalist John McCready, who insists that when he first met Atkins, May, and Saunderson, they considered techno simply as club music, party music. "I hate to look at the way it's written about now. There's no understanding of the personalities, there's no understanding of the dance history, of the humor of the people. It's been dried out and made European and claimed by a lot of intellectual knob-heads."

There's nothing wrong with a selective approach to music criticism, but don't think that techno's postpartum rationalizations give you any more reason to write about it than about house, funk or disco. Just because Detroit gave us tons of moody theories, while house brought us fluffy bras and the whooping of a lot of churchy queens, doesn't mean that techno should be portrayed as somehow superior. There has often been antipathy between the two scenes, but this has more to do with perceptions of purpose. In fact, much of the music ends up sounding remarkably close.

3 THE DJ TODAY

THIRTEEN
THE DJ AS ARTIST

Even Better Than The Real Thing

"1988 saw the latest would-be revolution happen in pop music. The DJ, with his pair of Technics and box of records, can make it to the top with a little help from a sample machine, squiggly bassline and beat box. Yet again this was interpreted as the masses finally liberating the means of making music from all the undesirables."

—Jimmy Cauty and Bill Drummond (KLF) in *The Manual (How To Have A Number One The Easy Way)*

"You can't make an omelette without breaking eggs."

—V.I. Lenin

So the DJ germinated rhythm and blues, he christened and disseminated rock'n'roll, he gave shape to reggae and he was the dazzling architect of the disco revolution. And then, from disco's hardy rootstock he singlehandedly bred hip hop, house, garage, techno and hi-NRG, not to mention all their offshoots and hybrids. But what else did he do?

What else? Not resting for a moment after a half-century building radical new genres, the DJ set off towards his current position as the most powerful creative force in popular music.

He became a producer, and given that he'd devised entirely new ways of conceiving and constructing music, he soon eclipsed the Luddite competition. His new postdisco genres gave unprecedented freedom to the nonmusician to make music, so of course it was DJs (as the cream of musical nonmusicians) who were best placed to take advantage. His star rose and rose. The music industry, which had never been too sure about the DJ, grew to love him for the way he could remix a song into any market; it adored him for the way his name could be used to sell collections of otherwise anonymous tracks. And when his dance revolution swept all other pop before it, the DJ found himself at the center of momentous social change, as he dramatically altered the way people consumed their music and enjoyed their leisure.

The DJ's craft and his skills were close to fully formed as long as twenty years ago. Disco and hip hop were his moments of true innovation. Most advances since then have come in his role as a producer, and in his possession of a good manager. But with wily representation and clever marketing, the DJ is now the hero of his age, a popstar, a crowd-draw, a reliable brand name. And he gets paid (like supermodels and movie stars, those other victors of late consumer capitalism) not according to how talented he is, nor how hard he works, but by the size of his franchise—how many ears he can reach and how many units he can shift.

How did all this happen?

The Arrival

The first explosion was loud, alien, devastating. It was the sound, between 1979 and '82, of hip hop announcing its British arrival: "Rappers' Delight," "Flash's Adventures On The Wheels Of Steel," Kurtis Blow, Tanya Winley, Funky Four (Plus One More), "Planet Rock"...

Matt Black of Coldcut, DJ and UK house pioneer, was hit square in the chest by the blast: "It just blew apart conceptions of what a song should be like. It was so far out, so radical."

"Everyone was completely like . . . 'Oh my god, what *is* this?'" recalls Dave Dorrell, DJ and another early UK house producer. "Rap, hip hop, was way beyond anything that you were accustomed to, or able to comprehend. It was a foreign language. What are these people doing? How do they do this? And what would it be like to see them doing it? It had just arrived here, and it was causing mayhem. Devastation. All of a sudden it was like, 'How can we get more of this drug?'"

The second impact, a few years later in 1985, '86, '87, came from house. Another alien musical language, equally devastating—Morse code from Mars. "Jack Your Body" and "Love Can't Turn Around," "Acid Tracks," "I've Lost Control," "Nude Photo," "Your Love," "Move Your Body."

"House just had a phenomenal impact," says Black. "Even straight away you realized that here was a new kind of music. As soon as you heard it you realized that here was a new form of energy that had materialized."

This wasn't just the latest batch of hot records from the States. This was revolution with no prisoners. The world was no longer flat. Blood was shed over the issue. Hip hop immediately drew a thick, inky line between the open-minded who—even though they didn't understand it—still got excited as soon as they heard its slaughtered beats, and the diehards in *Blues And Soul* who screamed "This isn't music," who couldn't believe the chiseling sound of scratching was rhythm, couldn't understand how someone talking in rhyme could replace singing. They just didn't get it; they just couldn't find its soul.

And house? House cleared dancefloors wherever it was played. Veteran DJ Johnny Walker was told, "You've gone right off the rails," when he introduced it to his funk crowd. When Maurice and Noel Watson started playing house at Delirium at London's Astoria, the management had to build a cage to protect them from the violent reactions of the hip hop heads. At another club, Jazzy M, the first to play house on British radio, was pulled off stage and threatened with a broken bottle for putting on house tracks. "What are you playing this gay music for, what are you doing? I wanna dance with my girl," shouted his attacker. When Mike Pickering came down to London from Manchester's Haçienda, a black guy handed him a note: "Stop playing this fucking homo music."

Dave Dorrell remembers getting his hands on three acid house records, some of the first to arrive—Phuture's "Acid Tracks," and "Frequency" and "Land Of Confusion," both by Armando. As soon as he played them, he knew how powerful this music would be.

"It was like a caveman with a spaceship. In the world of music, acid house was so far out there that it was beyond anything. There were no direction signs." Not only did the floor clear, but these records kept it empty for a full thirty minutes, even as the human pressure on the edges of the dancefloor grew to breaking point. Finally, he gave in and played them something they knew. "I had to play, I think, 'Across The Tracks,' and they literally *ran* onto the dancefloor. I thought, boy, this music is going to do something."

The Soul Mafia

At the beginning of the eighties, despite a healthy underground club culture, the British DJ lagged far behind his American counterpart. While the leading disco DJs in New York were already moving into production and remixing, in the UK the successful DJ was either a "personality" who chatted inanely between records, or a connoisseur who collected, appreciated and evangelized. The postdisco sounds of hip hop and house would soon revolutionize their craft, but before these new genres arrived, British DJs were largely unaware of the creative possibilities that disco had unleashed.

Even basic mixing techniques, *de rigueur* in New York since the start of the seventies, didn't make it over to the UK until 1978, when an American DJ called Greg James was imported to show how it was done. Brought over to play at London's newly refurbished Embassy Club, James stayed in England for several years and schooled many young DJs including Jazzy M, in American techniques (as well as running the Spin-Offs record store in west London).

There were several strong dance scenes existing at this time. The "Soul Mafia" was a small clique of soul and funk DJs centered around Chris Hill and Robbie Vincent. Younger mafiosi included Johnny Walker and Pete Tong, as well as Froggy, another of the DJs to whom Greg James had passed on his skills. Chris Hill had built a considerable reputation from the mid-seventies by playing a strong selection of hard-to-find black American imports first at the Goldmine in Canvey Island, and then the Lacey Lady in Ilford (both satellite towns to the east of London). He was quite a showman and thanks to his encouragement the Goldmine had a reputation for zany fashion fads. One brief period saw the clubbers dressing up in forties military fashion, with Hill obliging them by playing Glenn Miller.

The soul mafia coalesced around Hill's success. Its following was resolutely suburban and largely white. Here was a scene that elevated the smooth boogie of Kleeer and the bland soul of Maze to mythic status. Its dancefloors were usually filled with boys wearing alarmingly tight shorts, deck shoes and singlets, often brandishing cannon-sized air-horns. Although there were plenty of girls there, it was still a male-oriented scene. Initially no club owners would give up their prime weekend spots to them so the Soul Mafia's strength derived largely from all-dayers and Sunday events (like the "speed garage" scene years later). The all-dayers often attracted renegade northern soul fans who, despite the two scenes' considerable musical differences, would travel down to dance alongside the southern jazz-funkers. North also met south at soul weekenders like Caister and Bognor Regis, and all-dayers at Bournemouth, Birmingham and Leeds, where progressive northern jocks like Colin Curtis and Jonathan Woodliffe found common purpose with Chris Hill and with London DJs like Jay Strongman and Paul Anderson.

In the south underground club culture was fairly limited at this time so the Soul Mafia's influence was substantial. However, hip hop's arrival greatly eroded any notion of musical consensus and by 1987 there were massive fissures in the scene. Chris Hill wouldn't play rap or electro, claiming, "Just because it's popular with the black youth doesn't make it any good," and clung stiffly to a uniform sound of "real" soul. Pete Tong left the scene as a result: "When rap came along, me and Jeff Young became the embarrassment on the bill at those weekenders," he remembers. "Chris was like, 'Oh, fucking hell, here they are with that old racket!' And when house music came along, that was the last straw."

Rare Groove and the Warehouse Scene

Another significant UK scene through the eighties was to be found among the crumbling concrete of inner city London. Here imported Jamaican sound system culture had been put to fresh use by second-generation West Indians like Jazzie B, Norman and Joey Jay and Derek B. Inspired by club DJs George Power, Mark Roman and Greg Edwards, they largely eschewed their parents' dub and reggae tastes in favor of a grittier, more urban soundtrack. This mixed funk and soul together with the dramatic new U.S. import, hip hop, to make music perfectly suited to kids raised in the shadows of gloomy W11 tower blocks. Having been excluded from many west end clubs because of racist door policies, black kids found their entertainment in sound systems like Soul II Soul, Shake'n'fingerpop, Hard Rock, Funkadelic and Good Groove.

The sound crystallized around Norman Jay's "The Original Rare Groove Show" on Kiss FM—then a pirate station—where Jay reintroduced seventies funk tracks to an attentive audience. Although the warehouse scene was never wholly about such records (go-go, hip hop, electro and even early house were as likely to feature in its playlists), these were quickly used as a journalistic shorthand, and the music was dubbed "rare groove," after Jay's show.

As a largely retro form, rare groove picked up many of the same characteristics as northern soul. DJs searched rabidly for obscurities, paid huge sums for them and covered up labels to protect their identities. However, the fact that it was based resolutely in urban London gave it far greater cachet than the northern scene had ever enjoyed. Record companies leapt on it as a trendy way to market back catalogue material, its racially-mixed crowd and their funky seventies fashions were celebrated in the new "style" magazines, *i-D* and *The Face*, and rare groove grew into a fairly influential cultural force. And it was far from the whole story. There were weekend-long punk parties in docklands, the more unorthodox dance modes of Dirtbox and the chi-chi extravagance of Westworld's big-ticket parties. The presence of such a vibrant nightlife, enjoying the patronage of the capital's tastemakers, was the main factor delaying the acceptance of house in London.

"There wasn't really a need to change," remembers DJ/producer Terry Farley. "Everyone was running around wearing Duffer and flares, Norman Jay was carrying the swing with Gilles Peterson and the Young Disciples. There were great parties going on. Norman Jay did a Shake'n'fingerpop at the Town & Country Club in 1987 and there were 4,000 people in there. You'd go to a club and Bobby Byrd would be playing. It was brilliant. London was really, really happening in '87."

Eventually, as we'll see, the warehouse scene and many of its DJs would form a foundation for the acid house explosion, giving it the underground structures—unlicensed venues and an effective communications network—by which it would establish itself. However, for a long time rare groove prevented house gaining a foothold.

The Haçienda and Madchester

While the south was violently divided over house, the north had no such hesitancy. DJs Graeme Park at Nottingham's Garage and Mike Pickering at Manchester's Haçienda fell for it wholesale, as did their clubbers.

"They were more on it," says Pete Tong. "The day a house record came in, they chucked all the old ones out. They were looking at us, going, 'You fucking southern soul tossers!'"

The Haçienda was opened on May 21, 1982 by stone-age funnyman Bernard Manning. His famously bigoted jokes didn't go down too well and he returned his fee, saying, "Take my advice, never hire a comedian." The forward-looking musical policy was also a little out of sync with the clientele's expectations. The original resident DJ, Hewan Clark, programmed a mix of black funk, soul and disco, while sullen students mooched around the cavernous space in raincoats waiting in vain for Echo & the Bunnymen to be played.

The club was the brainchild of a group of Manchester music folk including Tony Wilson, supremo of Factory Records, and Rob Gretton, New Order's manager. It even had a Factory catalogue number, FAC 51. And it was modeled unashamedly on the great clubs of New York: the Paradise Garage and Danceteria. As Wilson put it: "I just thought, why hasn't Manchester got one of those? Fucking New York's got one, we should have one."

New Order were also among the club's directors, and as the band was regularly over in New York recording with Arthur Baker, they formed the lynchpin of the Manc-yank connection. "There's always been this big underground link with New York, because of New Order and Factory's early success there," Mike Pickering told Jon Savage in *The Haçienda Must Be Built.* "The most important thing about the Paradise Garage was that Larry Levan used to mix these underground New York records with records on Rough Trade or Factory, and that was what first got me really into New York. As far as I was concerned, the dream was that the Haçienda would be like that."

As well as these connections to New York's more progressive clubs, the scene in the north of England could claim close musical kinship with Chicago and Detroit. Northern soul had made earlier ties and, more recently, electronic bands from England's northern industrial cities—Human League, Cabaret Voltaire, ABC, New Order—had provided crucial inspiration for the pioneers of house and techno. The "new romantic" movement, as this became known, is nowadays derided for its chronic narcissism and overuse of Max Factor, but many of its records still stand as darkly electronic slices of futurism. Producers like Richard Burgess, Trevor Horn, Zeus B Held and Mute founder Daniel Miller fashioned protohouse and gleaming funk from huge machines that make today's synths look like pocket calculators. Mike Pickering's projects Quando Quango and T-Coy were among the arty experiments and pop confections, as were acts like Art of Noise, Fashion, Soft Cell, and Life Force, an outfit fronted somewhat improbably by Rob Davis, the ex-guitarist for glam-rockers Mud. As a result, in the north where this electronic pop had largely originated, there was a logic and continuity to the new music which London couldn't hear. To clubbers in places like Manchester and Sheffield, house completed a circle; it was their own music sent back to them with an injection of black funkiness. In the south by comparison, rare groove, hip hop and the short-lived go-go craze all but eliminated any love for the synth-pop bands of the early eighties.

By 1986, the Haçienda's Nude night—having started two years earlier—had switched to a playlist heavily weighted with Chicago house. With the recruitment of local boy John Hibert (aka Jon Da Silva) and Graeme Park from Nottingham, together with a batch of ecstasy courtesy of a gang from nearby Salford, the fuse was lit. Another night, Hot, despite only running for a few months in 1988, was also hugely influential. The sullen students who had populated the Haçienda in its early days were now replaced by a combustible tribal mix of dancers, many fueled by the strange new empathetic hug-drug.

Even after acid house had swept the UK, Manchester's take on the music remained distinctive. It was here, as the eighties closed, that "indie dance" was born, when local bands, led by the Happy Mondays, combined guitar-based rock with the new dancefloor aesthetic. Frontman Shaun Ryder confessed that in a reverse of accepted tradition the Mondays were a musical habit formed around some serious drug-taking, and their scratchy psychedelic rock-funk proved the point. Remixed by London DJ Paul Oakenfold their raucous reading of John Kongos's "Step On" became their first UK Top 10 hit in 1990. The Stone Roses followed in their wake, welding this baggy Mancunian rock to James Brown rhythms, as did bands like the Charlatans (the Small Faces without the faces), The Inspiral Carpets and the impossibly hopeless Northside. "All Manchester bands began sounding like 'Funky Drummer' played by the Velvet Underground," said one commentator. Manchester was dubbed "Madchester," A&R men descended on the city in droves, and the sound spread nationally. Scotland's Primal Scream had their "I'm Losing More Than I'll Ever Have" wrenched apart by Boy's Own DJ Andrew Weatherall to produce the supremely twisted remix, "Loaded," another key indie dance record.

After acid house, this sound was seen as a brief resurgence of band-driven music, but it was actually a clever reconstruction of rock to make it palatable to a market that had learned how to dance. That even guitar rock bowed to the dance revolution was an indication of the power unleashed when America's radical new DJ-forged music combined with Britain's long established club scene.

The Revolution Will Be Synthesized

Upon arrival in the UK, hip hop and then house did far more than just divide people along lines of taste. With them these new forms also brought radically new ways of making music. They brought amazing new ways of even *thinking* about music. Hip hop fostered the idea of sampling, of stealing rather than emulating, of making patchwork music from a multitude of sources. House encouraged this idea too, and house also showed—quite conclusively—that music made with drum machines and synthesizers could be as sexy, funky and downright danceable as anything made with wood, brass and steel.

Now, given that these new postdisco forms had been created by DJs, it was no surprise that DJs were best placed to adopt them. House and hip hop had both emerged as the DJ's response to the demands of his dancefloor, they were based on the DJ's peculiar understanding of music, and they were made in ways that most DJs could easily follow. House and hip hop were revolutionary for the jolt of novelty and excitement they gave the UK club scene, but they were also vitally significant because they made the DJ's move to production inevitable. With rare groove ruling the roost there was little pressure to venture into the studio: unless he was also a talented musician or experienced producer, a DJ in love with old soul records or polished jazz-funk didn't have much hope of making his own music. However, a DJ blown over by the sound collages of hip hop or energized by the synthetic beats of house might perfectly well expect to cook some up for himself. A generation of British DJs became remixers and producers as a result, and in the ever-fertile musical melting pot of urban Britain, a new era of dance music began.

Double Dee and Steinski

A brief clarification is needed here. While the first real hip hop records were nothing short of a mindfuck for most people, the way they were made was far too intimidating to inspire a cavalcade of UK copyists. This role instead fell to the records made by New York sound engineer Douglas DiFranco and advertising copywriter Steve Stein, aka Double Dee and Steinski, who showed that it was possible to make hip hop without having to spend years perfecting supernatural turntable skills.

Already an obsessive record collector, Stein realized that he could emulate a quick-mixing scratch DJ with the studio technology he used to make radio ads. "I didn't really want to become a scratchy guy, like a turntablist. It obviously took a lot of time to learn how to do, and I had a job." Instead, at the end of 1983, the duo took six crates of records into the studio, fired up the eight-track recorder, locked the door and emerged with "Lesson One" (aka The Payoff Mix), a frenzied masterpiece made from a bombardment of cutup chunks of other records—pieces of "Adventures On The Wheels Of Steel," a bit of James Brown, "Buffalo Gals," Funky Four's "That's The Joint," a little Culture Club, The Supremes, "Rockit," a snatch of Humphrey Bogart and a hundred more.

The catalyst for this project had been a remix competition sponsored by Tommy Boy records. Come up with the best remix of the G.L.O.B.E. and Whiz Kid track "Play That Beat Mr. DJ" and you'd have it broadcast on the radio.

"Six weeks later, after some meeting at the agency, my secretary goes, 'Hey, Tommy Boy just called, Tommy Boy himself.' And I went, 'Yeah, why?'"

"'You won that contest.'

"'We *won???*'"

Stein and DiFranco were whisked into hip hop society, they met all their DJ heroes (who all said "... but they're *white*!") and they recorded more tracks.

There was "Lesson Two," a James Brown megamix; "Lesson Three (History of Hip-Hop)," an amalgam of the most ubiquitous old school breaks; and then Steinski's solo project "The Motorcade Sped On," a satirical cutup based on the news soundtrack from the Kennedy assassination. Though these records could never be released commercially, due to their huge volume of illegal samples, Tommy Boy pressed a great many promotional singles and when a few made it to London, they were gold dust.

As well as the sheer number of different sources which had been combined in these records, it was because they were discernibly the result of tape-splicing rather than turntable skills which made them so exciting to British ears. Where Grandmaster Flash had wowed with his dexterity, Steinski's records suggested an easier method of construction. The absence of rapping was another key factor. Here was the green light to make a record for anyone who loved hip hop but a) couldn't scratch, and b) couldn't rap.

Coldcut and M/A/R/R/S

One group influenced profoundly by the Double Dee and Steinski collages was Coldcut, the musical partnership of ex-art teacher Jonathan More and computer programmer Matt Black, both DJs.

"They were actually *lessons*," says Black, explaining that, as their titles suggested, they saw Steinski's records as practical instruction. "This is how you can go about taking a bunch of old stuff and make it into something new. It wouldn't have happened without those blueprint records."

Inspired by what they heard, Coldcut became the first UK act to release a sample-built record—1987's "Say Kids, What Time Is It?" When the track was released, they upped its desirability by pretending it was an American import, even to the extent of scratching off the matrix numbers at the center of the records.

Another London DJ who couldn't wait to try his hand at the new music was Dave Dorrell. In spring 1987 he was approached by MTV to create some music for a series of video jingles for the channel's European launch. He teamed up with Martin Young from the band Colourbox, who had the necessary studio experience, and set out, as he says, "to put as many edits into fifteen seconds as possible." The resulting music, an intense montage of cut up sounds, graced screens for a few months, but it also whetted their appetite for further production. So, as part of a project involving Colourbox and another band A.R. Kane, and with the addition of CJ Mackintosh as their scratch DJ, they formed M/A/R/R/S (an acronym of the band members' names). With Coldcut's "Say Kids ..." and Steinski's records as admitted influences, they scraped together as many upfront tunes as they could find and put together "Pump Up The Volume," a rapid-fire collage of vocal snatches, including Israeli singer Ofra Haza, Criminal Element Orchestra chanting, "Put the needle to the record," Public Enemy shouting, "You're gonna get yours!" and some James Brown grunts, all cemented by an insistent dance beat. This rocketed to #1 (UK) in September 1987.

Just before this, Coldcut had put together "Beats And Pieces," a collage of sampled doorbells plus a bit of Vivaldi. Then, following fast behind M/A/R/R/S, and using almost all the same sampled elements, came Coldcut's remix of "Paid In Full" by U.S. rap group Eric B. and Rakim.

"With Eric B. and Rakim, we were kind of giggling all the way through it, thinking that we were making it so fucked up, people wouldn't be into it," confesses Coldcut's Jonathan More. "We thought, 'This'll fuck 'em up. They won't be able to handle this.'" Eric B. and Rakim themselves hated it, but the record-buying public shot it to #15(UK) in November 1987. In the wake of their success, Coldcut moved towards a more house-influenced style with records like "Doctorin' the House" featuring Yazz on vocals and "People Hold On" with Lisa Stansfield.

There was an explosion of energy as UK producers (nearly all of whom were DJs) took up the hip hop and house blueprints—readily fusing elements from the two genres—and made their own readings of the new dance aesthetic. In late 1987 and early '88 came a score of pop hits obviously built from these influences. Bomb the Bass with "Beat Dis," S'Express's "Theme From S'Express," A Guy Called Gerald's visionary "Voodoo Ray" and 808 State's "Pacific State" were some of the key moments. All made the charts.

Baby Ford made the first UK acid house record, "Oochy Koochy," and D. Mob gave the country a taste of London's acid club scene with the awful "We Call It Acieed," which went to #3(UK) and caused the BBC to ban all songs containing the word "acid."

KLF and the New Punk

Another lively impetus was punk, for its still-resonating do-it-yourself ideology and its guerrilla approach to the music industry. "The DIY record thing, that was very important," says Matt Black. "In the late seventies, the idea that you could actually make a record yourself was very powerful. I did that with my little band at college. I'm sure hundreds of other people did." Punk had spawned scores of tiny independent labels as people realized they didn't have to sell their soul to a major label to get a record released; these upstart independents provided a model that hundreds of dance labels would follow.

As well as their punky readiness to put out their own records, another reason for Coldcut's head start had been their familiarity with a piece of simple punk technology, the four-track recorder. "By the time I got round to doing 'Say Kids . . .' I had an advantage, which was that I knew what a four-track was," says Black. "Say Kids . . ." was done on a Portastudio and a cassette machine with an analogue pause button, two turntables and a DJ mixer, and some sound effects."

New technology was a vital force in Britain, as it had been in Chicago and Detroit. When the first wave of UK house broke, affordable digital sampling was yet to come, but tape sampling was easy enough and drum machines and synthesizers were becoming ever more commonplace. With these digital instruments, the punk manifesto that anyone could make music, no-experience-necessary, could be fully realized. Visionary composer John Cage had once written, "What we can't do ourselves will be done by machines and electrical instruments which we will invent." Now such machines were a reality and would-be producers were able to sidestep the fact that they had zero musical training (and sidestep studio fees of £1,000 a day) and immediately start putting music together in their bedrooms.

DJ/producer Norman Cook, then playing bass with the Housemartins, agrees that the punk do-it-yourself ethos was important: "There was an irreverence to the rules, like you can make a record that's really repetitive and isn't very musical and was made at home in your bedroom and doesn't have chords, drummers, singers, or anyone who can read a musical note."

Importantly, the sound everyone was chasing was quite lo-fi. Hip hop and Chicago house was all the more inspiring for the very fact that it was far from polished. As Matt Black says, "There was a nicely ignorant attitude which was that if it sounded fresh, you were in. So just by sampling one bass note off a JBs record into this £20 Casio sampler, you could play a bassline. Yeah, it sounded muzzy, but it actually had weight to it and a great sound. There must have been a lot of people that felt as we did at the time—Hey! Wow! We can do this. We can actually do this ourselves."

There were certainly plenty of old punks who saw the lure of this new music. Kris Needs, Andy Weatherall and Mike Pickering all had roots in punk, and would all enjoy success with house. Two others, Jimmy Cauty and Bill Drummond, came together as the JAMs (Justified Ancients of Mu Mu), and later KLF (Kopyright Liberation Front), which, in their mission to annoy, seemed to pick up where the Sex Pistols had left off. Bathing their projects in a rich web of mystic references taken from cult book *The Illuminatus Trilogy*, Drummond and Cauty attacked all that was sacred to the rock-based music industry. Playing the game by all the wrong rules, they assaulted the dull notion of originality, took free-for-all sampling to extremes, and released a series of outrageously copyright-infringing records. Then, in a blend of eager cynicism and inspired originality, they put a collage record together and took it to #1(UK). With a title—"Doctorin' The Tardis"—that was a piss-take of Coldcut's "Doctorin' The House," it combined glam rock, rapping and the theme tune from the TV show *Dr. Who.* It reached the UK's top slot in June 1988.

After their chart success, they wrote a book called *The Manual (How To Have A Number One The Easy Way)*, which described exactly what its title promised, giving an incisively amusing insight into the workings of the pop industry. At least one group copied their instructions to the letter and did indeed have a hit record. *The Manual* reminded that talent borrows, but genius steals:

"It is going to be a construction job, fitting bits together. You will have to find the Frankenstein in you to make it work. Your magpie instincts must come to the fore. If you think this sounds like a recipe for some horrific monster, be reassured by us, all music can only be the sum or part total of what has gone before. Every number one song ever written is only made up from bits from other songs. There is no lost chord. No changes untried. No extra notes to the scale or hidden beats to the bar. There is no point in searching for originality."

This could have been the manifesto for what was underway—nothing less than a revolution, precipitated by the DJ, in the acceptable way to make music.

DJ/Producer/Remixer

Since the DJ is an expert at making people dance, it was inevitable that he would eventually dominate the making of dance music itself. Most successful DJs now carry the job title DJ/producer/remixer. Making their own records, or reconstructing those made by others, is a natural extension of the club DJ's trade, a way to put his creative stamp on the world. It's a way of distilling the particular sound he favors in his club performances into a more tangible form and, importantly, it's how a DJ can most convincingly claim artist status.

"Most DJs become DJs because they love the music, and if you love the music, you feel you have some of it in you waiting to come out," says Norman

Cook. "You're playing tracks that are really simple. You think, this is just a couple of samples and a drum machine, I bet I could probably do that. And invariably, you can."

The DJ has a powerful advantage when it comes to making music digitally. Today, thanks to the (DJ-derived) concept of musical collage and the equipment which makes it possible, what a producer does in the studio to make a dance record is almost identical to what he would do to make a remix, and little different in principle from what a DJ does in a club. When a good DJ performs, he will be layering parts of records over each other, introducing snatches of one into a second, weaving and splicing different elements to make an original suite of music. Similarly, making or remixing a dance record is usually a case of playing around with relatively large chunks of sound (i.e. samples and predetermined rhythms), and combining them to make something new. The studio allows much greater levels of complexity, but at heart, constructing or reconstructing a dance record is very like a compressed version of DJing in a club.

The new methodology has the added bonus of being technically undemanding. With a good studio engineer to actually press all the buttons and achieve the desired results, it's perfectly possible for a complete novice to make a great dance record. All they need are workable musical ideas. And a good DJ, even the most technically clueless, will have a steady supply of those.

"When you're DJing, you spend untold hours just standing watching people dance," explains Cook. "And you begin to realize which bits of a record people react to and which bits get them going. You just learn what makes people dance." And this experience translates easily into inspiration for remixing and production. "When I'm in the studio, I think back to the night before and what kind of things worked with dancers. You remember how you felt when you put a tune on and it rocked the crowd; or when you played a groove that the crowd totally got into, even when they'd never heard the record before. It doesn't necessarily mean you make great pop music, but if your music's aimed straight at the dancefloor it gives you a head start."

Most DJs would agree that the leap from playing records to making them is a small one; few see the move from DJ booth to recording studio as anything other than a natural progression. "Everything I've learned is through playing records. It triggered everything," says Kenny "Dope" Gonzales, one half of Nuyorican duo Masters At Work, one of the most respected remix/production teams of the nineties. "DJing was our training and it still is," adds his partner "Little" Louie Vega. "Learning the structure of songs, the bars, the breaks, is all through DJing."

The Evolution of the Remix

Remixing was first done in Jamaica in the sixties when DJ/producers started to unravel songs into one-off versions and dub-plates, making them more effective for outdoor sound systems. A similar goal was at work in mid seventies New York when the disco and hip hop DJs started the technique of cutting rapidly from one record to another to extend the best passages, and began reconstructing songs on reel-to-reel for the same effect. Many of the disco DJs enjoyed careers as commercial remixers and in New York at least it was quickly an accepted part of the job—a way for the DJ to feed his dancefloor, to make his performance more distinctive and, by making nondancey songs suitable for a dancefloor, to enlarge his armory of records.

Remixing, at its simplest, is usually a straightforward process of sorting out a track's good elements from bad, relative to the dancefloor. As Paul Oakenfold puts it: "Someone'll play you something. You say, 'That's wrong, that's wrong, that's wrong,' take all of them out and replace them with this, this, this and this. Rearrange it—and it'll work."

This basic description belies the fact that the concept of the remix has evolved dramatically. A remix can be anything from a slightly different arrangement of a song to a track that bears hardly any relation to the original.

At first the remixer only made structural changes. Record companies were very protective of the original song and it was all you could do to add a conga.

"In the beginning, you remixed the original track," explains David Morales, one of the world's best-known remixers. "You used what was there to create the intro, your body, your break, your tag—the end of the song."

But remixers were soon allowed to add a few new elements.

"You might change the bassline, add percussion, or you added some other things, but you still had the song. You still had the artist intact."

A third stage came when the vocal track was used intact but the music accompanying it was replaced completely. "You started to put *new* music on remixes. And all you had left from the original was the vocal track. Now people expected to hear something totally different when they bought a remix."

Finally, remixers were given a free hand to scrap anything from the original and add anything they liked from other sources. In some, nothing of the original record remained except perhaps a tiny sampled snatch of vocals or instrumentation. Here, the remixer constructed an entirely new track and incorporated a few yelps from the singer, or a couple of stabs from a guitar. Strictly speaking, the remixer was now doing full production (although not getting any royalties or publishing fees for it, because contractually it was almost always only a remix). This is today's most common form of remixing. "It's totally leftfield now," says Morales. "It's totally in another place. I mean, let's not even call it remixing anymore. It's production."

Now that such radical remixing is so prevalent, the success of a dance record often has very little to do with the original artist or the original song. To a craftsman like Morales who prides himself on respecting the original, and who is one of a select few who are capable of full vocal remixes, this is overstepping the mark.

"Somebody says, 'I need a remix.' So you take a piece of a vocal: '*Bla*' and stick it on a rhythm track you have already sitting around. That's a remix? That represents the artist? That doesn't represent the artist, it represents *you*."

But for many an ambitious DJ/remixer, that is the whole point.

Remix and Restyle

Take a painting, cut it into pieces and rearrange the bits. How much do you have to change it before the end result is your work and no longer something made by someone else? Does it help if more people like your collage than liked the original painting? Can the collage be a genuinely new piece of art?

By the end of the seventies, DJs knew that the remix could go further than just make a song more *functional* for the dancefloor. It also offered them a route into the record industry and the means to finally gain recognition as creative artists. By adding stylistic twists, they could give a song the precise musical flavor they wanted, and if their enhancements were individual enough, these would mark out the remixer—rather than the original writer/musician—as the creative force behind a track. If their particular flavor was reasonably consistent over a series of records, a remixer could even develop a "sound," just like any other recording artist. And since a DJ's remixes were usually based on the kind of music he chose to play when he performed in a club, the musical style evident on his remixes would serve to reinforce and further distinguish the musical style of his DJing, and vice versa. Through remixing, the DJ had a way of pushing his music in a distinctive direction, both on the dancefloor and in the studio.

When remixes started being more successful than their originals (usually because they'd been made infinitely more danceable), the remixers started taking the limelight away from the original artists. And as remixes strayed further and further away from their originals stylistically, they started to look like completely new things. The new studio methods had made remixing and production more or less indistinguishable, as had the hip hop DJs who had started producing records by more or less recreating their live performance in the studio. By the mid-eighties, certain remixers were enjoying name recognition and both dancefloor and chart success, and as the DJ's new postdisco genres took hold, the lines between remixing and authorship started to fade.

The idea that a remixer can make something new, that he can do something as creative as original production, has its earliest precedent in Jamaica. Here, since the sixties, certain dub remixers had enjoyed equal recognition to the artists in their records. However, it took a while before this idea gained currency anywhere else. Disco produced several star remixers—pioneers like Tom Moulton, Walter Gibbons, Jim Burgess—but they never enjoyed star billing on their records: appreciation of their artistry was largely confined to the closed world of other DJs. Slightly later, figures such as Shep Pettibone, Jellybean, Larry Levan and François Kevorkian were recognized as having a magic touch, and often when they did a remix their names were fairly prominent on the credits. However, when Epic in the UK emphasized Kevorkian's name above all others on a compilation of his disco remixes, his U.S. label Prelude was incensed that the remixer's name should overshadow the acts themselves.

It was really only with the emergence of house that remixing was widely seen as a genuinely creative activity, when the key DJs of the period—Frankie Knuckles, David Morales, Tony Humphries—made having a reputation as a DJ and a reputation as a dance producer/remixer virtually interchangeable. A DJ's studio work started to become, as it is today, an important means of self-promotion and in the UK at least, the DJ/remixer had started his journey towards pop-star status.

Certain American jocks became gods in the UK, not by virtue of their DJ performances, but simply because of their studio work. Brooklyn producer/remixer Todd Terry exemplified this. In the middle of the nineties he commanded a DJ fee higher than anybody, yet his fame came not from playing records but from production and remixing. And his success in this came from marking himself out with a highly distinctive style. By grafting the hard New

York hip hop aesthetic onto house, he had brought a richer, stronger percussion palette to the genre in records like Royal House's "Can You Party" and Todd Terry Project's "Weekend" and "Bango" (all 1988). "That Chicago sound. I took it to the next level," he says. "You'd listen to it and say only Todd would do that, that's Todd's drum pattern, that's his *sound*, the dark, wild hype sound."

By 1990 the wider music industry felt ready to invest in the idea of the DJ as artist, and there was a signing frenzy in which Frankie Knuckles, Blaze, Robert Clivilles and David Cole, and Lil Louis were all awarded album contracts. On the whole they were marketed as producers who happened to be DJs, with different vocalists and musicians appearing on each track. But most of these album projects bombed commercially (only Clivilles and Cole, as C&C Music Factory, enjoyed any real success) and U.S. major labels once again saw dance music as a risky business, and the idea of the DJ as recording artist as something best left to the independents.

The DJ's rise to artist status was finally ratified in 1993, when a DJ's remix album was released with all the fanfare of a major artist and aimed, in the wake of the UK's dance transformation, squarely at the pop market. Sasha (Alexander Coe), a DJ who had risen to fame as resident at Shelley's, a club in the north of England, released an album made up entirely of remixes (*Sasha: The Remixes*). These weren't songs that he had originated in the studio. He wasn't presented as a producer who was incidentally also a DJ. These were songs originally written and recorded by other artists entirely, and many of them well-known, successful artists. Sasha, had only *remixed* the tracks. Despite this, these reconstructions were on *his* album, with *his* name in the title, and were to be considered *his* pieces of music. But most importantly, unlike the two or three remix albums that had predated it, it wasn't a small pressing aimed strictly at connoisseurs and other DJs. It was a major release. "Sasha is living proof of the dictum that DJs, as dance music's prime movers, are ideally placed to take that music to new levels as producers," declared Nick Gordon Brown's liner notes. "The lines between DJs and artists, remixers and producers are getting ever more blurred."

The Remix Goes to Market

Though it took them a while to recognize the DJ as an artist, the record companies hadn't been slow turning his remixing skills to their advantage. In the disco era they had quickly realized that having a dance version of a tune (which had originally been made for the radio) allowed them to promote it to a whole new audience via the clubs. In the nineties, when dance music had evolved into highly compartmentalized scenes, this idea of remixing for marketing purposes was taken even further.

A really radical remix can push a track into a whole new genre and make it appeal to a completely new set of fans. A Mariah Carey song which works great as a piece of radio pop could be remixed into a house record, there could be a hip hop version, you could even get someone to remix it so it worked in a techno club. In an effort to capture each segment of the fragmented dance world, labels started making the remix a vital part of their marketing strategies. Dance singles were issued in double and triple packs as no end of remixes were included. Michael Jackson's 1991 single "Jam" was released in no fewer than twenty-four different versions.

As a result, certain remixers—those perceived to have a strong style which could be targeted at a particular sector of the market—were in great demand.

David Morales was one such remixer, a young Brooklyn DJ who had risen to instant fame in fairytale fashion when he had been hired to stand in for the increasingly hazy Larry Levan at the Paradise Garage. Morales soon developed a very distinctive melodic style, influenced in equal parts by the classics of disco and the rawer sounds of Chicago. His first production work was the 1985 dance hit "Do It Properly" with David Cole and Robert Clivilles (who would later form C&C Music Factory) as Two Puerto Ricans, A Black Man And A Dominican, and this led to a series of remixes starting with "Instinctual" by Imagination. His Red Zone mixes, named after the Manhattan club where he was resident in the late eighties, sound fresh even when played today.

Through the early nineties, Morales's name could be found on a prolific stream of remixes, as the industry treated him as a surefire source of elegant vocal house. At times, the industry's marketing-based view of remixing has come into sharp conflict with his artistic judgement, and he's found himself at odds with record company people because they've expected some kind of trademark Morales style, and he's delivered something quite different. "I've had moments when they've said, 'But I wanted this style, I wanted it like this and like that!'" he admits. "What some A&R man hears in his head is totally different from what can actually work."

In 1995 he did what was then the ultimate remix: "Scream," the first single of Michael Jackson's new album. This was such a high-profile job that rather than send Morales the master tapes to work from (as is standard), he was flown out to Jackson's studio. "They wouldn't give me the masters. They flew me to L.A.; flew everybody over, money was no problem. I spent a week in Michael Jackson land." For three mixes he was paid a rumored $80,000. Today, even this huge sum has been superseded. Supercommercial hip hop mogul Puffy Combs supposedly demands $100,000 to put his name to a remix.

The DJ Rules the Roost

Arguably a DJ doesn't have to make records to be an artist—the greatest can express artistry in their club performances. However, it was by becoming a recording artist that the DJ escaped being seen as just "someone who puts records on." Today, thanks largely to this move, the DJ has dance music sewn up. DJs who don't make their own music are rare, as are dance music producers who didn't get their start by playing records. The two crafts are inextricably linked, the one inspiring the other. "Now I understand records more because I *make* records," stresses Morales. "And that just makes you all the more better as a DJ because you understand music better."

Significantly, while the DJ was showing off his new skills as a producer, rock adopted such a knee-jerk antitechnology stance that dance outstripped it in creative terms for many years. Samplers, sequencers and synthesizers were snapped up by the DJ because he was already familiar with the shapes they gave to music (and because he couldn't play any "real" instruments), while they were heavily criticized by rock-based musicians (who could). Only recently, when artists like Beck have embraced dance-derived approaches, has rock started to look innovative again.

In its directions for creating a number one single, Cauty and Drummond's *The Manual* makes it quite clear. "If you are already a musician stop playing your instrument," it insists, ". . . if in a band, quit. Get out. Now." Over the page, in the authors' list of essential tools, the only thing necessary for pop stardom which comes anywhere near being a musical instrument is a record player and a pile of 7-inch singles.

Since *The Manual* was written in 1988, the revolution it predicted in the way pop music is made has been fought and won. Thanks to the collision of black American music and British underground club culture, and specifically the energy released when house arrived in the UK, the world's pop has become ever more dance-oriented and the DJ's supremacy has been assured.

In 1992, with his star rising, Paul Oakenfold was invited to remix a track by rock giants U2. Retaining the bulk of the song, but sprinkling it with dancefloor magic, Oakenfold's remix was an instant and huge hit in the clubs. The remix shot into the charts a mere three weeks after the original release had slumped from its peak at #12(UK). The remix dramatically eclipsed sales of the original and reached #8(UK).

Its title?

"Even Better Than The Real Thing."

FOURTEEN
THE DJ AS OUTLAW

Renegade Snares

"Let us admit that we have attended parties where for one brief night a republic of gratified desires was attained. Shall we not confess that the politics of that night have more reality and force for us than those of, say, the entire U.S. government?"

—Hakim Bey, anarchist philosopher

"The introduction of a new kind of music must be shunned as imperiling the whole state, since styles of music are never disturbed without affecting the most important political institutions."

—Plato, *Republic*

Dancing is political, stupid.

You think you're just having fun, but when you're on the dancefloor, you're rejecting the rules and responsibilities of your daytime life, questioning the values that make you wait for the bus and smile at the boss every morning. Dance in a club and you are rebelling for a while. Your escape might come in a pill, a smoke, some beers. Or the music might be enough. Your escape might be from yourself. You're dancing with hundreds, maybe thousands of people; you're no longer just an isolated individual. A dancefloor is about collective action, making you an active participant, a vital component. You're creating the event, not just consuming it—the spectacle doesn't exist without you.

A good DJ has the power to suspend reality. Dance to his music and you forget your unpaid bills, your struggles for promotion. You shelve the motives that keep our good old capitalist democracies ticking over, and you replace them with a few more basic human—even animal—priorities. This puts the DJ in a powerful position. Politicians have always been scared by people gathering in large numbers, so you can bet they're suspicious of the figure who controls the event. If dancing at a rave is breaking the law, then a

DJ there is inciting a riot. Add illegal drugs to all of this and you've really started something.

In New York City early in Mayor Giuliani's reign of error, you started seeing signs in bars that read "NO DANCING," and they weren't kidding. In his mad monk mission to make the city resemble a quiet Connecticut suburb Giuliani began enforcing the long-ignored laws relating to cabaret licenses. Without such a license, even the most drunken gin-joint couldn't legally allow its customers to dance. If more than two or three barflies were seen to be moving rhythmically, the police were quite entitled to raid the place, fine it or even close it down. And they did.

In the UK, meet up with a few friends in the park and slam on a tape and, technically speaking, you're breaking a serious law. Luckily your average cop has more on his mind and is unlikely ever to use such broad-reaching legislation against you, although he's been quite happy to use the full force of it against ecology-minded antiroads protesters, or to restrict "new age" travelers' freedom of movement. The law in question forbids people spontaneously grouping together in public for any purpose. It's not one of those ancient irrelevancies like legally everyone must practice archery on Sundays; it was passed in 1994. It is the Criminal Justice Act, one of the most repressive measures ever passed by a modern democratic government. Part of it specifically refers to people coming together to listen to music, taking particular care to define music so that it includes dance music.

An earlier law, the 1990 Bright Act, which imposed penalties of up to £20,000 and six months' imprisonment for anyone throwing an unlicensed party, was responsible for the biggest mass arrest in British history. Just a week after this law became effective, police violently arrested 836 clubbers dancing in a warehouse near Leeds. Those arrested were driven away in a fleet of specially hired coaches, many were hurt, but only seventeen were charged. The DJ, Rob Tissera, because he had encouraged the dancers to barricade the doors and carry on partying, was sent to jail for three months.

Ecstasy, Shoom, Spectrum and Ibiza

America created the DJ and gave him his music. Britain, in its fertile club culture, gave him a home. Then, starting in 1988 (for many commentators dance music's year zero) the DJ and his music embarked on an unprecedented project of social change. A new kind of music met a new kind of drug and thousands, eventually millions, of young people discovered a new way of enjoying themselves. House music, having upturned the ways in which music is conceived and created, set about transforming the way it is consumed. And the communal psychedelic culture that grew around it proved to be an incredibly powerful force.

Ecstasy, E, X, methylenedioxymethylamphetamine, MDMA, the chemical compound which changed everything. It is hard to imagine a drug more conducive to the club experience. It gives you energy, it enhances light and sound and it can make a roomful of people drop their defenses, forget their insecurities and feel a sense of intense communion. Not for nothing is it classified as an empathogen, as in empathy, as in the transcendence of individuality.

Ecstasy arrived in the UK in around 1985, just as it was made illegal in the United States (it has been outlawed in Britain since 1977). Originally synthesized in 1912, it made a resurgence as a psychotherapy tool, and spread as a recreational drug via Texan hippies, international quasi-Buddhist sex communes and, of course, the transatlantic party animals of the music biz.

Ecstasy first met dance music on the floors of the New York gay scene. From here it was introduced to London by people like Boy George and by Marc Almond of synth pop band Soft Cell, who have the distinction of making the first ecstasy-influenced record, 1981's "Memorabilia." In its remixed version on their album, *Non Stop Ecstatic Dancing*, this insistent prototechno groove featured their dealer Cindy Ecstasy rapping.

As if the new music coming over from America wasn't enough to revolutionize British clubland, the arrival of a phenomenal new drug was certainly going to affect things.

Dave Dorrell, who was then part of a small inner circle in London who had tried ecstasy, remembers how the drug didn't really fit with the accepted leisure style. Here were people dressed in distressed Levis, polo necks and MA1 jackets being very cool listening to "rare groove" and to cocktail bands like Sadé and Blue Rondo A La Turk. When they tried E, it just didn't fit.

"The music was the wrong backing track to it," says Dorrell. "Everyone was just kind of wobbling around like Jell-O on a chair."

However, when ecstasy was combined with the formidably danceable sound of house music—complete with its heightened emotive force—the results were to be nothing short of seismic. It was the most potent combination yet of a particular drug and a particular music. The club scene cool was about to be blown.

Dave Rofe, a DJ at the Haçienda in Manchester, remembers the dramatic change it made. In March 1988 he visited the Trip in London's Astoria, the first large-scale acid house night. He was stunned by what he saw. "The whole club was dancing, from the bar to the dancefloor, onto the stage. Complete, hundred percent club euphoria, where you felt like a dick if you weren't dancing. Whereas before it was, 'Oh, look at him, dancing on the dancefloor,' now, being cool was dancing. So we went back to Manchester saying, 'Wow, down in London they're just going off their heads.'"

The Trip was Nicky Holloway's club. It was here that the explosive ecstasy experience emerged from the underground. Clubbers here were so fired up that when the night ended, they'd dance round someone's car stereo or in the fountains across the street. On one occasion, a police van arrived, siren blaring, and the crowd in Charing Cross Road chanted as one, "Can you party?" since the siren sounded just like the sample in Royal House's "Can You Party?"

The Trip's precursors were the defiantly underground Clink Street, Paul Oakenfold's Spectrum, and Shoom, the granddaddy of them all. When Spectrum moved to the huge main room of Heaven, on a Monday night, everyone expected disaster. And for the first weeks it was nearly empty. "But I knew something which everyone didn't," said Oakenfold, "which was ecstasy. So I knew Spectrum was going to go off. I knew it in my heart. That's why I stuck with it." Sure enough, by the fourth week it was crammed full.

But it was a club called Shoom that started it all. "Happy Happy Happy..." read the flyers, with a scattering of tumbling grinning pills, starting a craze for yellow smiley faces. Shoom was run by Danny Rampling and his future wife Jenni. It started in October 1987 at the Fitness Center in Southwark Street, a tiny venue with mirrored walls, lots of strawberry-flavored smoke and room for only about 200. "Everyone would turn up at midnight on a Saturday night," recalls Johnny Walker. "In. Lock the doors, and on with the smoke machines and strobes and the Balearic classics and the party would just go on until about six or seven in the morning."

"I got the name from Trevor Fung," says Rampling. "It's just through . . . um . . . through an experience I had and he said, 'Are you feeling Shoomy?' and I quite liked the word. It expressed the feeling of the club, the feeling of the club was up, positive energy."

All these clubs, the sacred sites of acid house, were attempts to reconstruct the unique atmosphere of Ibiza. In the summer of 1987, Johnny Walker, Paul Oakenfold (then known as a hip hop DJ), Danny Rampling and London party promoter Nicky Holloway had traveled to the island to visit Trevor Fung, who was out there DJing at a place called Project Bar in San Antonio. Here they discovered the island's bizarre club constituency of visiting celebs, Eurotrash, wily Brits and international gay party monsters. They also discovered a drug called ecstasy.

"I think that Nightlife in San Antonio was the club where we were first offered an E," recalls Walker. "I was very hesitant at first. But having seen Paul and Danny and Nicky do one and then go skipping and hopping around the club holding hands, going 'I *love* you,' I thought, well, this doesn't look too bad, I'll try one. And suddenly the whole night just sort of turned into this fabulous, sparkling, colorful night. I just felt so wonderful."

The other discovery that night was a beautiful open-air club called Amnesia and a DJ named Alfredo who played joyously eclectic music, much of which would have been anathema to the club scene back in London. Prince's "Sign Of The Times" or George Michael's "I Want Your Sex" would sit next to Chicago house like Ralphi Rosario's "You Used To Hold Me," next to an obscure indie record like "Jesus On The Payroll" by Thrashing Doves or the live version of the Woodentops' "Well, Well Well." (This style of music would be referred to as "Balearic" after the island group in which Ibiza is found.)

By the end of the night, the four had resolved to introduce this wondrous and life-affirming experience to London. Walker recalls the sense of mission that they all felt. And as they ran around trying to recreate the Ibiza vibe, it wasn't something that needed too much promotion. "I suppose people saw us running about having a good time, big smileys, you know. And everyone thought, 'Mmm, this looks interesting, what are they up to?' And it gradually started to happen."

The Acid House Revolution

"Acid house" was a blanket term given to the music being hungrily imported from Chicago at the time. Specifically it referred to a few records made using the distinctive mewlings of a distressed Roland 303 bassline machine. After Phuture's "Acid Tracks" set the mold, a bleeping flurry of similar records followed, both imported and UK-made, and "acid house" was soon shorthand for house and techno as a whole. The acid records were the name-makers because they were the weirdest, strangest of the lot, the tunes most likely to upset your parents, and because they were perfect for dancing on this new drug called ecstasy.

Ecstasy changed the way music was best experienced. It's a drug which concentrates on the physical, it emphasizes the fact that you have a body, and it drives even the most uptight stiff to the dancefloor. No longer was it about listening to music, it was about *feeling* it, about merging with the music's physicality. "Can You Feel It?" boomed the title of Mr. Fingers' huge club hit, and thousands of E-initiates screamed "Yes!"

More than this, ecstasy has a powerful ability to make an individual feel connected to the wider group. For many people leading late-twentieth-century lives tainted with isolation and suspicion, this was a very new sensa-

Smiley culture—a sly northern stylist named Barnsley reinvented the smiley badge as the icon of acid house, seen originally in Shoom and on the cover of *i-D* in late 1987.

tion. But as well as these powerful communal feelings, there was still room for individual interpretation. Ecstasy inspires, as Matthew Collin puts it in his evocative social history *Altered State*, "a culture with options in place of rules." It's not a dogmatic drug; it doesn't come with a new set of restrictions. As more and more people started popping E and got "on one matey," a strong collective spirit and a wave of personal revelation catalyzed dramatic changes in attitudes and behavior.

Acid house culture did much to sweep away the sectarianism which was always a part of British pop culture. It made people more tolerant of others, and as young men dropped their defenses and hit the dancefloor, and as girls and boys learned to appreciate each other as friends and not just alien opposites, it did much to erode the famously repressed British character. It reduced racism and homophobia and was even said (though largely erroneously) to have softened the behavior of football hooligans. People learned to show their feelings. Black danced with white danced with gay danced with straight. And because it encouraged self-belief and seemed to unlock possibilities, it launched a great many people into creative careers. Amazingly, the dance scene which started in 1988 is still in full swing, making it a uniquely enduring youth culture. The party started by acid house makes the swinging sixties look like a wet barbecue.

While our parents thought E was one step down from heroin, we thought it was one step up from beer. Eventually, ecstasy became an almost universal peak experience for young people, as much a part of growing up as your first cigarette. And so the feelings of individual awakening and communal joy which the ecstasy/house combination so powerfully fostered swept Britain clean. In a country whose national psyche was built on division (of class, of geography, of race, of accent, of football team), the acid house experience—dancing with thousands of smiling friends you'd never met before—was nothing short of revolutionary.

"We broke down a lot of barriers at the beginning of house music," says DJ Danny Rampling, one of the scene's key pioneers. "It broke everything down. It smashed down the walls."

But much of this culture was illegal. It was based around an illegal drug. The desire to take drugs and dance to house music in company with as many people as possible put the DJ at the center of a law-breaking movement. Whether he had clipped the locks to play in a warehouse in Holloway, or clambered down tractor tracks to spin for a field of ravers, or climbed up on the roof of a Hackney housing project to put up a pirate radio antenna, the DJ was now often an outlaw.

Rampling, DJing at Shoom, felt that he and his friends had created an alternative community, independent of the outside world. "When the doors were closed, you could do what you wanted. It was our own state of freedom. It was a free state, as it should be generally anyway. There were no restrictions in that club, at the beginning, *whatsoever.* All you wanted to do, that was conducive to that atmosphere, you could do it. Like all of the good clubs that have stood the test of time. So, in a sense, yeah, it was an outlaw period."

Raves

With acid house's compelling fever for togetherness, the DJ soon found himself at the heart of illegal events of unheralded size, conducting a dance communion of thousands. Raves were massive outdoor dance events, promoted and advertised in ways that kept them secret from the authorities, with vast arrays of sound and light equipment erected on the sly. Things started in 1988, known now as "the Summer of Love," with a few fairly spontaneous events thrown by the movers of the London acid house scene. The idea quickly caught the attention of some more money-minded promoters and over the next few years, raves expanded in size and ambition until they were huge encampments complete with car parking and fairground rides.

The first were centered around London, although there were later some large events in the north as well. Eventually, the movement would crash under the weight of police and government intervention and the overreaching greed of some of the organizers. But for three or four summers, in events like Sunrise, Biology and Back to the Future, you could find yourself sharing the time of your life with thousands of like-minded souls in an aircraft hangar or a muddy cowshed.

Johnny Walker recalls DJing a Biology event in June 1989 at the height of the movement. Here, in an open field in Hertfordshire, the night sky streaked with lasers, gathered an incredible 12,000 ravers. Walker, up on a stage, found himself DJing for a churning sea of people, all locked into the groove of his records. "It was breathtaking, to be onstage and look out and see that many people dancing to what you're playing, it was just incredible."

A rave was an idealized version of clubbing. It wasn't about visiting some purpose-built venue, it was about creating somewhere new; it was about building a city for a night. A club had a place in space and time, but a rave was made of possibilities. A rave existed in the minds of the people who danced together. Without them it was nowhere, just a field off a motorway exit. While Margaret Thatcher claimed, "There is no such thing as society," in her face were thousands of people making alternative one-night communities. Raves emphasized the ecstatic acid house ideal: it was people that counted above everything.

The first raves had been offshoots of the original acid house clubs, Shoom and Spectrum. Boys Own, a group of cultural hooligans from around Slough, evangelized by Shoom, organized a series of events. The Shoomers experimented with outdoor parties, taking clubbers on buses out to a farm and filling a barn with fire-engine foam. Then, with the success of big clubs like Spectrum and the Trip, the possibilities of ever larger venues looked exciting. After clubbing at Shoom and Spectrum, in the summer of 1988 a capitalist prodigy, Tony Colston-Hayter, began organizing warehouse parties, including one on Greenwich wasteland (now the site of the Millennium Dome and also where the battle scenes in *Full Metal Jacket* were shot) and several in Wembley Studios, which he called Apocalypse Now. However, when the tabloids started sniffing around the scene—there was a clueless story about "acid" dealers in Spectrum in the *Sun*—Colston-Hayter decided to get out of London altogether.

On October 22, 1988, ten coaches ferried clubbers from the BBC studios in west London to an equestrian center in Buckinghamshire for Sunrise, The Mystery Trip. Passengers included most of the acid scene's club promoters, as well as stars including ABC's Martin Fry, Wham!'s Andrew Ridgeley, and Boy George. They arrived to see strobe lights and flaming torches lighting up the sky and then, plunged into darkness except for a single laser, heard Steve Proctor play a set which started with the apocalyptic theme from *2001*. This was the beginning of the "orbital" or "M25" parties, so named after London's M25 orbital motorway, which had just been completed.

"In the morning, everyone was outside dancing," recalls Colston-Hayter. "All the Shoom kids were getting flowers and putting them in their hair and talking to all the horses, like they'd never seen a horse before. Some kids started walking home; they thought they'd get home eventually."

The direct antecedents of the acid house raves were the warehouse parties of the early eighties, part of a London club scene so vibrant and established, as we've seen, that it long prevented the wholesale acceptance of house, which was seen as little more than a novelty. While the industry expected go-go to become huge, they consigned house (along with hip hop and electro) to the box marked "fad." But the music's champions—the Watson brothers, Graeme Park, Mike Pickering, Mark Moore, and Colin Faver, not to mention a drug called ecstasy—soon changed that. And when acid house finally broke big, the warehouse scene provided it with clued-up promoters, plenty of illegal venues and, in pirate radio, a powerful communications network. Warehouses once full of kids dressed like extras from the set of *Shaft* were suddenly full of kids dressed like dayglo infants.

The venues were often in the most forsaken areas of London, in disused carpet warehouses, old theatres, boarded up cinemas, anywhere with a floor big enough to dance on. If a place couldn't be hired legally, then it would often be appropriated for the evening through either a friendly estate agent or, failing that, a crowbar.

There were close links with London's blossoming pirate radio stations, and in particular an enterprising station broadcasting out of southeast London called Kiss FM (a name unashamedly copied from New York's Kiss FM, whose Shep Pettibone Mastermixes were then floating around on bootleg tapes). Using coded messages, which you didn't need to be a wartime code-breaker to figure out, the DJs would advertise the latest secret party rendezvous.

Raves might well have remained quietly underground had it not been for the tabloids exaggerating things beyond all reason. In between selling its own smiley T-shirts and offering rabid moral condemnation, the *Sun* told the nation that a few thousand kids were dancing all night on drugs and having sex. The next day, of course, *half a million* kids were asking, "Where's the party?"

"SPACED OUT! 11,000 YOUNGSTERS GO DRUG CRAZY AT BRITAIN'S BIGGEST EVER ACID HOUSE PARTY."

With such effective free advertising, the rave phenomenon was suddenly of national interest. The drugs aspect was the papers' chief cause for concern, although confused by the name of the music, *acid* house, they had initially concluded it was an LSD scene. Immediately, the (initially fairly accommodating) police attitude to raves changed. The BBC banned acid house records from its airwaves and Parliament started brewing up legislation aimed at curbing this evil menace.

Meanwhile, the events got larger and more grandiose, with huge sound systems, amazing lasers and light shows, even funfair rides (including the infamous Moon Bounces). The promoters quickly realized the value of new technology like mobile phones and reprogrammable telephone message lines to keep the address secret until the last minute. Incredible scams were pulled off to secure sites and to deflect police interest.

Energy, in May 1989, showed the way. Held in a Shepherd's Bush film studio, it offered dancers the choice of five different rooms, each filled with lasers and built as lavishly as a film set. There was a Blade Runner room, Stonehenge, a Greek temple, an Egyptian room and even a sushi bar. Among the DJs were Paul Oakenfold, Trevor Fung, Grooverider, Jazzy M and Nicky Holloway. Jazzy, who was DJing from a twenty-foot-high platform, remembers it as the best gig of his life.

"We were twenty foot up on the scaffolding that was wobbling about, playing 'Strings Of Life' in the middle of the night and everyone going totally mad. Then I stopped it and played it again from the top. Lasers firing everywhere, everyone with their hands in the air. There were probably about 5,000 people there. It was amazing."

Dance Outlaws

If it feels good, don't do it. That was the message from government. As a knee-jerk reaction to the tabloid horror stories, the Tories passed MP Graham Bright's 1990 Entertainments (Increased Penalties) Act, which drastically upped the fines which could be imposed on rave organizers. Following a series of busts and mass arrests, Bright's law did much to curtail the rave phenomenon, but its long-term effect, as it forced the growing scene into properly licensed premises, was to encourage councils to grant clubs later licenses and to bring ecstasy into the mainstream.

Now that raves were clearly illegal, those sections of the great unwashed who thrived on anti-establishment action—travelers, pagans, squatters, eco-warriors—started throwing free parties, the bigger the better, as a continuation of the old hippie festivals. There followed some summer cat-and-mouse madness as the cops and the travelers played tag, and in 1992, when 25,000 people arrived to dance on Castlemorton Common in Worcestershire to 100 hours of techno-shamanism from the nation's collected sound systems, the government made it clear that they'd had enough. To set an example, members of the Spiral Tribe sound system were arrested and charged with "conspiracy to cause a public nuisance," only to win their freedom in a court case which cost the taxpayers £4 million. In frustration, John Major's government floored the gas pedal on the passing of their hot new item, the Criminal Justice Bill, a wide-sweeping set of laws which, among other things, overturned the centuries-old right to free assembly and greatly increased the powers of the police.

The Bill was an attempt to fight social change with the iron heel of legislation, and it united the outlaws as never before. Travelers, squatters and protesters of any kind all became targets of a single piece of legislation. Although Advance Party, a coalition of sound systems and civil liberties groups, did what they could to bring down the Bill, it became law in 1994.

The CJB was unique in that it was the first time the pop music of a youth culture had been specifically prohibited. Its famous definition of house and techno as any "sounds wholly or predominantly characterized by the emission of a succession of repetitive beats," showed just how seriously government saw the threat of dance culture, with its combination of music, drugs and hordes of lusty young people.

By the nineties, thanks to the cunning of policeman Ken Tappenden and his Pay Party Unit, promoters found it increasingly difficult to stay a step ahead of the police. Additionally ravers were soon used to paying for tickets to events that delivered a tenth of what they promised, or which didn't exist beyond the promoter's bank account. Also, by this time the club scene had expanded to accommodate the huge numbers of clubbers who had been turned on by the acid house explosion. There was little reason to spend the night driving round unlit highways in search of a party that probably didn't even exist.

By the time the Bright Act came into force in 1990, much of the excitement had already gone. By the time the Criminal Justice Act was law four years later, house music had transferred its energy to the clubs, and legal, mainstream clubbing was becoming a fact of life.

Jungle

Some rave promoters soldiered on and adapted their orbital blueprint for legal events, developing, in the process, a hothouse environment which eventually produced the fast, breakbeat-derived form known as jungle (drum'n'bass). As the raves moved from their original house soundtrack, they adopted harder and faster music. This was driven largely by an increase in the amphetamine content of the low-quality ecstasy pills dancers were taking. In time there was a thriving subculture based around a house/techno/hip hop derivative known as hardcore.

"People would boast about the amount of Es they'd dropped, in a way reminiscent of the fifteen-pints-a-night lager boys. Living on the absolute edge of reality, the ravers were all or nothing, 100 percent hardcore. The music reflected this extremity as beats and noises became more manic," wrote Martin James in *State of Bass*, his detailed history of jungle.

Like any scene left to its own devices, the music underwent a dramatic evolution, simmering in raves in the southeast, and in Midlands clubs like Eclipse in Coventry and Kinetix in Stoke-on-Trent (where jungle star Goldie is said to have taken his first E). DJs pitched records faster and faster (some tampering with their turntables to exceed the maximum plus-eight pitch change), and showed a predilection for breakbeats. The DJs' palette ranged from hip house records like Renegade Soundwave's "The Phantom" to the harsh vacuum-cleaner sounds of Belgian techno such as R&S artist Joey Beltram's "Mentasm."

Gerald Simpson, who as A Guy Called Gerald had produced "Voodoo Ray," one of UK house's earliest classics, was drawn to this sound after hearing London DJ Grooverider play a set at a rave in the Midlands.

"He was playing these really fast breakbeats and the kids were just going mad. I hadn't seen anything so manic before, I was totally mesmerized. Suddenly I thought, 'Shit, these beats are all at least 160 bpm and all my stuff is much slower.'" Afraid of bombing badly if he played his usual house style, Gerald tampered with some other music he had brought and improvised a performance which matched the speed and aggression of Grooverider's music. "I had these breaks already looped in my sampler, so I just sped them up to the right speed and increased the tempo on the backing tracks. It was totally spontaneous, but it went down really well."

Grooverider was the key force on the scene. He and his DJ partner Fabio inspired many of jungle's DJs and producers with their radio show on south London pirate Phase I and weekly Rage nights between 1990 and '93 at London's Heaven. Rage was the scene's first great club, a test bed for the emerging jungle sound. Future artists and DJs like Kemistry and Storm, DJ Rap, Photek, Dillinja and Ed Rush were in regular attendance, as was jungle's first recognizable star Goldie, a young Midlands graffiti artist.

"Goldie had made a tune, but I didn't think all that much of it," recalls Grooverider. "Some geezer gave me a copy of it and I thought it sounded OK, so I whacked it out at Rage. Then this guy with gold teeth comes up to me and says, 'Hey, that's my tune.'"

By 1991 there was the start of a definite split in the rave movement. The slower, more elegant house scene was leaving for the comfort of a more intimate club environment, leaving the hardcore ravers to their own devices. Rave companies like Raindance, Rezerection and Amnesia started throwing regular hardcore events, and rave fashions appeared including white gloves, Vicks inhalers (to enhance the ecstasy/amphetamine rush), dust masks and light-sticks.

By 1992 there were records being made specifically for this scene. These ranged from British techno like Altern-8's "Activ-8" to cartoon records like The Prodigy's "Charly" and Smart E's "Sesame's Treat," which pitted familiar childhood TV theme tunes against a crashing onslaught of manic rhythms. Another key moment was SL2's "On A Ragga Tip" and a series of releases on Hackney's Shut Up And Dance label, which added a heavy Jamaican influence to the gestating sound.

Rave peaked commercially in 1993 with crowds of up to 25,000 at (legal) Fantazia and Vision events. By now, DJs like Micky Finn, Randall, Kenny Ken and Jumping Jack Frost were conjuring a moodier, less playful sound in their sets. This became known as "dark." Grooverider championed this at Rage and a north London club night, AWOL, was another focus point, as was pirate radio. In London you could hardly avoid hearing the clattering of super-speeded snare drums, bottoming basslines and helium voices. Even at this point, when it was obvious that here was unprecedented music, the music press continued to deride the scene and its new sound. But in 1994, with Rob Playford's label Moving Shadow and distinctive tracks like Omni Trio's "Renegade Snares" and Deep Blue's "The Helicopter Tune," media interest was suddenly massive. When Goldie secured a powerful deal with London records for his *Timeless* album, jungle was the sound of the moment.

It has been claimed that the name "jungle" is racist, although the clearest explanation of its origins comes from a Jamaican MC's shout out to "alla da junglists," a term referring to inhabitants of Tivoli Gardens in Kingston. This entered the hardcore consciousness when sampled on a 1991 Rebel MC track. Nevertheless, most jungle artists were happy when the phrase "drum'n'bass" gained currency, as were journalists and music critics who had suddenly realized the importance of this music and needed a new term to distance themselves from the slagging they had given jungle for so long. As the music evolved towards far more sophisticated textural production, using jazz samples in place of the Minnie Mouse vocals of earlier, this was sufficient to distinguish the two styles. LTJ Bukem and then Roni Size did much to popularize the mellower, more ambient sounds. So drum'n'bass is really just grown-up jungle. When people got really pretentious about it, they added the prefix "intelligent."

Jungle, and the many forms within it, is of vital significance, as it was the UK's first genuinely indigenous form of black music—although the scene itself was truly interracial, and there are as many white jungle DJs and producers as black. It is, in many ways, Britain's answer to hip hop, which was always too culturally alien to sound convincing in a British accent. On the other hand, jungle is a defiantly British music. It has been massively influential, inspiring a whole range of subgenres, and giving stylistic impetus to such recent forms as speed garage (aka UK garage).

Women DJs

One cultural side effect of acid house was the freedom it gave to women to be DJs. In the rushing years at the end of the eighties, anything seemed possible, even the idea that a woman could enter this most male of professions and not be laughed out from behind the decks. In the decade since then women DJs have progressed from being rarer than fish-fur to being, if not a sizeable number, at least a number worth counting. And while some are content to exploit club culture's essential sexism to get ahead, thankfully there are plenty today who are judged on their music rather than their cleavage.

Throughout this book the DJ is "he" and this is not just a matter of grammatical simplicity. In DJing's 94 years, women have been largely frozen out of the picture, with precious few exceptions. Until recently the music world has always been very much a boys' club, with women restricted to turning out some vocals for the lads. Like musicianship, DJing is usually passed on from master to apprentice in an almost masonic manner, with little room for the ladies. It's also highly significant that much of early dance culture revolved around gay men, so in most of the important New York and Chicago clubs women were in the clear minority—they were hardly encouraged to step up and play a few tunes. In any case, club culture has never been much of a force for sexual equality. Just look at a few flyers or this month's dance mags to see what skills are sought in female clubbers. DJing is not at the top of the list. And of course the blame must also be leveled at the wider culture. The notion of girls tampering with anything that isn't a typewriter, oven or cash register is, sadly, relatively new.

The disco era mostly saw women confined to being decorous fixtures on the dancefloor, although New York's Fire Island circuit enjoyed the talents of Sharon White and, latterly, Susan Morabito. In Los Angeles in the early seventies British expatriate Jane Brinton (now Junior Vasquez's manager) ran a pioneering mobile disco. Later, given the freedoms of postpunk New York, Anita Sarko gained a solid reputation as DJ at Danceteria.

But arguably it was the advent of acid house in the UK, with its have-a-go spirit, that did most to encourage women to take up DJing seriously. Lisa Loud and Nancy Noise were two such pioneers, and in their footsteps there have been many more.

With the advent of new scenes, so new possibilities have arisen. It's no coincidence that one of the newest musical forms, drum'n'bass, has brought with it several leading DJs who happen to be female. Fewer ingrained prejudices, fewer gender barriers. DJ Rap quit her day job as a topless model and became the first female drum'n'bass producer signed to a major label. Admirably, other than a pneumatic album cover photo, she has blocked any attempts to use her past career as a promotional gimmick. And until Kemistry's tragic death in a car accident, the duo of Kemistry and Storm were rightly respected and admired for nothing more spurious than their music. In the U.S., techno threw up its own stars, with DJ Moneypenny a regular fixture in late eighties New York, while in Chicago there is the fierce duo of Teri Bristol and Psychobitch.

"I think the younger techno and drum'n'bass DJs are a lot different," says DJ Cosmo, one of the few credible female New York jocks. "Those scenes are more open to female DJs. These girls grew up with computers and electronics, so it was no big deal to them."

What about the notion that men have the *obsession thing* more than women, that the desire to collect things has a male bias? Cosmo thinks this is a myth. "Girls are into music. Big time. They're just as into music as boys are." (Mind you, if there is a genuine gender difference to trainspotting, having seen some of the pathetic vinyl junkie behavior of male DJs, women should be thankful.)

"Things are changing," says Cosmo. "It's not that big of a deal to be a female DJ anymore and I think that's great. The less people ask me about it, the better, I think."

Pirate Radio

In pondering the truth of the DJ's outlaw nature, pirate radio offers an intriguing insight. On the one hand, it's the embodiment of his drive to spread music, whatever the consequences. It's a vital underground service, the disseminator of all the tunes too hot and subversive for the legal stations. On the other hand, pirate radio often derives from surprisingly commercial motives, even when its programming is the exact opposite. Pirate radio is all about filling a gap in the market.

"Call up and put in your code for the reload."

Turn on the radio in London (and in most major UK cities) and wedged next to the latest from Elton John you'll hear a clattering of upfront beats and red-hot street slang: Kool, Fresh, Freek, Magic, London Underground or one of about twenty others that spring up and die down daily. Move your dial a whisker and the trebly tones of UK garage will blend into some kicking drum'n'bass. Move it another millimeter and you'll hear some ragga, or some militant R&B. If it's nighttime you'll probably hear the urgent grunts of an MC; if it's daylight there'll be some slightly dazed announcements delivered in gapped-out interracial cockney. And whenever the music gets too relaxing, there'll be some girl in an echoey housing project shouting at you to go to some Essex lockup for a party with fifty different DJs.

Pirate radio is a fast-paced test bed for new music, inextricably linked to whatever underground dance scene currently has the most momentum. It's here you'll find records belonging to genres that don't even have names yet, broadcast by DJs who are risking a lot to bring you them. If a station gets raided by the authorities, a DJ can face up to six months in jail. Worse, he could have his records confiscated.

Pirate radio takes its name from the outlaw stations of the sixties which actually broadcast from ships moored out in the North Sea and English Channel. These original pirates were started not by rebels, but by entrepreneurs breaking the law to create commercial radio. The airwaves were tied up by the nationalized monopoly of the staid BBC, so there was ad money in them thar ships.

The first challenger to the BBC was Leonard Plugge's Radio Normandie, which started transmissions to the south coast of England in 1931 from the small French town of Fécamp. In 1934 Radio Luxembourg followed suit, using a transmitter hoisted to the Eiffel Tower in Paris. Luxembourg, with Gus Goodwin in the fifties and Tony "The Royal Ruler" Prince through the sixties, was known for programming a fair amount of black music, and broadcast well into the nineties.

But most famous of them all was Radio Caroline, a ship-based station launched in 1964 by a flamboyant Irishman Ronan O'Rahilly, who had earlier run the Scene Club in Soho.

Such was the unmet demand for a pop music radio station that Caroline received 20,000 fan letters within ten days of its initial transmission and within three weeks had a listenership of seven million. The station was swiftly followed by a gamut of copyists, among them Radios Sutch, 390, England, Britain, 270, Scotland, and its more popular and closest rival, Radio London. "Nobody loves the Pop Pirates—except the listeners," wrote the *Daily Sketch* in 1965.

The government legislated against them, forcing them to close, and in 1967 the BBC's monolithic pop station Radio 1 was launched to take the last breath of wind out of the pirates' sails (Radio 1 hired most of its first DJs from the pirates). But Caroline and London had already shown that the airwaves didn't belong to the government. Anyone with minimal technical ability could broadcast whatever they wanted. In 1971, a schoolboy in Matlock was fined £5 for transmitting pop music to friends at school on equipment which had cost him just 50p to build. He was one of seventy-eight people prosecuted that year for pirate broadcasting.

In the seventies land-based pirates emerged, many serving London's growing black communities. One such station was Radio Invicta, the first to exclusively program soul. With its slogan "Soul Over London," Invicta started broadcasting in 1970 from a Mitcham lower-income housing unit. *Time Out* reported in 1972 that its aim was "to inform the audience of the freaky deaky discos." By the start of the eighties, there were over two dozen stations operating in the London area alone. As the decade progressed, these included Rebel Radio, based in Ladbroke Grove; LWR, where, thanks to Jazzy M's Jacking Zone show, many Londoners first heard house; and Dread Broadcasting Corporation, the city's most popular reggae station.

The acid house years gave a huge burst of energy to pirate radio and Kiss was at the forefront. The pirates were inextricably linked to the rave movement, promoting upcoming events and offering phone numbers to call for information. Danny Rampling has fond memories of broadcasting from a 23rd-floor flat of a Hackney housing project belonging to dub DJ trio Manasseh.

"It had this magnificent view all over the whole of London. And when house was blowing up, that whole energy and feeling and being twenty-three floors up looking out over the city—that was a very exciting moment for me. And people would be locked into Kiss during that time. It was very popular. I'd made this transition from playing independent soul to playing this wonderful new musical form that I'd embraced. Breaking that new music on Kiss, that just felt amazing." In autumn 1990 Kiss secured one of the government licenses and became fully legal, London's first dedicated dance music station.

Pirate radio is a very British phenomenon. America's airwaves were always commercial enough to tie up any holes, and in recent years the role of playing the most upfront, least preprogrammed music has been well served by the college and public stations, not to mention the growing channels of Internet radio. However, perhaps the roots are there somewhere: there are said to be hip hop pirates on the loose in Brooklyn and Philadelphia, broadcasting sporadic bursts of rugged, uncensored rap to anyone who knows the frequencies.

Outlaw?

The dance revolution which started in Britain in 1988 and which has since spread almost globally, has had an undeniable social impact. And in the structures it encouraged, like pirate radio, raves and festivals (and let's not forget an enormous trade in recreational drugs), it was a serious force for lawbreaking. But is the DJ intrinsically an outlaw? Or is it just coincidence?

The DJ has an envied ability to turn individuals into a collective mass, but does he ever use it to generate more than just escapist enjoyment? Well certainly he has in the past. Disco's early DJs strove to tell a message with their music, and though today the dancefloor ideals they propagated—of love, tolerance and equality—may sound banal after years of repetition, they are remembered by many as having a potent and tangible force back when racism and homophobia made them sorely needed. Hip hop, the defiant voice of black America that is consumed so eagerly by its white youth, has had an undeniable sociopolitical agenda ever since the DJ told his MC to rap about more than just the party. And, as we've seen, when they saw the power of collective action to create whole smiley cities for a night, the acid house DJs sincerely believed that they were changing the world.

If a DJ is doing his job right, there has to be an element of the rebel in what he does. A DJ should challenge the cultural establishment even if he stays within the law of the land. The first radio disc jockeys were seen as a dangerous threat to the status quo of the music business. Rock'n'roll propagator Alan Freed was treated as an outlaw scapegoat by the U.S. government. In Jamaica, amid the island's tumultuous politics, the sound systems were often seen as outlaws. The best DJs are always trying to break away from what is safe and accepted. At the very least this means a constant search for new music.

"You're playing rap and then six months later everyone is playing rap. Right, what's next?" says Paul Oakenfold, a DJ who's been through his share of different genres. "You're a fashion junkie in a sense. A music junkie of new trends. You're always looking for the next thing."

The DJ's desire to evangelize, his need to turn as many people as possible on to his choice of music, can also make him an outlaw. DJs become DJs precisely because they want to share great music with others. Often—especially with novel forms—the established channels are not open for this, so the DJ resorts to more underground, and often illegal ways to get his music heard. Raves, warehouse parties and pirate radio are only the most obvious examples; there is probably a DJ gene for spreading the word.

Oakenfold tells a story which illustrates this compulsion perfectly. On a recent holiday visit to Cuba, despite being one of the most established and successful DJs there is, he smuggled in some record decks and put on a tiny illicit rave. There was no practical reason for him to do this. He made no money from it and the Cubans were far from crazy about his music, but he feels very proud that he tried to expose them to new sounds. "You've got to have the education factor, because that's my stimulation from a DJ's point of view."

Often, a DJ's instinct to share his love of music is so strong that he forgets he is breaking the law to do it. Thinking back to his days as a pirate DJ, Pete Tong admits that it didn't seem like an illegal thing to do.

"It was like a hobby, and the fact that you were so bothered about doing it, and you would bother to go to such great lengths to do it, it seemed like, 'What do you mean, it's illegal?'"

But now that club culture is an established commercial force in most of the world, it is easy for a DJ to become successful by simply playing the game, without ever taking any risks. Some very famous DJs are content to champion whatever big tune the labels send out, confident that merely by being able to play it months before it's released, they will look brave and innovative.

"The majority of DJs are not subversive at all; they're extremely conventional," asserts Coldcut's Jonathan More, "because DJing's been completely co-opted by the establishment as a tool, as much as everything else has."

So while DJing has a rich history of subversion, there is much pulling the DJ in the other direction. Some of the most exciting musical revolutionaries end up as boring old farts. Once they taste success, they're happy to let the mainstream snap them up and package them for the masses.

Dom Phillips, former editor of *Mixmag*, agrees. "They're quite content to stay in with the record companies. They're quite content to stay in with the clubs, because it's their business." He points out that while the best DJs are cultural outlaws, they are far from rebels when it comes to business. "Throughout dance music's history it has always been ruthlessly opportunistic, entrepreneurial and capitalist. It's always been about making money."

"You can join the club or you can stand outside and stick two fingers up," adds More. "It just depends which type of DJ you want to be."

FIFTEEN
THE DJ AS SUPERSTAR

God Is A DJ

"The DJ for me was literally god. In the ghetto. To be coming of age in a time when that person was such a star was just incredible for me. It's affected my whole life. I can remember looking at a big stack of speakers and going, 'Money!—this shit is like some kind of altar!'"

—Fab 5 Freddy

"It's the coolest thing, the guitar. *Eric Clapton*: *Used* to be. It's DJs now."

—UK talk show host Frank Skinner

When Paul Oakenfold plays records in a club, every person on the dancefloor will be facing him. Just like they'd face a rock band on a stage. There's not much for them to see: a baseball cap maybe, a studious face leaning into a pair of headphones, some minimal arm movements as he slides in another flawless mix. Occasionally he might throw his hands up in excitement, smile out in response to a particularly grand track, or share a wink with some energetic fan, and when he does, there'll be a sea of hands aloft, a breakout of waving and grinning, an ocean of smiling dancers mirroring his every gesture.

For he is a superstar.

When he takes the stage, or rather when he gets behind the decks, he doesn't just mix his first tune into the warm-up DJ's last. Instead, he turns off the power and lets the other guy's record grind noisily to a halt. Then he waits. The silence announces his arrival, broken then by a deafening wave of cheers as a thousand clubbers realize who's going to put on the next record.

"When I DJ, I perform," Oakenfold says with measured seriousness. "It's not me. I get into character."

The readers of *DJ* magazine recently voted Oakenfold the best DJ in the world. The Guinness Book of Records lists him as the world's most successful DJ. He travels ceaselessly, jetting off to play in Argentina, Hong Kong or Japan, at the drop of a hat, embarking on grueling rock-style tours around the cities of America to promote his record label Perfecto and spread the gospel of British club culture.

"The DJ is a modern-day entertainer," he stresses. "There's no difference between a band and a DJ. People pay £15 to come and see me, they want the best night of their life. So that's why I have to get into character. I prepare myself mentally. If I've got a hangover or I'm sick, they don't want to know that. They don't want me up there, just standing there like this, mixing a few tunes in. When I perform, they're directly watching the DJ, so they're all watching every move. They expect you to deliver."

He claims he learned a lot about behaving as a star when he toured with U2. "You watch how the band conduct themselves, and you think, I can take a little bit of that and put it in my world."

Oakey makes a sum well into four figures for three hours of playing records.

Hands on—Paul Oakenfold and some of his dancefloor worshippers at Home in London.

A Star Is Born

In the nineties, the DJ became a superstar. The disc jockey has always enjoyed a certain power over the dancers in his club because of the amount of pleasure he can dispense, but away from the dancefloor he had mostly been a rather anonymous figure. Suddenly his status was magnified a thousandfold and he was treated like a rock god or a pop idol. DJs could play outside of their home town, even overseas, and draw a crowd, they were interviewed in magazines, clubbers began to know what they looked like. People even started describing their musical tastes not in terms of genres or records but by reference to particular DJs.

Capitalizing on this change, and indeed encouraging it, were the promoters, who vied with each other to have the most impressive DJ lineups, often hyping up visiting jocks to godlike status. Soon, the right name on a flyer could make or break a particular club night—and DJs' earnings rocketed accordingly.

"When I started DJing, the DJ was just below glass collector in order of importance in a nightclub," recalls Norman Cook. "You were just the bloke who stood in the corner and put records on." Nowadays, after his chart success as Fatboy Slim, Cook is such a massive draw that promoters often keep his name off a flyer, fearing crowds way in excess of their club's capacity. And he's aware that clubbers' response to him has as much to do with his fame as his DJing. "People go bonkers from the moment I walk on rather than me earning it," he says. "You only hope you're worthy of it."

He is in such demand that he is regularly offered what he considers "silly money" for a night playing records—figures so high that he finds it difficult to refuse.

"Sometimes, the money I get paid I think, '*Fuck*, this is just stupid.' I'm worth *some* money, and I've put in the years and paid my dues, but if there's a DJ getting paid £50 and I'm getting paid five grand, I couldn't say I was a hundred times better. I could say I was better than him. I might even say I was twice as good as him, but there's *no way* that I'm a hundred times better than him."

The preparations for Millennium Eve showed just how out of hand it had all become, with top-rank DJs demanding fees well into five, even six figures for a single performance. A far cry from the pioneers of the craft, who would play seven nights a week for less money than the bartender. When Francis Grasso was told that today's above-average DJ is paid about a grand he said, confused, "What . . . a month?"

Like playing a guitar onstage, playing records in a nightclub puts you in the spotlight. However much a disc jockey might try to submerge his ego and break down the artist/audience boundary, the DJ can't escape being the focus for the dancers' excitement. Clubbers—lost in a world of bodies, music and perhaps brain-altering chemicals—can't help but project their peak experiences onto the DJ. And when a DJ is particularly skilled at steering the emotions in a room, all kinds of heightened feelings can be directed his way.

Danny Rampling, now a fixture on Radio 1, remembers how this got a little out of hand at his pioneering acid house night, Shoom. People there were enjoying very powerful new experiences related to the drugs, the music and the feelings of communion which the club generated. Rampling's role as DJ made him the focus for all this.

"There was a period at Shoom where a group of people was trying to hail me as this new messiah. It quite frightened me, because it was so intense. One guy opened a page in the Bible, and my name—Daniel—was in the Bible in this particular paragraph. And he said, 'This is you! This is you! This is what's happening now!' And that completely flipped me out."

While they are rarely raised to such explicitly messianic status, most DJs have stories about the absurd lengths fans will go to to show their awe. David Morales remembers playing in Yellow, one of Tokyo's biggest clubs. The DJ booth was full of people watching his every move, trying to observe the source of his magic. He remembers feeling slightly embarrassed at the level of worship, wanting to defuse it, wanting to tell them, "I'm just playing records, I'm not doing anything. *You* can do this." But later in the evening, things got stranger. As the energy levels rose, the dancers down on the dancefloor started scrabbling at the high wall at the front of the DJ booth: "They literally wanted to climb over the walls, up to the box. It was amazing."

Many can report that playing records well has greatly increased their sexual attractiveness. Not a breed famous for their looks, DJs were quick to take advantage of this and welcomed their unlikely new role as sex symbols. Though they never reached the rock monster heights of figures like Van Halen's David Lee Roth (who, at the height of his fame in the 1980s, once took seventeen women to bed with him), DJs started to attract groupies. When DJ-mania was at its peak in the mid-nineties, it became the end-of-the-night norm to have a couple of underdressed club vixens carry your records and escort you to your hotel room. Some of these "jockey sluts" were quite serious about their collecting. A DJ friend admitted that he'd gone home for a night of passion with a British girl in a New York hotel room. In the morning, as she showered, he found a copy of dance magazine *Mixmag* opened at a page with his face shining out and a felt-tip ring around it. Worse—there was also a handwritten list of British DJs with his name at the bottom.

At Shelley's in Stoke-on-Trent, such was their admiration for the resident DJ's talents that the club's regulars built him into a real hero. At the end of each night, this DJ—a Welshman named Sasha—found a queue of people waiting to shake his hand. Guys even asked him to kiss their girlfriends.

Seeing this kind of DJ adoration, the industry—from record companies to promoters to magazines—sensed a lucrative trend and jumped aboard. In time Sasha would become red hot property as a guest DJ and the first to release a remix album under his own name. In December 1991, *Mixmag* put him on its cover with the line: "SASHA MANIA—THE FIRST DJ PINUP?" The magazine stood to benefit greatly if DJs became stars, and it pulled no punches in promoting Sasha, and others like him, from local nightclub legends to more stratospheric fame. "We were accused at the time of creating the idea of a DJ superstar," recalls Dom Phillips, then the magazine's Assistant Editor.

Sasha's stardom was quite genuine. His audience reacted as they did because his music—stirring concertos of a cappellas and piano-laden house—was generating very powerful emotions. Admittedly, ecstasy was a contributing factor, but it was his skill as a DJ, his ability to connect with his dancers, that made Sasha a star. In fact, he resented the way *Mixmag* overhyped him. In 1994 when the magazine put him on the cover as "SON OF GOD?" he argued so much with Dom Phillips, by then editor, that the two had an impromptu wrestling match outside Ministry of Sound.

There are several precedents for the kind of DJ stardom that happened in the UK. The New York disco DJs were famous in their own closed world, and as hip hop rocked the planet, many DJs, especially Grandmaster Flash, enjoyed considerable recognition although as Flash points out, most people were utterly confused by the notion of a famous DJ. "People still didn't know what I did, or thought I was a rapper," he says.

In the mid-eighties, John "Jellybean" Benitez became the first DJ to be signed as an artist for a major label album deal, after he had shot to worldwide fame for his early eighties remix work. There were several other New York star DJs—Shep Pettibone, Tee Scott, François Kevorkian and Larry Levan—who had name recognition as remixers, but Jellybean somehow eclipsed them all. Some suggest that it was because he was a rare straight guy in the gay world of New York dance music. Others put it down to the fact that he was Madonna's boyfriend. But most point to his club stardom as DJ at the wild, huge Funhouse. Here he was such a hero that girls would show up wearing T-shirts reading "LAST NIGHT JELLYBEAN SAVED MY LIFE." Certainly, anyone who can get James Brown to repeatedly grunt out their name on a record (as Jellybean did on "Spillin' The Beans") had to be doing something right.

Even then, the UK was much more accepting of the DJ's fame than the U.S. *Billboard*'s former Dance Editor Brian Chin remembers Jellybean telling him of visiting England and being hounded for autographs. "And I remember the week I saw his picture on the back of *Number One* magazine, I thought, 'Jeez, this would never happen in America.'"

Guest DJs and Visiting Americans

Perhaps the greatest single factor in making the DJ a star was the practice of hiring guest DJs. Promoters found that a big-name, out-of-town jock could give a considerable boost to a club night's fortunes. To keep up with the demand for their services, the best DJs started playing two, sometimes three gigs a night, eating up thousands of miles of motorway a week, and flying off to Germany, Italy and Japan, where DJ fever was also raging. It was soon standard for a top DJ to roll into a club, play for just two hours, collect his inflated fee and rush off to another engagement.

This was severely damaging to the craft of DJing, as it encouraged jocks to show up with a lot of bombastic tunes, flashy tricks and prepared mixes, rather than develop any real rapport with a crowd. And it severely limited the musical attention span of the average British clubber. However, this was undoubtedly what made the DJ a star. As he took over from the club's resident DJ for a brief couple of hours, the guest spinner was treated like a chart-topping band. The crowd applauded as he came on, watched his every move, and screamed whenever he did anything clever.

Soon there was a national circuit for guest DJs; even the tiniest towns with the pokiest clubs somehow hired a few big names once in a while. Agencies sprang up to organize their bookings, club magazines thrived by offering national listings of who was playing where, and clubbers took to driving to other cities to hear their favorite DJs, something that hadn't happened since the heyday of northern soul. DJs were regularly earning four-figure sums for each two-hour set they could squeeze in. Some admitted that the idea of earning so much money was ridiculous; others began to take themselves very seriously.

The notion of the DJ as guest star was helped in no small part by the fetish for visiting American DJs, which peaked around 1994. In the years after house music established itself throughout UK nightlife, clubbers dug deep into their pockets to hear its founding fathers perform. It was much the same as Chuck Berry playing the UK in the wake of fifties rock'n'roll fever. Bucketloads of hype were added to the equation—it wasn't cheap to fly someone over and money had to be recouped, so the American DJs were given all the hoopla of the second coming. Naturally, they jumped at the chance to make some real money—even the big guns were still only earning a maximum of $500 a night in their native land.

The biggest were all from New York: Masters At Work, David Morales, Todd Terry, Tony Humphries and Frankie Knuckles. Of these, Todd Terry earned the most money, anything between £7,000 and £10,000. And for this he played a two or three-hour set composed entirely of his own material. Todd, known by some as "God," remains ruthlessly sanguine about this, delighting in the fact that he can earn such money while shamelessly promoting his own productions. "I'm not a DJ. I am a producer," he says flatly. "I DJ for money, 'cause I get paid for it." Lesser stars of American dance music were also able to make a healthy living outside their own country. The leading lights of Detroit and Chicago, revered as they were by the connoisseurs, made occasional trips here and were treated as visiting deities by the trainspotters (as were certain European techno jocks like Sven Väth and Laurent Garnier).

At one stage, such was the draw of an American name on a flyer that several were able to earn money despite being pretty lousy DJs. British audiences knew them solely through their production and remix work, and quite a few producers who had never been DJs, once they realized how much they could earn in the UK, hurriedly learned some basic mixing skills and got on a plane.

Conversely, one talented DJ, Junior Vasquez, became a legend despite (or maybe because of) refusing to play in the UK. In 1994, he said, "I wouldn't ever go over there and play Ministry. It's just stupid, everybody does it." As a result, to British fans who knew him only by his production work and his mythologized reputation, Vasquez and his club the Sound Factory came to represent the ultimate in clubbing. In May 1997 (rather too long after UK fans' interest had peaked) he finally relented and for a large fee played a couple of much-publicized though anticlimactic nights at Cream and Ministry of Sound (in any case, Vasquez had DJed in London, promoting his album as Ellis D, back in 1989).

The Backlash

There was some method behind all the madness. Clubland is a supply and demand free-market economy and DJs are only paid what they are worth, in audience terms, to a promoter—just like a crap actress who gets paid $17 million to star in a movie because her superstar name ensures ticket sales. Certain DJs today enjoy such recognition that their marquee value has shot up way beyond that of the average rock group. It's not because they work hard, it's sometimes not even because they're any good, it's simply that they can pull in the crowds.

"Do DJs get paid too much money?" asks Pete Tong. "Well, not really because if they did, you wouldn't book them back, would you?"

"Promoters aren't stupid," says Norman Cook. "They aren't running an aging DJ charity. They're paying you that money because they know they'll make *more.* And they're making it because you're attracting crowds and entertaining them."

Having heavyweight DJs became a way of making a particular night seem special or memorable, a promoter's marketing tool. "One of the ways to give a night a badge of credibility was to put a name on it," argues Dom Phillips, offering the example of the first *Mixmag*-sponsored night in Bristol in 1990. "It was the first time Andrew Weatherall had come to town. Nobody had any idea who Andrew Weatherall was. Or what he played. Or what he stood for. But they *did know* that he was a DJ and he'd never been to town before so the whole city went out. It was rammed."

Most of the mid-nineties premier league DJs—Sasha, Carl Cox, Paul Oakenfold, Jeremy Healy—rose to prominence by virtue of their talent. However, once famous, they entered a spiraling world of high fees, wily agents and persona-hungry magazines. It became hard to book them directly, and many were seen to have priced themselves out of all but the largest venues.

As a result, there was a considerable backlash against the superjock. There had been a great many letdowns, as promoters falsely advertised big names in order to fill their clubs. And the honest promoters were paying so much for their star DJs that they had no money left for the other essential elements of a good night out.

"The letters are pouring into *Mixmag* complaining," declared the magazine in November 1996, "from people who spent a brilliant night dancing to DJ Unknown because the £15 queue for DJ Rich Bastard was too long."

Things looked bad. DJs' fees had shot well past the £1,000 mark; Jeremy Healy was asking £15,000 to play New Year's Eve. The large venue superclubs were strengthening their monopolies with the devious idea of the club tour: where a small club pays a lot of money for the privilege of hosting a "visit" by a much bigger club and their much bigger DJs. Then, in a move which summed up just how crazy things had got, magazines reported that a club in Japan had offered Junior Vasquez $150,000 to play.

Mixmag's pages were filled with reports on DJs' wages, on whether clubbers were getting value for money, on dance music's creeping commercialism. Corporate sponsors had moved in, helping to finance the rising cost of club nights in exchange for prominent displays of their products and logos. Clubs without name DJs started to suffer. Around the same time, dance music was all over TV commercials, and club records were regularly making the pop charts. Things looked sure to crash. "It was like the eighties before Black Monday," recalls Dom Phillips.

In fact, it didn't crash; instead things calmed down gradually. The guest superjock didn't die—since most could still rock a party like no other—but many clubs started to reemphasize everything else, from cabaret acts and more imaginative decor to fresh DJ talent and great underground music. Anything to get away from the cult of the superstar spinner. Judge Jules, a DJ well known for his show on Kiss FM, pointed out insightfully that "the unique phenomenon of dance culture is the way that commercial and underground clubs coexist."

This would be the way forward.

The Pedestal

Many who had been involved with clubbing since its 1988 rebirth felt that the rise of the superstar DJ signaled a real loss of innocence, a betrayal of dancefloor unity. As wages rocketed, it seemed that the original goals of equality had been lost. These goals, which were first expressed in David Mancuso's Loft back in seventies New York, were realized most powerfully in Britain in the muddy egalitarianism of the rave movement.

Dave Dorrell, one of the first generation of UK house DJs, admits to being disappointed that the DJ rose so far above his station.

"I bought in wholesale to the 'no division, DJ-dancefloor-we're-all-one' unity," he says. "I loved all that."

For Dorrell, one of the best things about the early acid house clubs was the smoke machines. These, he argues, were real levelers. "Nobody knew what was going on. It was great. You were just all in it together, you were just as much a part dancing in the DJ box as anyone dancing on the floor."

Nevertheless, he could see the seeds of stardom being sown.

"It was inevitable, of course, that being a couple of feet higher than everyone on a podium was going to lead some people's heads to get lost in the clouds. DJs suddenly thought they had to have a Ferrari, a Porsche, you know. And people would be carrying record boxes through the crowd like you're the king . . . Oh please!"

Some see the whole DJ stardom thing as patently ridiculous, pointing out that a guy who plays records is never going to have the same magnetic aura as a traditional performer like, say, James Brown.

"DJs just aren't able to get it up on that kind of level of god-hood," insists Coldcut's Matt Black. "And yet there's this huge pedestal. We're told, 'Here's the new star,' and there's this guy standing there looking sheepish, not really doing anything except fiddling with his headphones.

"Name the Jim Morrison of DJs," he challenges.

Marketing the Star DJ

The music business revolves around stars. They look good on record sleeves and magazine covers, they can do interviews, they have fans and most importantly, they have lasting and profitable album-based careers. As DJs acquired starlike attributes, the record industry's ears quickly pricked up.

The first time the major labels bought emphatically into club music was with disco. But they didn't have a clue how to market it, so they had their fingers badly burnt (almost all the disco hits were on independent labels). The majors couldn't get their head around music which had such a lack of recognizable faces. Disco was constructed by studio producers and session musicians, and with Donna Summer as a notable exception, it failed to produce anyone who could convincingly get teenagers writing teary-eyed, moist-pantied fan letters.

With house it was different.

By putting the star DJ at the center of its dance music marketing efforts, the record industry was able to do with house what, with one or two exceptions, it could never do with disco—sell albums of it to the masses, especially since the once-underground activity of intense, drug-assisted nightclubbing was fast becoming a conventional night out.

Here was the guitar hero for the end of the century, a face for all those faceless tunes.

Most early attempts to make the DJ an album artist as a *producer*, such as those by Frankie Knuckles and David Morales, had actually failed quite badly, but in 1992 the idea of the (legal) DJ-mixed compilation was born. These were

Hungry for endorsements—Junior Vasquez shows his taste for CDs.

collections not of a DJ's own productions but of other people's records mixed by the DJ as if he were playing in a club. DMC launched its *Mixmag Live* series with a Carl Cox and Dave Seaman mix album, and *Journeys By DJ* put out a mix album by Billy Nasty. The DJ was on his way to being an album star.

Up until the nineties, young people bought singles. Those 7-inch slices of excitement defined our lives. But now the soundtrack to youth, in Europe and increasingly elsewhere, is the mix CD, the latest *Ministry Annual* or Pete Tong's *Essential Mix*—CDs which sell hundreds of thousands of copies. These are marketed with the names of the world's biggest DJs, who get large amounts of money for their endorsement (often their name is all they are selling—in many cases the music is actually mixed by a studio engineer using a computer program called Pro-tools). Here the big name DJ acts as a trusted, recognizable figure who brings together some songs which we'd otherwise never buy—he's a musical *brand.* You buy an *Essential Mix* CD the same way you buy a pair of Nike trainers.

"People buy into trusting the Ministry of Sound logo or trusting Boy George, or trusting me or trusting Sasha," says Pete Tong. "I think that's a massive revolution in the last five years." He sees DJ-mix albums as snapshots of a DJ's set, as the legitimization of the booming early nineties trade in bootleg DJ tapes. "It's a really nice, succinct way of charting their ability to entertain."

Superclubs and Global Brands

We can thank the much-hated 1994 Criminal Justice Act for the rise of mainstream clubbing. With the government intent on outlawing large-scale unlicensed dance events, alternative outlets had to be found for all the young energy that had been unleashed. After the law knocked raves on the head, people flooded into the clubs. They swapped muddy fields for the carpet and chrome of the local Cinderella's and carried on partying. The underground scene was legalized (and largely sanitized), money was made and the whole thing was a grand victory for consumerism. Indeed, cynics have pointed out that ecstasy, far from being a liberating force, actually represents the ultimate in consumerism—not only do you pay for music and a place to dance, now you can also buy a great party mood whenever you want one. Whatever the validity of this view, commercial club culture as we now know it was born out of the ashes of loving, hugging E-culture.

At the start of the nineties, as alternatives to the evil raves, licensing boards had granted permission for later and later club-based dance events, provided alcohol wasn't served (hardly a problem for the E generation). Legal all-night dancing finally arrived at London gay club Trade, and then at the Ministry of Sound in late 1991.

Once dance music was indoors and respectable, it turned glamorous. Club fashion was born—not just trends for practicality's sake like acid house's baggy T-shirts, dungarees and Kickers, but for reasons of fab, decadent flashiness. Fluffy bras and fetish wear, silver miniskirts, techno robot gear, and no end of sexy teenage midriffs made their appearance. All were well documented in the pages of *Mixmag*, which was filled with photos of us enjoying our new club-based lifestyle.

Looking back, Dom Phillips insists that, even more than the 1988 acid house revolution, the real turning point in UK dance culture came in 1994 when clubbing got dressed up and turned its back on the sweaty rave movement that had spawned it. Suddenly, the epitome of clubbing was a glamorous mixed-gay club like Leeds' Vague, or Mansfield's opulent Renaissance, filled with neoclassical pillars and girls dressed in satin. In London there was Billion Dollar Babes and Malibu Stacey. "I remember thinking things are really changing," says Phillips. "At that point it was suddenly so accessible." As if to prove his point, club promoters recall 1995 as the year when they made the most money.

At one point things had come full circle. Everyone was dancing in the clubs that acid house and rave were supposed to have finished off. We noticed, with irony, that some of us were dancing round our handbags again. Thus was named "handbag house"—the easy-cheesy soundtrack to tacky, glitzy nights drinking trashy cocktails. In the UK, clubbing had become an ordinary thing to do. It was suddenly a "mainstream leisure activity," and it was increasingly the heart of young people's identities.

Market researchers declared that clubbers were excellent targets for advertising—"early adopters," "opinion formers" every one of them—and ad agencies hurried to learn the language of the dancefloor. Clubbers allegedly spent nearly twenty percent more cash than Miss and Mr. Average. As a result, TV ads filled up with rushing techno soundtracks, shiny clubwear babes and barely hidden drug slang. "Sorted," shouted the venerable Royal Mail, echoing the cry of a clubber who's just bought his pill.

The market in soft drinks like Ribena and Lucozade boomed as E-takers eschewed alcohol. The breweries fought a rearguard action against ecstasy's popularity (and an exodus from the pubs) by inventing alcopops, potent, colorful, young new ways of getting drunk. Fruit-flavored alcoholic beverages, designed and marketed to compete with the psychedelic experience, became one of the fastest-established new product sectors ever, the kings of dayglo underage vomit.

Long-established brands were "repositioned" (postclubbing cornflakes anyone?). Drinks and cigarette companies patrolled clubs like drug-pushers, giving out free samples to hook those "early adopters," and in 1994, with Pepsi's Ministry of Sound tour, started actually sponsoring club nights. Graphic designers gave undue emphasis to the letter e, something hilariously evident in the BBC's coverage of the 1997 e-lection. Even the staid world of book publishing tried co-opting club culture. Irvine Welsh showed that the dance generation can actually read, and bookstores were crammed with fluorescent flyer-type book jackets—alcopop fiction!

At the end of the nineties the commercialization process triumphed in the superclub, with Liverpool's Cream, the Midlands' Renaissance and London's Ministry of Sound as the leading examples. Originally started with an eye on the grand venues of New York by people who cared about providing the best sound, the best DJs and the finest treatment, the nation's biggest venues soon fell for the lure of money and the power that their "brand" had accumulated. The Ministry of Sound now exists as an actual, physical club only so that kids worldwide believe in the Ministry brand as a reliable indicator of cool. The old Etonians who run the place make far more money from stamping that portcullis logo on things than they make from the club's dancefloor. With its merchandise booth and its own-brand bottled water, Ministry is the Hard Rock Café of clubs, something that will become clear as it follows its stated aim of opening branches in other cities.

In such places, the DJ's main role becomes that of floor-filler. Whether it's the quality of his music or his superstar status that draws in the punters ceases to matter. Pete Tong, for one, laments that the pressure to keep things at fever pitch with popular tunes makes it almost impossible for him to educate a club audience towards new sounds.

"One of the problems of being Pete Tong or Judge Jules or whoever is that you have that huge responsibility to peak the night," he says. "I never forget that—you are there to entertain. When people are lining up to get in and paying their money, they just want to go doolally to their favorite records."

At his worst, a DJ in a superclub is just working to build a brand. He's the hired power behind the logo, and like that crap $17 million actress, he's not there to be creative or innovative, he's there to pull a crowd.

One side effect of this has been the personality jock, the DJ who is more famous than their music. Boy George is often held up as the obvious example here, although to be fair, he has been DJing since the early eighties and has earned his stripes behind the decks, even if his fame as a pop star gave him a head start. Similarly, the transvestite DJ Jon Pleased Wimmin is undoubtedly an accomplished DJ, though would he have become quite so famous if he didn't wear wigs and a frock?

Many others are just celebrities who have turned to DJing as an alternative career. When ex-boxer Nigel Benn announced that he was a closet DJ and he was available for bookings, there were plenty of groans. When big-league soccer players David Hughes and Daniele Dichio made the same revelation, they got the same reaction.

Similarly, in recent years we've been treated to a series of dollybird DJs, cleavage-heavy girlies who are at home in both porn mags and dance rags, but who do a disservice to the ranks of serious female DJs as soon as they switch on their decks. One took things to extremes and was rumored to have hired a real DJ to do all her mixing.

Selling Back the House

Few forms of pop music actually originated in Britain, but the country leads the world in the musical import-export business. Perhaps a hangover of its imperial past, the UK excels at looting styles and sounds from elsewhere, mutating and combining them and then selling them back as something new. The Stones took the blues and repackaged it with more volume and a psychedelic edge; The Beatles copied the soul sound of The Isley Brothers but gave it a clunking Liverpool thump. And America bought into these remixed versions of its own music wholesale.

Such trade benefits greatly from the grass-is-always-greener principle, the idea that an audience will always respond better to something it thinks has come from somewhere else. Usually the key to this has been making the re-exported pop appeal to a different set of consumers from the ones who enjoyed it in the first place. Historically, this has almost always meant the UK changing black American styles into forms that have wide appeal for white America.

And so with postdisco dance music. Having adopted and adapted the black forms of house and techno (and having thrown hip hop into the mix as a major influence), the British have started selling them back in much-altered incarnations. And the market for this in the U.S. is resolutely young, white and suburban. So far the acts which have had the most commercial success are those which have developed from anonymous studio ensembles into fully fledged live performers, capable of "proper" rock-style stage shows. These are producers who became bands thanks to the UK's increasingly dance-friendly rock festivals, especially Glastonbury: groups like The Prodigy, Leftfield and the Chemical Brothers. (Interestingly, this is a similar process that hip hop underwent when it was forced from its club/party origins into adopting a rock-concert mentality to fill halls and stadiums.)

Making middle America dance is not an easy task. It might nod its head and wave its arms around to hip hop (a very hetero, lyric-based style) but until recently, other dance forms were seen as too close to disco (i.e. too gay) for comfort. While house-based dance music became the cornerstone of the pop charts in Britain and the rest of the world, in the US it remained underground, preserved and continued by the same marginal scenes which had created it. These were the black, gay and ethnic club "families" whose lineage went back to the dancefloors of disco.

As the faster, less funky European forms started to gain a U.S. foothold, there were some interesting collisions. Many of the older generation of clubbers looked down on this invasion force, resenting the presence of what they saw as a lot of underage kids wearing impossibly baggy trousers and taking all the wrong drugs. DJs watched their audiences change dramatically. Someone like Junior Vasquez saw his crowd change from being almost exclusively black and gay to being overwhelmingly white, far younger and much straighter. And the older scenes found themselves losing venues to the new generation as club owners smelled the profit in these eager young clubbers.

These kids are set to be America's first overground dance generation. They are the first teenagers for whom dance music is a consumer choice rather than a well-protected lifestyle secret. House and techno are hardly yet mainstream musics in the U.S., but they are no longer the preserve of marginal big-city cliques.

US Rave

In the main this is down to the small but fast growing rave scene which has emerged in the USA over the past ten years. Ironically, house and techno's pioneers had little to do with this movement. The spread of UK house into America's suburbs was driven largely by Anglophiliac American DJs and ex-pat Britons who, having experienced acid house firsthand in England, evangelized it stateside from San Francisco to New York.

In the east, parties like Caffeine on Long Island (run by rave favorite Micro), the Storm raves (promoted by Brooklyn's Frankie Bones, who was said to have been inspired by his DJing trips to the UK, along with Heather Hart and Adam X) and DJ DB's NASA parties in New York gave U.S. clubbing a distinctive UK twist.

Launched in July 1992, NASA, perhaps because it was staged at Manhattan's Shelter (a club fueled on memories of the Paradise Garage) was a high-profile assault on New York's closed dance community. The music was hard, fast and unrelenting, with 150 bpm breaks the order of the day. The clientele, too, was younger, more suburban—kids that had grown up on rock and rap. DJ DB, a Londoner transplanted to America, remembers the polarizing effect his music had. "The English posse that I'd been hanging around with for the last two years in New York absolutely ditched me," DB recalls. "They couldn't handle the fact that the music was full on rave, at this point. It was trance, and banging hard breakbeats. So they ditched me and I got this new generation of kids who were up for anything really fast." Although it lasted for only one year, NASA was an important focal point (in the film *Kids*, the club scenes are meant to be NASA). It was also one of the early U.S. champions of what later became known as jungle.

Florida developed its own quirky scene, too, with DJs like Kimball Collins playing a style of music heavily influenced by John Digweed and Sasha's frequent trips to the Sunshine State. There was also a thriving "breaks" scene (a hybrid of house, using hip hop breaks, sometimes called "coastal breaks") led by jocks like DJ Icey.

On the Left Coast, both Los Angeles and San Francisco found themselves with burgeoning party calendars. The climate and geography encouraged outdoor events and there were lingering psychedelic traditions such as the Deadhead scene to draw on. In San Francisco there was The Wicked Crew and DJs like Doc Martin (since relocated to L.A.). In Los Angeles party organizers like OAP (One Almighty Party), Moonshine and Truth. In Orange County there emerged a satellite scene grouped around hardcore progenitor Ron D. Core.

Both Moonshine and Truth were promoted by the Levy brothers, Steve and Jonathan, a pair of Englishmen with a knowledge of acid house and an entrepreneurial zeal. "In 1989, we did one of the first raves in Los Angeles," says Jonathan. "Initially it was in an old TV studio in West L.A., but then we moved it downtown to various locations, the most famous of which was an old fish distribution center. On the map we gave out it said, 'Just look for the building with a tuna fish on the side. You'll smell it from a block away.'"

Although rave's spread in the U.S. hasn't matched the UK's flash-fire tendencies, there are now a generation of DJs, producers and promoters whose skills and music have matured within it. Many of the country's most exciting dance producers—Joeski, Onionz, DJ Garth, Halo Varga—cut their teeth on the American rave circuit. Those former centers of excellence—New York, Chicago and Detroit—are fast being outpaced thanks to DJs whose traditions stretch back no further than the last five years.

Another of the new wave of producer/DJs to make an impression is Dano. He freely acknowledges the influence of acid house on the American rave scene. "Well, the Wicked Crew are all English," he says. "And I would say a good amount of the sound that's coming out of San Francisco now is influenced by these guys who primarily came out of the acid house movement rather than Chicago or New York. I was definitely more influenced more by acid house than anything else."

Whatever its origins, U.S. rave now has a very distinctive flavor that sets it quite apart from anything happening in the UK or Europe. Indeed the British influence has now withered to the point where the scene can be reasonably described as truly American. Although the average age at these events has dropped somewhat, causing some commentators to dismiss many of the teenagers attending these events as "candy-ravers," there is no doubting the size of today's movement.

And since this underground world has been allowed space to grow, unhindered by the sensationalist press that thrust it overground in the UK, it is now handily poised for further expansion, aided considerably by net-literate promoters, and savvy DJs. Mick Cole of the Deconstruction America label, a veteran of the west coast party scene, claims that new technology has considerably aided this nationwide push. "It's expanded a lot; and the Internet has helped," he says. "It's pushing it way out of the window. The more organized of the promoters, like B3, focus on their Web site. They put pictures from previous parties up so people can check them out; they showcase the mixes of DJs that have played at their parties. I mean, people around here have just got so many computers."

"It's a whole different thing now," claims Jonathan Levy. "It's getting so large, and it's ready to explode. There are amazing raves taking place that you wouldn't believe. I was in Colorado Springs with Carl Cox, and there were 2,500 people in a little mountain town. And you're talking about *hardcore* ravers. Kids who are just so into it." Levy insists that the rave circuit, having lagged behind financially for years, has now got to a stage where it can even compete with the European market. "The promoters are bringing in money now. I know that Carl Cox, when he comes out here now, the idea of taking a cut in money from European levels is not an issue anymore."

America is also getting to grips with its own DJ stars, among them Terry Mullan, DJ Dan, Josh Wink, Derrick Carter, Taylor, as well as Keoki, perhaps the one DJ with genuine star potential (and a peculiar predilection for missing glaring opportunities).

"If you look at Sasha or Oakenfold in the UK, they're basically fucking rock stars," says Levy. "There are various DJs out there who this might happen to, but I don't think it will be an English DJ. By the same token, a lot of American DJs aren't interested in going over to Europe anymore. The smart ones don't give a fuck about Europe because they want to make a name out here."

There are still many hurdles to cross. The size of the country is certainly a factor slowing down the transmission of this new music, especially since there is no national radio station as there is in the UK. And as yet, apart from a few notable (British-run) exceptions, the U.S. recording industry has shown little faith in dance, probably because it can't deal with its inherently ephemeral nature, but also because no one has taken the necessary leap of faith. Having had its fingers badly burned by the disco backlash, when the record industry was guilty of flooding—and killing—a dance scene that had previously been both genuine and pure, its reticence to throw itself fully onto the dance bandwagon may actually bode well for the long-term health of dance music in the U.S. After the hype of the "electronica" boom of four years ago, the industry has settled back into its traditional inertia, and continued to peddle a relentless (and often tedious) succession of R&B and hip hop in the knowledge that this music has already proved its profitability.

Brian Chin, formerly *Billboard*'s Dance Editor, puts the blame at the feet of the executives. "In the end I would have to say there is no business figurehead who would have institutionalized dance the way they did in Europe. Over there, all the captains of industry were perfectly willing to make media stars out of DJs."

This has left the field clear for the independents. Jonathan and Steve Levy's L.A.-based company, Moonshine, who specialize in DJ-mix compilations, are happily cashing in on this rapidly-expanding market. Their turnover for this year is expected to exceed $10 million.

Another reasonable indicator of rave's gradual incursion into the mainstream can be seen in some of the corporate sponsorship it has enjoyed over the past few years: Levi's, Red Bull, Camel and vodka companies like Absolut have all spotted the potential for a captive malleable youth audience. Whether this translates into artists crossing into the *Billboard* charts remains to be seen, especially after the many false starts of the past decade. However, looking at the way the industry has twisted hip hop into a hideous parody of itself in order to wring money from it, its continual shunning of dance music may actually be a *good* thing.

Overpaid and Over There

Consider that into the fertile ground of this expanding rave scene comes a concerted effort by certain big-name British DJs to "break America," and a U.S. dance future looks inevitable. And remember that as established British DJs gain success in the states, they're also opening doors for homegrown talent to prosper—in much the same way that The Rolling Stones' championing of singers like Muddy Waters thirty-five years ago helped reawaken America to blues music.

The UK dance press is currently filled with articles describing how DJs such as Oakenfold, Sasha and Norman Cook (Fatboy Slim) are finally making inroads, the latter having recently joined The Prodigy and Chemical Brothers as a recognizable album act and seeing his song "Praise You" all over ads for the Gap. "Any person I switch off from Hootie and the Blowfish is another soul saved," laughs Cook, as he continues his ridiculously successful one-man British invasion.

Sasha, who has been a regular visitor to U.S. shores for many years (and who now enjoys a residency at New York's Twilo with longtime DJ pal John Digweed) claims that at the beginning of 2000 a real acceleration is noticeable in America's acceptance of dance. "Recently I've started to notice the difference," he told *Ministry* magazine. "There's more dance music in adverts. You see it more on films too," he adds, pointing out the dance-leaning soundtrack to such movies as *Go*.

"This is the year," beams Paul Oakenfold. "We've been hammering away at it for the last few years, and now it looks as if we're going to break it wide open. We're going to take America to the next level."

Oakenfold's methodology has been to talk to America in a language he was sure it understood. Speaking in 1996 announcing his mission to break his Perfecto label in the States, he was adamant that the only way to do this was through the age-old rock methods of touring and live shows. "We're not interested in the clubs," he said. "We're going straight at it from the college, alternative route. I've got acts who can come out there and tour, just like Oasis."

And perhaps this is the common factor of the few British dance acts who have so far seen transatlantic success: they are examples of dance music made into rock music, bands with computers that are happy onstage, neat new presentations of dance music in a way that the U.S. rock mind can understand.

Norman Cook agrees that the dance acts who have crossed over in America have something rocky in common. "There's a little element of rock'n'roll in all of us," he says. "We're not just studio boffins, we're caning rock'n'roll animals that *Rolling Stone* and *Spin* can write stories about. We've all had brushes with rock music. There's a couple of guitars in there and that's all the Americans needed to latch on to!"

Cook is grateful that the door has been opened, that U.S. major labels might now take dance acts seriously and invest in promoting and developing them. However, such is America's confusion about DJ-produced dance music, he is regularly asked if he is *in* Fatboy Slim, and he is often referred to as "the *band* of the nineties." Even his American record company remains confused about what it is he actually does.

"They're always trying to make me put a band together and play as a band," he sighs.

"I've got to the point now in America, where I'm like, 'Look this is as far as we can take it where it's still dance music. I don't wanna cross over and be a rock act. I don't wanna play in a band. I don't wanna tour. It's nice that you're promoting me and we're selling albums, but let's not forget that this is what I do.'"

Such confusion even led to him having to turn down TV appearances.

"I got offered to do *Letterman* and *Saturday Night Live*, which is a lovely idea, but what would I do? I'm a DJ and it takes two hours to DJ. You can't do it in three minutes."

Future DJing

If the DJ/producer pretending to be a band is a step backward, what does future DJing look like? It seems certain that DJing will start to outgrow the 12-inch single. Affordable CD-burners are here and many DJ/producers now play their work-in-progress from a test CD rather than an expensive (and delicate) acetate. It's easier to learn, too. With bpm counters and clever synchronization facilities, CD mixers can take much of the necessary skill out of mixing. DJs will cling to the sexy tactile nature of vinyl, and stress the warmth of its analogue sound, but digital DJing will become ever more attractive—not least for the fact that digital music is far more easily obtained than vinyl. A CD DJ can play from an album as readily as a single (whereas most vinyl albums are cut too quietly to play in a club), and so a wealth of material is immediately open to them on compilations and reissues, without spending hours rooting around used record stores. They could also go to one of several Internet sites and choose tracks from the entire back catalogue of a vast series of dance labels. Those ordered are pressed onto a custom CD and shipped out by return mail. Alternatively they could download any number of MP3 dance tracks posted by the globe's bedroom producers.

In most third world countries, CD DJing is already the norm. It offers far more music and is much more practical than vinyl in a hot and dusty climate. From Kenya to Cuba you'll find talented DJs making a great night's music with a CD mixer and maybe a shoe box full of discs.

Digital DJing has other attractions. By multiplying the sonic possibilities immediately available to a DJ playing live, it further blurs the line between DJing and musicianship. Several DJs have recently emerged—such as London spinner Pure Science—who play nothing but their own compositions, tailoring them live using a host of beats, samples and MIDI equipment.

Coldcut, an act who always have the latest toys, believe that the advances in DJing will come in presentation. They talk of ways to make the event more responsive—like having the dancers somehow trigger elements of the music by the way they move (perhaps using floor pads or laser sensors). Their VJamm software allows a DJ to cut and mix video samples while simultaneously playing music. They have also devised a MIDI interface for a turntable, a device they call the "dextractor," which allows a DJ to use the back and forth scratch movements of a record to trigger other instruments. With the dextractor, a DJ can scratch any chunk of digital sound he chooses (or even video)—you could scratch a drum beat, a piano riff, a nightingale singing or a film clip of *Debbie Does Dallas*. You can even synchronize a video projection to a record you're scratching.

Other technologies will have an impact, too. Pretty soon if you're in a club and you hear a song you like, you'll be able to hit a key on your organizer/cell phone and have it downloaded immediately to your hard-drive. Broadcasting is becoming narrowcasting and thousands of highly targeted online channels of specialist information will become the norm. Instead of radio you'll be able to go to the Salsoul channel, or the Twisted network and hear whatever track you want, on demand. Or you'll switch on your own personal channel which automatically sequences the music you like best, according to your mood, and even goes out and buys new things according to what it knows you like. Forget having an actual physical music collection, you'll just have a stereo system that works like your own personal DJ.

In that sense, technology will have a fairly insidious effect on the DJ's craft. You can already buy software which automates the mixing skills of a DJ. Buckingham's Databeat Digital Music Systems markets just such a system to pub chains across the country. Yes, DJ Robot is here. And not only can he mix, he can be programmed to address audience behavior. "Pubs like to program faster music for their peak hours because it makes people drink more," says the machine's spokesman. It could save fortunes on DJ fees and it won't be demanding free drugs or groping the promoter's girlfriend, but it's unlikely such software would ever be used to expand listeners' tastes, or recontextualize a piece of music, or juxtapose two really unlikely records to great success. When was the last time you were surprised or challenged by a piece of in-store muzak?

House Sucks (Pessimistic Conclusion)

Now we've let the DJ become a superstar, have we stopped listening to the music?

We have DJs who are so famous that we'd go crazy for their first record even if was utter rubbish. We have DJs who let the club tell them what to play. We have personality DJs who can draw a crowd even though they're crap. Porno DJs who have someone else to put on their tunes. Novelty jocks. Ex-boxers as DJs, soccer heroes behind the decks, washed-up pop stars desperate for new credibility. DJs who are shit but they've got a record in the charts.

We go to superclubs that only exist to support a lucrative brand name so that a company run by people who don't dance can make millions from T-shirts, compilation CDs and alcohol and tobacco sponsorship. We listen to a few big-name DJs on the radio and let them totally rule our tastes. When their name's on a mix album we trust it without thinking and rush out to buy it. The DJ is a corporate whore.

The DJ has chopped and mixed and merged every kind of music until there's no chance of a "next big thing." All we can expect is the next remix, a variation on a theme. And the music is so *effective* now, especially when consumed with drugs, that no one cares whether it's actually any good. It's just an infallible, Pavlovian technology of pleasure. At the end of the seventies people decided "disco sucks"; at the end of the nineties, house, trance, garage . . . SUCKS! (techno and drum'n'bass are just boring). The only difference is we haven't noticed how much it sucks yet, because the commercial club industry has got us in the palm of its hand. As long as it gets me throwing my fists in the air with my eyes glued shut on my Friday night podium, I don't give a fuck whether it has any artistic value.

Our precious, once-underground culture has been co-opted into a great mainstream capitalist hegemony.

Is going clubbing special anymore, or is it just like going to the pub?

The greatest success of dance culture is supposed to be that it now has acts who are at home playing American stadiums. But it's not a triumph for dance music to disguise itself as something that's existed for 35 years or more. The Prodigy are just The Rolling Stones for a new generation. The record labels have just squeezed them into the rock-star rulebook so they can market them better. They'll go on tour when the album comes out. We'll all scream when they come onstage and the music biz is happy.

Dance revolution . . . Where?

Club culture was built on togetherness, on participation, equality, communion. When it works you shouldn't be able to tell the dancer from the dance. It was founded on the idea that the clubbers are the stars, not the short guy who fiddles with the record player. If we're on a dancefloor but we're all watching the DJ, or if we're in an arena all looking at the stage, we are no longer doing what it's all about: we are once more an audience and no longer the event.

Dance culture has been completely stolen by the forces of commercialism.

OK?

Good.

That's the pessimistic conclusion over with.

The Global Underground (Optimistic Conclusion)

But the dialectic saves the day.

In dance music there's always an underground.

This is at its most creative just after things have got horribly commercial. The mainstream picks up on something, burns it up, and declares it dead. But meanwhile, the pioneers have moved on and are free to push things further, to reclaim the momentum and come up with something new.

So rail about supercommercial club culture all you like. It's all true, every pessimistic word, but it doesn't matter because there's always an underground, always something fresh on the horizon.

For every cheesy commercial DJ who's happy to play what the record pluggers send him, who charts records he doesn't like just so he stays on the mailing list, who plays records he hates because everyone else is playing them, and who has no problem with a club giving him "guidelines" on what and what not to play, there's another DJ who loves music, who searches out and *buys* records rather than just playing promotional freebies, who develops his own style, who throws his own parties, who generates his own following, who creates new music.

There'll always be an underground and it will always be filled with people who love music, not as a job but as the centerpiece to their life—even if manipulative drug pop seems to rule the day and even if most clubs are clogged with DJs who have abandoned their missionary zeal to return to the safe job of musical waiter. The exceptions are where the energy lies.

The fragmentation of dance music into scores of specialized genres is another reason for excitement. This works directly against the idea of the superclub and the prostitute DJ, and can only encourage experimentation and creativity. You can bet that sooner or later, out of these devious little scenes will come something interesting, and inevitably something momentous. That's how we got disco, hip hop, house, and in recent years that's how jungle emerged, and drum'n'bass, UK garage (speed garage), two-step, coastal breaks...

What's next? Who knows—all that's certain is that something somewhere is busy evolving, just like it's always done.

We spent the last forty years recording pop music, now we're gonna have incredible fun recycling it into any form we want. The band is dead, long live the DJ. No more waiting for the next big thing, let's look forward to the next amazing tweak, the next gut-wrenching new noise, the next unbelievable collision of sampled sound.

And dance music is now truly international, and internationalist. Musical possibilities have become global. The established centers of our story have splintered so much that the next great record might just as likely come from Norway as from New York. And with words losing out to the universal beat, we all speak the same language. French people can finally make music that English people like. In fact you can bet that any really radical new styles of dance music will emerge from somewhere truly bizarre, far away from the intense scrutiny of the dance media and the commentators who swoop on anything novel before it has a chance to spread its wings.

Abetting this dramatic crashing of borders is the rise of the Internet as a force for musical distribution. If house music was the fulfillment of the do it yourself punk ethos, then netcasting and clever compression formats like MP3 take things even further. The means of music production have long been in the hands of the masses; now we have the means of distribution too, and record companies—who were only ever banks stupid enough to lend money to musicians—are redundant. Any DJ can create a global community of listeners on the Net. DJs in a club in New York can play to the dancefloor of a club in London. A DJ can make music in his own home, transmit it to another DJ across the world, who can press it himself onto a CD and play it when he goes on in a club in Singapore in a couple of hours.

The Buzz Remains

The disc jockey has been with us for almost a century now. In that time he has been ignored, misunderstood, despised, worshipped and adored. He has stayed in the forefront of music, twisting and shaping it into fresh forms, perverting technology and forcing from it stunning new sounds. He has conjured a long series of novel genres in his endless search for material to keep his dancers moving. In the U.S. the DJ created amazing music, then the UK gave him a home and made him a star. He continued his magic and around him there grew a musical culture more revolutionary and more enduring than any before.

After the 1988 summer of love, kids in Britain were finally enjoying the transcendent rituals on which the U.S. evolution of dance music had been based. They finally understood the real power of a DJ, and in large numbers. Now, having conquered Europe and much of the southern hemisphere, the music is spreading back across the Atlantic. Having forged music more truly universal than any preceding it, the DJ is arguably a conduit for celebration and communion on a global scale. It's possible that the DJ is the ultimate expression of the ancient shamanic role; that the DJ is the greatest witchdoctor there has ever been, unmatched at shaking us out of the drudge of the day and into the life of the night.

Why do we worship at the knees of the record-slinger? Because he is occasionally capable of divinity. When it all connects in a club, there's nowhere you can have more fun.

"A really great DJ is totally capable of making a bad record sound okay, a good record sound great, and a great record sound fantastic—by the context they put them in, and what they put around them. How they steer them. They can do all kinds of tricks. A great DJ can make people spontaneously cheer just for a little squelchy noise. Which is quite insane really. A little noise like *wha-wha-wha* and people go, 'Yeeeaaah!' They can have people clapping along to a cymbal, just by the way they're bringing it in. When it's done well, it's fantastic. If it's done really well, it can be quite transcendental."

It's a mystic art indeed. It seems so banal, but it holds the potential of phenomenal, inexpressible power. A great DJ can arouse more raw emotion in his audience than the composer of the most bittersweet opera, or the author of the most uplifting novel, or the director of the most life-affirming film.

When you're DJing and you're great at it, you're not playing records, you're playing the dancefloor. You're not just mixing tunes, you're mixing energy and emotions, mixing from surprise into hope and happiness, cutting from liberation to ecstasy to love. When it goes right, you're inside the bodies of everyone in the room, you know what they're feeling and where they're going, and you're taking them there. You're sweeping them off the earthly plane and transporting them to a higher place. You're moving their bodies and their souls with the music that flows from your fingertips.

You're putting them in the moment.

"Sweaty palms. Huge smiles. That kind of intenseness when you're in the zone, when you're in the box on your own. Oh my God! What's the next record? Frantically searching, making sure your instinct's right, changing your mind, then going back to your first choice, and then ripping that out and putting it on at the last minute… and it works!

"And seeing people smiling.

"And singing.

"And going crazy."

SOURCES
CLUB CHARTS
INDEX

Sources

ORIGINAL INTERVIEWS

All conducted by the authors, except *transcripts lent by Matthew Collin.

Abbatiello, Sal 5.10.98
Aletti, Vince 12.10.98
Baker, Arthur 25.1.99
Bambaataa, Afrika 21.12.95, 6.10.98
Barrow, Steve 10.9.98
Beedle, Ashley 4.9.96
Bellars, Rob 25.3.99
Berkman, Justin 5.9.97
Blow, Kurtis 27.9.98
Byrd, Gary 20.11.98
Carpenter, Kenny 11.1.99
Carter, Derrick 24.2.95
Casey, Bob 1.2.99
Chase, Charlie 1.10.98
Chin, Brian 5.10.98
Clinton, George 17.5.95
Coldcut 14.4.99
Cole, Mick 10.2.00
Combs, Sean Puffy 17.4.95
Cook, Norman 19.3.99
Cosmo 25.5.99
D'Acquisto, Steve 5.10.98
Damier, Chez 23.2.95
Dano 9.2.00
DB 3.2.00
Dean, Farmer Carl 28.3.99
deKrechewo, Nick 8.10.98
Dewhirst, Ian 14.9.98, 2.4.99
Dexter, Jeff 18.2.99
Dorrell, Dave 3.3.99
Dynell, Johnny 8.10.98
Eagle, Roger 10.9.98
Evison, Dave 1.5.99
Fab 5 Freddy 5.10.98
Farley, Terry 2.11.94*
Farley Jackmaster Funk 22.2.95
Gillett, Charlie 5.3.99
Godin, Dave 21.9.98
Gomes, Michael 2.2.99
Grabel, Richard 2.2.99
Grandmaster Flash 8.10.98
Grand Mixer D.ST 7.10.98
Grand Wizard Theodore 2.10.98
Grappone, Charlie 7.10.98
Grasso, Francis 4.2.99
Hayden, Terry 9.1.99
Holman, Michael 20.11.99
Islam, Afrika 27.9.98
Jay, Norman 23.2.99
Jazzy Jay 7.10.98
Jazzy M 1.10.97
Jefferson, Marshall 8.9.94*, 22.2.99
Kevorkian, François 6.10.98, 9.1.99
Knuckles, Frankie 27.2.95, 2.4.96
Kool DJ Herc 30.9.98
Kool Lady Blue 29.9.98
Krivit, Danny 6.10.98
Levine, Ian 20.10.97, 2.3.99
Levy, Jonathan 10.2.00
Leybold, Yvon 9.1.99
Lil Louis 10.9.92
McCready, John 17.5.99
Mancuso, David 3.10.98
Mangual, Bacho 7.10.98
Marsh, Jon 26.10.94*
Moore, Mark 2.12.94
Morales, David 4.2.99
Moulton, Tom 30.9.98

Neal, Cedric 22.2.95
Noel, Terry 30.9.98
Oakenfold, Paul 13.6.96, 7.4.99
Peel, John 7.4.99
Phillips, Dom 20.5.99
Piccioni, Dave 12.9.97
DJ Pierre 22.3.95, 17.2.99
Q-Bert 17.3.99
Rampling, Danny 6.5.99, 14.9.94*
Roberts, Kev 21.9.98
Roc Raida 2.10.98
Rosner, Alex 5.10.98
Rushton, Neil 10.2.00
Samwell, Ian 23.2.99, 24.2.99
Savile, Jimmy 22.9.98
Siano, Nicky 7.10.98, 29.1.99
Sicko, Dan 20.11.99
Simmons, Russell 24.8.94
Spanky 19.5.99
Steinski 30.1.99
Tenaglia, Danny 1.10.98
Terry, Todd 3.11.94, 21.5.96
Tong, Pete 13.5.99
Tyree 20.2.95
Vasquez, Junior 2.11.95
Walker, Johnny 1.10.97
Wesker, Lindsay 10.2.99
Winley, Paul 2.10.98
Woodliffe, Jonathan 23.9.98

(The uncredited quotes on the last page of the narrative belong to Dom Phillips and Dave Dorrell.)

BOOKS

Adler, Bill, *Rap* (St. Martins, 1992)
Barrow, Steve & Dalton, Peter, *The Rough Guide to Reggae* (Rough Guides, 1997)
Beadle, Jeremy J., *Will Pop Eat Itself?* (Faber & Faber, 1993)
Benson, Richard (ed.), *Night Fever* (Boxtree, 1997)
Boy George with Spencer Bright, *Take It Like a Man* (Sidgwick & Jackson, 1995)
Brewster, Bill & Broughton, Frank, *The Manual* (Headline, 1998)
Bromberg, Craig, *The Wicked Ways of Malcolm McLaren* (Harper & Row, 1989)
Broughton, Frank (ed.), *Time Out Book of Interviews* (Penguin, 1998)
Burchill, Julie, *Damaged Gods* (Arrow, 1986)
Bussman, Jane, *Once in a Lifetime* (Virgin, 1998)
Cale, John & Bockris, Victor, *What's Welsh For Zen?* (Bloomsbury, 1999)
Cantor, Louis, *Wheelin' on Beale* (Pharos, 1992)
Cauty, Jimmy & Drummond, Bill, *The Manual* (KLF Publications, 1988)
Chanan, Michael, *Repeated Takes* (Verso, 1995)
Chapman, Rob, *Selling the Sixties* (Routledge, 1992)
Clarke, Donald (ed.), *The Penguin Encyclopedia of Popular Music* (Penguin, 1990)
Cohn, Nik, *Awopbopaloobpalopbamboom* (Minerva, 1969)
Collin, Matthew, *Altered State* (Serpent's Tail, 1997)
Cox, Harvey, *The Feast of Fools* (Harvard University Press, 1969)
Dannen, Frederic, *Hit Men* (Vintage, 1991)
Davis, Stephen & Simon, Peter, *Reggae Bloodlines* (Anchor Press, 1979)
Davis, Stephen & Simon, Peter, *Reggae International* (R&B New York, 1982)
Dawson, Jim, *The Twist* (Faber & Faber, 1995)
Diebold, David, *Tribal Rites* (Time Warp Publishing, 1988)
Eisenberg, Evan, *The Recording Angel* (Picador, 1988)
Eure, Joseph & Spady, James G., *Nation Conscious Rap* (PC International, 1991)
Fernando, S. H. Jr., *The New Beats* (Anchor, 1994)
Fleming, Jonathan, *What Kind of House Party Is This?* (MIY, 1995)
Floyd, Samuel A., *The Power of Black Music* (Oxford University Press, 1995)
Frith, Simon, *Sound Effects* (Pantheon, 1981)
Garratt, Sheryl, *Adventures in Wonderland* (Headline, 1998)

George, Nelson, *The Death of Rhythm and Blues* (Plume, 1988)
George, Nelson, *Hip Hop America* (Viking, 1998)
Gillett, Charlie, *The Sound of the City* (Sphere, 1970)
Godfrey, John, *A Decade of i-Deas* (Penguin, 1990)
Goldman, Albert, *Disco!* (Hawthorn, 1978)
Green, Jonathon, *Days in the Life* (Pimlico, 1998)
Guinness Book of British Hit Singles (Guinness, 11th Edition, 1997)
Haden-Guest, Anthony, *The Last Party* (William Morrow, 1997)
Hager, Steven, *Hip Hop* (St. Martins, 1984)
Hamblett, Charles & Deverson, Jane, *Generation X* (Tandem, 1964)
Hebdige Dick, *Cut 'n' Mix* (Comedia, 1987)
Hibbert, Tom, *Who the Hell?* (Virgin, 1994)
Hilmes, Michelle, *Radio Voices* (University of Minneapolis Press, 1997)
Holleran, Andrew, *Dancer from the Dance* (Penguin, 1978)
Jackson, John, *Big Beat Heat* (Schirmer, 1991)
Jahn, Brian & Weber, Tom, *Reggae Island* (Da Capo, 1998)
James, Martin, *State of Bass* (Boxtree, 1997)
Joe, Radcliffe A., *This Business of Disco* (Billboard, 1980)
Jonas, Gerald, *Dancing* (Harry N. Abrams, 1992)
Kaiser, Charles, *The Gay Metropolis* (Harcourt Brace, 1997)
Keith, Michael C., *Voices in the Purple Haze* (Praeger, 1997)
Kempster Chris (ed.), *History of House* (Sanctuary, 1996)
Knoedelseder, William, *Stiffed* (HarperPerennial, 1993)
Krivine, J., *Jukebox Saturday Night* (Buckleberry Press, 1977)
Larkin, Colin (ed.), *Guinness Encyclopedia of Popular Music* (Guinness, 1993)
Larkin, Colin, *Virgin Encyclopaedia of Reggae* (Virgin, 1998)
Lee, Martin A. & Shlain, Bruce, *Acid Dreams* (Grove Press, 1992)
Martin, Linda & Segrave, Kerry, *Anti Rock* (Da Capo Press, 1993)
McKenna, Pete, *Nightshift* (S. T. Publishing, 1996)
Melly, George, *Owning Up* (Penguin, 1965)
Melly, George, *Revolt into Style* (Penguin, 1970)
Middles, Mick, *Red Mick* (Headline, 1993)
Mietzitis, Vita, *Night Dancin'* (Ballantine, 1980)
Musto, Michael, *Downtown* (Vintage, 1986)
Needs, Kris, *Needs Must* (Virgin, 1999)
Passman, Arnold, *The Deejays* (Macmillan, 1971)
Perkins, William Eric (ed.), *Droppin' Science* (Temple University Press, 1996)
Post, Steve, *Playing in the FM Band* (Viking, 1974)
Reynolds, Simon, *Energy Flash* (Picador, 1998)
Romanowski, Patricia & George-Warren, Holly, *Rolling Stone Encyclopedia of Rock & Roll* (Fireside, 1995)
Rose, Tricia, *Black Noise* (Wesleyan University Press, 1994)
Rutledge, Leigh W., *The Gay Decades* (Plume, 1992)
Savage, Jon, *The Haçienda Must Be Built* (International Music Publications, 1995)
Savile, Jimmy, *As It Happens* (Barrie and Jenkins, 1974)
Scott, Ronnie, *Some of My Best Friends Are Blues* (W. H. Allen, 1979)
Selvin, Joel, *Summer of Love* (Plume, 1994)
Shapiro, Harry, *Waiting for the Man* (Quartet, 1988)
Sicko, Dan, *Techno Rebels* (Billboard, 1999)
Smith, Joe, *Off The Record* (Warner Books, 1988)
Southern, Eileen, *The Music of Black Americans* (W. W. Norton, 1983)
Stanley, Lawrence A. & Jefferson, Morley, *Rap: The Lyrics* (Penguin, 1992)
Tee, Ralph, *Soul Music, Who's Who* (Prima, 1992)

Théberge, Paul, *Any Sound You Can Imagine* (Wesleyan University Press, 1997)
Thornton, Sarah, *Club Cultures* (Polity, 1995)
Toop, David, *Rap Attack 2* (Serpent's Tail, 1984)
Troy, Sandy, *Captain Trips* (Thunder's Mouth, 1994)
Wexler, Jerry & Ritz, David, *Rhythm and the Blues* (St. Martins, 1993)
Whitburn, Joel, *The Billboard Book of Top 40 Hits* (Billboard, 1996)
Winstanley, Russ & Nowell, David, *Soul Survivors* (Robson Books, 1996)
Wolfe, Tom, *The Electric Kool-Aid Acid Test* (Bantam, 1968)
Wolfe, Tom, *The Pump House Gang* (Bantam, 1968)

MAGAZINES & PERIODICALS

Billboard, Black Music, Blues & Soul, Cashbox, Collusion, DJ, Downbeat, Evening Standard, The Face, i-D, Life, Melody Maker, Melting Pot, Ministry, Mixmag, Mix/Master, Mojo, Music Technology, Muzik, NME, New York, New York Post, New York Sunday News, The New York Times, Nightlife, Out/Look, Penthouse, Popular Music, Q, Rolling Stone, Spin, Time, Time Out, Time Out New York, Togetherness, Variety, The Village Voice.

MISCELLANEOUS SOURCES

Austin, Brian Todd, *The Construction and Transformation of the American Disc Jockey Occupation, 1950-1993*, University of Texas at Austin PhD dissertation, 1994
Fikentscher, Kai, *"You Better Work!" Music, Dance and Marginality in Underground Dance Clubs of NYC*, Columbia University PhD dissertation
BBC TV, *Beat This* (Arena), 1984
BBC TV, *Dancing in the Street*, 1996
Granada TV, *The Wigan Casino Story*, 1998
WMAQ-TV (Chicago), *What is House?*, 1991
Chin, Brian, sleevenotes to *The Disco Box* (Rhino)
Gordon Brown, Nick, sleevenotes to *Sasha, the Remixes* (Stress)
McLaren, Malcolm, sleevenotes to *Duck Rock* (Charisma)
Wilson, Frank, sleevenotes to *Eddie Kendricks: The Ultimate Collection* (Motown)
Garage Remembrance Web site: http://www.ingress.com/~garage2/postingsz.html
Ian Samwell Web site: http://www.saber.net/~orb/
Disco Inferno Web site: http://heml.passagen.se/discoguy/tributes/larry.html
Terry Noel Web site: http://www.fidelibus.com/noel (netscape)
International Turntablist Federation Web site: http://www.turntablism.com

Picture Sources

Epigraph page: S. Weir
6: The Granger Collection, New York
23: © BBC
37: © Peter Hastings
38: Joe Scherschel/*Life* magazine, © Time Inc.
47: Courtesy Gaslight Advertising Archives
68: © Jeff Dexter 1966
79: Redferns Music Picture Library, London
110: © Peter Simon
132: © Frank Broughton
141: © 1975 The Estate of Peter Hujar, courtesy Matthew Marks Gallery, New York
147: From the collection of D. Krivit
157: Courtesy of Bob Casey/*Melting Pot*
183: From the collection of D. Krivit
187: Sonia Moskowitz © Bettmann/CORBIS
191: Gaslight Advertising Archives, reprinted by permission of Studio 54
193: Courtesy of *Billboard*
219: V. Richard Haro © Newsday, Inc. 1993
227: David Corio © S.I.N./CORBIS
249: Courtesy of KLB Productions
253: © Laura Levine
277: © Tina Paul
285: From the collection of D. Krivit
288: From the collection of D. Krivit; artwork © The Estate of Keith Haring
299: © Simon Witter
303: From the collection of C. Neal
323: RIP
365: Collection of the authors
368: © *i-D*
385: © Jason Manning
394: Courtesy of Philips Electronics and Junior Vasquez

Club Charts

WIGAN CASINO TOP 50

The Adventurers—Easy Baby
Lee Andrews—I've Had It
Paul Anka—I Can't Help Loving You
Yvonne Baker—You Didn't Say A Word
Frankie Beverly & The Butlers—If That's What You Wanted
George Blackwell—Can't Lose My Head
Mel Britt—She'll Come Running Back
Doni Burdick—Bari Track
The Carstairs—It Really Hurts Me Girl
The Casualeers—Dance Dance Dance
Johnny Caswell—You Don't Love Me Anymore
Lorraine Chandler—I Can't Change
Freddie Chavez—They'll Never Know Why
The Checkerboard Squares—Double Cookin'
Morris Chestnut—Too Darn Soulful
Connie Clark & Orchestra—My Sugar Baby
Eula Cooper—Let Our Love Grow Higher
Dean Courtney—I'll Always Need You
The Del Larks—Job Opening
The Detroit Executives—Cool Off
The Dynamics—Yes I Love You Baby
Epitome Of Sound—You Don't Love Me
The Four Perfections—I'm Not Strong Enough
Edward Hamilton & The Arabians—Baby Don't You Weep
Joe Hicks—Don't It Make You Feel Funky
Willie Hutch—Love Runs Out
Gloria Jones—Tainted Love
Tamiko Jones—I'm Spellbound
Tobi Legend—Time Will Pass You By
Little Richie—Just Another Heartache
Joe Mathews—Ain't Nothing You Can Do
Jodi Mathis—Don't You Care Anymore
Garnett Mimms—Looking For You
Dean Parrish—I'm On My Way
Jimmy Radcliffe—Long After Tonight Is All Over
Saxie Russell—Psychedelic Soul
The Salvadores—Stick By Me Baby
Larry Santos—You Got Me Where You Want Me
The Sherries—Put Your Arms Around Me
The Silhouettes—Not Me Baby
R. Dean Taylor—There's A Ghost In My House
Don Thomas—Come On Train
The Tomangoes—I Really Love You
The Velvet Satins—Nothing Can Compare To You
The Volcanoes—The Laws Of Love
Sam Ward—Sister Lee
Jerry Williams—If You Ask Me
Maurice Williams—Being Without You
Billy Woods - Let Me Make You Happy
The World Column—So Is The Sun

Compiled by Ian "Frank" Dewhirst

LOFT TOP 100

Andwella—Hold On To Your Mind
Ashford & Simpson—Stay Free
Atmosfear—Dancing In Outer Space
Babe Ruth—The Mexican
Barrabas—Woman

Archie Bell & The Drells—Let's Groove
Blackbyrds—Walking In Rhythm
Black Rascals—Keeping My Mind
Brass Construction—Music Makes You Feel Like Dancing
James Brown—Give It Up And Turn It Loose
Candido—Thousand Finger Man
Cassio—Baby Love
Central Line—Walking Into Sunshine
Code 718—Equinox
Crown Heights Affair—Say A Prayer For Two
Deep Vibes—A Brand New Day
Alfredo De La Fe—My Favorite Things
Manu Dibango—Soul Makossa
Dinosaur L—Go Bang!
Don Ray—Standing In The Rain
Double Exposure—My Love Is Free
Lamont Dozier—Going Back To My Roots
D Train—Keep On
George Duke—Brazilian Love Affair
Ian Dury—Spasticus Autisticus
Earth Wind & Fire—The Way Of The World
Easy Going—Baby I Love You
Fingers Inc—Mystery Of Love
First Choice—Doctor Love
Forrrce—Keep On Dancing
The Gap Band—Yearning For Your Love
Joe Gibbs—Chapter 3
Eddy Grant—Living On The Frontline
Johnny Hammond—Los Conquistadores Chocolates
Damon Harris—It's Music
Ednah Holt—Serious Sirius Space Party
The Holy Ghost—Walk On Air (Sun & Moon Mix)
Frank Hooker & The Positive People—This Feeling
Instant House—Lost Horizons
Tamiko Jones—Can't Live Without Your Love
Kat Mandu—Don't Stop Keep On
Eddie Kendricks—Girl You Need A Change Of Mind
Gladys Knight—Friendship Train
Bo Kool—Money No Love
Patti Labelle—The Spirit's In It
Lil Louis—Music Saved My Life
Luna—I Wanna Be Free
Man Friday—Love Honey Love Heartache
Chuck Mangione with Hamilton Philharmonic—Land Of Make Believe
Rita Marley—One Draw
Janice McClaine—Smack Dab In The Middle
Harold Melvin & The Bluenotes—Wake Up Everybody
MFSB—Love Is The Message
Dorothy Morrison—Rain
Van Morrison—Astral Weeks
Idris Muhammad—Could Heaven Ever Be Like This
Nicodemus—Boneman Connection
Nightlife Unlimited—The Love Is In You (No. 2)
Nuyorican Soul—Nervous Track
Odyssey—Inside Out
The O'Jays—Love Train
The O'Jays—Message In Our Music
Babatunde Olatunji—Jingo-Bah
One Way with Al Hudson—Music
The Orb—Little Fluffy Clouds
Ozo—Anambra
Pal Joey—Spend The Night
Pleasure—Take A Chance
Powerline—Double Journey
Prince—Sexy Dancer
Psychotropic—Only For The Headstrong
Resonance—Yellow Train
Rinder & Lewis—Lust
Risco Connection—Ain't No Stopping Us Now
Demis Roussos—L.O.V.E. Got A Hold On Me
Sandee—Notice Me
Bunny Sigler—By The Way You Dance
Slick—Space Bass
Lonnie Liston Smith—Expansions
Soft House Company—A Little Piano
Larry Spinoza—So Good
Nick Straker Band—A Little Bit Of Jazz
Sun Palace—Rude Movements
Sylvester—Over And Over

Ten City—Devotion
Third World—Now That We Found Love
The Trammps—Where The Happy People Go
280 West featuring Diamond Temple—Love's Masquerade
Miroslav Vitous—New York City
Dexter Wansel—Life On Mars
War—City Country City
Fred Wesley—House Party
The Whispers—And The Beat Goes On
Lenny White—Fancy Dancer
David Williams—Come On Down Boogie People
Winners—Get Ready For The Future
Edgar Winter—Above and Beyond
Jah Wobble, Jaki Liebezeit & Holger Czukay—How Much Are They
Stevie Wonder—All I Do
Michael Wycoff—Diamond Real

Compiled by DJ Cosmo & David Mancuso

GALLERY TOP 50

Barrabas—Woman
The B-52s—Dance This Mess Around
The B-52s—Rock Lobster
Blue Magic—Look Me Up
Bonnie Bramlett—Crazy 'Bout My Baby
James Brown—Give It Up And Turn It Loose
Jeannie Brown—Can't Stop Talking
Lynn Collins—Think
Dinosaur—Kiss Me Again
Doctor Buzzard's Original Savannah Band—Cherchez La Femme
Double Exposure—My Love Is Free
Double Exposure—Ten Percent
Fantastic Johnny C—Waiting For The Rain
First Choice—Doctor Love
Loleatta Holloway—Dreamin'
Loleatta Holloway—Hit And Run
Loleatta Holloway—We're Growing Stronger The Longer
Isley Brothers—Get Into Something
The Jacksons—Forever Came Today
Margie Joseph—Prophecy
Eddie Kendricks—Date With The Rain
Eddie Kendricks—Girl You Need A Change Of Mind
Labelle—Messin' With My Mind
Labelle—What Can I Do For You
Harold Melvin & The Bluenotes—Bad Luck
Harold Melvin & The Bluenotes—The Love I Lost
MFSB—Love Is The Message
MFSB—TSOP
Midnight Movers—Follow The Wind
Mighty Clouds Of Joy—Mighty High
Dorothy Morrison—Rain
The O'Jays—For The Love Of Money
Teddy Pendergrass—You Can't Hide
Realistics—How Can I Forget
Diana Ross—Love Hangover
Southshore Commission—Free Man
Gloria Spencer—I Got It
The Supremes—Let My Heart Do The Walking
The Supremes—Up The Ladder To The Roof
Sylvester—Mighty Real
Temptations—Law Of The Land
Traffic—Gimme Some Loving (live)
The Trammps—Disco Party
The Trammps—Love Epidemic
The Trammps—That's Where The Happy People Go
Undisputed Truth—Law Of The Land
Martha Velez—Aggravation
War—City Country City
Betty Wright—Where Is The Love
Zulema—Giving Up

Compiled by Nicky Siano

WAREHOUSE TOP 50

Ashford & Simpson—It Seems To Hang On
Roy Ayers—Running Away
Peter Brown—Do You Wanna Get Funky With Me
Donald Byrd—Love Has Come Around
Candido—Thousand Finger Man
Change—Paradise
The Clash—Magnificent Dance
Tony Cook & The Party People—On The Floor

Dinosaur L—Go Bang!
Dr. Armando's Seventh Avenue Rumba Band—Deputy Of Love
Ecstasy, Passion And Pain—Touch And Go
ESG—Moody
Taana Gardner—Work That Body
Eddy Grant—Timewarp
Gwen Guthrie—It Should Have Been You
Jimmy Bo Horn—Spank
Geraldine Hunt—Can't Fake The Feeling
Imagination—Burning Up
Indeep—Last Night A DJ Saved My Life
Inner Life—Caught Up (In A One Night Love Affair)
Howard Johnson—So Fine
David Joseph—You Can't Hide Your Love
Kat Mandu—The Break
Chaka Khan—Ain't Nobody
Chaka Khan—I'm Every Woman
Klein & MBO—Dirty Talk
Patti Labelle—Music Is My Way Of Life
Loose Joints—Is It All Over My Face?
Machine—There But For The Grace Of God Go I
Gwen McCrae—Funky Sensation
Sergio Mendes—I'll Tell You
MFSB—Love Is The Message
Giorgio Moroder—E=MC2
The Originals—Down To Love Town
Phreek—Weekend
Positive Force—We Got The Funk
Powerline—Double Journey
Prince—Sexy Dancer
Diana Ross—The Boss
Paul Simpson Connection—Use Me, Lose Me
Skatt Brothers—Walk The Night
Slave—Party Lights
Gino Soccio—Dancer
Sparque—Let's Go Dancing
Nick Straker Band—A Little Bit Of Jazz
Tantra—Mother Africa
Harry Thumann—Underwater
Two Man Sound—Que Tal America
Unlimited Touch—In The Middle
Yello—Bostich

Compiled by the Committee

PARADISE GARAGE TOP 100

Affinity—Don't Go Away
Ashford & Simpson—No One Gets The Prize
Carl Bean—I Was Born This Way
Hamilton Bohannon—Let's Start The Dance
Dee Dee Bridgewater—Bad For Me
James Brown—Give It Up And Turn It Loose (live version)
Peter Brown—Do You Wanna Get Funky With Me
David Byrne & Brian Eno—The Jezebel Spirit
Central Line—Walking Into Sunshine
Chicago—Street Player
The Chi-Lites—My First Mistake
Chocolette—It's That East Street Beat
Martin Circus—Disco Circus
The Clash—Magnificent Dance
Company B—Fascinated
Dinosaur L—Go Bang!
D Train—You're The One For Me
Ian Dury—Spasticus Autisticus
ESG—Moody
ESG—Stand In Line
Marianne Faithfull—Why D'Ya Do It
Family Tree—Family Tree
Fingers Inc—Mystery Of Love
First Choice—Double Cross
First Choice—Let No Man Put Asunder
Front Line Orchestra—Don't Turn Your Back On Me
Funk Masters—Love Money
Taana Gardner—Heartbeat
Manuel Gottsching—E2E4
Eddy Grant—Living On The Frontline
Eddy Grant—Nobody's Got Time/ Timewarp
Gwen Guthrie—Padlock

Gwen Guthrie—Seventh Heaven
Loleatta Holloway—Hit And Run
Loleatta Holloway—Love Sensation
Ednah Holt—Serious Sirius Space Party
Thelma Houston—I'm Here Again
Imagination—Just An Illusion
Inner Life—Ain't No Mountain High Enough
Instant Funk—Got My Mind Made Up
Jackson 5—I Am Love
Mick Jagger—Lucky In Love
Marshall Jefferson—Move Your Body
Grace Jones—Pull Up To The Bumper
Grace Jones—Slave To The Rhythm
Tamiko Jones—Can't Live Without Your Love
Kebek Elektrik—War Dance
Eddie Kendricks—Girl You Need A Change Of Mind
Chaka Khan—Clouds
Chaka Khan—I Know You, I Love You
Klein & MBO—Dirty Talk
Kraftwerk—The Robots
Labelle—What Can I Do For You
Patti Labelle—The Spirit's In It
Lace—Can't Play Around
Loose Joints—Is It All Over My Face?
M—Pop Muzik
Man Friday—Love Honey, Love Heartache
MFSB—Love Is The Message
Steve Miller Band—Macho City
Modern Romance—Salsa Rappsody
Melba Moore—You Stepped Into My Life
Alicia Myers—I Want To Thank You
Stevie Nicks—Stand Back
Nitro Deluxe—Let's Get Brutal
Northend—Tee's Happy
Nu-Shooz—I Can't Wait
NYC Citi Peech Boys—Don't Make Me Wait
NYC Citi Peech Boys—Life Is Something Special
Yoko Ono—Walking On Thin Ice
Phreek—Weekend
Pleasure—Take A Chance
The Police—Voices In My Head
Will Powers—Adventures In Success
Rockers Revenge—Walking On Sunshine
Sharon Ridley—Change
Alexander Robotnick—Problèmes d'Amour
Diana Ross—Love Hangover
Salsoul Orchestra—Love Break
Sister Sledge—Lost In Music
Sister Sledge—We Are Family
Sparque—Let's Go Dancing
Cat Stevens—Was Dog A Doughnut
Nick Straker Band—A Little Bit Of Jazz
Strikers—Body Music
Sugarhill Gang—Rappers' Delight
Donna Summer—I Feel Love
Sylvester—I Need Someone To Love Tonight
Sylvester—Over And Over
Syreeta—Can't Shake Your Love
Talking Heads—I Zimbra
Talking Heads—Once In A Lifetime
Tom Tom Club—Genius Of Love
Touch—Without You
Two Tons of Fun—I Got The Feeling
Visual—The Music Got Me
The Weather Girls—Just Us
Womack & Womack—Baby I'm Scared Of You
Yazoo—Situation
Yello—Bostich

Compiled by the Committee

MUSIC BOX TOP 50

Adonis—No Way Back
Armando—Land Of Confusion
Armando—151
Roy Ayers—Running Away
Brother To Brother—Chance With You
Brother To Brother—In The Bottle
Chip E—It's House
Chip E—Time To Jack
ESG—Moody
Fingers Inc.—Mystery Of Love
Fingers Inc.—Washing Machine
First Choice—Doctor Love
First Choice—Let No Man Put Asunder

Fun Fun—Happy Station
Dan Hartman—Vertigo/Relight My Fire
Isaac Hayes—I Can't Turn Around
Hercules—Ways To Jack
Loleatta Holloway—Catch Me On The Rebound
Steve Silk Hurley—Jack Your Body
Steve Silk Hurley—Jungle DJ
Jack Master Dick's Revenge—Sensuous Woman
The JBs—Doin' It To Death (Funky Good Time)
Jungle Wonz—Time Marches On
Eddie Kendricks—Girl You Need A Change Of Mind
Eddie Kendricks—Going Up In Smoke
Chaka Khan—Clouds
Chaka Khan—I'm Every Woman
Klein & MBO—Dirty Talk
Frankie Knuckles & Jamie Principle—Baby Wants To Ride
Frankie Knuckles & Jamie Principle—Your Love
Liquid Liquid—Optimo
Cheryl Lynn—You Saved My Day
Harold Melvin & The Bluenotes—Bad Luck
Harold Melvin & The Bluenotes—The Love I Lost
Mr. Fingers—Can You Feel It?
Alicia Myers—I Wanna Thank You
On The House—Move Your Body
Phuture—Acid Tracks
Jamie Principle—Bad Boy
Rhythim Is Rhythim—Strings Of Life
Diana Ross—Love Hangover
Sleezy D—I Lost Control
S.L.Y.—I Need A Freak
Southshore Commission—Free Man
Sylvester—You Make Me Feal (Mighty Real)
Talk Talk—It's My Life
Third World—Now That We Found Love
Visage—Frequency 7
Bobby Womack—I Can Understand It
Stevie Wonder—As

Compiled by Spanky

ROXY TOP 100

Abaco Dream—Life And Death In G & A
Afrika Bambaataa And Family—Bambaataa's Theme
Afrika Bambaataa & The Soul Sonic Force—Planet Rock
Afrika Bambaataa & The Soul Sonic Force—Renegades Of Funk
The Aleems—Release Yourself
Art Of Noise—Beat Box
Babe Ruth—The Mexican
The B-52s—Mesopotamia
Blondie—Rapture
Kurtis Blow—The Breaks
Chuck Brown & The Soul Searchers—Bustin' Loose
James Brown—Papa Don't Take No Mess
Tyrone Brunson—The Smurf
The Bus Boys—Did You See Me
Bobby Byrd—I Know You Got Soul
Cameo—Flirt
Chic—Good Times
The Clash—Rock The Casbah
George Clinton—Loopzilla
Lyn Collins—Think
Culture Club—Time
Dead Or Alive—You Spin Me Round (Like A Record)
Defunkt—Razor's Edge
Manu Dibango—Soul Makossa
Dominatrix—The Dominatrix Sleeps Tonight
Shirley Ellis—The Clapping Song
ESG—Moody
Fab 5 Freddy with B-Side—Change The Beat
Falco—Der Kommissar
Foreigner—Urgent
Aretha Franklin—Rock Steady
Freeze—I.O.U.
Friend And Lover—Reach Out In The Darkness
"Fusion Mix": Mohawks—Champ, James Brown—Get Up, Get Into It, Get Involved, Dyke & The Blazers—Let A Woman Be A Woman, Let A Man Be A Man
Peter Gabriel—Shock The Monkey

Graham Central Station—Now Do U Wanna Dance
Grand Funk Railroad—Inside Looking Out
Grandmaster Flash—Larry Love
Grandmaster Flash & The Furious Five—The Message
Eddy Grant—California Style
Hall & Oates—I Can't Go For That
Herbie Hancock—Rockit
Hashim—Al Naafiysh (The Soul)
The Incredible Bongo Band—Apache
Jackson 5—Dancing Machine
Michael Jackson—PYT
Rick James—Superfreak
Joan Jett—I Love Rock'n'Roll
Grace Jones—My Jamaican Guy
Herman Kelly—Dance To The Drummer's Beat
Kool & The Gang—Jungle Jazz
Kraftwerk—Numbers
Kraftwerk—Trans Europe Express
George Kranz—Din Da Da
Fela Ransome Kuti—Shakara
Cyndi Lauper—Girls Just Wanna Have Fun
Liquid Liquid—Cavern
Lisa Lisa & The Cult Jam—Head To Toe
Little Sister—You're The One
LL Cool J—Rock The Bells
Madonna—Everybody
Man Parrish—Hip Hop Bebop
Malcolm McLaren—Buffalo Girls
Vaughan Mason—Bounce Rock Skate
Michigan & Smiley—Diseases
The Miracles—Mickey Monkey
New Edition—Candy Girls
Nicodemus—Boneman Connection
Gary Numan—Cars
The O'Jays—Money
Parliament—Atomic Dog
Phase 2—The Roxy
Pointer Sisters—Automatic
Prince—Controversy
Queen—We Will Rock You
Ram Jam—Black Betty
Rock Steady Crew—Hey You Rock Steady Crew
Rolling Stones—Start Me Up
Run DMC—It's Like That
The Sequence—Funk You Up
Shalamar—A Night To Remember
Shango—Zulu Groove
Shannon—Let The Music Play
Sister Nancy—Bambam
Sly & The Family Stone—Family Affair
SOS Band—Just Be Good To Me
Jimmy Spicer—Bubble Bunch
Steppenwolf—Magic Carpet Ride
Strafe—Set It Off
Sugarhill Gang—Rappers' Delight
Donna Summer—I Feel Love
Talking Heads—Once In A Lifetime
Tom Tom Club—Genius Of Love
Treacherous Three—Yes We Can Can
Trouble Funk—Trouble Funk Express
West Street Mob—Breakdance
Yazoo—Situation
Yellow Magic Orchestra—Firecracker
Yellowman—Zuzuzangzang
Zapp—More Bounce To The Ounce

Compiled by Kool Lady Blue & Afrika Bambaataa

HAÇIENDA TOP 50

A Guy Called Gerald—Voodoo Ray
Bam Bam—Give It To Me
Bamboo—Bamboo
Coolhouse—Rock This Party Right
Delite—Wild Times
808 State—Pacific State
ESP—It's You
Farley Farley Farley—Give Yourself To Me
Roberta Flack—Uh Oh Ooh Ooh Look Out
Siedah Garrett—K.I.S.S.I.N.G.
Loleatta Holloway—Love Sensation
House Master Baldwin—Don't Lead Me
Inner City—Big Fun
Jago—I'm Going To Go (Knuckles Mix)
Arnold Jarvis—Take Some Time Out
Kenny Jammin' Jason—Can U Dance
Maurice Joshua—I Gotta Big Dick
Landlord—I Like It
Liaisons D—Future FJP
Lil Louis—French Kiss

Mantronix—King Of The Beats
Mark The 45 King—The 900 Number
Nayobe—I Love The Way You Love Me (Dub)
New Fast Automatic Daffodils—Big (Baka)
Nightwriters—Let The Music Use You
Orange Lemon—Dreams Of Santa Anna
Orbital—Chime
Paradox—Jail Break
Phase II—Reachin'
Phuture—Acid Tracks
Phuture—Slam
Precious—Definition Of A Track
Rhythim Is Rhythim—Nude Photo
Rhythim Is Rhythim—Strings Of Life
Risque 3—Essence Of A Dream
Ce Ce Rogers—Someday
Rusty—Everything Is Gonna Change
Shaker Song—Shaker Song
Sha-Lor—I'm In Love
S.L.Y.—I Need A Freak
Joe Smooth—Promised Land
Sterling Void—It's Alright
Sueño Latino—Sueño Latino
Sweet Exorcist—Test Four
T Coy—Carino
Ten City—Right Back To You
The LP—Acid Trax
28th Street Crew—I Need A Rhythm
Unique 3—The Theme
Virgo—Mechanically Replayed

Compiled by Jon Da Silva

SHOOM TOP 50

A Guy Called Gerald—Voodoo Ray
Adonis—No Way Back
Adonis—The Poke
Art Of Noise—Crusoe
Bang The Party—Release Your Body
The Clash—The Magnificent Dance
CLS—Can You Feel It?
Code 6—Drop The Deal
DJ Pierre's Fantasy Club—Dream Girl
Elkin & Nelson—Jibaro
Fallout—The Morning After
Fingers Inc.—Distant Planet
Gentry Ice—Do You Want To Jack
Paris Grey—Don't Lead Me
Richie Havens—Going Back To My Roots
Inner City—Good Life
It's Immaterial—Driving Away From Home
Arnold Jarvis—Time Out For Lovin'
Kenny Jammin' Jason—Can U Dance
Marshall Jefferson—The House Music Anthem
MFSB—Love Is The Message
Mr. Fingers—Stars
Nightwriters—Let The Music Use You
Phase II—Reachin'
Phuture—Acid Tracks
William Pitt—City Lights
Jamie Principle—Baby Wants To Ride
Raze—Break 4 Love
The Residents—Kaw Liga
Rhythim Is Rhythim—Strings Of Life
Rickster—The Night Moves On
Ce Ce Rogers—Someday
Rolling Stones—Sympathy For The Devil
Ralphi Rosario—You Used To Hold Me
Paul Simpson & Adeva—Musical Freedom
Joyce Sims—Come Into My Life
Taja Seville—Love Is Contagious
S*Express—Theme From S*Express
Mandy Smith—I Just Can't Wait
Joe Smooth—Promised Land
Split Second—Flesh
Ten City—Devotion
Ten City—Right Back To You
Todd Terry—Black Riot
Mac Thornhill—(Who's Gonna) Ease The Pressure
U2—I Still Haven't Found What I'm Looking For
Barry White—It's Ecstasy When You Lay Down Next To Me
The Woodentops—Why Why Why
Pete Wylie—Sinful
Laurent X—Machines

Compiled by Danny Rampling

SOUND FACTORY TOP 50

African Dreams—It All Begins Here
Aphrohead—In The Dark We Live

Black Traxx—Your Mind Is So Crazy
Cajmere—Percolator
Mariah Carey—Dreamlover
Doomsday—Atom Bomb
Doop—Doop
DSK—What Would We Do (Farley & Heller's Eight Minutes Of Madness)
East Village Loft Society—Manhattan Anthem
E. G. Fullalove—Divas To The Dancefloor
Factory Kids—I'm Simian Dammit!
First Choice—Doctor Love
KC Flight—Voices
Rosie Gaines—Exploding All Over Europe
Happy Mondays—Stinkin' Thinkin' (Junior Style Mix)
Headrush—Underground
Hed Boys—Boys And Girls
Nick Holder—Erotic Illusions
Whitney Houston—I'm Every Woman
Kiwi Dreams—Y?
Kristine W—Feel What You Want
Lectroluv—Dream Drums
Lectroluv—Struck By Love
Lidell Townsell—Get With You
Lidell Townsell—Nu Nu
Livin' Joy—Dreamer
Madonna—all tracks
Billie Ray Martin—Your Loving Arms
Vernessa Mitchell—Reap
Moraes—Welcome To The Factory
Outdance—Reality
Pascal's Bongo Massive—Père Cochon
Karen Pollack—You Can't Hurt Me
Roxy—Get Huh
Frank Ski—Tony's Bitch Track
The Soundman—The Factory
Sugarcubes—A Leash Called Love
Danny Tenaglia—Bottom Heavy
Thompson Twins—The Saint (8th Street Dub)
Barbara Tucker—Beautiful People
Underground Sound of Lisbon—So Get Up
U2—Lemon
Armand Van Helden—Witch Doktor
Junior Vasquez—Get Your Hands Off My Man
Junior Vasquez—X
Waterlillies—Never Get Enough
Melanie Williams—Not Enough
X-Press 2—London X-Press
X-Press 2—Music X-Press
Yo Yo Honey—Higher (DJ Pierre Mix)

Compiled by Rob Di Stefano

STEALTH TOP 50

Air Liquide—Robot War
Tori Amos—God (Joi Remix)
A Reminiscent Drive—Flame One
Atavistic Rhythms—Snackwitch
Boom Boom Satellites—Dub Me Crazy
Coldcut—Atomic Moog
DJ Food—Scratch Yer Head (Squarepusher Mix)
Dr. Rocket (live performance)
The Dust Brothers—Chemical Beats
Fat Boy Slim—The Weekend Starts Here
Fearless 4—Rockin' It
4E—Temple Trax
Gescom—Mag
Glowball—Frequency
Happy Campers—No Mind
Pierre Henry—Psyche Rock
The Herbaliser (live performance)
Dick Hyman—Give It Up Or Turn It Loose
Innerzone Orchestra—Bug In The Bassbin
Jedi Knights—May The Funk Be With You
Jedi Knights—Ruak Et & Kok-Bah
Jhelisha—Friendly Pressure (a cappella mixed over anything)
Kid Koala (live performance)
Fela Kuti—any track
La Funk Mob—La Doctoresse
Derrick Laro & Trinity—Don't Stop Till You Get Enough
Idris Muhammad—Power of Soul
Multiplication Rock—Three Is The Magic Number
Nicolette—No More Government
Ocean Colour Scene—The Riverboat
Photek—Seven Samurai/Hidden Camera
Pointer Sisters—Yes We Can Can
Primal Scream—Don't Fight It, Feel It

Primal Scream—Trainspotting
Red Snapper—Hot Flush
Red Snapper—In Deep
Alex Reece—Jazz Master (Kruder & Dorfmeiter remix)
Talvin Singh (live performance)
Solaris—Slow Burn Dub
Space Time Continuum—Sea Biscuit Pressure
Squarepusher (live performance)
Squarepusher—Male Pills mixed with . . . Dream Warriors—My Definition Of A Boombastic Jazz Style (a cappella)
Peter Thomas—*Chariot Of The Gods* (soundtrack)
Peter Thomas Orchestra—The Obelisk of Karak
Tipsy—Nude On The Moon
2 Player—Extreme Possibilities (Wagon Christ Mix)
Ultra Magnetic MCs—Papa Large
Warp 69—Natural High (Global Communications Mix)
Witchman—Leviathan

Compiled by Jonathan Moore & Matt Black

Index

BREEDER

BT

LTJ BUKEM

SANDRA COLLINS

DJ DAN

JOHN DIGWEED

GRACE

MAX GRAHAM

HYBRID

PAUL OAKENFOLD

DAVE RALPH

PETER RAUHOFFER

SASHA

STARECASE

SUBMARINE